Jungian
Analysis

Jungian Analysis

Edited by Murray Stein
Foreword by June Singer

SHAMBHALA
Boulder & London 1984

SHAMBHALA PUBLICATIONS, INC.
1920 13th Street
Boulder   CO   80302

© 1982 by Open Court Publishing
Foreword © 1984 by June Singer
9 8 7 6 5 4 3 2 1
First Shambhala edition
Distributed in the United States by Random House and in Canada by
Random House of Canada Ltd.
Distributed in the United Kingdom by Routledge & Kegan Paul Ltd.
London and Henley-on-Thames.
Printed in the United States of America

Library of Congress Cataloging in Publication Data
Main entry under title:

Jungian analysis.

   Reprint. Originally published: La Salle, Ill. : Open
Court, c1982. (The Reality of the psyche series ; v. 2)
   Includes bibliographies and index.
   1. Psychoanalysis.   2. Jung, C. G. (Carl Gustav),
1875-1961.   I. Stein, Murray, 1943-   . II. Series:
Reality of the psyche series ; v. 2.
BF173.J86   1984b   616.89'17   83-27092
ISBN 0-87773-262-0 (pbk.)
ISBN 0-394-72333-3 (Random House : pbk.)

ACKNOWLEDGMENTS

The publisher gratefully acknowledges the use, in the Glossary, of excerpts from the following volumes of *The Collected Works of C. G. Jung,* trans. R. F. C. Hull, Bollingen Series XX. The excerpts are reprinted by permission of Princeton University Press:

Vol. 1: *Psychiatric Studies,* copyright © 1957, 1970 by Princeton University Press.

Vol. 2: *Experimental Researches,* copyright © 1973 by Princeton University Press.

Vol. 4: *Freud and Psychoanalysis,* copyright © 1961 by Princeton University Press.

Vol. 5: *Symbols of Transformation,* copyright © 1956 by Princeton University Press.

Vol. 6: *Psychological Types,* copyright © 1971 by Princeton University Press.

Vol. 7: *Two Essays on Analytical Psychology,* copyright 1953, © 1966 by Princeton University Press.

Vol. 8: *The Structure and Dynamics of the Psyche,* copyright © 1960, 1969 by Princeton University Press.

Vol. 9: I, *The Archetypes and the Collective Unconscious,* copyright © 1959, 1969 by Princeton University Press.

Vol. 9: II, *Aion: Researches into the Phenomenology of the Self,* copyright © 1959 by Princeton University Press.

Vol. 10: *Civilization in Transition,* copyright © 1964, 1970 by Princeton University Press.

Vol. 11: *Psychology and Religion: West and East,* copyright © 1958, 1969 by Princeton University Press.

Vol. 12: *Psychology and Alchemy,* copyright 1953, © 1968 by Princeton University Press.

Vol. 13: *Alchemical Studies,* copyright © 1967 by Princeton University Press.

Vol. 14: *Mysterium Coniunctionis,* copyright © 1965, 1970 by Princeton University Press.

Vol. 15: *The Spirit in Man, Art, and Literature,* copyright © 1966 by Princeton University Press.

Vol. 16: *The Practice of Psychotherapy,* copyright 1954, © 1966 by Princeton University Press.

Vol. 17: *The Development of Personality,* copyright 1954 by Princeton University Press.

Vol. 18: *The Symbolic Life,* copyright 1950, 1953, copyright © 1955, 1958, 1959, 1963, 1968, 1969, 1970, 1973, 1976 by Princeton University Press.

The publisher is also grateful to Routledge & Kegan Paul Ltd. (London), publisher of the above-mentioned edition of *The Collected Works of C. G. Jung* in England, for permission to reprint the excerpts referred to earlier.

Finally the publisher thanks Pantheon Books, a division of Random House, Inc., for permission to reprint, in the Glossary, an excerpt from *Memories, Dreams, Reflections* by C. G. Jung, recorded and edited by Aniela Jaffé, translated by Richard and Clara Winston, copyright 1961.

*The right way to wholeness
is made up of fateful detours
and wrong turnings.*

—Jung

CONTENTS

FOREWORD

June Singer

Jungian Analysis could not have been written before now. The concepts of C. G. Jung were seminal, but they had to go through a period of dormancy, to reemerge on American soil, and then to ripen. We have in hand one outcome of that process, a collection of essays written by Jungian analysts that offers the most complete discussion in English to date on the background, practice, and new developments in Jungian psychology.

I wonder how Jung would have reacted to this book. I never had the privilege of knowing Jung, although I was a student at the Jung Institute in Zurich when he died in June, 1961. I belong to the generation of Jungians who were trained by that small band of Zurich analysts who had known Jung intimately. I use the word "intimately" deliberately, for there is no greater intimacy than that in which one shares dread secrets and, in doing so, makes oneself fully open and vulnerable. Jung was "companion to the soul" for that first group of Jungian analysts. Listening to them speak about him, one gained the impression that for them he was a man of heroic dimensions. They had been close enough to "the old man" to experience his profound greatness of spirit. Unlike the contemporaries of Jung—Emma Jung, Toni Wolff, and Freud—the second generation had little opportunity or desire to observe the shadowy aspects of Jung's being: his emotional storms, his internal struggles, his difficulties managing the multiple levels of consciousness and the unconscious. My analysts, my teachers, constantly quoted Jung. I recall, for instance, how Barbara Hannah never delivered a lecture at the old Jung Institute in Zurich without at least half a dozen sentences commencing with "Jung says...."

The Jungian analysts whose essays comprise this volume belong to the third generation of Jungians, the generation in which I count myself. Exceptions are Joseph Henderson and the Wheelwrights, who did most of their analytic work with Jung. My generation had been steeped in the "mystique" of Jung, it is true, but we also have gained some distance. We look upon Jung as an historic personage, rather than as a personal mentor. Our generation has not been so closely entangled with Jung's life and thought as was the second generation of Zurich analysts. We have been exposed to Freud's thinking in his later years and to the revisions of the psychoanalytic movement in England and America, as well as to a wide variety of other psychological approaches.

Those of us who received our analytic training in the old ivy-covered building on Gemeindestrasse in the sixties and seventies returned to a

United States that was decidedly not receptive to Jung's ideas. When his autobiographical statement *Memories, Dreams, Reflections* was first published, negative criticism ran high. Jung was "vague," "abstruse," "mystical," the reviewers said. The only favorable critique I read at that time was that of Lewis Mumford, a man who could track with the visionary mind. Nevertheless, *Memories, Dreams, Reflections* captured the imagination and enthusiasm of a delighted American readership. Not too surprisingly, this consisted mostly of people under thirty.

By the early sixties, psychology in the United States had been parceled out between two groups, the behaviorists in the academic institutions, and the psychoanalysts in their private offices and postgraduate institutes. These two forces in psychology had been clearly defined and systematized. Each had its own body of literature. Its schools of thought were firmly established. Its tenets had become cultural values.

I knew all this before I left for Switzerland; but when I returned to the United States in 1964 to begin practice as a Jungian analyst, I discovered that another powerful force had emerged in society that I had not known when I went abroad—the counterculture. This consisted mostly of bright young people who were not so much interested in acquiring a specific corpus of knowledge or in accepting unquestioningly the traditional mores, as they were in coming to know their world and themselves through their own experience. Faced with one awesome reality of American involvement in Vietnam, and the alternate awesome reality of the collective unconscious as it had been unveiled with the aid of psychoactive drugs, they were looking for new ways to understand themselves and their experience of the world. Around this time Jung's *Collected Works* were beginning to appear in English translation. Although these were not assigned by their professors, many college students bought them and read them with great interest.

Jung offered a psychology that acknowledged the reality of the psyche as the medium through which we perceive our inner and outer worlds. He validated the individual's own experience of unconscious material. He offered an open system in which the unconscious was represented as a realm of unlimited potential for growth and decay, good and evil, order and chaos. Jung offered a psychological approach that was not primarily based on a pathology model. Rather, it was oriented toward the purposive movement of the psyche in the direction of enlarging the scope of consciousness. Students of Jung learned that Jung regarded the psyche as an inherently self-regulating system with a tendency toward balance and wholeness. He taught that when the person's equilibrium becomes disturbed and an imbalance between consciousness and unconscious complexes occurs, the complexes may assume autonomy. When this happens, the complex areas can become highly energized, and may then lead to neurotic or even psychotic developments.

In the ensuing years, more and more people sought out Jungian analysts with whom to work on their own issues. Sometimes these had to do with psychological disorders, sometimes with developmental patterns, and sometimes with a desire to increase in self-knowledge through a carefully guided individuation process. Jungian institutes in the United States grew in size and influence (cf. Henderson's chapter on the history and practice of Jungian analysis). During the past two decades I have experienced much of this growth firsthand. I joined the New York Association of Analytical Psychologists when I first returned from Zurich, then became a founding member of the Inter-Regional Society of Jungian Analysts and later of the Chicago group, and, most recently, I have joined the Society of Jungian Analysts of Northern California. From these varied perspectives, what strikes me as most remarkable is the unique character of each group of analysts and of the training institute it operates. Every society of Jungian analysts is autonomous, although a collegial relationship exists among them all. Within each group of Jungian analysts, it is evident that the members are clearly individuals, all with their own characteristic styles of analytic practice.

This book bears witness to the imagination and creativity of the analytic process and of those whose professional work has been shaped by that process. The aim and purpose of Jungian analysis is to help the analysand to discover the nature of those archetypal configurations that give form and shape to the personality, and that activate its dynamism. The analysts who have contributed to this volume have themselves experienced many of the dimensions of the analytic process of which they write. Nor is this process ever finished, for, as Jung taught, analysis works only when both persons, analyst and analysand, are transformed in their encounter. As long as the analyst works on himself or herself, the transformative process continues. What you will read here is a description of "the state of the art" of Jungian analysis as it is practiced today in the United States. What comes through between the lines may be even more important, though. For here you may discover, concealed behind the expositions of the analyst/ writer, traces of the trickster, the old wise man, the dancer, the doctor, the cleric, the divine child, and the fool.

When Jung uttered his now famous statement, "Thank God I am Jung and not a Jungian," he may have been afraid that his followers would carve his words in stone and refuse to depart from them. This book is evidence that this has not occurred. The writers have followed the spirit, not the letter, of Jung's teachings. That spirit does not deal in rules or theories, but seeks the liberation of the human soul from ignorance, fragmentation and self-delusion. The task has not been to say what Jung said, but to move forward as Jung did—meeting new challenges in new ways, always inquiring, always remembering that where light falls, also must there fall shadow.

What would Jung have thought of this book? I suspect he would have been surprised at some of it, and taken issue with some of it, but that on the whole he would have been quite pleased with the productions of his offspring.

EDITOR'S PREFACE

The plan for this book evolved out of an idea for a handbook of analytical psychology and Jungian analysis, envisioned as numerous encyclopedialike entries organized into three large sections: theory, psychopathology, and practice. The intent of such a reference work would have been to answer questions about the field's conceptualizations of the basic dynamics and structures of the human mind, about its understanding of the forms of psychopathology, and about its methods for conducting psychotherapy and analysis. What finally emerged, however, as the result of many discussions with fellow analysts and students, is a book focused primarily on practice, with theoretical concerns brought in only as required.

Over the past fifty years, Jungian analysis has taken its place in the United States among the accepted forms of psychological treatment offered by professionals in the various branches of the field of mental health. In the popular view, however, Jungian analysis still retains an esoteric aura, bearing the overtones of a cultic experience and a ''mystical'' approach to psychological life. The Jungian concept of the psyche's reality, to cite just one source for this popular view, places Jungian thought for some readers at the borderline of occultism. Persons who enter Jungian analysis are often surprised to find that it is analytically tough-minded and mostly devoid of cultic or mystical qualities, that it is not always supportive of lofty spiritual strivings, and that it is usually geared more toward mundane psychological conflicts than toward purely symbolic inward journeys.

A major goal of this book is to spell out how Jungian analysts actually work and how they understand what they are doing. As the reader will see, these accounts have the effect of distancing Jungian analysis from the mystical and occult traditions, with which it has been too closely identified by misguided or misinformed lay persons and professionals, and of relating it to the broad spectrum of modern psychotherapies and to other schools of psychodynamic thought and research. As a body of thought, analytical psychology has wide and numerous applications; as a professional discipline, Jungian analysis belongs to the helping professions and is committed to the goal of psychological healing.

Jungian analysts today enjoy a rich heritage of respect and regard accumulated through the dedicated work of the first generation of analysts, who were trained by Jung himself. Today's graduates of the various Jung

Institutes are the beneficiaries of the high reputation of Jungian analysis established by such figures as Eleanor Bertine, Werner Engel, Esther Harding, Joseph Henderson, James Kirsch, and Jane and Joseph Wheelwright in the United States, as well as by a host of other distinguished analysts in Europe. Through their writings and practices, these analysts have established the Jungian approach as a highly valued option for psychological treatment in many parts of the world.

As a Jungian work, this book is unusual by virtue of the fact that all the contributors are analysts who live and practice in the United States. It is an American book. Most of the authors are not professional teachers or writers, although many teach and have published books and papers. All of them, however, are professional psychotherapists and analysts. Coming to this vocation through clinical psychology, pastoral counseling, psychiatry, and other disciplines, they now share the Jungian approach to treatment. Approximately one-half of them received Jungian training in European Institutes (Zurich, London, Berlin); the other half were trained in American Institutes (New York, San Francisco, Los Angeles, and the Inter-Regional). Their experience as Jungian analysts ranges from five to forty years.

Some of the authors who were invited to write chapters were selected because they are recognized in the field as authorities on a particular subject; others were chosen on the recommendation of the board of advisors; still others were selected because in my judgment as editor they promised excellence. All were asked to perform three general tasks in their individual chapters: to include a critical review of the Jungian literature on the subject under discussion; to raise questions that could lead to further thought and research in the field; and to provide a reasonably comprehensive list of references for students who want to pursue the topic in greater detail. Beyond the constraints of these tasks, the authors were given full freedom and encouragement to state their own positions, in their own styles. What would come of this, it was hoped, would be a comprehensive statement from the field of analytical psychology regarding the practice of analysis, as well as a representative sampling of the diversity of perspectives and personalities among the members of the field. In this way, I tried to combine the objectives of a textbook on analytical practice with the more stimulating tone created by the vigorous expression of individual opinion and argument. The reader will be the judge of the success of this attempt.

In a number of important respects, this book is different from other works in the field of analytical psychology. Unlike much of the Jungian literature, the focus of this book is not on the interpretation of cultural themes or archetypal material as these appear in myths, fairy tales, religious ideas, or stories and images from traditional or modern cultures. It is a book intentionally limited to the practice of analysis. It is also a systematic work, and thus different from such collections of papers as the International Congress series. It is organized in such a way that it can be read through from beginning to end, providing an orderly presentation of the history of Jungian analysis, its aims and goal, its structures, its methods, various special topics, and, in conclusion, a discussion of training. Alternatively, it can be consulted as a reference work on individual topics.

An additional hallmark of this book is that each chapter is an attempt to represent the field rather than only the perspective of an individual author. As a whole, therefore, the book represents the ''state of the art'' of Jungian analysis as it exists in the United States today.

The hope of the editor and authors is that the diverse audience to which this book is addressed—analysts, students, therapists of other schools— will find here a work that represents some of the best contemporary thinking in the field of analytical psychology in the United States and one that will serve the field by stimulating further development in it.

MURRAY STEIN

JANUARY 1982

NOTE ON REFERENCES TO WORKS BY C. G. JUNG

I should here add a note about the form of entries referring to works by Jung himself in chapter reference lists: The date following Jung's name is the date of original publication of the work, and the date at the end of the entry is the date of publication of the volume of the *Collected Works* in which it appears. In a reference to an entire volume of the *Collected Works* that originally appeared as a separate work, the first date given is that of original publication and the second is that of publication of the volume of the *Collected Works*. If a reference is to an entire volume of the *Collected Works* that did not appear previously as a separate work, the single date given is that of publication of that volume of the *Collected Works*. This system is intended to distract the reader as little as possible, while providing as much bibliographic information as possible to the student who wants it.

M. S.

EDITOR'S ACKNOWLEDGMENTS

For a book of this kind, which is a statement from the field of analytical psychology and Jungian analysis, the list of persons who deserve to be thanked for their help and advice is a long one. Many individuals shared time and attention generously as this book grew and took shape over the past two-and-one-half years. The editor owes a particular debt of gratitude to the following persons:

To John Mattern of Zurich for a seminal idea for this book and to Louise Mahdi, editor of The Reality of the Psyche Series, and Howard Webber, Publisher and General Manager of Open Court Publishing Company, for supporting that idea as it was changed and transformed into the present book.

To the following persons who took time to visit with me and to discuss the book's original outline in detail: Gerhard Adler (London), Helmut Barz (Zurich), Ean Begg (London), Hilde Binswanger (Zurich), Werner Engel (New York), Toni Frey (Zurich), Liliane Frey-Rohn (Zurich), Adolph Guggenbühl-Craig (Zurich), Elie Humbert (Paris), Mario Jacoby (Zurich), John Johnson (New York), John Nicholas (San Francisco), Richard Pope (Zurich), and Leland Roloff (Chicago).

To Aniela Jaffé, who, through a long afternoon of conversation in Zurich, helped me find the way to a workable outline and who, more than any other member of the Jungian community, encouraged me to continue working on this book.

To the five senior Jungian analysts who acted as an advisory board for this book and who spent valuable time making numerous suggestions: James Hall (Dallas), Joseph Henderson (San Francisco), Russell Lockhart (Los Angeles), June Singer (San Francisco), and Edward C. Whitmont (New York).

To the three perspicacious "readers" whose detailed comments to the authors stimulated much soul-searching and improvement in the chapters: Mary Hendricks (Chicago), William Goodheart (San Francisco), and Caroline Stevens (Chicago).

Several contributing authors, too, gave useful suggestions for the book as a whole: John Beebe (San Francisco), Thomas Kirsch (San Francisco), Harriet Machtiger (Pittsburgh), and Ann Ulanov (New York).

Mary McNelis of Open Court has been a particularly cogent critic; her piercing sensibility has helped to purge the dross. Patty Green, Managing Editor of Open Court, and Kate Engelberg, copy editor, have made an invaluable contribution in their caring and careful attention to the countless details of preparing the manuscript for publication.

Finally, my wholly delightful wife, Jan, has been a constant resource throughout this long voyage, acting as secretary, muse, counselor, and companion in many unpredictable circumstances.

MURRAY STEIN

INTRODUCTION

PART ONE

$$\left[\begin{array}{c} 1 \end{array}\right]$$

REFLECTIONS ON THE HISTORY
AND PRACTICE OF JUNGIAN ANALYSIS

Joseph L. Henderson

FREUD AND JUNG

WHEN I first went to Zurich in 1929 to be analyzed by Jung, I was only twenty-six and as yet completely without psychological knowledge or scientific experience. I therefore had little or no objective judgment concerning the relative merits or failings of depth psychology. No doubt I supposed that analysts, like gods, had no human failings. Consequently I was all the more vulnerable to the Freud-Jung controversy, which was still very much alive. At that time it was generally supposed that the rupture of their relationship was due to a father-son conflict, Freud being the father and Jung the son. Since we all know, thanks to Freud, that all sons experience ambivalence toward the father in their early years, and that most fathers try to keep a certain control over their sons' development, it was natural that the father-son aspect of the Freud-Jung relationship mobilized my own ambivalence toward the father. In the light of my early transference to Jung, I was inclined to see him as the misunderstood son of an authoritarian father; but then, since Jung was a father figure, too, I found plenty of room for considerable resistance to him. In such a state of resistance, I felt that Jung was the bad (or at least unsympathetic) father and Freud the good (or, shall we say, misunderstood) father. And then it all turned around, and Jung became the good father again.

Joseph Henderson, M.D., a founding member of the C. G. Jung Institute of San Francisco, is in private practice in San Francisco. He is a Special Lecturer (Emeritus) in Neuropsychiatry, Stanford University Medical School, and a former vice-president of the International Association for Analytical Psychology. Dr. Henderson is the author of "Ancient Myths and Modern Man" in *Man and His Symbols*, edited by C. G. Jung, *The Wisdom of the Serpent* (with Maud Oakes), and *Thresholds of Initiation*.

I soon realized that the Freud-Jung controversy was inhibiting the process of separation from, or repair of, my own parent images and, if allowed to go on, could become itself a kind of false parent. Jung was very good about understanding this problem and helping me to disidentify with what was in the projection of my father image. But in spite of his help, a certain problem remained, because I felt that some of the personal suffering that C. G. and Emma Jung experienced following the break with Freud still existed. And one only had to read between the lines of Freud's *History of the Psychoanalytic Movement* to know how much he, too, had suffered. Because of this situation, I realized I could not expect total objectivity from any of them.

Today, the publication of their correspondence (McGuire) reveals, on the personal level, how their break came about, and how deeply, even tragically, they must have experienced it. But it still does not reveal what I think is the best way of understanding their unresolved separation. To save myself from introjecting their personal conflict, I began to study the history of the psychoanalytic movement, and Jung's deviation from it, from a cultural point of view. I soon began to notice that this conflict was much larger than a clash of personalities or an unresolved father-son complex. Rather, I saw their relationship as the inevitable result of cultural forces at work behind the scenes, bringing these two great men together and then inevitably and, I think, meaningfully sending them on their separate ways.

Freud's medical career began during the full tide of nineteenth-century scientific materialism in the form of the "movement best known as Helmholz's School of Medicine" (Jones 1953, p. 40). His teacher was Ernst Brücke, in whose physiology laboratory Freud says, "I found rest and satisfaction—and men, too, whom I could respect and take as my models . . ." (p. 39). These men, according to Ernest Jones, were "driven forward by a veritable crusading spirit," expressed by one of them in the following manifesto:

> " 'No other forces than the common physical-chemical ones are active within the organism. In those cases which cannot . . . be explained by these forces one has either to find the specific way or form of their action by means of the physical-mathematical method or to assume new forces . . . inherent in matter, reducible to the force of attraction and repulsion.' " (Pp. 40–41)

The "transformation and interplay of physical forces in the living organism," according to Jones, "correspond closely with the words Freud used in 1926 to characterize psychoanalysis in its dynamic aspect: 'The forces assist or inhibit one another, combine with one another, enter into compromises with one another . . .' " (pp. 41–42).

Freud's original scientific identity was very closely connected with this dynamic aspect of Brücke's physiology. Jones tells us:

> In this evolution of life, no spirits, essences, or entelechies, no superior plans or ultimate purposes are at work. The physical energies alone cause effects— somehow. . . .
>
> This . . . was part of the general trend of Western civilization. Slowly, continuously, it had risen and grown everywhere through the preceding two or three hundred years, steadily gaining momentum from the end of the eighteenth century. . . . (P. 42)

This gives one a striking picture of Freud's scientific superego, but it does not account for an inherent opposition that crept into the whole movement from the Romantics. In fact, according to Jones, "Freud himself, inspired by Goethe, . . . passed through a brief period of the pantheistic *Naturphilosophie.*" But then, "in his enthusiasm for the rival physical physiology, he swung to the opposite extreme and became for a while a radical materialist" (p. 43). Out of this strife of opposites, psychoanalysis was born, or at least the scientific foundation upon which psychoanalytic theory was constructed. Jones writes:

> . . . in his famous wish theory of the mind, [he brought] back into science the ideas of "purpose," "intention," and "aim" which had just been abolished from the universe. We know, however, that when Freud did bring them back he was able to reconcile them with the principles in which he had been brought up; he never abandoned determinism for teleology. (P. 45)

It is precisely at this point that we find the major difference between Freud's background and that of Jung. Jung was to criticize Freud for what he called his reductive method of interpretation of unconscious contents, while he claimed for his own method the superior efficacy of a teleological approach. He demonstrated this approach by according a "prospective" or "synthetic" interpretation to dreams that pointed the way to solutions of problems. But just as Freud entertained ideas of "purpose," "intention," and "aim," so Jung agreed that a reductive approach to unconscious material, by the method of psychoanalysis, did reveal levels of childhood memory that it was necessary to recover. It may therefore seem that their initial disagreement, at least concerning method, disappeared in the course of time. But the deeper cultural differences remained, in response to which Jung later created a method that had very little in common with psychoanalysis. As it used to be said, Jung at first seemed only to change the hilt of the sword representing psychoanalysis, but later changed the blade as well.

If Freud derived his determinism from physiology based on a Darwinian model, where, we may ask, did Jung get his tendency to prefer teleology? It came not from science but from philosophy. While he was at medical school, he read philosophy in his spare time. In fact, he told me that he had no spare time for anything else during that period. He, too, had been influenced by Goethe, and there was even a legend, for what it is worth, that one of his grandfathers was a natural son of Goethe. But he was not influenced in the same way as Freud, who seems to have responded to the Romantic aspect of Goethe's philosophy, the *Naturphilosophie*. Thomas Mann, for instance, pointed out the existence of a certain likeness between Freudian concepts, such as the principle of Eros, and the half-scientific, half-mystical sentiments to be found in the writings of Novalis. It was to Goethe's mature, classical period that Jung responded, avoiding the Romantic emotionalism of *Naturphilosophie*. He tells us that his philosophic reading extended from Descartes and Leibnitz to Kant, Schopenhauer, Carus, von Hartmann, and Nietzsche, covering a period of over two hundred years—from the end of the seventeenth century to the beginning of the twentieth (1933–34, pp. 7–21).

Jung saw in the writings of these philosophers many of the elements that were later to support his theory of the collective unconscious. In Leibnitz's "unconscious perceptions" and Kant's "dark representations," he saw ideas that approached those of modern psychology; but of much greater importance to Jung was Schopenhauer, of whom he says:

> Before his time the belief was widely held that the psyche could be rationally understood, being principally composed of rational processes. The genius of Schopenhauer brought an answer to the world which thousands had been obscurely groping for and for which they had looked to the empiricists in vain. This new note is the voice of *suffering:* the human psyche is not only order and purpose; it is suffering. . . . He thus brings a point of view into the psychological situation which we must not lose sight of for it concerns modern man most closely. (Ibid.)

In his first English seminar, Jung shows how this study of philosophy influenced his psychological investigations before he knew of Freud. He writes:

> Out of the reading of Schopenhauer I got a tentative explanation of the possible psychology of the case I was studying. . . . From this I became convinced of the tendency of the unconscious material to flow into quite definite molds. . . . (1925, p. 3)

He acquired still further enlightenment about the nature of the unconscious from von Hartmann, Schopenhauer's successor:

> Following Hartmann, I held that our unconscious is not meaningless but contains a mind. After I had taken this position I found much contradictory evi-

dence, and so the pendulum swung back and forth. At one time it seemed as though there must be some thread of purpose running through the unconscious, at another I was convinced there was none. . . . (P. 4)

He continues:

After this period, which contains the origin of all my ideas, I found Nietzsche. I was twenty-four when I read *Thus Spake Zarathustra*. I could not understand it but it made a profound impression upon me, and I felt an analogy between it and the girl I had been studying. (P. 6)

This was a mediumistic girl whom Jung had been studying during his last years as a medical student. She exhibited the phenomenon of multiple personality while in a state of trance. He made the case the subject of a dissertation on occult phenomena (1902), which at this early period had begun to awaken his interest in psychology. He had intended to specialize in internal medicine but was turned away from this path by a chance reading of Krafft-Ebing's *Textbook of Insanity* (1890). This book awakened his determination "to work out the unconscious phenomena of the psychoses" (1925, p. 7) as being the cause of blockage in conscious-unconscious interaction. This interest led him to his meeting with Freud, who had been working on the same problem.

It was the recognition of the complex, which each had arrived at independently, that brought them together; it was the sexual theory that kept them from full agreement. Thus arose the conflict I have described between the cultural traditions in which they had been brought up, a conflict between philosophy and physiology. In the nineteenth century, two men of such different cultural conditioning could hardly have met at all, much less become close companions and coworkers. The strict physiological (that is, neurological) model of Freud's education and the broad philosophical model of Jung's would have alienated them from the start. But at the beginning of the twentieth century, the cultural atmosphere had so changed that they could find common ground. In retrospect today, the physiological tradition and the philosophical tradition seem like two ships sailing at a great distance from each other but heading for the same port. Freud and Jung both reached that port about 1903, and today we would call it psychology, if by that term we mean depth psychology in the widest sense. There was to be ample room in this new port for numerous other contributions to psychology besides those of Freud and Jung. There were also important pilot ships that conducted them into this port.

It is significant that both Freud and Jung were helped in finding their new direction by men outside the German-speaking world. The man who meant the most to Freud in this respect was Charcot, who, even though firmly entrenched within neurological medicine, opened the door to a new kind of empiricism. Jones tells us that Charcot "was a true follower of Galileo! This empirical attitude was to stand Freud in good stead in the years of his startling discoveries" (1953, p. 208). Charcot's description of repressed sexuality in hysteria was a revelation to Freud. Jung found his own introduction to empiricism in William James' *The Principles of Psychology* and in James' subsequent formulation of pragmatism. Of him Jung said: "He led psychology away from academic circles to the investigation of the personality itself and into the realm of the doctor" (1933–34, p. 21).

Since Freud was the older man, he was, of course, less responsive to the new developments that the early twentieth century had to offer, by which I mean such breakthroughs as were achieved by Bergson, Whitehead, Einstein, and others, in fields ranging from science to philosophy. Nevertheless, Freud and Jung enjoyed from 1906 to 1913 what I would call the same cultural optimism about the development of science, philosophy, and art, all of which were flourishing at that time. After all, they were both well educated in the humanities. The first decade of this century was a strange mixture of decadence and creativity. Nineteenth-century intellectual rigidity and emotional repression were all too apparent in the lives of middle-class people of the time. It was, of course, Freud's work, above all, to expose and offer a cure for this cultural neurosis. But as the title of Whitehead's famous book implies, it was also a time that was ripe for new "adventures of ideas." During the early phase of their association, Freud and Jung basked in the sunshine of an enlightened atheism permitted by the cultural weather of that period.

One of the happy products of their association, also fostered by their contemporary culture, was the emergence of something that was neither scientific nor philosophic. It was aesthetic. In different ways they both affirmed that their work was concerned with human development as a process of creative discovery. They both show that the interpretation of dreams or fantasies may awaken in the analyst an aesthetic response, to the nature of certain patterns or images that promote the kind of apperception evoked by artists in the greatest literature, painting, and music. Freud was himself a superb literary artist in his descriptive passages and in the clarification or summation of his patients' symptomatology. Allen points out that what Freud said of Charcot could well be said of him:

> He had the nature of an artist . . . a *visuel*, a man who sees. . . . He used to look again and again at things he did not understand . . . till suddenly an

understanding of them dawned on him. In his mind's eye the apparent chaos presented by the continual repetition of the same symptoms then gave way to order. . . . (P. 110)

Some such process was at work in Freud's great discovery, and caused him to break out of his physiological (first) world. Jones locates this break at the end of the Breuer period, quoting Freud as follows: " 'If hysterics trace back their symptoms to fictitious traumas, this new fact signifies that they create such scenes in phantasy, and psychical reality requires to be taken into account alongside actual reality' " (1953, p. 267). This statement may seem like a truism today, but it was sensational in 1895.

Quite early, Jung was impressed by the aesthetic aspect of the language of the psyche. In a letter to Karl Abraham in 1908, he wrote: "Seldom in my analytical work have I been so struck by the 'beauty' of neurosis as with this patient. The construction and course of the dreams are of a rare aesthetic beauty" (1973, p. 5).

Jung and Freud might have found some reconciliation in the creative synthesis of science, art, and philosophy had Jung not been drawn away by his own particular genius for exploring the religious aspect of psychic experience. This interest may be what really brought about their final separation, since Freud quite rightly could not accept it in the psychoanalytic framework he had created. Jung's essay "Freud and Jung: Contrasts" (1929b) expresses his view of their impasse concerning religion. And so Freud remained true to the scientific spirit in which he had been nourished, while Jung entrusted his future to the seemingly irrational guidance of mythology and worldwide myth-related religious patterns.

At first, however, Freud viewed Jung's struggle to understand mythology with interest and a kind of benevolent fatherly approval. After all, he was about to have a shot at interpreting mythology himself, in *Totem and Taboo*. But when Freud turned in this direction, he followed the path already traveled by his own contemporaries, men like Robertson Smith and Sir James Frazer, who had the same scientific detachment from their material that Freud had from his. Explorers of mythology at that time were interested in myths not for their content but for their usefulness in pointing the way back to the origins of human culture. As represented by Durkheim and the École Sociologique, or by the English archaeologist and Greek scholar Jane Harrison, they were looking for one thing and one thing only: the social origin of all culture. Religion, philosophy, even science itself, were no longer of interest to these scholars, who considered them to be merely later developments; the origin of culture *had to be a "total social fact,"* as Lévi-Strauss phrases it. In other words, they were moving away from the study of mythology as such, and into sociology, which was a dead end from the point of view of any further psychological research in the understanding of myth and ritual.

In contrast to this trend, Jung, though unconsciously at first, was one of a group of avant-garde champions of myth not only as a language of ancient cultures, but also as a universal language of the modern psyche. These men were so far ahead of their time that the movement to which they belonged could not begin to manifest itself until the 1920s and 1930s. Only in the 1940s did Jung cautiously publish *Essays on a Science of Mythology,* in collaboration with Kerényi, the author of many works on Greek mythology. At this time, like-minded writers from many fields— religion and art historians, such as Mircea Eliade and Herbert Read, cultural anthropologists, and structural anthropologists—were producing a rapidly growing body of literature. Two of Freud's own followers, Eric Fromm and Erik Erikson, responded to this new trend; on the Jungian side, the writings of Heinrich Zimmer (as introduced by Joseph Campbell) and Erich Neumann began to appear at the same time.

Freud and Jung had already, inevitably, experienced a cultural parting of the ways before their final break, which occurred soon after the publication of Jung's *Symbols of Transformation* and Freud's *Totem and Taboo.* These two works appeared in the same year (1912), but on different sides of a distinct cultural watershed. And so we are left to reconcile these two great, but rather disjointed, traditions as best we can—traditions that, in their lifetimes, Freud and Jung, being themselves such important instruments of the whole process of cultural change, could not bring together.

JUNGIAN ANALYSIS IN THE UNITED STATES

C. G. Jung first came to the United States in 1909 with Sigmund Freud, at the invitation of Stanley Hall, to speak about the new science of psychoanalysis at Clark University. Everyone who met Jung was impressed with the dynamic quality of his personality. Therefore it seems suitable today to refer to his type of analysis in the United States as Jungian rather than by the formal designation, analytical psychology, which he chose in order to distinguish it from psychoanalysis. In later years, Jung himself said that the whole of his psychology could be understood as a personal confession. This statement used to trouble me when I was still one of his students. I wanted, and indeed needed, to believe that his psychology was scientifically valid and independent of the idiosyncracies of its creator. This turned out to be my misunderstanding, and it was fully resolved through Jung's exposure of the truly personal aspects of his life and thought in his auto-biographical work *Memories, Dreams, Reflections.* What he describes there is personal but so mixed with transpersonal imagery that it demonstrates the validity of his discovery of the collective unconscious, which, by definition, is independent of race, history, or creed. So I found that the most important scientific foundation of his work stood firm and separate from his own personal experience of it after all.

Where Jung's personal experience does, however, still color certain aspects of his writing, we individual practitioners have had to reformulate our therapeutic experiences when they differ from those of the master. This is to be expected since individuation (Jung 1921) implies that no psychotherapist can be called Jungian without first becoming as differentiated an individual as he or she can be in response to his or her own personal analysis.

From about 1918 onward, Jungian analysis began to acquire its own tradition, with its theory and methodology more clearly defined each year. By 1930 it began to draw practitioners from many countries other than Switzerland. During the 1930s, however, the presence of Jung still dominated his school. Following World War II, this changed. The personal influence of Jung on his immediate followers gave way, as independent Jung Institutes and groups of practitioners began to appear. I was a participant-observer during the transitional period that followed, and I will try to indicate the basic guidelines that were set down at that time.

On one of my visits to Zurich, I became acquainted with two impressive women staying at my hotel. The older of the two was Dr. Beatrice Hinkle, a Jungian analyst from New York, and her companion was Alice Raphael, a Goethe scholar. It was somewhat awesome to realize what a strong influence American women had been in the movement associated with Jung. Dr. Hinkle first introduced Jung in his own right, apart from Freud, to his American audience by her translation of the book that marked his separation from Freud, *Transformations and Symbols of the Libido,* the English title of which was *Psychology of the Unconscious* (now called *Symbols of Transformation*). Although I never knew her well, I always heard Dr. Hinkle spoken of with special approval among members of the psychiatric profession as one of the most effective analysts (whether Freudian or Jungian) of the early period in the United States. She was not as well known in Jungian circles as she might have been, since she tried to alter Jung's theory of typology in a book that failed in its purpose and did not survive a first printing. She had tried to add two subtypes which she called the emotional introvert and the subjective extravert.

A younger group of women, also in New York, then took up the task of founding the school of Jungian analysis. These women were anxious to practice this form of analysis following as closely as possible the model set by Jung himself. Dr. M. Esther Harding, Dr. Eleanor Bertine, and Dr. Kristine Mann established their practices in the 1920s but returned separately each year for a two-month period of further training-analysis with Jung in Küsnacht. They founded the first American analytical psychology club, in New York, and this encouraged a number of interested people, most of whom were analysands, to pursue their study of Jung beyond their own personal need for understanding themselves. Dr. Harding herself became the leading expositor of Jung in the United States during the following years with her easy, semipopular style of writing. The work of these strongly dedicated, remarkable medical women was rewarded in a public manner when Jung came to lead a conference in 1937 in the small community of Bailey Island, Maine, where they spent their summers. He then gave a public lecture in New York that was sponsored by the analytical psychology club.

There were two other women analysts in New York who had stable practices. One was Frances Wickes, a lay analyst who became well known through her book *The Inner World of Childhood* (1927), which attracted Jung's interest, followed later by *The Inner World of Man* (1947) and *The Inner World of Choice* (1965). She had a special skill for working with patients gifted in the arts. This type of work was not so much analytical as inspirational. Her intuitive wisdom rescued many people from those blocks to creativity that psychiatrists so often fail to recognize for what they are and try to explain with useless diagnostic labels. Another, rather self-effacing woman analyst in New York, Dr. Margaret Nordfeld, had a similar talent. Certain creative people seem to sense this quality in a therapist and intuitively seek out one who can cure them of such blocking. This condition can only be removed by a person with an aesthetic attitude who can meet them on their own ground. Two patients of mine who started with Nordfeld later accomplished outstanding works, one as a writer, the other as a teacher and art therapist whose work was widely recognized for its understanding and treatment of preschool children.

All the Jungian analysts I have mentioned were women. There were no men in the field except Dr. James Whitney (not to be confused with his son, James Whitney, who later became a Jungian analyst), but he is the exception that proved the rule. He was much less active than his wife, Dr. Elizabeth Whitney, another outstanding Jungian analyst, who had a large, successful practice in San Francisco that began in 1928 and continued well into the 1950s. Her husband, a former general practitioner, lived only a short time after becoming an analyst.

Why, it may be asked, were women so much more responsive to Jungian analysis than men? Numerous answers came to mind at the time this phenomenon was occurring, the 1920s and 1930s, but no one of them seemed to me adequate to explain it. We wondered whether it was due to Jung's emphasis on the role of the mother in the Oedipus complex, in contrast to Freud's emphasis on the role of the father. Was the United States heading towards matriarchy? Were American men afraid of acknowledging their feminine nature in accordance with Jung's concept of the anima? Was Jungian psychology too introverted for Americans, who love action and heroic achievement and mistrust introversion? Did Jung's inability to establish lasting relationships with men have something to do with it?

Only now at the beginning of the 1980s can we perhaps review this trend with some new insight. Did these women not sense in Jung's psychology a new valuation of woman's position in the culture? Did they not also see how much it would mean to men to understand the "archetypal feminine" to be found in them no less than in women? The United States, especially the area around New York City, was the logical place for this to happen, because the problems of estrangement and tension in the man-woman relationships of our time were felt more acutely there, perhaps, than anywhere else in the Western world. These problems were a perennial theme in the outstanding American writings and plays of that time, works by Hemingway, O'Neill, Dreiser, Fitzgerald, and Wilder. At the Second Bailey Island Conference in honor of Dr. Harding's eightieth birthday, she voiced this opinion in her final speech at the banquet. Acknowledging that the lack of men in the field had been a limitation to their work, she went on to say that one meaning of their contribution, as women, was that of pioneering a new attitude toward the feminine.

These women found in Jung a man who honored the principle of relationship in which neither sex is limited to playing a stereotyped role. Although he thought that women excelled in the use of Eros as a function of relatedness and that men excelled in the use of Logos as a function of intellection, Jung believed that any development of Self, over and above the claims of the ego, brought both men and women into the same field of consciousness with an equal sharing of their capacities. Thus it was not in "women" but in one woman at a time, in her individual experience, that he examined the problems of women. The cultural problem as such concerned him very much less, though he approached it effectively in his essay "Woman in Europe" (1927) when he described how cultural changes had psychological effects.

Meanwhile, an interest in Jung's psychology on the part of men, already existing in Europe, was beginning to awaken here in response to the influence of the English analyst, Dr. H. G. Baynes, who had been one of Jung's assistant analysts in Zurich. He was a stimulating and joyous visitor to the West Coast in 1928. I learned a great deal from him, and he encouraged me to go to Zurich to be analyzed by Jung the following year. He had a strong personal influence on certain academic men in the United States, especially at the University of California and in Cambridge, Massachusetts. Soon the engaging presence of a Harvard psychologist, Henry Murray, was also felt. Together with Christiana Morgan, an analysand of Jung, Murray contributed to the spread of Jungian psychology to the clinical branch of American psychologists. He devised the thematic apperception test, or TAT, and other testing programs and wrote brilliantly about the relevance of the collective unconscious to an understanding of early American literature, especially that of Melville.

Toward the end of the 1930s, various men trained as Jungian analysts began to work in the United States. Dr. Archibald Strong, formerly of Rigg's Sanitarium, started practicing in New York. By 1942, Dr. Joseph Wheelwright and Jane Wheelwright (husband and wife, both trained by Jung) and I began our practices in San Francisco. Soon after that, Dr. James Kirsch and his wife, Hilde Kirsch, whose training likewise began with Jung, and the psychologist Dr. Max Zeller came from Germany to Los Angeles. In the early 1950s, Dr. Edward Edinger and Dr. E. Whitmont became active in New York, after training with Drs. Harding and Bertine. They added their own formulations of analytical psychology to those of Dr. Harding, Marie-Louise von Franz, Erich Neumann, Gerhard Adler, and the other writers who represented the best in Jungian thought, in a yearly journal, *Spring,* edited in New York and supported by Jane Abbott Pratt.

Meanwhile the Bollingen Foundation, established in New York by Paul and Mary Mellon, under the direction of Jack Barrett and Vaun Gilmore and the editorial acumen of William McGuire, was beginning to provide an excellent library of Jung's collected works and of research in the related fields of mythology, philosophy, poetry, art, and anthropology. A specific collection of pictures on religious art and archaeology had been started by Olga Froebe-Kapteyn to illustrate the archetypal themes discussed at the yearly Eranos conference in Ascona, Switzerland. It was developed further by Jessie Fraser with the assistance of Jane Pratt and the Bollingen Foundation. This project, known as the Archive for Research in Archetypal Symbolism, or ARAS, is housed at the C. G. Jung Foundation in New York, with duplicate copies at the San Francisco and Los Angeles Institutes.

In recent years the appearance throughout the United States of many analysts, too numerous to list, trained at the Zurich Institute, has led to the formation of new institutes, centers, and associations. These developments have produced a new ferment of ideas that suggests what Jungian analysis will one day become. The present collection of papers edited by Murray Stein is a valuable indication of the liveliness of the Jungian movement in the United States at this time.

THE PRACTICE OF JUNGIAN ANALYSIS

Jungian analysis in the United States has never departed so far from its European origins as to change the foundation and structure of C. G. Jung's basic concepts: the collective unconscious, the ego, the shadow, the Self, and the personality types and functions. But certain revisions of the psychodynamic application of his theories have been made from time to time in recent years. The most important of these revisions relates to Jung's early tendency to associate the development of the ego with the first half of life, while the influence of the Self upon the psyche was reserved for the second half of life. This distinction implied that the individuation process could only be found in a mature person. However, clinical observations have provided extensive proof that the Self may be experienced by a child or an adolescent, while a complete formation of ego-identity may not take place until much later than might be considered normal (Dunn, p. 55). Individuating experiences, though not individuation in its mature phase, may occur at any age, even in young children (Fordham 1970).

Other revisions have not so far drastically altered the practice of analytical psychology, which shows a wholesome consensus, even though it has spread from Zurich to Germany, France, Belgium, Italy, the United States, Canada, Brazil, Israel, Venezuela, Australia, South Africa, Japan, England, Austria, Denmark, Holland, New Zealand, and Korea. The only essential distinction is whether the Jungian practitioner is an analyst or a psychotherapist. Jung himself frequently spoke of analysis and psychotherapy in a way that implied that each required a different method. Analysis implied intensive work involving patient and doctor over a long period of time with frequent sessions. Psychotherapy implied an alliance between therapist and patient that was not binding as to time or as to frequency of sessions, and that could be adjusted to meet immediate needs for psychological insight or crisis intervention; it could, however, turn into an analysis at any time.

Jungian analysis, no less than Jungian psychotherapy, departs from the

Freudian model of closed-system analysis, in which the analyst maintains an impersonal and essentially passive position vis-à-vis the patient (Fordham 1978, p. 107). Jung introduced a dialectical procedure "based on an open-system theory: the patient and analyst were conceived to interact all the time" (ibid., p. 107). The open-system method may correspond, at times, to the Adlerian method of reeducation. But analysis in any full sense of the word does not wholly abandon classical psychoanalysis, insofar as it provides certain patients with a protective setting in which to regress to early childhood in order to reexperience and correct disorders in their object relations. But the Jungian treatment of regression, following Jung's theory of the role of the Self, goes further; it expects to find regression occurring not just in the service of the ego, but also in the service of the Self.

I find that what happens during deep regression is a fresh encounter of the ego with its dimly remembered "primal" Self-image, following which the ego separates itself from that primal image in collaboration with the analyst. The patient is thus able to be aware of the process by which separation occurs, and of how it inevitably leads to a reunion with original parent figures, as a healing experience. This process is followed by a new sense of parent-child separation mediated by the analyst, in the analytical "container" or "temenos" (Meier).

A period of redevelopment then occurs, spontaneously enabling the patient to use the educational patterns of the culture in his or her own, not society's, way. This process involves an activation of the archetype of initiation as the transitional means of arriving at a mature ego-and-Self development (Edinger). The psyche moves toward maturity as a kind of "ultimate" Self-image (Henderson 1967). The paradoxical use of the word *Self* with both *primal* and *ultimate* merely emphasizes the transitional nature of the analytical process in general. The conflict experienced by anyone in such an induced "rite of passage" is mediated by the creation of symbols, which suggests that there is a symbolic method that may be used to describe this kind of analysis (Goodheart). I recall an alchemical saying Jung was fond of quoting to express this:

In Habentibus Symbolum Facilior Est Transitus

which I have translated as:

It is easier for those who have a symbol to change.

Those of us who were analyzed by Jung, and many others who have followed the Zurich model, are most comfortable using the symbolic method not only for our patients but for ourselves, in our efforts at self-analysis. It is implemented by the use of amplification of dream or fantasy contents in order to draw upon the archetypal source of all inner imagery. In contrast, there is an alternative method, which has always existed in Jungian analysis or psychotherapy as a sort of reaction-formation to the symbolic method. It is a purely clinical method of dealing directly with the patient's personal problems. This method has been given a more official kind of recognition and sponsorship by Fordham and those members of the London school of analytical psychology whose practice consists mainly of children and regressed adults. It is also being taken up by some of the younger analysts in the United States. Those analysts who favor the clinical method are working mainly in a neo-Freudian style and are at variance with those who use the symbolic method—or seem to be, until one talks to them about specific cases. Then the clinical and symbolic methods seem at times identical, or at least overlapping. However, there is still some danger that these two different styles may become theoretically polarized into two quite different schools of Jungian thought, the clinical-personal and cultural-anthropological. In fact, some writers have expressed the opinion that this has already occurred (Hubback, p. 219).

I prefer to think that, for the most part, any such split is to be found in certain individual therapists at certain times and not in the movement as a whole. I also prefer to use a term that better defines what we usually mean by *cultural*. A symbolic attitude arises from certain cultural roots that foster imagination instead of focused thought. This imagination might be likened to what we hear today about the activity of the right hemisphere of the brain, in contrast to the activity of the left hemisphere. This symbolic thinking may be diffused but not confused. It is in fact clear thinking, when true to its own intrinsic nature, and therefore is an activity of consciousness just as much as the focused thinking of the left hemisphere (Kenevan). When this symbolic attitude becomes habitual in the diagnosis and treatment of psychological disorders, one can use it to understand symbolically even those psychopathological states that used to be considered the exclusive province of the traditional psychiatrist.

As an example, let us take a patient suffering from a severe depression. If we approach this problem with a symbolic attitude, we try to find a metaphor to express the essence of the mood of the depressed person. Perhaps we feel that he or she is under the influence of some sinister senex-figure, a personification of the planet Saturn as in the astrological symbolism, that brings with it a feeling of repetitive limitation and a sense of defeat. But if the patient has accepted the depression as a necessary and welcome escape from a state of hypomanic excitement, we might recall the figure of "veiled Melancholy" in Keats' "Ode on Melancholy," with its suggestion of a feminine image of inwardness. This image symbolizes a wholesome attitude of introversion for relieving and healing the patient's suffering. Keats suggests this in the last lines of the poem; a state of depression is transformed in accordance with a suitably contemplative mood:

Ay, in the very temple of Delight
   Veil'd Melancholy has her sovran shrine
      Though seen of none save him whose strenuous tongue
    Can burst Joy's grape against his palate fine;
His soul shall taste the sadness of her might,
    And be among her cloudy trophies hung.

Such a use of symbolism need not conflict with a clinical method, provided the analyst relies upon the actual mood, affect, and dream imagery of the patients and does not impose his or her own fantasies upon them. The Keats poem was in fact the association of a patient of mine at the time of realizing such a symbolic change of mood. A strict analytical clinician may object that any amplification of a symbolic nature is to be avoided because it might interfere with the patient's spontaneous recovery and that, in any case, no amount of psychological intervention without drugs ever shortened a depression, which must run its course. But it can also be claimed that a symbolic attitude helps the analyst to be ready to find meaning in the symptom when none is apparent to the patient.

I have mentioned depression because it is one of the most difficult conditions in which to find any symbolic content. We meet many other conditions in our practice, especially in borderline states, in which dreams or fantasies are overflowing with imagery that can be used for interpretation in meaningful ways. Since most of this material comes from a primordial level of the unconscious and is pre-Oedipal, it then becomes important to look for the particular form the Oedipus complex takes in the subsequent development of the patient. Following Freud's original insight into Sophocles' famous tragedy *Oedipus Rex,* and its alternate version as represented in *Hamlet* (Jones 1949), many Jungian analysts have vastly expanded this practice, learning to use Greek mythology for help in defining all sorts of character disorders in a cultural-archetypal context (see Malamud; Hillman and Roscher; Stein; and Berry, among others).

If, however, the imaginal activity invested in this symbolic approach becomes an end in itself, it may have the aesthetically seductive effect of concealing, instead of curing, the original problem for which the patient sought help. In this sense, it merely sets up another line of defense against facing the personal shadow. Hence it has become an essential part of analytical technique to analyze the mutual empathy, or sense of sharing something secret, that takes place between analyst and analysand in the phenomenon of transference and countertransference. Because this process requires making conscious what was unconscious, the symbols are replaced by new realities. This transformation is brought about by means of a "transcendent function of the psyche" (Jung 1957), which amounts to a psychological mutation whereby the ever-changing, repetitive symbolism of the unconscious is transformed into the specificity of consciousness.

Jung once gave me a simple example of this during a conversation on the subject of the transcendent function. He described a patient who was a gifted but uneducated artist. This man had reached the limit of his powers and could not progress without more knowledge of his craft and his relation to the larger spirit of his time, the *Zeitgeist*, as it is known in the German language. Then in a dream he saw emerging from the earth some prehistoric forms of life that suggested the beginning of a transformative process, from lower to higher forms of life. Jung saw this dream, with its powerful imagery of new beginnings, as an inner impulse for some radical change. Shortly afterward, the patient experienced a profound change of attitude with a concomitant release of new energy that allowed him to undertake the studies he needed. He began to educate himself for the creative work he had yet to produce, and subsequently did produce.

Once a realization has occurred of the symbolic nature of the process that unfolds in the course of a typical Jungian analysis, the transference of the analysand and the countertransference of the analyst take on a more symbolic meaning. There is an urgency to resolve the compulsive fascination with the archetypal patterns involved in the relationship. Jung described this aspect of the transference by referring to the pictorial representations of a *hierosgamos*, or sacred marriage, in the *Rosarium Philosophorum*, an alchemical manuscript. In "Psychology of the Transference," he examined many archaic patterns of kinship relationships to show how an apparently straightforward erotic attraction conceals a regressive incest wish, and how, in the formation of a fourfold union of opposites (the marriage *quaternio*), a biologically binding experience is transformed into a spiritually liberating one.

The perennial question now occurs of whether Jung's approach to the unconscious is basically religious. Does he encourage a metaphysical solution to life's problems or does he merely psychologize the life of the spirit? Jung's own statements as early as his "Commentary on 'The Secret of the Golden Flower' " should leave no doubt that he faced this question squarely both as a scientist and as a humanistic philosopher. He says:

> . . . I strip things of their metaphysical wrappings in order to make them objects of psychology. In that way I can . . . discover psychological facts and processes that before were veiled in symbols and beyond my comprehension. In doing so I may perhaps be following in the footsteps of the faithful, and

may possibly have similar experiences; and if in the end there should be something ineffably metaphysical behind it all, it would then have the best opportunity of showing itself. (1929a, pp. 49–50)

Working with individuals in this spirit becomes an adventure for both analyst and patient; the nature of the unconscious, opened to consciousness, is felt to be personal, yet appears in an impersonal way. Again let me quote Jung in a late paper, "The Philosophical Tree." The trickster figure, called Mercurius in alchemy, appears in the "great work" as a spirit of paradox, which in psychotherapy begins with a "confrontation with the personal unconscious and then leads to archetypal symbols." In the process of therapy, this confrontation temporarily abolishes "the dissociation" between these two worlds, the personal and the archetypal:

This means not only bringing the conflict to consciousness; it also involves an experience of a special kind, namely, the recognition of an alien "other" in oneself, or the objective presence of another will. The alchemists, with astonishing accuracy, called this barely understandable thing Mercurius. . . . he is God, daemon, person, thing, and the innermost secret in man; psychic as well as somatic. He is himself the source of all opposites, since he is duplex. . . . (1954, p. 348)

These statements have given that overused word *depth* a much more specific meaning than was possible in the early days of analytical psychology. At that time a certain obscurity veiled the process of development and many practitioners were thankful not to have to think about such "barely understandable" factors. It was common then for therapists to criticize Jung for his "mystical" ideas and to bolster their patients' morale with the "commonsense" formulations of other schools of psychology. But Jung persisted in maintaining that the spirit of paradox had to be faced if we are to resolve basic conflicts, and he expressed it as follows: "So we should not begrudge Paracelsus and the alchemists their secret language. . . . The protean mythologem and the shimmering symbol express the processes of the psyche far more trenchantly . . . than the clearest concept . . . " (1942, p. 162).

Throughout these alchemical studies we see how Jung responded to the poetry inherent in the process of psychic change. Although he made no recommendation that other practitioners follow his example, the psychological validity of this response is shown in an early passage from "Commentary on 'The Secret of the Golden Flower.' " There, "circulation of light" and the appearance of a "germinal vesicle" suggest to Jung his work with his patients, in which the transcendent function is best symbolized by the emergence of light out of darkness: ". . . out of the 'lead of the water region' grows the noble gold; what is unconscious becomes conscious in the form of a living process of growth" (1929a, p. 24).

Before leaving the subject of alchemy, I can say in support of Jung's enthusiasm for its symbolic content that in my seminars at the Institute in San Francisco and elsewhere, I have found that a translation of alchemical imagery (as represented in such manuscripts as the *Rosarium Philosophorum* and the *Splendor Solis*) into the language of psychodynamics has been received by my students as a much more practical form of teaching than any other in my repertoire.

In an article on this subject (1978, p. 248), I made passing reference to the difference between students whose primary personality function is intuition and those whose primary function is sensation. We know from Jung that intuition in this sense means greater interest in future possibilities, in contrast to sensation, which is chiefly concerned with present actualities. In a philosophic sense, intuition, as a function of the mind, affirms the principle of becoming, and sensation, the principle of being. Bradway and Wheelwright, in their testing of a large number of Jungian analysts, found that "the overwhelming majority of analysts in all . . . geographical locations are introverted rather than extraverted in attitude and more at home with intuition than with sensation" (p. 214).

This does not, however, mean that these introverted intuitive analysts are only concerned with inner possibilities. They show a "high regard for role-playing, non-verbal art forms, family therapy, group therapy, body involvement techniques and marathon therapy." In contrast to them, the introverted sensation types appear to favor formal analysis and "like to work with character disorders more than do intuitives" (p. 223).

The extraverted analysts, according to this survey, are more inclined to enter into intense relationships with patients, comfort the patient by touching, and use typology in making connections or interpretations. Although astrology is infrequently used by analysts, those who do use it are much more likely to be extraverted than introverted.

Although these statistics are not surprising to those who have had a Jungian analysis, anyone else is bound to wonder why so many analysts in this field are of the intuitive introverted type. It may mean that there is so little regard for the realities of everyday life that these problems are left to future "ideal" solutions and are not fully tested in present time or with appropriate care to assessing the effects of past conditioning. I once had a patient whose problems were certainly very real in every outer sense of the word. His marriage had collapsed; security in his business had declined; he was threatened with alcoholism; and he himself felt that rather than analysis what he really needed was therapeutic "first aid." He asked friends what they knew of Jungian analysis and reported that they said it was fine for some people, but for the most part was only "frosting on the cake." Then, during a period when I was away, he consulted other psychotherapists more actively engaged in family counseling and marriage counseling, and in treating drug abuse. He found that their advice to him was in no way different from mine, except that with me he had access to dream interpretation. This aspect of his analysis threw his practical problems into high relief, so he could see them more clearly and feel their deeper impact. It is to this inner dimension of any problem that the intuitive analyst responds naturally.

If the intuitive analyst were true to his or her original type reaction and to no other, his or her effectiveness would indeed be only ''frosting on the cake.'' But if the analyst has been analyzed, that inner change has occurred that renders the inferior function (in this case, sensation) accessible to consciousness in such a way as to compensate the one-sidedness of the superior function, intuition. The person who has undergone this change is a very different kind of person from an uncompensated intuitive. In like manner, an analyst with sensation as a superior function has undergone a similar change so that intuition is available to consciousness to form a similar compensation. Ultimately, whatever the superior function may be, the end result of any full analysis convinces both therapist and patient that they live with that diversity represented by all four functions, and not exclusively from one or two, however dominant these may previously have been (cf. chapter by Quenk and Quenk, below).

A somewhat harder bridge to cross is the one joining the polar opposites of introversion and extraversion. It is deceptively simple at first to acknowledge them, and the Jungian analyst who is working with a patient of the opposite type is likely to assume that all difficulties in communication may be abolished by recognizing this difference. The patient is also inclined to minimize this difficulty, enjoying, as it is so easy to do, a sense of companionship with a therapist who so admirably complements his or her own type. In my experience this is the vehicle of an illusion. No matter how well they understand each other's type reaction, there will be endless misunderstandings and feelings of being judged from the other's point of view.

This potential for misunderstanding is especially marked in the very conduct of the analytical sessions. The introverted analyst enjoys the intimacy and privacy of the sessions; they seem natural. The extraverted analyst wants to feel the dynamism of relationship, unlike the introvert who feels most comfortable with its reflective, uninvolved interchange. The introverted analysand may want to remain too long in the analytical container, whereas the extraverted analyst may want to push him or her out into life too soon, and this may work similarly the other way around. For the most part, however, patience and open discussion of therapeutic procedure resolve such problems, since both therapist and patient are, by this time, partners sharing a tension of opposites that helps the patient to discover "a reconciling symbol" (Jung 1921). This method honors both principles, separation and union, leading the analyst to a working hypothesis that transcends the typological bias of either.

I have actually found in many cases that I need only use the Jungian type theory sparingly, since it may lead to hair splitting about how extraverted or introverted certain people appear to each other to be. This was Jung's own cautionary advice. In other cases, the type difference is obvious from the first, and it becomes part of the therapy for the patient to learn how this influences his or her relationships and attitudes to society.

Here we meet a larger issue of cultural conditioning that is a whole subject in itself, one that sooner or later comes into any therapeutic discussion. This issue may lead to a study of those ethnic traditions that promote differences of cultural attitude as well as of function or type. Awareness of such differences becomes therapeutically desirable when, as we see so often in the United States, analyst and analysand have grown up in different traditions. Thus the introverted quality of social custom as it is found in New England, Scotland, or Switzerland contrasts strongly with the highly extraverted quality of social life in the younger frontiers, such as the Middle West or Far West of the United States, Australia, or Israel. Besides a difference in type reactions, there are other cultural attitudes to be considered in any process of psychological change, attitudes that I have found it useful to classify roughly as religious, social, aesthetic, and philosophic (1962). This subject is still too speculative to be discussed as a typical part of a Jungian analysis, but such speculations at least open a window through which new patterns, formed by the meeting of psychology and anthropology, may be perceived.

One aspect of the Jungian approach to culture that has already borne fruit is the study of shamanism as an archetypal pattern underlying any deep engagement in the process of healing. There was a time when the appearance of shamanic patterns in the unconscious was said to denote a tendency to schizophrenic dissociation. Thanks to the comparative method of studying shamanism, so well exemplified in Eliade's classic work, several Jungian analysts have presented case material (for example, Henderson 1967) in which shamanic patterns appear, and others (Sandner; Reed) have explored actual shamanism. These studies have rescued this subject from the tundra of Siberia and the deserts of Australia and given it an important place in our analytic way of perceiving the material of our patients.

Although no Jungian analyst would call himself a shaman, there is a parallel between depth analysis and shamanic healing that we cannot fail to respect and value when it has been called to our attention. Sandner rightly points out that a kind of "symbolic shamanism," such as we find in the chantways and sandpaintings of the Navaho Indians, is similar to the material we deal with in our work of exploring certain kinds of archetypal imagery. The difference lies in the roles played by the participants. The Navaho medicine man performs the active role of priest, and the patient is an essentially passive recipient of the healing power of the ceremonial. In Jungian analysis, it is the patient who produces the material. Aided by the analyst, who applies his or her interpretive skill in the role of participant-observer, the patient may then experience analysis as an active process of self-healing.

Our main concern as therapists is to learn to use these archaic rituals to perceive the origin of archetypal conditioning in the psyche and distinguish between this origin and later cultural developments. All too frequently the modern patient, as well as the psychotherapist, even one technically skilled in neo-Freudian methods, takes refuge in traditional cultural attitudes that do not allow the most basic changes of the psyche to occur. An important characteristic of this type of analyst, in contrast to the Jungian analyst, lies in his or her conviction that all essential change comes from within the culture pattern itself as it has been established by tradition and formal education.

We should not, however, minimize the importance of studying the culture patterns for their influence on the early unconscious conditioning of our patients. We may also use them to conceptualize the archetypes before meeting them at their affective source. Jungian psychology in this sense is like a quest undertaken with religious feeling for the mystery to be unveiled in the process of discovering our way to this source. It cannot be identified exclusively with the study of instinctual drives or characterological configurations. However well we may have analyzed our patients for personality disorders or assisted in separating them from the ill effects of parental influences in childhood, there remains the unknown source of psychic conditioning in the region of the primal Self to be tapped wherever we can find it. The shamanic model offers the best opportunity for understanding the nature of this activity.

REFERENCES

Adler, G. 1965. Methods of treatment in analytical psychology. In *Psychoanalytic techniques*, ed. B. B. Wolman, pp. 338–78. New York: Basic Books.

Allen, D. 1974. *The fear of looking*. Charlottesville, Va.: University Press of Virginia.

Berry, P. 1975. The rape of Demeter/Persephone and neurosis. *Spring* 1975: 186–98.

Bradway, K., and Wheelwright, J. 1978. The psychological type of the analyst in its relation to analytical practice. *Journal of Analytical Psychology* 23/3: 211–25.

Dunn, J. 1961. Analysis of patients who meet the problems of the first half of life in the second. *Journal of Analytical Psychology* 6/1:55–67.

Edinger, E. F. 1972. *Ego and archetype*. New York: Putnam.

Franz, M.-L. von. 1970. *The problem of the puer aeternus*. New York: Spring Publications.

Freud, S. 1938. *On the history of the psychoanalytic movement*. New York: Random House, The Modern Library.

———. 1950. *Totem and taboo*. New York: Norton.

Fordham, M. 1970. *Children as individuals*. New York: Putnam.

———. 1973. The empirical foundation and theories of the self in Jung's works. In *Analytical psychology: a modern science*, ed. M. Fordham; R. Gordon; J. Hubback; and K. Lambert, pp. 12–38. London: Heinemann.

———. 1978. *Jungian psychotherapy*. New York: Wiley.

Goodheart, W. B. 1980. Theory of analytical interaction. *San Francisco Jung Institute Library Journal* 1/4:2–39.

Groesbeck, C. J. 1978. The shaman from Elko. In *The shaman from Elko*, ed. G. Hill, pp. 54–58. San Francisco: C. G. Jung Institute of San Francisco.

Harding, M. E. 1947. *Psychic energy*. New York: Pantheon.

———. 1963. *Journey into self*. New York: Pantheon.

———. 1965*a*. *The I and the not-I*. Princeton: Princeton University Press.

———. 1965*b*. *The parental image*. New York: Putnam.

Henderson, J. L. 1962. The archetype of culture. In *The archetype*, ed. A. Guggenbühl-Craig, pp. 3–14. New York: Karger, 1964.

———. 1967. *Thresholds of initiation*. Middletown, Conn.: Wesleyan University Press.

———. 1978. Practical application of alchemical theory. *Journal of Analytical Psychology* 23/3:248–51.

Hillman, J., and Roscher, W. H. 1972. *Pan and the nightmare*. New York: Spring Publications.

Hubback, J. 1980. Development and similarities, 1935–1980. *Journal of Analytical Psychology* 25/3:219–36.

Jones, E. 1949. *Hamlet and Oedipus*. New York: Norton.

———. 1953. *The life and work of Sigmund Freud*. Vol. 1. New York: Basic Books.

Jung, C. G. 1902. On the psychology and pathology of so-called occult phenomena. In *Collected works*, vol. 1, pp. 3–88. 2d ed. Princeton: Princeton University Press, 1970.

———. 1921. *Psychological types*. *Collected works*, vol. 6. Princeton: Princeton University Press, 1971.

———. 1925. *Seminar notes*. Privately circulated. Zurich: C. G. Jung Institute.

———. 1927. Woman in Europe. In *Collected works*, vol. 10, pp. 113–33. New York: Pantheon, 1964.

———. 1929*a*. Commentary on "The secret of the golden flower." In *Collected works,* vol. 13, pp. 1–55. Princeton: Princeton University Press, 1967.

———. 1929*b*. Freud and Jung: contrasts. In *Collected works,* vol. 4, pp. 333–40. New York: Pantheon, 1961.

———. 1933–34. *Modern psychology.* Notes on lectures given at the Eidgenössische Technische Hochschule. Mimeographed. Zurich: C. G. Jung Institute.

———. 1938. *Modern psychology.* Vols. 1 and 2. Privately circulated. Zurich: C. G. Jung Institute, 1959.

———. 1942. Paracelsus as a spiritual phenomenon. In *Collected works,* vol. 13, pp. 109–89. Princeton: Princeton University Press, 1967.

———. 1946. Psychology of the transference. In *Collected works,* vol. 16, pp. 163–323. New York: Pantheon, 1954.

———. 1954. The philosophical tree. In *Collected works,* vol. 13, pp. 251–349. Princeton: Princeton University Press, 1967.

———. 1957. The transcendent function. In *Collected works,* vol. 8, pp. 67–91. New York: Pantheon, 1960.

———. 1961. *Memories, dreams, reflections.* New York: Random House.

———. 1973. *Letters.* Vol. 1. Ed. G. Adler. Princeton: Princeton University Press.

Keats, J. 1920. *The poetical works of John Keats.* London: Oxford University Press.

Kenevan, P. 1981. Eros, logos, and androgeny. *Psychological Perspectives* 12/1: 8–21.

Lévi-Strauss, C. 1967. *The scope of anthropology.* London: Jonathan Cape.

McGuire, W., ed. 1974. *The Freud-Jung letters.* Princeton: Princeton University Press.

Malamud, R. 1971. The amazon problem. *Spring* 1971:1–21.

Meier, C. A. 1967. *Ancient incubation and modern psychotherapy.* Evanston: Northwestern University Press.

Munn, T. 1936. *Freud und die zukunft.* Vienna: Fischer Verlag.

Neumann, E. 1959*a*. The psychological stages of feminine development. *Spring* 1959:63–97.

———. 1959*b*. The significance of the genetic aspect for analytical psychology. *Journal of Analytical Psychology* 4/2:125–37.

Reed, W. 1978. Shamanistic principles of initiation and power. In *The shaman from Elko,* ed. G. Hill, pp. 39–53. San Francisco: C. G. Jung Institute of San Francisco.

Sandner, D. 1979. *Navaho symbols of healing.* New York: Harcourt Brace Jovanovich.

Stein, M. 1980. Hephaistos: a pattern of introversion. In *Facing the gods,* ed. J. Hillman, pp. 37–86. Irving, Tex.: Spring Publications.

Weston, J. L. 1957. *From ritual to romance.* New York: Doubleday.

Whitmont, E. C. 1969. *The symbolic quest.* New York: Putnam.

Wickes, F. 1927. *The inner world of childhood.* New York: Appleton.

———. 1947. *The inner world of man.* New York: Farrar and Rinehart.

———. 1965. *The inner world of choice.* New York: Harper & Row.

[2]

THE AIMS AND GOAL
OF JUNGIAN ANALYSIS

Murray Stein

IN a paper entitled "Psychoanalysis and the Cure of Souls" (1928), Jung spoke of the goal of analysis and drew some parallels and contrasts between analysis and pastoral care. He noted that both share the goal of "curing souls." The difference is that, in analysis, this goal is pursued by working with the unconscious. Rather than trying to help persons reconnect to the symbols and meanings of traditional religions, the analyst seeks to help them relate to their own sources of vitality and symbolic meaning in the unconscious. So, while analysts and clergy may share a similar goal, their methods and approaches are quite different.

Whether this goal of curing souls is undertaken by priests and pastors or by analysts, however, one thing is usually true. The individuals who are seeking help must experience many, often seemingly small, changes in their conscious attitudes, in their patterns of behavior, and in what we call their psychological structures and dynamics, if their growth is to continue and be genuinely effective over an extended period of time. It is for the many small changes in attitude and behavior that the analyst works most of the time, using the therapeutic and analytic tools at his disposal.

For many Jungian analysts, the practice of analysis becomes such a concrete and emotionally immediate experience of daily life that it costs them considerable effort to become, or to remain, fully aware of its larger

Murray Stein, M.Div., is President of the Chicago Society of Jungian Analysts and maintains a private practice in Willmette, Illinois. A graduate of Yale College, Yale Divinity School, and the C. G. Jung Institute of Zurich, he is a founding member of the Inter-Regional Society of Jungian Analysts and the Chicago Society of Jungian Analysts. He is the translator of Karl Kerènyi's *Hermes* (1976), *Athene* (1978), and *Goddesses of the Sun and Moon* (1979), and of Adolph Guggenbühl-Craig's *Marriage—Dead or Alive* (1977). His published papers include "The Devouring Father" (1972), "Hephaistos: A Pattern of Introversion" (1973), "Narcissus" (1976), and "Hera: Bound and Unbound" (1977).

aims and its overall goal. Conversation among analysts is often full of
shoptalk about methods and analytic experiences, but relatively empty of
reflection on the goal of curing souls. In this respect, analysts are no different from members of the other professions; it is just as easy for doctors
and teachers to become so immersed in the particular tasks presented to
them every day, and in their need to perform them well, that they neglect
the question of what ends their efforts are serving. Even priests and pastors
frequently lapse into technical professionalism. All of these professionals
are directed, however, by the more or less unconscious purposes of their
professions. Occasionally one or another member of the profession will
"come up for air," for an overview of the daily round of work, and will
try to reflect on his or her practice and its ends. And so we ask: can we
spell out in some detail the Jungian analyst's goal of curing souls?

When a person enters the Jungian analyst's consulting room and brings
his or her problems to the analyst's professional attention, a relationship
begins and a process of treatment is set in motion. The most obvious goal
of this process is the alleviation of psychological suffering. Sometimes this
is a fairly simple, even though not necessarily brief, matter of guiding an
individual through a psychological crisis with skilled support and understanding. After the emergency has passed, the inherent psychological
health of the person takes over and does the rest. But the analyst routinely
confronts persons for whom this is not the case, for whom "health" in the
usual sense of adequate functioning and psychological well-being is either
not so easily attainable or not the real issue. Deeper psychological questions and problems are involved. It is these people who call for the greatest
and most sustained efforts the individual analyst can make. Of course they
must be similarly motivated to make the greater efforts demanded by analysis, and must be developmentally adequate to the task (cf. chapter by
Sandner and Beebe, below; see also chapter by McCurdy, below). In the
long-term treatment that ensues, the question of aims and goal does arise
in many subtle forms, often voiced as a challenge by analysands.

Before proceeding to my definition of the goal of analysis, a few words
about terminology in this chapter are in order. When speaking of *aims,* I
am referring to the small, specific changes in attitude, behavior, and perception that an analyst works and hopes for in analysis. By the *goal* of
analysis, I mean the overarching, general end point toward which the analytic work as a whole is oriented. In the day-to-day practice of Jungian
analysis, the sense of specific, limited aims tends to occupy the foreground
of consciousness for both analyst and analysand. This situation is actually
necessary and desirable. Many small battles are fought and either won or
lost as analysis goes on, and they will add up to significant changes in a

person's psychological patterns if more are won than are lost or severely compromised. When the eye is kept fixed on a long-range goal, the result is usually failure to meet the specific demands for insight and change as they present themselves in analysis and in life. These many small aims, which are intimately related to a person's existence in and out of analysis, can be grouped under a few large-scale aims. These, in turn, can be seen in a still longer perspective: the goal.

A survey of the Jungian literature would quickly reveal a wide range of opinion on the aims of analysis. In the following definition, which is highly abstract, I have attempted to state a goal that could be agreed upon by most Jungian authors and analysts, even if they would, individually, generate many different aims in formulating the more concrete applications and amplifications of this statement. With this definition I am starting with the most abstract and general statement of a goal:

> *Jungian analysis takes place within a dialectical relationship between two persons, analyst and analysand, and has for its goal the analysand's coming to terms with the unconscious: the analysand is meant to gain insight into the specific unconscious structures and dynamics that emerge during analysis, and the structures underlying ego-consciousness are meant to change in their dynamic relation to other, more unconscious structures and dynamics.*

This formula will serve as a guideline for pressing on in our reflections on the aims and goal of Jungian analysis.

> *Jungian analysis takes place within a dialectical relationship between two persons, analyst and analysand . . .*

The Jungian use of the term *analysis* is a legacy of Jung's history. Jung spent the formative years of his psychiatric career as a member of the nascent psychoanalytic movement; he continued to use the term *analysis* to describe his practice even after he had broken with Freud in 1913 and had founded his own distinctive approach to psychotherapy. His attachment to the term is further reflected in the name he preferred for his own body of thought, *analytical psychology.*

The Jungian approach to treatment can justifiably be called analysis because it does, like psychoanalysis, place primary emphasis on revealing the fundamental and often unconscious ''building blocks'' of the personality. In Jungian analysis, an effort is made to perceive the psyche's composition and its ways of functioning by uncovering the relationship between consciousness, and the experiences that disturb it, and unconscious contents and dynamics. (The *unconscious contents* are called complexes and archetypes, depending on their topological depth in the psyche. The term *dynamics* refers to the relations of unconscious contents to each other and to ego-consciousness, as well as to the prospective meaning of these relations for psychological development.) If chemical analysis reveals the chemical composition of a physical substance, psychological analysis discloses the basic patterns, processes, and contents of a human psyche.

Analysis is also descriptively appropriate as a term for Jungian treatment. Within a properly secured and maintained analytic framework (cf. chapter by McCurdy, below), analysands can afford to experience a degree of psychological dissolution. (The word *analysis* is derived from the Greek *analyein*, "to dissolve.") As the fixed attitudes, identifications, and psychological dynamics underlying ego-consciousness and supporting its sense of identity are raised into conscious awareness, and as the unconscious contents that were repressed or left out of a self-image begin to enter the field of consciousness, analysands often feel themselves released into a state of psychological fluidity. This experience of "being in analysis" is necessary if structural change is to come about, because only when the organization of ego-consciousness becomes loosened can the blocked and repressed contents, along with the unconscious strivings for new development, enter the field of consciousness and become available for integration. But the danger of analysis lies here as well, and Jung was acutely aware that analysis could release a latent psychosis (1928a; cf. also chapter by Sandner and Beebe, below). For this reason, careful training for analysts is critically important. Ideally, however, the experience of psychological dissolution in analysis leads to a new synthesis of ego-consciousness (Jung 1966a, p. 80ff.), one that will be more affectively related to the Self, the central organizing agency of the personality, and more structurally reflective of the personality's whole reality than was the earlier formation.

A significant aspect of Jungian treatment, however, is not described so well by the term *analysis*. This is the experience of the Self that often occurs in, or as a result of, Jungian therapy. Jungian analysis results not only in Self-knowledge but also in a new kind of Self-experience. People who enter Jungian analysis may do so because they wish to know more about themselves, but if the analysis actually works, they come to experience themselves in a way that was previously not possible. This new kind of Self-experience takes place as the rigidities of ego-consciousness dissolve, and as the unconscious responds and is acknowledged within the security and understanding of the analytical framework. What actually creates the therapeutic effect in Jungian analysis is the increasing amplitude of a person's experience of the Self. This experience, moreover, usually brings with it an influx of energy and vitality, so that one common result of analysis is more creativity in one's responses to life and its challenges. Further, synchronistic events—that is, meaningful coincidences—are often noticed to surround experiences of the Self. What these events contribute to the analysis, when attention and value are given to such phenomena, is a sense of meaning, future direction, and destiny. For this aspect of the experience of Jungian treatment, the term *analysis* seems inadequate. Perhaps *therapy*, with its connotation of healing, is more suitable (cf. Meier 1967).

In the Jungian understanding, analysis, as a method both for furthering Self-knowledge and for increasing Self-experience, takes place within the context of a dialectical relationship between analyst and analysand. This relationship is dialectical in the obvious sense of being a two-way interaction, not one-way only: the action of Jungian analysis is understood to be reciprocal (Jung 1966*b*, p. 8). Normally the effects of this relationship are greater on the analysand than on the analyst, but it is true that the analyst's personality can also be deeply affected by a long-term and psychologically engaging analytical relationship. Jung recognized that analysts can become "infected" by analysands' illnesses and may even occasionally get "assimilated" by their personalities (ibid., p. 72). The strength of the analyst's personality and conscious standpoint are critical for holding up the analyst's end of the dialectic.

The dialectical relationship between analyst and analysand is not the same in every case or at every stage of the analytical process. (Many of the complexities of this dialectical relationship are discussed in the chapters below on transference/countertransference, by Ulanov, and on countertransference/transference, by Machtiger, as well as in the chapter on psychological typology, by Quenk and Quenk.) Jung describes four "stages of treatment" (1966*b*, pp. 53–75): confession, elucidation or interpretation, education, and transformation. These stages are not necessarily sequential. They characterize several types of relationship analysts and analysands have at various points in analysis, occurring in almost any order or duration. The nature of the dialectical relationship between analyst and analysand is subtly different in each of these stages.

In the first three of the stages as I have listed them, the dialectic comes into play as the knowledge and conscious standpoint of the analyst meets the analysand's conscious attitude and standpoint in a compensatory fashion. This dialectic of compensation can range from empathic mirroring in the first stage, to direct opposition in the second stage, to "filling in missing pieces," by pointing out the options and perspectives that have remained unconscious for the analysand, in the third stage. The aim of this compensatory dialectic between analyst and analysand is to remove distortions, balance attitudes, and improve psychological functions, for the purpose of facilitating the ego's more complete view of and better approach to the Self and reality.

On the other side of the dialectic, the analyst's own one-sided attitudes are often confronted in a compensatory fashion by the analysands' attitudes. It has often been observed that analysts get the analysands they need for their own further psychological development! Frequently the problems and unconscious material brought into analysis by analysands have an uncanny relationship to the psychological issues an individual analyst needs to face and work through in his or her own individuation process. It is generally recommended that analysts do this by arranging for further analysis themselves, or by using the knowledge and methods they have acquired through analysis earlier.

In some, but by no means all, analytical processes the depth of engagement between the personalities of analyst and analysand penetrates to a level considerably deeper than that of ego-consciousness. The dialectic between them, therefore, extends past their conscious intentions and draws on responses and counterresponses from the deeper, unconscious layers of their personalities. Both personalities become profoundly engaged in the process that is taking place, and the dialectic is then between two persons reacting with, against, and for each other on many levels. The atmosphere is thick with unconscious material, and there is engendered a potential for profound union, and for insight and differentiation, as well as for wounding betrayal. If managed with skill and blessed by good fortune *(Deo concedente),* the dialectic at this level can enter what Jung calls the fourth stage of treatment, transformation. For the dialectical relationship to work therapeutically at this depth, the personality of the analyst is far more critical than any technical know-how he or she may have, although solid training and experience help the analyst avoid many pitfalls (cf. chapters by Singer and Kirsch, below).

|| *. . . and has for its goal the analysand's coming to terms with the* ||
|| *unconscious . . .* ||

The question of the aims and goal of Jungian analysis is a complex one, and it can lead to considerable confusion and misunderstanding. In the literature there is a tangle of opinions. The discussion of what can be counted as ''success'' and ''failure'' in analysis, for instance, exemplifies this complexity and often leaves the student in about the same place as when he or she began reading (cf. Guggenbühl-Craig 1972; Adler 1974).

This disarray of opinion is a reflection of the complexity of every analyst's practice. There is no such thing as a typical Jungian analysis, and analysts find themselves involved in such a large variety of issues and specific aims that the idea of a single goal for their work does not seem appropriate. Jung and some Jungian authors have, however, tried to formulate some generalizations about analysis, and the question of general aims and a goal can be approached from this angle.

Much of the apparent confusion in the literature may result in part from the absence in Jungian clinical thought of an agreed upon and precise distinction between short-term, issue-oriented psychotherapy and long-term, transformational analysis. Differentiations among the various "stages of analysis" outlined by Jung may also seem vague. Each of these stages could be seen as having a different set of aims while still sharing in the same general goal. An important step toward making such clarifications has been taken by Goodheart.

Guggenbühl-Craig's rough-and-ready distinction between the goal of psychotherapy, "well-being," and the goal of analysis, "individuation," is another attempt at clarification of goals (1977, pp. 23–24). Psychotherapy is understood by him to be short-term psychological treatment oriented toward resolving specific conscious issues, crises, or problems, and thus toward achieving relaxation of tensions and conflicts. These resolutions bring about a sense of well-being. Analysis, a long-term psychological treatment engaged intensively with material from the unconscious, has a different goal than therapy and therefore has different strategies as well. The pursuit of individuation through analysis, Guggenbühl-Craig points out, requires that the ego go further into intrapsychic tensions, that it endure the inner conflicts that result from the play of opposites in the Self, and that it submit to the processes of healing and resolution of conflict that originate in the Self. As the ego comes to terms with the unconscious, the result is not necessarily a pleasurable sense of well-being, but rather a more conscious sense of the Self. In this view, the goal of psychotherapy is ego-oriented, while the goal of analysis is Self-oriented.

A more important reason, therefore, for the lack of consensus in the field on specific aims for analysis is that its outcome is not governed by the ego-intentions or the conscious knowledge of the analyst. Persons in analysis are meant to stay receptive to the unconscious—to the less rational, more ambiguous, and often mysterious side of the personality— rather than being directed by specific ego-intentions. For this reason, Jung avoided stating a precise set of aims for analysis:

> As far as possible I let pure experience decide the therapeutic aims. This may perhaps seem strange, because it is commonly supposed that the therapist has an aim. But in psychotherapy it seems to me positively advisable for the doctor

not to have too fixed an aim. He can hardly know better than the nature and will to live of the patient. The great decisions in human life usually have far more to do with the instincts and other mysterious unconscious factors than with conscious will and well-meaning reasonableness. The shoe that fits one person pinches another; there is no universal recipe for living. Each of us carries his own life-form within him—an irrational form which no other can outbid. (1966b, p. 41)

This statement typifies Jung's viewpoint and shows his high regard for individual solutions to psychological conflicts, as well as his lesser trust in the wisdom of professional ego-intentions.

Jung instructs us to be careful about setting up specific therapeutic aims for analysis, partly because they are so often based on a culturally biased opinion of what is psychologically normative. His views, however, do not proscribe consideration of such aims at every level of generality. The book is not closed. In a discussion of the aims and the goal of Jungian analysis, it is important to be aware of several factors: the level of generality or abstraction one is moving at; the stage of the analytical process one is discussing; and the kind of case and form of psychopathology one is dealing with (cf. Goodheart; see also chapter by Sandner and Beebe, below). Our statement of a goal—"coming to terms with the unconscious"—is a high-level abstraction, and it can be maintained while still holding to the view that analysis does not, and should not, have "too fixed an aim."

Since analysis stays open to the autonomous workings of the unconscious and to the unique personalities of both partners in the dialectical relationship, no one brings to it a preprogrammed agenda of specific aims. Yet it is possible for either partner to put forward a concrete aim in the course of the work. Such aims might involve, for example, the need to work on specific symptoms, issues, or problems; to alter the psychological depth of the discussion from the concrete to the symbolic, and vice versa; and to shift the focus to, or away from, the transference or countertransference. Termination, too, whether full stop or pro tem (cf. chapter by Wheelwright, below), comes up as an aim of analysis at a certain point, and this aim may originate with either the analyst or the analysand. Naturally the discussion of whether or not to pursue a specific aim, of why it is being stated as an aim, and of its possible psychological meaning, is itself an important aspect of analysis.

Jungian analysts have personally experienced, in their own analyses, the challenge of coming to terms with the unconscious (cf. chapter by Kirsch, below). They are familiar with the rigors and strains of this psychological labor. This experience, along with their other clinical and theoretical training, is meant to prepare them to assist analysands in their efforts to do the same. "Together the patient and I address ourselves to the 2,000,000-year-old man that is in all of us," Jung relates. "In the last analysis, most of our difficulties come from losing contact with our instincts, with the age-old unforgotten wisdom stored up in us" (McGuire and Hull, p. 89). But analysts need, and usually have, a developed sensitivity for when they and their analysands are addressing the unconscious at this level and when they need to face up to the influences of personal unconscious complexes and defenses. To consult the latter in the same way would mean detouring away from the goal of coming to terms with the unconscious and would simply dignify old neurotic patterns with false meaning. Those patterns are stumbling blocks in the way of individuation, and it is the task of analysts—and one of their aims—to help analysands confront and overcome them. This can be done by interpreting the neurotic patterns and trying to correct for their distortions and disturbances of consciousness.

Understanding the aims and the goal of Jungian analysis requires seeing them in the light of its theory. The practice of Jungian analysis is intimately linked to, if not justified by, its theory. It does not necessarily follow, as is sometimes suggested, that what comes about in analysis is produced, or even significantly controlled, by the analyst's ideas about what should happen. But an analyst's understanding of what he or she sees and experiences in an analytical relationship is unmistakably marked by the viewpoint that provides the framework for interpretation. The terms *Self* and *collective unconscious,* for example, are attached to theoretical constructs whose living psychological expression is the "2,000,000-year-old man" spoken of by Jung; these theoretical terms and constructs supply the tools for exploring the meaning of such an image and its appearance in analysis. A psychologically sound interpretation of the meaning of images from the unconscious is seen by Jungian analysts as critical for therapy and for the "cure of souls" (cf. Stein 1978).

It is important to recognize that when Jungians speak of "the unconscious," they mean not only a lack of awareness, "unconsciousness," but an area of the mind that is unconscious by nature. It is true that certain contents, such as thoughts, feelings, fantasies, and images, do pass over from the unconscious into ego-consciousness. Nevertheless, the unconscious per se continues to exist as a dynamic factor and source of new contents no matter how conscious an individual may become of such contents. Coming to terms with the unconscious, the goal of anal-

ysis, means establishing a more vital and aware relationship between two
enduring components of the mind, the unconscious and ego-consciousness.

> *. . . the analysand is meant to gain insight into the specific uncon-*
> *scious structures and dynamics that emerge during analysis . . .*

The methods used by analysts to make headway toward the goal of analysis are also related to theory. Dream analysis, active imagination, interpretation of behavior patterns in relation to complexes and archetypes, amplification, and so on, are used to help the analysand contact and come to
terms with the unconscious. Analysis keeps pointing a person toward the
unconscious and, ultimately, it is hoped, toward a glimpse and an experience of the Self. Analysts listen and watch for the appearance of the unconscious and for areas where unconsciousness exists, and they direct attention to those areas because they believe that the causes and meaning of
symptoms, as well as the seeds of future psychological development, lie
there.

Coming to terms with the unconscious, the goal of Jungian analysis,
means that an individual gains insight into the dynamic relations between
the ego and the contents of the unconscious (the complexes and archetypes), and that he or she acquires some conscious control and mastery
over the psychological interference caused by the personal complexes and
defenses.

This psychological mastery and control is achieved by means of insight
(cf. von Franz 1978, pp. 165–69). In the context of Jungian analysis, the
term *insight* means cognitive understanding that is connected to the emotional background of the content or dynamic being understood. When this
understanding is lost in favor of a more purely cognitive meaning, the term
can take on an excessively rational coloration and leave the impression of
an emotionally detached "analytical attitude." Insight does imply, quite
rightly, a degree of psychological "distance" between ego-consciousness
and the unconscious. An aim of analysis, therefore, is to establish and
maintain an appropriate degree of this analytical distance, but without losing the connection to the emotional background of the content or dynamic
being understood. Insight is in fact not complete until this connection is
fully conscious and integrated.

A somewhat artificial distinction, though one that is classically Jungian, is drawn between two phases of analysis. First, there is a period of
gaining insight into the material belonging to the personal unconscious
(personal complexes and issues of emotional development). Second, there

is a phase of encounter with archetypal material arising from the deeper layers of the unconscious. An extension of this idea holds that the success of analysis as a whole depends upon the first of these phases being largely accomplished before the second is entered. Gaining insight into the infantile tendencies of the personality, and thereby freeing oneself from them, is a precondition for meaningful engagement with the archetypal layers of the psyche (cf. Adler 1967, p. 342).

Jung makes this point in *Psychology and Alchemy,* in a passage in which he also explains how and why psychotherapeutic insight can actually free a person from infantile residues:

> It is of course impossible to free oneself from one's childhood without devoting a great deal of work to it. . . . Nor can it be achieved through intellectual knowledge only; what is alone effective is *a remembering that is also a re-experiencing.* The swift passage of years and the overwhelming inrush of the newly discovered world leave a mass of material behind that is never dealt with. We do not shake this off; we merely remove ourselves from it. So that when, in later years, we return to the memories of childhood we find bits of our personality still alive, which cling round us and suffuse us with the feeling of earlier times. Being still in the childhood state, these fragments are very powerful in their effect. They can lose their infantile aspect and be corrected only when they are reunited with adult consciousness. This "personal unconscious" must always be dealt with first, that is, made conscious, otherwise the gateway to the collective unconscious cannot be opened. The journey with father and mother up and down many ladders represents the making conscious of infantile contents that have not yet been integrated. (1944, p. 62; italics added)

Like the phenomenon that William James called "knowledge-about" something, as distinct from "knowledge by acquaintance" (pp. 221–223), insight is, by nature, detailed, intimate, affective awareness. Insight has two features that give it psychologically transformative power: it is a "remembering that is also a re-experiencing," and it is a connecting of such memories with current adult consciousness. When the complexes that disturb consciousness can be affectively linked up with conscious memories of the events and patterns from childhood that played an important role in emotional development, the complexes lose much of their ability to disrupt and distort consciousness. The affect generated by the complex can be contained by the detailed memory image.

Jungian analysts, unlike their Freudian colleagues, do not generally engage in a meticulous reconstruction of childhood. Nevertheless, as the statement quoted above indicates, a certain amount of re-membering childhood and adolescence does commonly occur in Jungian analysis. It is typical for considerable time to be spent tracing the history of various personal complexes from infancy to the present and becoming aware of how they have affected ego-consciousness in the past and continue to do so in the present (cf. Dieckmann 1971).

Lambert notes that the purpose of reconstruction is the recognition of oneself "in a continuing context in which [one's] present modes of experiencing and of dealing with [one]self and others are a logical outgrowth" of one's past (p. 24). Linking up current experience and patterns of consciousness with re-experienced moments from childhood in this fashion is referred to by Jungians as the reductive aspect of analysis. Typically, Jungian analysts will take this reductive approach to treatment when it is indicated by compensatory dreams or by what they evaluate as a pathological, unadapted, or inflated ego attitude. The effect of this kind of analysis on an analysand is to free him or her from "excessive anxiety and crippling defensiveness" and to allow him or her "to experience new feelings and potentialities" (Lambert, p. 29).

Jungians understand the "release" of such "new feelings and potentialities" as due to the activation of archetypal layers and contents of the personality. To gain insight into these contents and their psychological meaning, the analyst will employ the symbolic approach, using an "archetypal model" (Whitmont 1971). The purpose of this interpretive approach is to raise the finalistic, or forward-looking, meaning of these contents to consciousness. Here the term *insight* has another nuance of meaning: it signifies the affectively connected understanding of the relation between a psychological pattern or image and its archetypal dimension. This dimension gives it greater meaning and indicates its significance for future psychological development (ibid.).

"Coming to terms with the unconscious," then, means gaining insight in both of these areas: mastering the personal complexes to some extent on the one hand, while grasping the symbolic meaning of emerging archetypal contents on the other. Analysis creates an ongoing dialogue between the ego and the unconscious (Jung 1966a, p. 80), which produces a dialectical tension of opposites within ego-consciousness, between ego strivings on the one hand and unconscious disturbances and archetypally based demands on the other. This dialogue is mirrored in the dialectical structure of analysis itself. This dialectic, in turn, reflects the Self, which actually consists of a dialectical play of the opposites. For ego-consciousness to come to mirror the Self more completely is another way of expressing the goal of analysis.

In addition to insight, the other major component in my statement of the goal of Jungian analysis is psychological change. Coming to terms with the unconscious involves changing the relationship between ego and unconscious. Hence the last part of our formula:

> . . . *and the structures underlying ego-consciousness are meant to change in their dynamic relation to other, more unconscious structures and dynamics.*

Here we are speaking of "deep change," rather than the host of small adjustments of ego-attitude that take place in analysis.

This kind of change may seem more orderly and clear when discussed in the abstract than when actually experienced in analysis, and yet it can be regularly observed in long-term analytical practice. It appears as a subtle change in dream motifs and themes, as well as in an analysand's conscious attitudes towards him- or herself and in his or her relations with others. To facilitate this change and to make it a conscious process, analysis is aimed at building a bridge over the gulf between consciousness and the unconscious, a split caused by repression, psychological defensiveness, or inadequate conscious structures. Closing the gap between these two parts of the psyche, itself an aim of analysis, makes it possible for the unconscious to compensate consciousness more effectively. New energies and contents are released from the unconscious, and individuation is allowed to move forward. "My aim," Jung writes, "is to bring about a psychic state in which my patient begins to experiment with his own nature—a state of fluidity, change, and growth where nothing is eternally fixed and hopelessly petrified" (1966*b*, p. 46). When such a state of fluidity has been brought about, traffic is free to pass from the unconscious into ego-consciousness. It thus becomes easier for contents from the unconscious to challenge the structures underlying ego-consciousness. This dialectical encounter energizes the individuation process and helps activate the mystery of the soul's alchemy and achieve its transformation (cf. Hillman, p. 28).

To clarify the terms I am using in this discussion of the kind of change sought in Jungian analysis, the following very brief definitions are offered. The ego, itself a complex, is the conscious agent and actor of the personality, as well as the center of reflective awareness. The ego ("I") exists in a field of associated psychological contents, such as memories and familiar thoughts, feelings, and fantasies (earlier "I's"); together they make up ego-consciousness. This ego-consciousness is a structured psychological entity—a "character structure" made up of habitual tendencies of thought, impulse management, and so on. Its underlying principle of organization is called a "dominant" (Jung 1955–56, p. 358ff.). Ego-consciousness, in

turn, is in the orbit of the central organizing agency of the personality, the
Self. The dominant pattern of organization shown by ego-consciousness is
made up of both innate, instinctual/archetypal trends, which are parts of
the Self, and social/cultural influences and introjects; this pattern is the
result of the foregoing developmental history (see Neumann for a complete
developmental theory). The core of the dominant pattern underlying ego-
consciousness is made up of a selected number of the many potentialities
for psychological development within the Self, and therefore it exhibits the
property of "one-sidedness" relative to the psyche as a whole (Jung 1969,
p. 292).

The dominant pattern of organization underlying ego-consciousness
shapes the ego's identity, channels its available energies, and structures its
behaviors. Along these same lines, Hall speaks of a "dominant ego image"
made up of "a persistent association of complexes" (p. 173). This association of complexes is, in my view, held together by archetypal patternings
and can often be related to specific archetypal images, as has been shown,
for example, by the work of Dieckmann (1971).

Because there seems to be an innate striving within the personality to
overcome partial Self-expression and the condition of conscious one-sidedness, analysis supports this trend. In analysis, ego-consciousness and its
underlying structures are brought into an intensely conscious relation to
other, unconscious and unintegrated aspects of the personality. This process may take several forms: the realization of "shadow" aspects of the
ego, both negative and positive (Jung 1928b); the encounter with the ego's
unconscious contrasexual opposite, the anima (for men) and the animus
(for women) (cf. E. Jung); or the recognition of the ego's less developed
and inferior functions and their distortions (von Franz 1971). These aspects
of the unconscious may be brought into analysis as dream contents, or they
may enter as experiences of projection in the transference and countertransference, or in other current life situations. One purpose of bringing them
into a conscious relationship with the ego complex is to dislodge the ego's
identification with its dominant underlying pattern. A change in ego-consciousness is brought about as the ego ceases to identify with old structures, and as new aspects of the personality are assimilated. A new dominant pattern of organization for ego-consciousness is formed. As a result,
the ego's identity is shaped by a more multifarious set of structures, and it
therefore more approximately represents the whole Self (cf. Stein 1980,
pp. 82–86).

In the analytic process, the ego's attachment to an earlier, underlying
dominant pattern of organization is dissolved as it is brought into an intensely conscious relationship with other, more unconscious parts of the

Self. This experience is emotionally painful and the ego usually resists it. A person's ego prefers to maintain its familiar psychological identifications and arrangements of inner objects, even after these have been recognized as outmoded, one-sided, and Self-defeating patterns. This is resistance to individuation, and in analysis, as our statement of the goal implies, one faces such resistance and seeks to diminish its inhibiting effects. The ego resists transformation for a reason: it is threatened with the erasure of a former construction of identity. This process is perceived as the threat of regression to earlier, more helpless, psychological states, and ultimately to extinction of a conscious standpoint.

Some regression is inevitable within the analytic process; optimally it is experienced as a period of safeguarded destructuring. Later it is seen as having prepared the way for a new and more complete integration of psychic contents in the structures that underlie ego-consciousness and shape conscious identity. "The process that at first sight looks like an alarming regression," Jung writes reassuringly, "is rather a *reculer pour mieux sauter,* an amassing and integration of powers" that will develop into new structures (1966*b*, pp. 15–16). The change sought in analysis, which is born from psychological regression, is not a revolutionary replacement of one set of dominant contents with another wholly different group. It is, rather, a transformation that combines the earlier psychological formations with new contents from the unconscious. This transformation comes about through "recanalization of libido" (cf. Jung 1969, pp. 41–61), with psychic energy ("libido") now flowing along revised instinctual-archetypal pathways. These new expressions of libido are a combination of some old and some new forms, and the changes in behavior, attitude, and ways of experiencing mirror this reorganization of psychic energy.

The restructuring of libido along new psychic gradients is not purely a product of analysis. Its occurrence is a combination of the intentional work done in analysis and the spontaneous cooperation of the unconscious. The unconscious cooperates by producing symbols that represent the restructuring process and the archetypal groundwork for it. If genuine change in the structures underlying ego-consciousness is actually to come about, the deliberate and conscious action of analysis must be matched by the corresponding participation of the unconscious. Otherwise, the "cure of the soul" that seemingly occurs in analysis will be psychologically superficial, based perhaps only on a personal transference and likely to disappear shortly after termination. Psychological change does not become an effective, long-term change in functioning unless it is the product of structural change that itself has an archetypal basis.

In addition to this change in psychological structures, however, analysis seeks to create a change in the way the major parts of the psyche are related to each other. Together the analyst and analysand try to build channels of permanent openness between ego-consciousness and the unconscious. To accomplish this aspect of the goal, the ego must arrive at a location that is not wholly embedded in the structures of consciousness, a position from which the dynamic relations between consciousness and the unconscious can to some degree be registered and monitored. Jung called this observation point within the psychological universe the "transcendent function." It consists of a type of self-observing ego that is alert but not overly self-conscious or critical; receptive, yet discriminating about emerging psychic contents; knowledgeable about the personal workings of the psyche without being inflated or dogmatic; stable, but flexible. With the ego in this position, the unconscious can percolate through and continue affecting the attitudes and structures of consciousness, despite their tendency to rigidity.

Guggenbühl-Craig has suggested, somewhat ironically, that changes resulting from analysis may come about in great part through the "analytic ritual": visiting an analyst once or twice a week for a number of years; attending regularly to dreams during that period; taking time for serious introspection and inner work; and, thereby, forming new habits of conscious attentiveness to the psyche and its workings (1972). He may overemphasize the impact of the formal aspects of analysis at the expense of the personal content of the analytic experience, but his comments highlight an important point. Although analysis represents only a small portion of an entire individuation process, it can be critically important for making that process a conscious experience. If analysis has succeeded, it will have been a time in a person's life when the complexes and defenses that blocked his or her most intense, profound, and honest relation to life were rendered less effective, and when a rich appreciation of the soul's reality and of its depth and genius was amply nurtured.

REFERENCES

Adler, G. 1961. *The living symbol*. New York: Pantheon.
_____. 1967. Methods of treatment in analytical psychology. In *Psychoanalytic techniques*, ed. B. B. Wolman, pp. 338–78. New York: Basic Books.
_____, ed. 1974. *Success and failure in analysis*. New York: Putnam.
Dieckmann, H. 1971. The favorite fairy tale from childhood as a therapeutic factor in analysis. In *The analytic process*, ed. J. B. Wheelwright, pp. 77–84. New York: Putnam.
_____. 1980. On the methodology of dream interpretation. In *Methods of treat-*

ment in analytical psychology, ed. I. F. Baker, pp. 48–59. Fellbach: Verlag Adolf Bonz.

Edinger, E. F. 1973. *Ego and archetype.* Baltimore: Penguin Books.

Fordham, M. 1978. *Jungian psychotherapy.* New York: Wiley.

Franz, M.-L. von. 1971. The inferior function. In *Lectures on Jung's typology,* by M.-L. von Franz and J. Hillman. New York: Spring Publications.

———. 1980. *Projection and re-collection in Jungian psychology: reflections of the soul.* LaSalle: Open Court.

Frey-Rohn, L. 1974. *From Freud to Jung.* New York: Putnam.

Goodheart, W. B. 1980. Theory of analytical interaction. *San Francisco Jung Institute Library Journal* 1/4:2–39.

Guggenbühl-Craig, A. 1971. *Power in the helping professions.* New York: Spring Publications.

———. 1972. Analytical rigidity and ritual. *Spring* 1972:34–42.

———. 1977. *Marriage—dead or alive.* Zurich: Spring Publications.

Hall, J. 1977. *Clinical uses of dreams.* New York: Grune and Stratton.

Henderson, J. L. 1967. *Thresholds of initiation.* Middletown, Conn.: Wesleyan University Press.

Hillman, J. 1978. *The myth of analysis.* New York: Harper & Row, Harper Colophon Books.

James, W. 1950. *The principles of psychology.* Vol. 1. New York: Dover.

Jung, C. G. 1928*a.* Psychoanalysis and the cure of souls. In *Collected works,* vol. 11, pp. 348–54. 2d ed. Princeton: Princeton University Press, 1969.

———. 1928*b.* The relations between the ego and the unconscious. In *Collected works,* vol. 7, pp. 127–244. 2d ed. New York: Pantheon, 1966.

———. 1940. The psychology of the child archetype. In *Collected works,* vol. 9, part 1, pp. 151–81. 2d ed. Princeton: Princeton University Press, 1968.

———. 1944. *Psychology and alchemy. Collected works,* vol. 12. 2d ed., rev. Princeton: Princeton University Press, 1968.

———. 1946. Psychology of the transference. In *Collected works,* vol. 16, pp. 163–323. 2d ed., rev. New York: Pantheon, 1966.

———. 1955–56. *Mysterium coniunctionis. Collected works,* vol. 14. 2d ed. Princeton: Princeton University Press, 1970.

———. 1966*a. Two essays on analytical psychology. Collected works,* vol. 7. 2d ed. New York: Pantheon.

———. 1966*b. The practice of psychotherapy. Collected works,* vol. 16. 2d ed., rev. New York: Pantheon.

———. 1968. *The archetypes and the collective unconscious. Collected works,* vol. 9, part 1. 2d ed. Princeton: Princeton University Press.

———. 1969. *The structure and dynamics of the psyche. Collected works,* vol. 8. 2d ed. Princeton: Princeton University Press.

Jung, E. 1978. *Animus and anima.* Zurich: Spring Publications.

Lambert, K. 1970. Some notes on the process of reconstruction. *Journal of Analytical Psychology* 15/1:23–41.

McGuire, W., and Hull, R. F. C., eds. 1977. *C. G. Jung speaking.* Princeton: Princeton University Press.

Meier, C. A. 1967. *Ancient incubation and modern psychotherapy.* Evanston: Northwestern University Press.

———. 1971. Psychological types and individualism. In *The analytic process,* ed. J. B. Wheelwright, pp. 276–89. New York: Putnam.

Neumann, E. 1970. *The origins and history of consciousness*. Princeton: Princeton University Press.

Redfearn, J. W. T. 1980. The energy of warring and combining opposites: problems for the psychotic patient and the therapist in achieving the symbolic situation. In *Methods of treatment in analytical psychology*, ed. I. F. Baker, pp. 206–18. Fellbach: Verlag Adolf Bonz.

Stein, M. 1978. Psychological interpretation. *Dragonflies* 1:91–105.

————. 1980. Hephaistos: a pattern of introversion. In *Facing the gods*, ed. J. Hillman, pp. 67–86. Irving, Tex.: Spring Publications.

Whitmont, E. C. 1971. The destiny concept in psychotherapy. In *The analytic process*, ed. J. B. Wheelwright, pp. 185–98. New York: Putnam.

Whitmont, E. C., and Kaufman, Y. 1973. Analytical psychotherapy. In *Current psychotherapies*, ed. R. Corsini, pp. 85–118. Itasca: Peacock Publishers.

THE
STRUCTURE
AND
DYNAMICS
OF
ANALYSIS

PART TWO

[3]

ESTABLISHING AND MAINTAINING
THE ANALYTICAL STRUCTURE

Alexander McCurdy III

ANALYTICAL structure, and the process that evolves within it, develops in the context of a particular dialectic between two people. Structure is not an a priori entity used or provided by an analyst, but rather a complex of several interrelated areas of the analytical process, involving issues that range from the atmosphere of interchange to the technique of the analyst. Further, structure is influenced and shaped by several variable factors, including the patient's individual needs and psychological situation. In order to discuss analytical structure, one must consider its three major components: the patient, the analyst, and the theoretically based methods and techniques of analysis. Let me begin by saying something in general about each; then I will move to a more detailed exposition of the relationship of all three elements.

In considering the person seeking analysis, it should be noted that it is important for the analyst to have a psychodiagnostic understanding of the patient not only as the analytical situation unfolds, but from the very start. When the Jungian analyst begins with a diagnostic attitude, the intent is not only to generate a prognosis; neither is it merely to sort out those people accessible to analysis from those who are not, nor to diagnose definitively according to the familiar clinical formulations of depth psychol-

Alexander McCurdy III, M.Div., is in private practice in Philadelphia, Pennsylvania, and teaches at the C. G. Jung Center in Philadelphia and at the Philadelphia Jung Seminar, of which he is a cofounder. A graduate of Wesleyan University, the Episcopal Divinity School, and Wayne State University, he completed his training as a Jungian analyst with the German Society for Analytical Psychology at the Institute for Psychotherapy in Berlin. He is a member of the Inter-Regional Society of Jungian Analysts as well as of the New York, German, and Italian Associations for Analytical Psychology.

ogy. All these intentions must be considered to some extent by the analyst from the start. But the need for a general diagnostic attitude is based on the fact that Jungian analysis has traditionally been inclusive in its working definition of the treatable person. This is true even though those accessible to what might be termed the "classical symbolic-synthetic" form of Jungian analysis may be as relatively few as those accessible to the "orthodox" form of psychoanalysis (Fenichel). Jung and his followers have emphasized the importance of sorting out the therapeutic needs of patients by giving careful consideration to their present psychological and real-life situations, their stages of development, their intelligence, and their ego-strength, as well as their ability to be introspective. All these factors will determine the approach to be taken (Jung 1935, p. 19).

Of course the analyst cannot be absolutely sure of any of these things from the beginning. Jung pointed out, somewhat ironically, that the really correct diagnosis is to be made only at the end of treatment (1945, p. 87). He never ceased to counsel against having too sanguine an attitude about knowing a patient's diagnosis precisely and definitively. "There are only individual cases," he wrote, "with the most heterogeneous needs and demands . . . for which reason it is better for the doctor to abandon all preconceived opinions" (1929a, p. 71). Yet at the same time he qualifies this somewhat "liberal" statement by adding: "This does not mean that he should throw them [his preconceived opinions] overboard, but that in any given case he should use them merely as hypotheses for a possible explanation" (ibid.).

It is typical of Jung's thought in general that he finds answers in the tension between opposites. Jung strongly resisted schools of psychology and their representatives who claimed to have a corner on the truth and to have the correct and definitive way of conceiving and treating the psyche. Indeed, anyone who reads psychology is aware of the considerable temptation to imagine that he or she knows a good deal after becoming only a bit familiar with a particular psychological system. The potential for psychological inflation is considerable. Jung warned repeatedly that "nothing is more deleterious than a routine understanding of everything" (1945, p. 87). Yet it is important to understand the basic intent of statements such as these: the intent is balance. On the one hand, there is the clinical responsibility of the analyst to be well trained in the fundamentals of depth psychology and psychopathology; to understand and be able to apply insights from the basic schools of psychological thought; and, above all, to have had experience in these ways of diagnosing and working with people. If these essentials are absent, there is a considerable danger of inflation of another kind—the assumption that one can do without theories, methods, and techniques that are based on systematic attempts to understand the psyche and how it develops.

On the other hand, as a result of this broadly based foundation of knowledge and experience, the analyst has the ability and responsibility to "forget" all of this information and to orient him- or herself to the person in analysis as an individual. It is much like the artist, who, after great efforts and much time spent in mastering the fundamentals of a medium, can produce art without "thinking" of fundamentals. It is a matter of "letting go" and "holding on" at the same time, for without the underlying technique and understanding, the artist cannot create. This is also the case with the analyst. Speaking of the alchemists in this connection, Jung repeats their warning: " 'Rend the books lest your hearts be rent asunder,' and this despite their [the alchemist's] insistence on study. Experience, not books, is what leads to understanding" (1944, pp. 482–83).

The analyst is the second factor in the analytical structure; it is the analyst who creates its overall shape. Rather than stressing the details of couch, chair, number of weekly sessions, or other elements existing independently of the analyst using them, Jung believed that the most important features of analytical structure to be created and maintained in analysis were those that would facilitate the patient's individuation. They could be developed only by a person who was him- or herself well analyzed and psychologically mature. Thus, when Jung spoke of creating an analytical structure with a patient, he referred to a process that had begun in the analyst years before the actual meeting with the patient. As he once put it: "Every psychotherapist not only has his own method—he himself is that method. . . . The great healing factor in psychotherapy is the doctor's personality" (1945, p. 88).

Jung's emphasis on the importance of the analyst's personality went beyond "good intentions," of course, and focused centrally on the analyst's actual psychological development. This was a critical factor because of what he felt to be the dialectical nature of the analytical situation, in which "the personalities of doctor and patient are often infinitely more important for the outcome of the treatment than what the doctor says and thinks (although what he says and thinks may be a disturbing or a healing factor not to be underestimated)" (1929a, p. 71).

The importance of the person of the analyst and its potential for influencing a patient and the structures of analysis were early insights of Jung's. He was convinced that analysts themselves should be analyzed before analyzing others. This viewpoint was based on Jung's personal and clinical experience. He observed clearly that analysts' personal development—that is, their degree of consciousness and the depth of their relationship with their own unconscious, as well as their knowledge of, if not freedom from, their own infantile neurotic complexes—was the central factor in their being able to create and maintain a structure in which analysis and development could take place for others. "Indeed it is sufficiently obvious," Jung reminds us, "and has been confirmed over and over again by experience, that what the doctor fails to see in himself he either will not see at all, or will see grossly exaggerated, in his patient; further, he encourages those things to which he himself unconsciously inclines, and condemns everything that he abhors in himself" (1951, p. 115).

In addition to the need for the analyst to be well advanced in the process of his or her psychological development, Jung also called for a general breadth of life experience on the part of the analyst. He saw this as an essential for working with people whose problems went beyond neurosis and life adjustment, people who were dealing with basic human, religious, and existential questions. As he once put it: "be the man through whom you wish to influence others" (1929a, p. 73).

In turning to the third factor of structure, the issue of the theoretically based methods of analysis, I would like to consider two general directions in Jungian analysis. First, there is what might be called the "classical symbolic-synthetic" treatment. Second, there are nonclassical forms that rely heavily on the use and interpretation of transference and countertransference and that serve as vehicles for the better-known forms of psychoanalytical work.

Jung himself was concerned mainly with the classical symbolic-synthetic approach. He did not give precise directives about how analysts should structure their work or deal with the numerous details that inevitably confront them, such as the physical setup of the office or the beginning of an analysis. It should be noted that Jung concentrated much of his attention on a particular type of person who consulted him analytically. "The clinical material at my disposal," he wrote in 1929, "is of a peculiar composition: new cases are decidedly in the minority. Most of them already have some form of psychotherapeutic treatment behind them. . . . About a third of my cases are not suffering from any clinically definable neurosis. . . . Fully two thirds of my patients are in the second half of life" (1929b, p. 41). As a consequence, the way Jung structured analysis for these people probably took a form much different from what might have been required with patients who were indeed suffering from a "clinically definable neurosis." A different analytic structure would be especially needed for those in the first half of life, or for those older people who were still psychologically dominated by unresolved infantile and developmental neurotic structures, and therefore in no way prepared, or able, to analyze in the way Jung probably worked with many of his cases.

In fact, as Fordham points out (1969*a,* p. 265), the kind of analysis Jung described in terms of a dialectical procedure might really be termed nontechnical, with its emphasis on the personal equation and on the analyst being in analysis as much as the patient. Therefore, the various methods of which Jung spoke—for example, his technical recommendations on how to work with dreams or with active imagination—are clearly of secondary importance in his writings. The emphasis is not so much on details of the actual day-to-day, week-to-week management of particular kinds of cases, but on the types of symbols contained in his patient's dreams, fantasies, or active imaginations, and their archetypal amplifications. Drawing on symbolic material from mythology, religion, alchemy, and literature, Jung not only demonstrated the relevance of this material to the unconscious products of the human mind, but also pointed to its actual therapeutic effectiveness for the individual, once psychologically comprehended and assimilated.

Jung's aim was to work toward a person's wholeness by a furthering of the "dialectical discussion between the conscious mind and the unconscious" (1944, p. 4). As he put it: "My aim is to bring about a psychic state in which my patient begins to experiment with his own nature—a state of fluidity, change and growth where nothing is eternally fixed and hopelessly petrified" (1929*b,* p. 46). From a technical point of view, we know that Jung did not hesitate to comment on and to amplify directly the unconscious material of his patients: "Not only do I give the patient an opportunity to find associations to his dreams, I give myself the same opportunity. Further, I present him with my ideas and opinions" (ibid., p. 44). The structure that Jung provided for his patients consisted to a great extent in his assisting them in their ongoing process of making sense of the varied images from the unconscious, some of them shocking and distressing, others deeply moving to his patients: "It is absolutely necessary to supply these fantastic images that rise up so strange and threatening before the mind's eye with some kind of context so as to make them more intelligible. Experience has shown that the best way to do this is by means of comparative mythological material" (1944, p. 33).

It has been observed in Jungian analysis that directly experiencing the amplified images is, with certain patients, very moving and therapeutic: ". . . the 'mythical', i.e. archetypal, experience *happens* to the patient as an immediate realization which has a transforming effect" (Adler 1961, p. 14). In this connection, Hillman warns against analyses that proceed only in an Apollonian manner in theory, technique, and interpretation: explaining, formulating, interpreting, and labeling, instead of experiencing what is symbolized. The alternative he refers to as a "bisexual consciousness" is characterized by "a world undivided into spirit and matter, imaginal and real, body and consciousness, mad and sane" (Hillman 1978, p. 293). The analytic structure here is maintained by finding and staying with metaphors that overcome splits and unite mind and body in a symbolic expression. For an example of this, Hillman turns to the language of alchemy and to an "alchemical mode of imagining" (1974, p. 125). This is, of course, precisely the kind of imagery that Jung often found in dream material.

Of Jung's earlier students, there are four—Gerhard Adler, H. G. Baynes, Esther Harding, and Frances Wickes—whose writings demonstrate in some detail the practical therapeutic application of the kind of work in which Jung himself was most interested and for which he laid the foundations in great depth. As Adler expresses it in the introduction to *The Living Symbol:* ". . . I hope to have shown in this case study how 'practical' Jung's so-called 'theoretical constructions' are and to what extent they are related to the individual" (1961, p. 7). Drawing out the archetypal dimensions of their patients' material, as contained in the dreams and to a lesser degree in the transference, these authors rely heavily on mythological amplification. Their interest is focused on the individuation process, particularly as it occurs in the second half of life, although they affirm the significance of the same processes in the first half of life in connection with ego development, adaptation to outer realities, and instinctual development. But, as Harding recognizes, it is only after considerable work on the personal problems of a patient that "deeper and more fundamental issues will be sensed" (1965, p. xviii).

One gets the impression from these studies that a relatively advanced state of psychological maturity allows an analytical structure to be developed that is not particularly concerned with neurotic transference and countertransference. It is a structure in which the analyst can openly engage in a kind of educative function: ". . . the patient must be informed of the fundamental principles of self-realization . . ." (Baynes 1937, p. 28). In this kind of analytical work and structure, the emphasis is on what Adler calls the "sublimation" of the patient's personal transference. This is understood "as an act of transmutation of libido produced by the emergence of transpersonal images behind the personal ones" (1961, p. 216).

Adler emphasizes that "in analysis, central importance must always be given to the relationship between analysand and analyst" (ibid., p. 6). It is in the actual "interview" that, as he puts it, a "dynamic experience of realization" occurs (ibid.). This experience, he maintains, is accomplished through interpretation to the patient, first, "of the processes of the objective psyche," and second, "of the transference relationship" (ibid.). Here again it is clear that a special kind of analytical relationship has been established. If resistance should develop, Adler illustrates how the patient's unconscious will immediately raise the issue in a dream or in parapraxis, which can then be interpreted by the analyst to the patient. Most significantly, this interpretation can be understood and accepted by the patient and the resistance will be overcome. Here it seems that an analytical structure has been established in which the patient's resistances are, as it were, interpreted by his or her own unconscious in a way that can be pointed out by the analyst, then accepted and integrated by the ego. In this connection, Adler mentions also the dimension of ''mutuality'' that is basic to this kind of structure, referring to a paper by Henderson in which the ''capacity for symbolic friendship'' is identified as the structure that ultimately leads to the resolution and internalization of the transference.

In order to establish the analytical relationship, Jung had at one point recommended seeing the patient up to four times a week, until the beginning of what he called the ''synthetic treatment'' (1935, p. 20). At this stage, he usually reduced frequency to one or two hours weekly. The reason given for this was that ''the patient must learn to go his own way'' (ibid.). The intent was also to allow time in the periods between consultations for the assimilation of the contents of the unconscious brought up in the analytic sessions. Adler echoes this approach in his essay on technique (1948, pp. 26–27), and also raises a few other general technical principles that are part of ''classical'' Jungian technique. Speaking of the ''*external* relationship of psychotherapist and patient,'' he mentions the preference of Jungian analysts for sitting opposite their patients, who are also asked to sit rather than to lie down on a couch. One intention of this is to make it easier for the patients to test the degree of reality in their projections onto the analyst. Adler is against the practice of having the patient lie on a couch with the analyst sitting behind him; he stresses the importance of keeping the patient from assuming a passive role. Sitting up and facing the analyst makes it less possible for the patient ''to shut himself off in an artificial vacuum'' (ibid., p. 27). The object is to diminish the difference between analyst and patient, thus making it possible to relate the analytic experience to everyday life.

This point raises the question of what is meant by the ''real human contact'' between analyst and patient. A depth psychologist of any school knows only too well the difficulty of developing comprehensive, intimate relationships with patients. The inevitability of the patients' projections, originating in their neurotic complexes and archetypal layers (not to mention the analyst's side of the matter), diminishes the possibility for fairly clear, mutual, human relationships for long periods of the analyses. Speaking of two sorts of relationship—one as transference with "its artificial and somewhat pathological character," the other as "human rapport"—Adler stresses that "it is rather the normal human rapport which is always necessary before two human beings can readily communicate with each other" (ibid., pp. 34–35).

This idea suggests Greenson's "working alliance," a term he coined for "the relatively nonneurotic, rational rapport which the patient has with his analyst" (p. 192). Greenson traces this concept back to Freud. Indeed, the idea has been used and relied upon by Freudians and by Jungians in their work over the years. The existence of a working alliance is necessary for the functioning of classical psychoanalytical technique and is characterized by the patient's identification with the analyst, based on his or her capacity to form object relationships, as well as on his or her capacity "to split off a relatively reasonable object relationship to the analyst from repressive transference reactions" (ibid., p. 207). For the Jungian analyst, working with "the clinically definable neurosis"—that is, not in a classical synthetic way—the relevance of what is discussed by Greenson is clear. But, when working with other patients at a later stage of development or stage of life, the quality of the "working alliance" takes on greater breadth and is described and experienced in a way that people find less pathological and mechanical and more "human." "For twist and turn the matter as we may," Jung writes, "the relationship between doctor and patient remains a personal one within the impersonal framework of professional treatment" (Jung 1929a, p. 71).

However, we must recognize the perception, shared by Jungians and Freudians alike, that not all, or even most, of the people seeking treatment from an analyst are accessible to what we have referred to as the classical symbolic-synthetic approach. What Jung discovered and elaborated on regarding the integration of the collective unconscious took place in the context of an advanced kind of personal relationship between analyst and patient that modeled and paralleled the patient's dialectical relationship to his or her own unconscious. It was apparent to Jung from a very early point that this approach was not something indicated for everybody. When Jung describes the four stages of analysis (1929a), he implies a progression through analytic structures corresponding to these stages. In his writings, he repeats the recognition that his is only one way of approaching the psyche, and that in certain instances or stages of development the psychologies and methods of other schools are more appropriate for certain people. He even says he used them himself; for example: "The severer neuroses usually require a reductive analysis of their symptoms and states. . . . according to the nature of the case [one] should conduct the analysis more along the lines of Freud or Adler'' (1935, p. 19). Since the time that Jung made these observations, Freudian and neo-Freudian thought have undergone much expansion and development, quite a bit of which has been significant and practical for the Jungian analyst faced with patients who were neither suited for, nor actually open to, a classical Jungian analysis.

Parenthetically, it should be noted that the Jungian analyst is very familiar with patients seeking a classical analysis who in fact do so for neurotic and defensive reasons, being unconscious of their need to resolve issues of certain basic personal complexes. The analyst must be keenly aware of the dangers and futility of attempting to conduct a classical analysis with such individuals. It would merely become the enactment, albeit on a very elevated and heady plane, of a massive defense mechanism à deux.

Fordham and his associates in England have made great strides over the last thirty years in the development of Jung's ideas in several areas relating to the structure of analysis with patients who have standard neurotic disturbances. Their investigations have dealt with individuation processes in early infancy and childhood, with the relating of Jung's concepts to Freudian and neo-Freudian ideas, and finally with attempts to examine more closely the actual analytical process in terms of ''the microscopic study of the analyst-patient interaction'' (Fordham 1969a, p. 260). These observations have led to more precision about details of the technical procedure of analysis and to a great appreciation and valuation of transference/countertransference phenomena, not only as therapeutic and diagnostic tools, but also as the immediate situational structure in which neurotic behavior and ideation can be observed, experienced, and worked through.

The work done by Jungians in observing and elucidating early childhood developments has been aided by the insights of non-Jungians such as Spitz, Klein, and Winnicott (1951). These studies have led to an understanding of individuation processes in early childhood and to an increased comprehension of pathologizing influences early in life that lead to blocks in development or eventually to neurosis. Frieda Fordham puts it as follows: ''For instance, by paying attention to a patient's infancy one can discover the flaws in his environment which distorted his later development, led to a weak ego structure and consequent excessive influence of the archetypes'' (p. 114). The interest thus focused on early emotional development and its later effects has led to ''a style of analysis somewhat different from what has been considered the strictly classical Jungian one . . . [and] the expression of affects (often violent emotion) in the safety of the analytical setting is one of its results'' (ibid., p. 115).

It is clear from this description that the analytical structure needed in some cases cannot be characterized mainly by a discussion-type dialectic between patient and analyst. Rather, the analyst must have structured the analysis in such a way as to allow for the patient's projections. To facilitate this process, the analyst is appropriately reserved and discreet in terms of self-revelations, while gently insisting on the analysis of the patient's fantasies and projections.

It is, of course, of primary importance that in the creation and maintenance of an analytical relationship the analyst be well aware, and in control, of countertransference reactions. It will be in relation to the analyst, often "against" or "for" him or her, that the emotions of the patient will be mobilized. A structure must be provided in which this may occur. Jung spoke of the need to control retaliatory impulses in the countertransference: "It is no loss, either, if he [the analyst] feels that the patient is hitting him, or even scoring off him: it is his own hurt that gives the measure of his power to heal" (1951, p. 116). Jung is not here endorsing masochism on the part of the analyst, but rather a tempered openness toward the patient. Such an attitude permits the patient to express the feelings that arise in the safety of the analytical setting, and it permits the analyst to understand the patient at a "gut" level and to make use of this understanding in responding to the patient. Lambert, referring to the work of the psychoanalyst Racker (1968), addresses himself to the activation in the analyst of "talion law impulses," and he discusses the therapeutically effective ability of the analyst to contain the operation of these impulses and to interpret them back to the patient without retaliating (1972). For example, in the case of a patient's negative transference, the analyst "manages to understand the complementary negative counter-transference and also to master his feelings in such a way as to be able to make useful interpretations out of a renewed concordant counter-transference. If he does so he may succeed in making a breach in the patient's vicious circle either in part or wholly . . ." (p. 321). Lambert goes on to compare Racker's insights to basic Jungian principles in a way that is both pragmatic and profound. One gets the feeling from this article that some of the general views Jung emphasized have now been researched and demonstrated in the details of the working dialectic between analyst and patient.

Viewing the maintenance of constructive analytical structures as a product of the consciousness of the analysts and of their facility in working with their own feelings and countertransference reactions, Fordham makes a distinction between "illusory counter-transference" and "syntonic counter-transference." In the former, the analyst's unresolved conflicts are projected onto the patient, whereas in the latter, "psychic contents pass unconsciously from the patient into the analyst,'' providing the analyst who is sensitive to these phenomena with valuable perceptions about the patient (1960, p. 248). Since analysts can thereby perceive—that is, take into and feel in themselves—aspects of the patient's unconscious, they ''experience them often long before the patient is near becoming conscious of them'' (1969a, p. 275). Gordon succinctly describes the kind of active countertransference structure analysts must maintain for the microanalytical work in this field:

> . . . each analyst must constantly ask himself whether what he feels in relation to the patient stems from his own still unconscious and unintegrated conflicts or whether it is a necessary and matching reaction to the unconscious drama the patient needs to re-enact. And he must decide whether to communicate to the patient his own emotional reactions and, if so, in what form and when. (P. 181)

Here Jung's statements on the dialectical relationship in analysis, in which the analyst is as much in analysis as the patient, find very clear expression.

The problems that arise for the analyst and patient when countertransference—either syntonic or illusory—is not made conscious to the analyst are expanded upon by Kraemer. ''Unless transference and counter-transference is experienced, understood and incubated,'' he writes, ''carnal and spiritual ignorance and the lack of differentiation between the personal and collective events all tend to prevent the formation of an ego and its growth towards the integration of the self'' (pp. 238–39).

The reference to incubation is linked to Jung's many references to the alchemical *vas* as a symbol of the basic structure of analysis: ''The *vas bene clausum* (well-sealed vessel) is a precautionary rule in alchemy very frequently mentioned, and is the equivalent of the magic circle. In both cases the idea is to protect what is within from the intrusion and admixture of what is without, as well as to prevent it from escaping'' (1944, p. 167).

Goodheart relates Jung's work and his concept of the *vas,* or therapeutic structure, to the writings of two present-day psychoanalysts, R. Langs and H. F. Searles. Their work presents, he says, ''a view of clinical interaction, the unconscious and therapy which lies much closer to Jung's formulations than to Freud's'' (p. 3). In connection with Jung's emphasis on the *vas bene clausum,* he discusses Langs' insistence upon the analyst's being able to create and maintain an appropriate ''therapeutic frame'' (Langs 1978, p. 434). Goodheart sees this ''frame'' as a clinical elaboration of Jung's ideas and remarks on the *vas.*

Quite in keeping with Jung's emphasis on the depth and intensity of the dialectic between analyst and patient, Goodheart points out the effects of what is done or not done in a technical sense. These actions have important symbolic value, in his view, and their influence on the process will be reflected not only in the progress of the analysis, but also in the conscious and unconscious material the patient presents. He espouses the point of view that the analyst must take great care to maintain "a stable frame or container" (p. 12), pointing to alterations in the holding environment as the result most often of a detrimental "acting-out" on the part of the analyst (albeit under the cloak of "humanness" or flexibility). Under such negative alterations of the frame, he includes the following:

> missed visits, late arrivals, overstaying, contact by the analyst with any of the patient's family, friends or other third parties (including even insurance companies), allowing unpaid fees, contact between analyst and patient outside of analysis, breaking of confidentiality in any way by the analyst, [and] outside interruptions during the hour, such as phone calls. (Ibid., p. 13)

Agreeing with Langs, Goodheart feels that allowing such alterations in the basic structure of the frame tends to reduce the safety of the therapeutic space and "its full potential as a container for genuinely archaic and primitive archetypal affects and images" (ibid., p. 14). The result of failure to maintain the frame leads to a situation in which a certain amount of progress can continue to occur, but of a limited sort. This limited progress is the result of mutually shared blind spots and areas where complexes are acted out, rather than made conscious. Here reference is made to Langs' concept of the "therapeutic misalliance," which is described as

> a situation in which the patient and therapist join together in an interaction not designed primarily for inner change and conflict resolution through structural change within the patient. The interaction has as its conscious, and more often unconscious, purpose some other goal, such as bypassing such inner change, offering substitutes for adaptive inner change that are maladaptive, and offering pathological defenses to the patient—and to the therapist as well. (Langs 1976, p. 81)

While concurring with much of the spirit of Goodheart's and Langs' position on a firmly established and maintained analytical setting, I would highlight two points. First, it is important to have a realistic attitude about intending to provide a structure that is "good enough." Second, there is value in the proper and advantageous handling of mistakes and misunderstandings.

On the issue of the "good enough" analytical environment, Jungians have made extensive use of Winnicott's discussion of early childhood development, viewing the mother-child relationship as one paradigm for the *vas*—the holding-nurturing aspect of the analyst-patient relationship. Winnicott speaks of how the mother establishes a good enough environment by allowing her child the "full course of an experience" (1941, p. 67). This idea refers primarily to instinctual development, in which the drive for discharge and satisfaction is recognized by the mother and leads her to provide an environment where satisfaction is not one-sidedly emphasized and frustration levels are not allowed to reach too great a level. In analysis something similar happens. Analysts allow their patients the full range of an experience in a good enough environment. They maintain a structure that permits freedom of expression and experience, but that is not permissive. There is a sensitive alternation between allowing patients to be alone and requiring them to relate to the analyst as a quasi thing, or to what Winnicott calls a "transitional object" (1951). In this situation, patients can let go of rigid persona structures in themselves and allow impulses from the unconscious to arise and be experienced in the safety of the holding dialectic. The analyst can also be present in a more active "feeding" way, by offering such things as empathy, interpretations, and amplifications in relation to patients' symbolic material.

In this process it is inevitable, and implicitly understood, that mistakes by the analyst, and misunderstandings between the analyst and the patient, will at times occur. Strauss points out that rather than seeking to eliminate these phenomena, analysts should provide a context in which they may be dealt with properly. This means regarding them "as any other manifestation of the unconscious" (p. 256). It becomes, then, a matter of analysts either working their mistakes through on their own, or allowing the patients to join in the process. Insofar as patients are allowed to see and experience firsthand how analysts recognize their own mistakes, the analysts are able to demonstrate how unconscious issues are realized and integrated safely in connection with material that is highly relevant to the individual patient. Strauss points to what she sees as the particular value to the patient of this way of bringing her own mistakes into the process. Plaut takes a similar approach to the handling of the misunderstandings that crop up from time to time between analyst and patient, also emphasizing the value of approaching such occurrences analytically and treating them as relevant and therapeutically useful material (1971, p. 193).

Particular care and technical flexibility are called for on the part of the analyst who sets out to create and maintain an appropriate structure for persons whose disturbances are fundamentally narcissistic. Some Jungians, including Strauss, have observed that "borderline cases feel particularly attracted to analytical psychology" (p. 256). Quite different technical responses need to be employed here, based on an understanding of the psychopathology of this kind of patient and this kind of disturbed area in any patient. For authors approaching this subject from the psychoanalytic position, the reader is referred to Balint, Kohut, Kernberg, and Grunberger.

These authors provide a theoretical and technical exposition of the personal aspects of the narcissistic character disorder, and of the kinds of structures that they deem necessary for the proper therapeutic handling of these people. Schwartz, who relates the psychoanalytic and Jungian approaches to narcissism, distinguishes between the personalistic and archetypal aspects of such disorders and emphasizes that both perspectives are necessary for understanding and treatment. He stresses the necessity of activating the curative levels of the collective unconscious if the healing of narcissistic disorders is to be complete and stable.

We have reviewed structural issues pertaining to the analytical treatment of people accessible to a classical symbolic-synthetic kind of Jungian analysis, as well as of those people whose disturbances are centered more in the areas of transference and narcissistic neuroses. Considering these disparities, the analytical structure that needs to be created and maintained must be flexible enough (Zinkin) to respond appropriately to the varying needs of patients and to movements in their development, while at the same time providing certain basic elements common to all needs.

There are also some general and microtechnical questions to which the Jungian analyst does in fact pay a great deal of attention. This may not be immediately apparent, because Jungian technical procedures appear rather flexible, and indeed are so. However, this flexibility does not occur at random; it is rather a specifically "response-oriented" type of flexibility. Models for response-oriented behavior occur all about us. The good mother demonstrates it, as does the good linebacker in football. The basic position is one of potential action, starting from an attitude of poised reserve. Being in relative balance, the analyst can go in any one of several directions, depending on the situation that develops. Analysts must be able to diagnose and anticipate intuitively what might happen in the analytic field and in the patient, as well as within themselves.

A general fundamental feature of analytical structure can be summed up in terms of the words *experiencing, understanding,* and *incubating.* Essential in the first place to analytical work is the breadth and depth of the analyst's experiencing of the patient. Breadth includes all those perceptions that are immediately and continuously available to the analyst's consciousness. Experiencing implies not just cognitive, but also affective, kinds of perceptions, grounded in the analyst's typology. Basic to all of these perceptions is the analyst's attitude that everything a patient communicates, verbally and nonverbally, and evokes in the analyst, has potential significance. Further, as Plaut puts it: ". . . if we can find a way of appreciating the positive aspect of any psychological manifestation, be it a symptom or a defence, this positive understanding based on theory as well as empathy will come across to the patient in the voice and wording of our responses and interpretations'' (1971, p. 192).

The implication of this formulation for the behavior of the analyst could best be summed up by the word *reserved*. *Reserved* does not mean cold and withdrawn, nor does it suggest that one is intending to be a blank projection surface for the patient. Fordham states the Jungian position on this latter point when he says, ''Analytical psychologists all follow Jung in rejecting the idea that the analyst can possibly act only as a projection screen'' (1957, p.118). Bion's remarks cited by Lambert (1973, p.19) suggest some of the things that are occurring when the analyst retains an essentially reserved attitude, concentrating on experiencing the patient: ''. . . the analyst deals with each session without desire, without memory and without understanding[,] . . . a way designed to enable his patient to develop in his own way and in his own time'' (ibid.). What *reserve* implies, then, is providing from the start and conscientiously maintaining an atmosphere of open acceptance of the patient as he or she is in the present and can become potentially in the future.

Layard discusses this kind of reserved, nurturing experiencing under the rubric of the mother archetype. It provides, he says, the necessary context for, and bridge to, eventual interpretations and interactions with the patient on a more active level, under the rubric of the father archetype: ''It is the role of mother nature to bring forth, without criticism of what is *being* brought forth. This is the first stage biologically, as it is also the first stage in analytical treatment and remains the *underlying* level throughout all later stages in analysis . . .'' (p. 3).

Practically, this means that analysts must be careful in areas where they feel compelled to ''do.'' At many points they are called upon to provide a creative matrix, but not to imagine that they are the creators. Certainly patients will be consciously or unconsciously testing the analytical situation from the start, perhaps projecting the creator or healer archetype onto the analyst. At times these are unconscious attempts to test analysts' abilities to retain their nurturing reserve and not be lured into activity due to their own unresolved power or helper complexes (Guggenbühl-Craig). To be reserved certainly does not mean to do or say nothing. Depending on the communications of the patient and how the analyst experiences them, any number of appropriate responses may be indicated. Plaut discusses the importance of the analyst's being able and willing to be reserved and to incarnate the archetypal image being projected on him by the patient: ''. . . if I can allow myself to incarnate the animus without resistance and without identification on my part, this transference will—in the fullness of time—become undermined by a movement in the patient's unconscious'' (1956, p. 159).

To experience their patients in "depth," analysts need to allow their unconscious processes to surface and to observe them, in particular their projections, introjections, and identifications. As Fordham points out, "When practising this 'technique,' information is being collected and the analyst is finding out, through the activity of his attention based on unconscious processes, what is near the surface in the patient at the same time" (1969a, p. 272). As analysts allow themselves to project themselves onto their patients and, alternately, to take the patients introjectively into themselves, the depth of their ability to experience through empathic identification is increased. This will eventually lead to a deepened understanding of the individual patients, with their particular needs and their personal ways of individuation.

Some interesting research in this area has been done by a group of Jungian analysts in Berlin. They kept exact records not only of all the patient's material and associations during an hour, but also of their own associations to this material and to any other images arising from their unconscious. The careful examination of this material produced impressive results on the coordination of the two psyches, and, most significantly, on the therapeutic intentionality of the symbols arising from the unconscious of *both* parties. They found that "every fantasy, emotion and so on, arising out of the analyst's unconscious (sometimes very personal) was connected either with the patient's associations that he was describing at a specific moment or else shortly following the patient's fantasy" (Dieckmann, p. 26). It was further shown to what extent resistance is a mutual matter between two interacting persons. The research revealed the depth to which the synchronistic process goes and, most importantly, the concrete therapeutic efficacy of the analytic process when experienced, understood, incubated, and communicated. The analytical situation is "governed by the archetype of the self which is synchronizing the chains of associations, that means all the psychic events between two persons" (ibid., p. 31). Essentially, then, the experiencing of the patient is intended to lead to a breadth and depth of understanding in both its cognitive and feeling dimensions.

Expressing to the patient what the analyst has understood, however—correct as it may be—when the patient is not prepared to integrate the insight, will be unsuccessful at best, inhibiting to or destructive of the process at worst: ". . . it is here that the analyst has to prove his discipline. To know more but to say less is a necessary principle for the initiated . . .'' (Kraemer, p. 232). This point is related to Freud's concept of analyzing the defense before the content behind it; in his terms, the ego before the id. A period of incubation is implied, a period where the experienced and comprehended information is held and ripened to its proper age of birth.

This approach to analysis, in terms of experiencing, understanding, and then incubating to the point of birth, is consonant with a basic postulate of Jung's perception of the nature of the psyche. As Whitmont has put it:

> Eventually the unconscious will begin to provide not only descriptions of the existing impasse but also positive suggestions for possibilities of development which could reconcile the opposing positions, showing us what avenues of development are available to us, what paths are required of us or closed to us, according to the inherent plan of the Self. (P. 294)

Only when a proper period of psychological incubation has taken place will a person be able to comprehend the material arising from the unconscious in a nontheoretical way, in a way that can affect the course of development to produce real change and reorientation.

Finally, there are some technical issues that are related to the structure of Jungian analysis. This chapter is not an attempt to give final answers to detailed technical questions. Any consideration of specific questions such as these can be done only in conjunction with the individual analyst and patient.

Areas where we see obvious evidence of flexibility in structure are in the matters of the duration of the analysis and the frequency of analytical sessions. Different responses depend on many factors (Jung 1944, pp. 4–6). To discuss this issue in detail goes beyond the scope of this chapter. Suffice it to say, the same Jungian analyst might work four to five times weekly with some patients, once or twice weekly with others, and at even greater intervals with still others. Cahen describes his positive experience based on seeing certain patients intensely for periods of one or two months, followed by regular two-month pauses.

Any number of apparently minor details of structure turn out to be important as visible symbols of inner psychological realities. For example, the decoration and ''feel'' of the consulting room is certainly significant. The impact on different patients of over- or underpersonalization of the room must be considered.

Other technical issues, such as the contract, payment, vacations, personal revelations from the analyst, and whether the patient should sit or lie, must be thought through and resolved, but always in context. The analyst's realities are an integral part of this context and, if consciously faced, can be made an effective part of a therapeutic structure. Realities include "real" physical/material limitations beyond the analyst's present control and the analyst's psychological, if not neurotic, realities. Fordham puts it aptly: "Through consciousness, the analyst's neurosis, though not dissolved, is made flexible and usable" (1969b, p. 197). Analysts are called upon not to be perfect, but to integrate their whole selves as consciously as possible into the setting, wounded aspects included, without denial or rationalization. In saying this, though, one must immediately beware of allowing it to permit undue license in the structure. While using their wounds means they do not hide or deny them, it certainly doesn't mean that analysts should symbolically "bleed" on their patients.

Another area of flexibility, although a very limited one, has to do with the sealed integrity of the *vas*. Confidentiality must be absolutely protected. There can be no communication with third parties on the part of the analyst, such as routine kinds of sharing information about patients with colleagues or with the analyst's or patient's family. Kirsch addresses herself to the absoluteness of confidentiality, although for research and training, inflexibility cannot be maintained and "leakage" is unavoidable; in these cases, it must be handled with great discretion.

Flexibility aside, there are some absolutes, and they should be mentioned. One of these has to do with the analyst's personal health and well-being. It is probably true that if their analysts do not take care of themselves, patients will not learn to do so either. That an analyst's personal needs be taken care of apart from work is crucial. The how of it varies. On a small scale, some analysts refresh themselves with a ten-minute break after every hour, while others work through several sessions before needing to pause. The analyst's vacations and private life are also important as necessary refreshing and compensatory experiences to analytical work.

A second absolute is continuing study as a cornerstone of the analyst's capability to provide good structure. Jung's opinion—"The analyst must go on learning endlessly" (1951, p. 116)—is perhaps the one inflexible rule that cannot be taken literally enough.

If the analysts themselves are considered as the basic structure in and through which the work takes place, they will need to provide as many facilities in themselves as possible for the "containment" of the process. At times this means taking the patient's sickness in, holding and touching it to the point of risking infection from it. But, as the foregoing has suggested, a kind of "rubber gloves" surgical analysis can only lead to sterile results. So, when engaging in this kind of work, analysts, themselves the *vas*, need all the internal and external assistance they can acquire in terms of knowledge, experience, emotional development, and reasonably compensating personal lives. Ultimately, the way particular analysts create and maintain their working structure, in conjunction with the individual needs of specific patients, will be only as sound as their personal development and their theoretical convictions permit.

REFERENCES

Adler, G. 1948. A comparative study of the technique of analytical psychology. In *Studies in analytical psychology*, pp. 22–91. New York: Putnam, 1966.
———. 1961. *The living symbol*. New York: Pantheon.
Balint, M. 1968. *The basic fault*. London: Tavistock.
Baynes, H. G. 1937. A demonstration of analytical practice. In *Analytical psychology and the English mind*, pp. 19–33. London: Methuen, 1950.
———. 1955. *The mythology of the soul*. London: Routledge and Kegan Paul.
Bion, W. R. 1970. *Attention and interpretation*. London: Tavistock.
Blomeyer, R. 1971. Die Konstellierung der Gegenübertragung beim Auftauchen archetypischer Träume: Kasuistik. *Zeitschrift für analytische Psychologie und ihre Grenzgebiete* 3/1: 29ff.
Cahen, R. 1976. Abwesenheit und Rhythmus als therapeutische Faktoren. *Zeitschrift für analytische Psychologie und ihre Grenzgebiete* 7/2:123–51.
Dieckmann, H. 1976. Transference and countertransference: results of a Berlin research group. *Journal of Analytical Psychology* 21/1: 25–36.
Fenichel, O. 1945. *The psychoanalytic theory of neurosis*. New York: Norton.
Fordham, F. 1969. Some views on individuation. In *Analytical psychology: a modern science*, ed. M. Fordham; R. Gordon; J. Hubback; and K. Lambert, pp. 110–24. London: Heinemann, 1973.
Fordham, M. 1957. Notes on the transference. In *Technique in Jungian analysis*, ed. M. Fordham; R. Gordon; J. Hubback; and K. Lambert, pp. 111–51. London: Heinemann, 1974.
———. 1960. Counter-transference. In *Technique in Jungian analysis*, ed. M. Fordham; R. Gordon; J. Hubback; and K. Lambert, pp. 240–50. London: Heinemann, 1974.
———. 1965. The importance of analysing childhood for assimilation of the shadow. In *Analytical psychology: a modern science*, ed. M. Fordham; R. Gordon; J. Hubback; and K. Lambert, pp. 95–109. London: Heinemann, 1973.
———. 1969a. Technique and counter-transference. In *Technique in Jungian analysis*, ed. M. Fordham; R. Gordon; J. Hubback; and K. Lambert, pp. 260–88. London: Heinemann, 1974.
———. 1969b. Book review. *Journal of Analytical Psychology* 14/2:196–97.
———. 1971. Maturation of ego and self in infancy. In *Analytical psychology: a modern science*, ed. M. Fordham; R. Gordon; J. Hubback; and K. Lambert, pp. 83–94. London: Heinemann, 1973.
Goodheart, W. B. 1980. Theory of analytical interaction. *San Francisco Jung Institute Library Journal* 1/4: 2–39.

Gordon, R. 1968. Transference as a fulcrum of analysis. In *Technique in Jungian analysis*, ed. M. Fordham; R. Gordon; J. Hubback; and K. Lambert, pp. 178–87. London: Heinemann, 1974.

Greenson, R. R. 1967. *The technique and practice of psychoanalysis*. New York: International Universities Press.

Grunberger, B. 1979. *Narcissism*. New York: International Universities Press.

Guggenbühl-Craig, A. 1971. *Power in the helping professions*. New York: Spring Publications.

Harding, E. 1965. *The parental image: its injury and reconstruction*. New York: Putnam.

Henderson, J. L. 1955. Resolution of the transference in the light of C. G. Jung's psychology. In *International congress of psychotherapy*, ed. M. Boss. New York: Karger.

———. 1974. The therapeutic value of alchemical language. In *Methods of treatment in analytical psychology*, ed. I. F. Baker. Fellbach: Verlag Adolf Bonz, 1980.

Hillman, J. 1978. *The myth of analysis*. New York: Harper Colophon Books.

Jung, C. G. 1921. The therapeutic value of abreaction. In *Collected works*, vol. 16, pp. 129–38. 2d ed., rev. Princeton: Princeton University Press, 1966.

———. 1929*a*. Problems of modern psychotherapy. In *Collected works*, vol. 16, pp. 53–75. 2d ed., rev. Princeton: Princeton University Press, 1966.

———. 1929*b*. The aims of psychotherapy. In *Collected works*, vol. 16, pp. 36–52. 2d ed., rev. Princeton: Princeton University Press, 1966.

———. 1935. Principles of practical psychotherapy. In *Collected works*, vol. 16, pp. 3–20. 2d ed., rev. Princeton: Princeton University Press, 1966.

———. 1944. *Psychology and alchemy*. *Collected works*, vol. 12. 2d ed., rev. Princeton: Princeton University Press, 1968.

———. 1945. Medicine and psychotherapy. In *Collected works*, vol. 16, pp. 84–93. 2d ed., rev. Princeton: Princeton University Press, 1966.

———. 1951. Fundamental questions of psychotherapy. In *Collected works*, vol. 16, pp. 111–25. 2d ed., rev. Princeton: Princeton University Press, 1966.

Kadinsky, D. 1970. The meaning of technique. *Journal of Analytical Psychology*, 15/2: 165–76.

Kernberg, O. 1975. *Borderline conditions and pathological narcissism*. New York: Jason Aronson.

Kirsch, H. 1961. An analyst's dilemma. In *Current trends in analytical psychology*, ed. G. Adler. London: Tavistock.

Klein, M. 1932. *The psychoanalysis of children*. London: Heinemann.

Kohut, H. 1971. *The analysis of the self*. New York: International Universities Press.

Kraemer, W. P. 1958. The dangers of unrecognized counter-transference. In *Technique in Jungian analysis*, ed. M. Fordham; R. Gordon; J. Hubback; and K. Lambert, pp. 219–39. London: Heinemann, 1974.

Lambert, K. 1972. Transference/counter-transference: talion law and gratitude. In *Technique in Jungian analysis*, ed. M. Fordham; R. Gordon; J. Hubback; and K. Lambert, pp. 303–27. London: Heinemann, 1974.

———. 1973. The personality of the analyst in interpretation and therapy. In *Technique in Jungian analysis*, ed. M. Fordham; R. Gordon; J. Hubback; and K. Lambert, pp. 18–44. London: Heinemann, 1974.

Langs, R. 1976. *The bipersonal field*. New York: Jason Aronson.

_____. 1978. *Technique in transition*. New York: Jason Aronson.

Layard, J. 1950. Initial stages of analysis: leading to the problem of opposites. Paper read to the Analytical Psychology Club, 13 June 1950, London. Copy in Kristine Mann Library, New York.

Neumann, E. 1962. *The origins and history of consciousness*. New York: Harper & Row.

Plaut, A. 1956. The transference in analytical psychology. In *Technique in Jungian analysis,* ed. M. Fordham; R. Gordon; J. Hubback; and K. Lambert, pp. 152–60. London: Heinemann, 1974.

_____. 1971. What do we actually do? Learning from experience. *Journal of Analytical Psychology* 16/2: 188–97.

Racker, H. 1968. *Transference and counter-transference*. London: Hogarth.

Schwartz-Salant, N. 1982. *Narcissism and character transformation*. Toronto: Inner City Books.

Spitz, R. A. 1965. *The first year of life*. New York: International Universities Press.

Strauss, R. 1960. Counter-transference. In *Technique in Jungian analysis,* ed. M. Fordham; R. Gordon; J. Hubback; and K. Lambert, pp. 251–59. London: Heinemann, 1974.

Whitmont, E. C. 1969. *The symbolic quest*. New York: Putnam.

Wickes, F. G. 1959. *The inner world of man*. New York: Farrar and Rinehart.

Winnicott, D. W. 1941. The observation of infants in a set situation. In *Through paediatrics to psycho-analysis,* pp. 52–69. London: Hogarth, 1975.

_____. 1951. Transitional objects and transitional phenomena. In *Through paediatrics to psycho-analysis,* pp. 229–42, London: Hogarth, 1975.

_____. 1965. *Collected Papers*. London: Tavistock.

Zinkin, L. 1969. Flexibility in analytical technique. *Journal of Analytical Psychology* 14/2: 119–32.

[4]

TRANSFERENCE/COUNTERTRANSFERENCE: A JUNGIAN PERSPECTIVE

Ann Belford Ulanov

TRANSFERENCE and countertransference are universal in human experience. Defined most simply, *transference* is a phenomenon that occurs when one person becomes the carrier for an unconscious content activated in another person. That content carries into the present moment conflicting and unassimilated feelings about figures in the past that distort the perception of the present person or situation. *Countertransference* describes a similar phenomenon flowing in the opposite direction (Jung 1966, p. 64; Stein, p. 40). Jung notes that the carrier need not always be a person, but could "be a book, a piece of hearsay, or a legend" (1975, p. 504). And we are all familiar with transferences to places and things, such as childhood houses, pieces of furniture, kinds of food, schools we loved, and so on, transferences that can invade our perceptions of present surroundings and set them askew.

Analysis is a situation in which the phenomenon of interlocking transference and countertransference is examined with particular care. In recent years it has become a center of attention in psychoanalytic literature of all schools of thought, not only as a clinical tool used in the daily work of analysis, but also as a metaphysical concept used to think about the nature of human beings and their relationships to each other and to what they value.

As a clinical tool, the transference-countertransference interaction be-

Ann Ulanov, M.Div., Ph.D., is a Jungian analyst practicing in New York City, a member of the board of the C. G. Jung Training Center there, and Professor of Psychiatry and Religion, Union Theological Seminary. She is the author of numerous articles and of *The Feminine in Jungian Psychology and in Christian Theology* (1971), *Receiving Woman: Studies in the Psychology and Theology of the Feminine* (1981), and, with her husband, Barry Ulanov, *Religion and the Unconscious* (1975) and *Primary Speech: A Psychology of Prayer* (1982).

comes a focus for investigating the early stages of a relationship. By registering the way the patient makes him or her feel, the analyst can give back to the patient insight into what the patient is unconsciously transferring into present relationships from unresolved past conflicts. If, for example, the analyst feels the patient is subtly controlling interactions by standing back and searching the analyst's face for clues indicating how to react, the analyst can say this in appropriate form to the patient. What may come to light then is the analysand's discovery that this is the way he always felt with his mother; he *did* withhold his spontaneous responses in order to adapt to her expectations. Such a wounding of self in order to please another blights the patient's capacity to be a full person. Kohut's work on the narcissistic, idealizing, and mirror transference explores such early damage to an individual's ability to esteem the self and carry it forward into life (pp. 37, 78, 116, 203). Kernberg examines the rage and envy that defeat formation of a self capable of relating to another self (pp. 60, 69, 322). Searles suggests that the assault an analyst feels in the primitive love and hate of the transferences of patients suffering from schizophrenia shows, in grossly exaggerated forms, the tasks all of us face in relating to each other. We all must come to know and to tame these forces of love and hate in ourselves. To do this we need another person; we do this in relation to another person (1965, pp. 273–83; 1979*a*, p. 22; 1979*b*, pp. 53–4).

As a metaphysical concept, the transference-countertransference phenomenon has been used as a way to conceptualize the human tendency to personalize any relationship, even one to transpersonal realities such as God, society, or the values and truths held to be of supreme worth by individuals or groups. No human relationship can avoid the impact of the human unconscious, whether it is deemed a positive or negative contribution. Freud, for example, understood the father transference as the psychic root of religious belief. Leowald, a Freudian, understands transference to be the root of psychoanalysis itself, a discipline he considers to be a value system in its own right and one that has, in this country, strongly influenced our understanding of the construction of human values.

Dieckmann, a Jungian, finds a nonpersonal, collective theme dominant in any transference-countertransference interaction, and suggests that it is fundamental in shaping the way personal issues between analyst and patient come up and are resolved. Thus he reverses the usual direction of thought, in which a patient's personal conflicts lead the analyst to speculate about the human condition. Instead, he sees certain universal human themes as arranging the kinds of transference-countertransference conflict that occur between patient and analyst. For example, the unconscious hu-

man tendency to cast the authoritative figure of the analyst in a parental
role activates in the patient a father transference.

Fordham, another Jungian, posits progressive stages of transference, in
which a shift occurs from earlier, ego-centered concerns to the eventual
displacement of the ego in favor of a more comprehensive center of the
psyche that Jung calls the Self (Fordham 1978, p. 87). For example, a
patient's concern in analysis about whether an analyst likes the patient or
not can move through the memories of early attempts to gain a father's
approval, into deeper layers of the human longing for a felt connection to
some power at the source of life. What is at first sought as approval from
the analyst becomes a move to establish a secure relation to life itself, to
a center that is not felt to belong to either the patient or the analyst. The
patient can now see through the whole interaction with the analyst around
the issue of approval to a deeper purpose—securing a durable emotional
connection to an inner authority that is no longer projected onto the analyst
or any other individual. Jung would say it is a glimpse of the Self.

Despite differences of approach among analysts of conflicting schools,
firm agreement exists in two areas. The first is the uniqueness of every
transference-countertransference relationship. As Jung puts it, each case is
"pioneer work" because of the unrepeatable nature of each person (1946,
p. 177). General trends are evident, but each transference has its own
singular quality. Winnicott captured this uniqueness in his exchange with
a three-year-old girl as treatment drew to a close: "W: 'So the Winnicott
you invented was all yours and he is now finished with, and no one else
can ever have him.' . . . G: 'I made you.' " (1977, pp. 189–90).

The second area of agreement focuses on levels of transference and
countertransference. Winnicott describes three levels of countertransference (1975, p. 195): "abnormal," meaning those areas that arise from the
analyst's past unresolved conflicts that intrude upon the present patient;
"normal," meaning those reactions that describe the idiosyncratic style of
an analyst's work and personality; and "objective," meaning those reactions evoked in an analyst by a patient's behavior and personality that can
provide the analyst with valuable internal clues about what is going on in
the patient. Transference reactions would customarily fall into the "abnormal" category, but the other two categories are never entirely excluded.

Jung adds a fourth level of transference-countertransference interaction—the archetypal—and it is upon this level that I will concentrate,
without, however, altogether excluding the other levels and the analytic
systems that stress them (Fordham 1974, p. 6; 1978, p. 83). For, just as
Jung built upon the work of Freud and Adler (Jung 1966, p. 41), seeing
his own emphasis as adding an extra dimension to their systems, so many

Jungians today use the insights of workers in other schools to deepen their own.

The "extra" element Jung and Jungians see operating in transference is the archetypal. In addition to the projection of infantile conflicts onto the analyst, transference activates what Jung calls the archetype-centered process of individuation (Edinger 1957, p. 33; Paulsen, p. 203). In this process, the ego is radically changed as it comes into increasingly cooperative relation with the Self, that center and goal of the whole psyche that Jung describes as "both ego and non-ego, subjective and objective, individual and collective. . . . the 'uniting symbol' which epitomizes the total union of opposites. . . . not a doctrine or theory but an image born of nature's own workings . . ." (1946, p. 264).

Individuation involves the transformation of the analyst as well as the patient, stirring up in his or her personality the layers that correspond to the patient's conflicts and insights (Jung 1946, p. 176; Fordham 1957a, p. 62; Fordham 1958, p. 172; Lambert, p. 33). In the midst of infantile issues, the archetypal core breaks open, calling the patient not only to resolve issues of personal identity and functioning in the world, but also to come into a better relationship with potentialities that are not properly the possession of any one person, but are part of a shared human culture. The analyst then will find personal issues constellated in response to the patient's material. Ideally, those issues will be familiar to the analyst and nonobtrusive in the treatment because of the analyst's own long work as a patient. Archetypal dynamics will affect any analyst, but particularly one whose life is not fully lived and needs to be (Jung 1975, p. 172).

An example can be given from the analysis of a woman who suffered from intense anxiety stemming from a negative mother complex. As she was growing up, her mother criticized and belittled her harshly. As a result, her self-confidence was severely blighted and she became aware of radical self-doubt. She also harbored a lot of repressed anger, of which she became aware only as the treatment progressed.

In the transference, she needed now to please me the way she used to try to please mother. The whole mother issue was there with us and I could feel different parts of the mother role in its archetypal form come alive in me at different times. Sometimes I would find myself wanting to react as the good mother the woman never had. Other times her frantic anxiety aroused in me the thought of brusque responses with which to put a swift end to all her dithering. Other times, such as the day the patient greeted me at the door with "I'm sorry" before she even said hello, I wanted to laugh and just get out from under the whole mother constellation.

The patient's transference took her back into her actual relationship with her mother in the past. Because the patient perceived me as different from her real mother, she could risk facing her repressed angry reactions to her mother. In addition, she came to see how her mother's criticism continued to live in her own belittling attitude toward herself.

The issue of relating to the mother archetype arose in the midst of all of her personal struggles. For around associations and memories of her real mother, and mixed in with transference feelings to me as a mother figure, appeared images and affects, behavior patterns and fantasies, connected to relating to the archetypal mother. The patient reached to feelings of happy dependence, which she did not experience with her real negative mother, but which can be an authentic response to the mother image. She reached to a deep sadness that her mother was so anxiously distressed herself that she could not be a secure refuge for her child. Thus she went beyond her own bruises to perceive her mother's damaged state and to feel genuine compassion for her parent. The patient could wonder about where all this led, at moments seeing her mother problem as an important thread in her own destiny, setting her specific tasks to solve. She could accept the relationship now, with all its hurts, as an essential part of her own way of life.

On the countertransference side, I found my patient's material touched issues of my own, experienced with my own mother, some finished and easy to keep from intruding upon the treatment, others needing more work and attention so that they did not interfere. The life issues around "the mother," good and bad, were posed for me as well, to think about, to feel again, to work on.

Jung lays great emphasis on the importance of the relationship between analyst and patient, which accounts for his sitting face-to-face with his patients and confining sessions to no more than three a week. (Some Jungians of the English school, influenced by Freudian and object relations theory, do use a couch and a greater frequency of sessions.) In transference-countertransference, archetypes are constellated and both personalities are changed in the process of coming to terms with them. The aim of Jungian analysis is to secure greater connection to all the contents that properly belong to a patient's ego and to connect the ego to the Self, the center of the whole psyche. One needs a setting that mirrors the otherness of the Self in the otherness of the person sitting across from oneself, and time between sessions to digest the effects of archetypes in the analyst-patient relationship. Jung says of the connecting process, "That is the core of the whole transference phenomenon, and it is impossible to argue it away, because relationship to the self is at once relationship to our fellow-man and no one can be related to the latter until he is related to himself"

(1946, p. 233; see also Edinger 1957, p. 41; Fordham 1974, p. 15; Plaut, p. 19).

Jung's recognition of the pivotal place of the archetypal element in transference, or in any content of analysis for that matter, accounts for his development of the synthetic-constructive method of interpretation. The method addresses the archetypal potentiality hidden in a vexatious symptom (Jung 1944, p. 80). In practice, we feel this archetypal element as an unknown, as "something" that seems to us precious and on no account to be lost sight of even when embedded in gross perversion or degrading compulsion (Hillman, p. 186; Khan, p. 14). Awareness of this archetypal component quiets the clamor of judgment in both analyst and patient and makes room for the patient to breathe. We can discover the archetypal element urging growth that has been hiding in the distress of personal dysfunction.

Awareness of that element reveals what Jung calls the prospective function of the psyche (1948, p. 255), one we experience as a power that summons us, if it does not drag us, in a certain life direction. With sufficient consciousness of this power, we come to ask basic questions. What does this problem make me discover about my whole direction in life? What does it show me that must be dealt with if I am to go forward? To what banished area of life has this distress sent me back? The importance of this perspective cannot be undervalued, not only in building a bridge between the ego and the psyche's archetypal contents, but also in rescuing for the ego a sense of its dignity in the midst of a humiliating illness. The illness has a purpose and it was not to be avoided, even if one had had just the "right" attitude, the will power, or better luck.

In the transference, this perspective can yield particularly good working space. An example is a patient who asks what purpose can possibly be served by the intense attraction he or she feels to the analyst, who is clearly not available for any romantic or sexual relationship. Unfinished entanglements with parent figures from the past can be reductively analyzed. And the value of such an apparent impasse for the patient's growth into a realistic maturity can also be underscored.

The fact that the analyst is not available for social or sexual relationship turns out to be the centrally important fact. Only where outer action cannot be taken does the inner demand for greater consciousness urge itself upon the patient. In the analytical relationship, the projections of anima and animus can be worked on directly, so that the patient becomes more aware of what attraction to the analyst represents in the patient's own psychology.

Jung remarks that the sexual attraction is always used by the unconscious to represent the urge toward reconciliation with split-away parts of ourselves (1976, p. 173). The sexual transference, then, is a spontaneous way by which the psyche seeks to bridge a gulf between the patient's ego-identity and the contrasexual contents projected upon the analyst (von Franz, VI, pp. 3–4). What would otherwise be a humiliating fixation upon the analyst is redeemed by its hidden purpose—to bring to light the patient's relation to the anima or animus, depending upon the sex of the patient. Patients in this position need not then just go on feeling foolish for desiring someone they cannot have, and indulging in childish sulks, mopings, or resentments when refused gratification. Instead, such patients see the task set them by this welling up of emotion, impulse, and aspiration, and the sense of soul with which they cloak the analyst figure. When patients long for the analyst, it is their first direct experience of their strong longing to be reconnected to a missing part of themselves, to some aspect of their own souls.

It is precisely in transference interpretations that Jung's distinction between subjective and objective levels of interpretation makes its worth felt (1948, p. 266). For the analyst figure makes visible and accessible heretofore unconscious affects and value-laden instincts. The analyst also embodies aspects of the patient's psyche that must be claimed as part of the territory of the patient's own depths (Jacoby, p. 17). When a male patient dreams, for example, after the first session that he is having a session while a female analyst is seated in a tub having a bath, interpretation must follow two lines, each with its own individual effects on the patient's ego. It must look backward into the patient's attitudes toward his mother that may be recaptured or corrected in the dream image, and it must look forward to discover a solution that has some significant connection to the dreamer's life attitude.

In the reductive stage of analysis, such a patient withdraws his projections onto the analyst and assimilates them to his ego, an action that enlarges his ego and his responsibility for his own psyche's contents. In the synthetic stage, the patient is called beyond his ego concerns to build a stronger connection to his anima. He relies on his ego as one pole in the developing relationship. The analyst figure in the dream must be interpreted objectively as a real person to whom the dreamer is transferring unfinished issues with women, as well as a personification of anima content in the dreamer's own psyche. Amplifying the symbolic connections of this dream to include the symbolic meaning of bath, immersion, water, cleansing, baptism, and so on, will clarify the content the unconscious urges upon the dream-ego (Jung 1944, p. 220; Edinger 1978, p. 34).

One possible meaning of such an intimate dream scene might be to

compensate the dreamer's actual life attitude, his too-strict compartmental-
izing of his responses to women and to the feminine parts of himself,
segregating them from the rest of his life. Sitting with a woman while she
bathes suggests easy intimacy, relaxed interchange, and, in the image of
water, a dissolving of separating formalities and uncovering of feminine
presence.

Fordham correctly warns us against the tendency of patient and analyst
alike to use the symbolic-synthetic perspective as a defense against uncovering the infantile roots of a complex (1978, pp. 84, 93; see also Guggenbühl-Craig, p. 65). Jungians can easily waft themselves upward into
mythological spiritualizing, with talk about "the goddess" and "the gods,"
and thereby avoid the tough work involved in analyzing the anger that may
be present in the transference, the envy, the sexual attraction, the embarrassment, and so on. For example, when a patient dreamed of me as an
embodiment of presence and love, I was too quick to reject that projection.
I insisted upon seeing the projection as an aspect of his own inward reality,
something he should claim for himself and not project onto women as if it
were to be found only in and through them. The patient quite rightly
caught me up, sensing my unwillingness to see and deal with his feelings
about me. I thought of Searles' point about parents who deny their children
the experience of all-out lavish loving, because their own low self-esteem
cannot tolerate it (1965, pp. 230, 232–33), and of Jung's point about the
archetypes of king or queen that lurk in the midst of parental imagoes. But
we do not get to such understanding except through the concrete details of
specific personal relationships.

It is also fair to say that the fascinating work of exploring the early
dynamics of introjected objects can be used as a defense against the pull
of the archetype on the ego to get it out of placing itself, its wounds, its
past, and its purposes at the center of the analytical universe. The product
of this exaggeration is not a positive cooperation of ego and Self resulting
in generosity to others, but rather an increasingly narrow and narcissistic
concentration on the intricacies of the psychic process.

The reaching of the ego toward relation with the Self is the central
issue in analysis for Jungians, whether with negative or positive effect.
The movement of ego toward Self is involved in any transference, but
nowhere so strongly as when the contrasexual anima or animus is activated, stretching consciousness to make space for all that arrives from the
unconscious. The contrasexual archetypes galvanize the deepest issues of
individuation—that process of differentiating out of unconsciousness one's
individual personality in relation to other persons. Mess or grand experience, connection or disruption, a relation of love or one of hostility—our

sexual life is a constant drama in which the contrasexual archetypes play a major role. These are the archetypes that open onto the Self in the individuation journey. They touch all aspects of human life: our past experiences and future hopes, our sexuality, our bodies, our souls, our sense of purpose or purposelessness. An indication of how profoundly anima and animus reach into us in the transference-countertransference relationship can be seen in the way they constellate the backward and forward strivings of the incest motif.

Anima and animus introduce a sexual tonality into the relationship that symbolizes the urgency of the underlying impulse toward "union with one's own being . . . individuation or becoming [one's] self" (Jung 1946, p. 218). To become all of one's self means to connect consciously with unconscious parts of one's personality, such as personal memories from one's childhood that have been forgotten and need to be remembered, and impersonal unconscious contents like images that arise spontaneously in the psyche to accompany autonomous instinctive processes. The joining of the opposites of anima or animus and ego that Jung calls the *coniunctio* pulls the patient backward into his or her personal history through incestuous longings to be joined once again to those large and fascinating parental figures, with their interesting shapes, smells, tastes, and textures. The patient feels again in the transference the strong pull of small child to large adult, of infant to containing parent, of dependent self to encompassing other.

The sexualized tone of these feelings underscores their urgency by enlisting the body instincts in the movement of the psyche's longings. Sexual imagery is particularly well suited to conveying unconscious material, for it is a preverbal, nondiscursive language of images, emotions, and body drives. It includes autoerotic imaginings alongside efforts to build intimacy with another. It is almost impossible to forget a sexually charged dream!

The transference of anima or animus to analyst pulls the patient forward into the crucial work of *coniunctio,* the inner marriage of ego and contrasexual archetype that "brings to birth something that is one and united." Longing for "union on the biological level is a symbol of the *unio oppositorum* at its highest," of finding how to put together into a whole all the parts of oneself (Jung 1946, pp. 248, 250). The contrasexual archetype is particularly well suited to personifying contents of the collective unconscious, because it is so vivid in its appearance in the images of those "other" humans, those of the opposite sex. They are both so like us and so unlike us. Relating to contrasexual figures demands that we somehow put at our ego's disposal identification and differentiation, the psychic processes that encourage acceptance of sexuality in its entirety, our own sex and its opposite, both in ourselves and in others.

If the analyst receives the full transference of the contrasexual arche-type, a most intense and flammable situation will ensue. This is the case regardless of the patient's level of psychic development. The Self—the center of one's potential wholeness—is elicited and the ego feels its pull. The contrasexual archetype, though differently presented from stage to stage, will nonetheless always display its potentiality to connect ego and contents of the objective psyche, that realm of unconscious psychic life out of which the ego originally emerges (Hubback, p. 231; Fordham 1978, p. 87). To illustrate this connecting function, I will take an extreme ex-ample, one that amounted to a transference psychosis. That is a particular danger in this sort of transference, just because the anima or animus opens onto the Self, which then may threaten to overpower the ego. The patient feels the Self is at stake, in its smallest terms as personal ego functioning, in its largest terms as the center of authentic being.

A woman barely established as a person in herself entered treatment with a male psychiatrist and fell totally in love with him. She experienced herself as an infant coming to her divine parent, unawakened female to her hero-prince, love-starved middle-aged woman to her soul-mate. The treat-ment ended and a sexual relation ensued, but it soon dwindled to infre-quent meetings. When she entered treatment with me, she felt all but crazed by the experience. Our work for many months centered around her feelings for him, her intense transference. She felt that her love for him represented her most essential, true self, which she needed in order to exist at all. She felt he connected her to the center of life. But now he was withdrawn from her. The withdrawal recapitulated with explosive force deprivations in her early life. She felt in danger of annihilation, either from loss of him or from her rage over the loss.

She had not just transferred to her therapist the animus that might con-nect her to that authentic Self. He *was* the animus; hence, the delusional aspect of the transference. The experience was so powerful that it threat-ened to overwhelm her ego. The Self was glimpsed before the ego was strong enough to relate to it. She saw the promise of being loved and of loving, of feeling alive and real, of being connected to what she experi-enced as life's meaning and truth. But the promise was broken. It fell apart, in ruins. The ego was then in danger of being plowed under, swept away, or invaded by rageful animus opinions. Some unlived part of the analyst had also apparently been ignited in the dynamics operating between them. The analysis was lost and with it the relationship between them, and for her, the relationship to her own inward center.

Acting out the transference-countertransference, instead of analyzing it, is one of the greatest dangers in the transference of anima or animus, for in the long run the patient is robbed of the analytical container in which to forge connection to this inner "other" (Ulanov 1979, pp. 101–4). In such acting out, analysis presumes to replace a life relationship. As a result, analysis loses its own rightful place and only very rarely does a real personal relationship develop.

The other major danger with such a transference is that of talking it to death instead of experiencing it (Guggenbühl-Craig, p. 65; Newman, p. 122). That, too, is a sort of defense, but it is done verbally, with an excess of theorizing and an amplification of imagery that seduces the patients into a symbolic bond that sucks the libido out of all their intimate life relationships (Ulanov 1979, p. 109). Where acting out the transference robs the patient of realizing its symbolic significance, talking it to death steals the patient's right to experience instinct and affect and put together a creative solution (Winnicott 1971a, p. 57). Both prevent the potential transformation of the patient from going forward because, from different sides, both split apart the instinctive and the spiritual urges. The opposites are sundered instead of united.

Proper handling of a transference-countertransference that takes shape around anima or animus requires more vigor than either of the negative extremes of acting or talking it out. I will give some examples of anima transference in which one central theme is constant. In each, the anima acts as bridge between ego and objective psyche; it mediates the contents of the objective psyche to the ego; it functions as a connecting point; it opens the ego to experience of otherness. Personal concerns get linked to life concerns. One's conscious sexual identity gets in touch with opposite sex characteristics in one's own personality. Ego purposes and values—all that one asks of life—are confronted with what life asks of oneself. We meet up with less familiar parts of ourselves, sometimes parts that are unknown to us, but that nevertheless belong to us and that we must accommodate. This changes the whole. Thus in the transference, the analyst who receives the anima projection is experienced, whether positively or negatively, as one who facilitates the connection of the ego to its own deep resources in the Self.

When a man gains consciousness of anima contents, his ego changes. It enlarges and becomes more spacious and more flexible. His ego opens to contents that are not properly part of his masculine identity, but that his ego houses, so to speak, letting these contents enter and pass through. He does not identify with them. He experiences the anima contents as quite other than himself, yet as part of his larger personality. His ego becomes more flexible as he simultaneously takes notice of the anima qualities and impulses and stands aside from them. He sees them, but does not become them; holds them, but does not possess them, and is not possessed by them. He can look them over as something both within and outside himself, to be considered alongside his own more familiar points of view.

A man dreamed that he came for a session with his analyst, and she made him wait while she attended to a frail girl who had worms in her hair (Ulanov 1981, p. 72). In associating to the dream, the man evidenced that peculiar doubling up of consciousness so characteristic of coming into awareness of unconscious contents. It is particularly true of anima contents, because they present themselves in forms so different from the dreamer's ego-identity, so opposite from it. The man saw himself in the dream as robust, purposively directed, healthy, and male. He saw the anima figure as sickly, dependent, with disgusting hair, and female. Yet she touched him. She irritated him by keeping him waiting, and yet stirred some remote and painful sense of dependency in himself. She belonged to him, he felt, though he did not want her. The analyst took care of her in the dream, thus previewing the fact that this phase of the analysis (and transference) would be much occupied with this figure of otherness. He did not identify with his anima, but his ego-awareness enlarged to make room for her and her side of things, so opposite to his own.

Another man's experience in a session illustrates the flexibility this doubling up of consciousness engenders in the ego. He spoke of his pleasure in beginning a friendship with a man whom I knew and whom the patient knew that I knew. Suddenly, the patient thought I had some reservation about this mutual acquaintance. He asked me point blank and I said no, that in fact I liked the man. The patient, long used to dealing with his own projections, was astounded by the contrast between the certainty of his intuition and the fact of my reply. He felt simultaneously two opposed reactions. He saw in me a response that he had projected onto me, which contrasted sharply with the response to this man that he had thought was the only one he had.

In fact he had two responses. Where he was pleased, this "other" reaction was fearful, hesitant. We explored this second response in the context of an anima figure who recurrently appeared in his dreams as frightened, even disturbed. I commented that "she" might find the new friend's directness overwhelming and intrusive. Again, suddenly, the patient's experience repeated itself. He had been sure this was my reaction, but he knew that it was not, that it was his own. For the moment he cloaked me, the analyst, in the reactive guise of his anima. By claiming my own reaction, I enabled the patient to see his anima's view. He saw it, then lost it, then saw it again, experiencing that doubling up of perspective—his and the anima's—that occurs when one becomes conscious of the opposite that dwells within each of us. This simultaneity of experiencing and standing

aside, of owning one's own view and perceiving its opposite, develops
flexibility in the ego.

The connecting function of the anima can reveal itself from the countertransference side, too. For example, I felt my attention wandering in a
session, which is uncharacteristic of my reactions. I reviewed whatever
complexes in me might have been touched off by what the patient was
saying, but that led nowhere. Then I considered whether my reaction was
being evoked by something going on in the patient himself. My sense of
wandering evaporated, but I got no further than feeling negated, as if my
own consciousness, comments, and interpretive remarks were being cancelled by the patient's refusal to connect to them. The "wandering" revealed itself now as trying first this way, then that, to reach the patient,
but no door opened. I felt connection between us was being nullified. I
held this feeling and did not use it for interpretation at that time.

A few days later I received a letter from the patient in which he wrote
of a painful insight that came to him soon after our session. He too felt
disconnected. Tracing that feeling, he came upon an envious destructive-
ness in his attitude toward me that resented my having anything good at
all to give him. By not taking in anything from me, he in effect cancelled
my goodness. It was as if his anima made her presence felt negatively by
disrupting the connection between us, spurred to do so by envy of the
nourishing role in which he had cast me. His insight proved most fruitful
for our subsequent work. Klein comments that envy of the opposite sex
can sometimes be a split-off mad part in any of us that would destroy or
spoil the goodness that one missed getting from one's mother (as was in
fact true for this man), so that no one else can have it either (pp. 208–
11; see also Winnicott 1971*b*, pp. 73–75).

Just as a man's ego is changed by admitting anima contents, so we
may hazard that the anima is changed by connection with consciousness.
It is the securing of the ego-anima connection that comprises *coniunctio*.
That is the way we achieve the inner marriage that opens us to the Self,
beginning a process "whose goal is complete individuation" (Jung 1946,
p. 260). The ego changes. It is no longer center stage nor entirely intact.
It has something like a permanent hole in it that opens onto another center.
For some people, the original hole in their ego-identity, which caused so
much suffering and pathological distortion, is precisely what becomes
transformed into an opening onto what Gerard Manley Hopkins called the
"yonder, yonder, yonder" of being, for the sake of which, finally, we live
(pp. 53-54). The anima also undergoes transformation, becoming less
blurred and more defined in character. Moreover, "she" may take a more

vigorous role in dreams or active imagination in order to get her point across.

For example, a man who was given to angry outbursts of critical judgment against a woman with whom he was deeply involved, discovered, after some painstaking reductive analysis, that these scenes always erupted from his own hurt feelings when he felt his own sensitivities had been utterly disregarded. Who had disregarded them, however, remained the question. He berated his woman friend for this crime, while remaining clear in himself that she was a very important friend and a beloved companion.

His recounting of these episodes left me with my own puzzled reaction. I felt passing through me reactions of anger at being left out and a sense of ''What about me?'' that I could not account for in my personal reactions to this man. Nor did I find any significant abnormal transference of activated complex from my side. I felt as if I were having someone else's reaction, not my own. I was feeling, I believe, the reaction of the patient's most sensitive anima, a piece of objective countertransference originating in the patient. ''She'' felt jealous of his increasing affection for his woman friend; ''she'' felt left out, not taken into consideration, not dealt with directly by him. He was unconscious of this missing part of his own reactions and projected it onto me, and I found myself temporarily identifying with it. Fordham calls this ''identifying with a patient's projective identification'' (1978, p. 92; see also Klein, p. 11). For the moment, I was carrying a piece of the patient's psychic reality of which he was not yet conscious and so could not experience as his own inner conflict.

This bit of objective countertransference gave me a valuable clue as to what was going on in the patient and his resultant behavior. For no matter how solicitous his woman friend might be, the possibility of his feeling utterly disregarded remained, for he was himself the culprit in his dealing with his own anima. Working on this led to a change, summed up best by a dream fragment (Ulanov 1981, p. 57). In the dream, someone knocks angrily at the door. The dreamer opens it and is confronted by an angry woman who says that she wants to come in, that he has left her out and not cared about her feelings. She wants to know what he is going to do about it. The change this dream signified was the initial mending of the split in him between sensitive feelings and angry attack. Both arise together, and are clearly connected with each other, instead of the anger hiding the hurt. The woman says right out that she is hurt and angry. The issue is clearly between him and her, no longer split into pieces, some of which are projected onto the woman friend and some of which remain with

himself. He was connected now with an element of himself, and the anima
had made connection with him.

A last example illustrates an extreme anima transference that took
shape around the anima's function of connecting the ego-world to the otherness of the ego-transcending dimension of the psyche. Here both analyst
and patient were opened to the otherness of death. The patient had worked
intensively in analysis for several years on a radical split-anima condition
that was being lived out both internally and externally (Ulanov 1981,
p. 168). A dream best sums up the extreme nature of this split and its
seeming insolubility. The dreamer saw himself in a room between two
other rooms, in each of which stood a woman who represented one of
the opposite poles of his anima fascination. The rooms were so arranged
that the women could see him and each other. Each woman held a re-
volver in her hand, threatening to shoot either the other woman or the
dreamer, yet each was stayed in her action by the fact that the other
could see her take aim and perhaps shoot first. The dreamer was trapped
between them, in a menacing and divisive relation to different figurations
of his anima.

The patient's transference to me was to anima as a trusted sister
or colleague, even spiritual guide, who made space for both sides of the
anima split. After some years of work, this split softened. The dreamer
felt, at last, that he could live with it, a very different feeling from his
attitude when he entered treatment. At that time, he had felt close to
suicide, desperate over the gap between his public life—where he was
respected by all and was, in his small sphere, famous—and his secret
private life.

Against my counsel, the man terminated treatment, feeling he had gone
as far as he could go at least for the moment, though he kept in touch over
the ensuing years until I was again brought into sustained contact with
him. That contact was initiated by his phoning to announce that he had
just learned he was gravely ill with an incurable and fast-moving disease.
Indeed, he was to be dead within three months. The transference now
moved into the deep waters of spiritual direction, as the man put the question to me bluntly of whether or not he should kill himself before the
disease ravaged his brain and made him psychotic, its predictable course.
Here the analyst was crowded with questions about the ultimate value of
life, proper preparation for death, and the fate of the soul after death,
particularly one that had contemplated or even committed suicide.

As in the examples above, this case also recommended itself for reductive analysis and synthetic-constructive treatment. On the personal level,
the man feared his long-held, secret anima complex and behavior would

be what would spill out from him for all to see if he became psychotic before death. His thought of suicide was a defensive maneuver to protect his secret. Locating his fear and defining it brought him some relief. The prospective question, however, of what to do then and how in fact to move toward death loomed all the larger.

For my part, I felt the impact of larger questions about the value of consciousness, analytic methods, countertransference reactions, and so on. I found in myself deeper convictions than ever about the value of these activities, which really are important to me, and yet at the same time saw their emphasis shift, not in the sense of any loss of value, but loosened from their moorings, less fixed, less simply defined. I saw the positive qualities involved in giving over, opening up, remaining less anchored in method or procedure. This was a small mirroring of my patient's great loosening of his hold on his life, with all its rich values. His dying and, particularly, and centrally, his manner of resolving the issue of suicide, affected me in a permanent way. We asked the synthetic questions: What might the meaning be? To what end still not clearly in view might this particular disease's threat of psychosis be tending? What could be the purpose in the threat of exposing a long-hidden secret life, with which he had worked so hard to live, yet had not fully accepted?

In the midst of these groping questions, another way opened. He voluntarily—and completely—gave up the escape route of suicide by offering it up to the source of life from which he had come and from which he had received all that he had known of life. He felt this as an intensely personal offering of what he had to give, all he feared and wished for, back into the hands of God, of life. He offered even his sanity, letting go of everything—his fear of losing his sanity, his fear of exposure—releasing all to the power that had created him. In dying, he reached a depth of acceptance he could not reach in life. He reached beneath the split of public and secret life to deliver himself over utterly, as he was, fears, splits, and all.

One could say it would have all been taken from him anyway, which is true, for the disease took one function, one sense after another from him—his balance, his sight, his muscular coordination, his hearing, his voice. All the difference occurred as a result of his voluntarily bringing what he had and offering it up, all of it. That difference manifested itself outwardly in the surprising fact that he did not become psychotic before his body gave out, that, far from falling apart in spirit or psyche, he held together magnificently. Thus he was spared what he most deeply feared, but only because he faced the fear and willingly submitted to it. For my part, since this experience, there always has been a space between the analytic methods I cherish and my commitment to them, an empty space where questions can appear that may challenge the whole analytic endeavor, while at the same time confirming it.

REFERENCES

Carotenuto, A. 1980. Sabina Spielrein and C. G. Jung: some newly discovered documents bearing on psychotic transference, counter transference, and the anima. *Spring* 1980:128–45.

Dieckmann, H. 1976. Transference and countertransference: results of a Berlin research group. *Journal of Analytical Psychology* 21/1:25–36.

Edinger, E. F. 1957. Some manifestations of the transference phenomena. *Spring* 1957:32–45.

———. 1978. Solutio. *Quadrant* Winter 1978:32–44.

Epstein, L., and Feiner, A. H., eds. 1979. *Countertransference*. New York: Jason Aronson.

Fordham, M. 1957a. Notes on transference. In *New developments in analytical psychology,* pp. 62–104. London: Routledge and Kegan Paul.

———. 1957b. Note on a significance of archetypes for the transference in childhood. In *New developments in analytical psychology,* pp. 181–88. London: Routledge and Kegan Paul.

———. 1958. The objective psyche. London: Routledge and Kegan Paul.

———. 1974. Jung's conception of transference. *Journal of Analytical Psychology* 19/1:1–21.

———. 1978. *Jungian psychotherapy*. New York: Wiley.

Franz, M.-L. von. 1970. *Interpretation of fairy tales*. New York: Spring Publications.

Groesbeck, J. 1978. Psychological types in the analysis of the transference. *Journal of Analytical Psychology* 23/1:1:23–54.

Guggenbühl-Craig, A. 1971. *Power in the helping professions*. New York: Spring Publications.

Hillman, J. 1972. *The myth of analysis*. Part 2. New York: Harper & Row.

Hopkins, G. M. 1948. The leaden echo and the golden echo. In *Poems of Gerard Manley Hopkins*. London: Oxford University Press.

Hubback, J. 1980. Development and similarities, 1935–1980. *Journal of Analytical Psychology* 23/3:219–37.

Jacoby, M. 1971. A contribution to the phenomenon of transference. In *The analytic process: aims, analysis, training,* ed. J. B. Wheelwright, pp. 10–17. New York: Putnam.

Jung, C. G. 1944. *Psychology and alchemy. Collected works,* vol. 12. New York: Pantheon, 1953.

———. 1946. Psychology of the transference. In *Collected works,* vol. 16, pp. 163–323. New York: Pantheon, 1954.

———. 1948. General aspects of dream psychology. In *Collected works,* vol. 8, pp. 237–80. New York: Pantheon, 1960.

———. 1966. *Two essays on analytical psychology. Collected works,* vol. 7. 2d ed. New York: Pantheon.

————. 1968. *Analytical psychology, its theory and practice*. New York: Pantheon.

————. 1975. *Letters*. Vol. 2. ed. G. Adler. Princeton: Princeton University Press.

————. 1976. *The visions seminars*. Vol. 1. Zurich: Spring Publications.

Kernberg, O. 1975. *Borderline conditions and pathological narcissism*. New York: Jason Aronson.

Khan, M. M. R. 1979. *Alienation in perversions*. New York: International Universities Press.

Klein, M. 1975. *Envy and gratitude and other works 1946–1963*. New York: Delacorte.

Kohut, H. 1971. *The analysis of the self*. New York: International Universities Press.

Kraemer, W. P. 1958. The dangers of unrecognized countertransference. *Journal of Analytical Psychology* 3/1: 29–43.

Lambert, K. 1972. Transference/countertransference: talion law and gratitude. *Journal of Analytical Psychology* 17/1:31–51.

Loewald, H. 1977. Transference and countertransference: the roots of psychoanalysis. Book review essay on the *Freud/Jung Letters*. *Psychoanalytic Quarterly* 46:514–27.

Moody, R. 1955. On the function of countertransference. *Journal of Analytical Psychology* 1/1:49–59.

Newman, K. D. 1980. Countertransference and consciousness. *Spring* 1980:117–28.

Paulsen, L. 1956. Transference and projection. *Journal of Analytical Psychology* 1/2:203–7.

Plaut, A. 1970. "What do you actually do?" Problems in communicating. *Journal of Analytical Psychology* 15/1:13–22.

Racker, H. 1968. *Transference and countertransference*. London: Hogarth.

Searles, H. F. 1965. *Collected papers on schizophrenia and related subjects*. New York: International Universities Press.

————. 1979a. *Countertransference*. New York: International Universities Press.

————. 1979b. The self in the countertransference. *Issues in Ego Psychology* 2/2:49–57.

Spiegelman, J. M. 1980. The image of the Jungian analyst. *Spring* 1980:101–17.

Stein, R. M. 1971. Transference and individuation: reflections on the process and future of analysis. *Spring* 1971: 38–50.

Ulanov, A. B. 1979. Follow-up treatment in cases of patient/therapist sex. *Journal of the American Academy of Psychoanalysis* 7/1:101–10.

————. 1981. *Receiving Woman*. Philadelphia: Westminster Press.

Winnicott, D. W. 1971a. Playing: creative activity and the search for the self. In *Playing and reality*, chap. 4, pp. 53–64. London: Tavistock.

————. 1971b. Creativity and its origins. In *Playing and reality*, chap. 5, pp. 65–85. London: Tavistock.

————. 1975. Hate in the countertransference. In *Through paediatrics to psychoanalysis*, pp. 194–203. New York: Basic Books.

————. 1977. *The piggle: an account of the psychoanalytic treatment of a little girl*. New York: International Universities Press.

[5]

COUNTERTRANSFERENCE/TRANSFERENCE

Harriet Gordon Machtiger

THE intimately interwoven process of countertransference and transference is, in its archetypal bipolarity, a focal point in the theory and practice of analytical psychology. While recognizing the extent to which the two poles of this process overlap, and the impossibility of considering them as two discrete entities, one can nevertheless restrict the discussion to countertransference as it is experienced by the analyst, and as it is used within the analytic process. Various views of the countertransference and its current use in treatment will be presented here, along with a discussion of the influence of the analyst's personality and specific countertransference reactions.

HISTORICAL BACKGROUND

Although it is true that the actual term *countertransference* was originally introduced by Freud in 1910, it was Jung who, though rarely using the term in his writing, managed to incorporate its meaning actively within the context of analysis. He called attention to the possibility of the analyst's becoming psychically disturbed or injured by the patient: "The countertransference phenomenon is one of the chief occupational hazards of psychotherapy . . . and brings the therapeutic process to a standstill" (Jung 1937, p. 329). Jung likened countertransference to the old notion of the

Harriet Machtiger, Ph.D., is a Jungian analyst practicing in Pittsburgh, Pennsylvania. A diplomate of the Child Development Center of the University of London, she received her Ph.D. in psychology from the University of London. She was an associate trainee in child psychotherapy at the Tavistock Clinic and completed the Jungian Adult Psychotherapy Training Program of the British Association of Psychotherapists. Dr. Machtiger is a member of the New York Association of Analytical Psychologists; the Inter-Regional Society of Jungian Analysts; the British Psychological Society; and the American Psychological Association.

demon of sickness. The sufferer is able to transmit the disease "to a healthy person whose powers then subdue the demons—but not without impairing the well-being of the subduer" in the process (Jung 1931, p. 71).

Jung saw that analysts are put under stress during the analytic process, and also that analysts who do not avail themselves of countertransference data deny themselves the use of a highly relevant therapeutic device. It was with this in mind that Jung asserted that analysts should themselves be analyzed. He acknowledged his debt to Freud for discovering that analysts, too, had blind spots and complexes that could interfere with the progress of an analysis.

While Jung fully accepted the analyst's experience of countertransference as a vital ingredient within the analytic process, Freud saw it as an unnecessary contaminant. With the passage of time, the psychoanalytic understanding of the processes of countertransference and transference has evolved from an emphasis on the negative aspects and a perception of these processes as a hindrance, to a more positive acceptance of their role as a valuable therapeutic instrument for understanding the patient's unconscious by making constructive use of the analyst's own psyche.

Most of the revisions in current psychoanalytic literature concerned with countertransference/transference have been derived from studies in which analysts deal with the borderline and psychotic states of their patients. Although some of this thinking appears to be moving closer to the frame of reference of analytical psychologists, Freudians and Jungians continue to operate out of different paradigms. The basic differences emerge from the fact that Jungians postulate an archetypal dimension to the phenomena of countertransference/transference, in addition to a personal aspect. It is this postulation of an archetypal aspect to the unconscious, and the possibilities such a hypothesis presents, that not only led to Jung's parting with Freud, but continues to permeate the differing perspectives of the respective schools.

THE USE OF THE TERM COUNTERTRANSFERENCE

It is easier to write about the differences between Freudians and Jungians than to discuss countertransference/transference from the perspective of analytical psychology. Although they are inseparable, and what we say about one can largely be applied to the other, much more has been written on the transference.

One of the problems encountered in discussing the countertransference is that there is no consensus among analytical psychologists on the definition of the term, on its derivatives and content, or on its relevance and/or its applicability to treatment. It is all too easy to slip from one meaning to another, as the word itself is used in a variety of ways. A further complication is that the methods and theory of analytical psychology, like those of other approaches in depth psychology, are undergoing change. During this period of paradigm change, there appears to be a great divergency between those analysts who adhere to a more classical, orthodox approach, with its strict definition of countertransference, and the proponents of a wider, more comprehensive interpretation of countertransference.

Those analysts who embrace a strict definition of countertransference would limit the term to the unconscious projections of feelings incurred by the analyst in reaction to the attitudes and products of the patient. They would not include either conscious or preconscious attitudes of the analyst. When countertransference is defined in this narrow sense, the personal relationship aspect, with its accompanying positive and negative reactions, is ignored. The analyst is perceived as attempting to master some unconscious aspect of his or her own psyche in the therapy session with the patient.

At the other end of the continuum are those analysts who favor a broad definition of countertransference. They would consider everything that transpires within an analytic session to be a manifestation of the countertransference/transference. The analyst's conscious, personal response toward the real or imagined behavior or attitudes of the patient is utilized, along with the unconscious, to understand the interpersonal process between patient and analyst. As the sum total of the analyst's reactions to the patient, the countertransference is very much a statement of the psychic reality of the analyst, and encompasses all of the analyst's behavior in the therapeutic work.

It seems to me that those who limit the definition of countertransference to the involuntary projection of unconscious contents are in essence establishing a distinct line of demarcation between conscious and unconscious. In actuality, it is no more possible to achieve this than it is to differentiate clearly between the contents of the personal unconscious and those of the transpersonal or collective unconscious. When archetypal images are constellated, the analytic material reflects permeable boundaries with resultant fluidity between conscious and unconscious material, and between personal and transpersonal, archetypal material.

Jung conceptualized analysis as a dialectical process that "is not the simple, straightforward method people at first believed it to be, but, as has gradually become clear . . . a dialogue or discussion between two persons" who enter into a reciprocal relationship (1931, p. 3). Both patient and analyst are partners in the center of a dynamic process, in which there is a relationship between two total psyches encompassing conscious and unconscious, verbal and nonverbal, normal and pathological components in varying proportions.

It is out of this dialectical relationship, with its resultant therapeutic field, that countertransference/transference with its positive and negative potential emerges. At a central point in the dialectical process, each possibility evokes the other. This is not to say that they emerge like Venus out of the sea: they are derived from the projection and introjection of archetypal and personal contents within the countertransference/transference. These processes originate primarily within the sphere of the unconscious. No one consciously creates countertransference/transference projections or introjections. Yet as the analyst brings his or her whole person to the therapeutic encounter, the countertransference implies that the analyst's consciousness is brought to bear on the therapy too.

Countertransference and transference projections are not composed of old contents alone, but also include contents that have yet to be evoked. The point where they meet is in the interstitial area of a shared experience. As mentioned earlier, the archetypal aspects of the countertransference/transference have their roots in the shared unconscious relationship between analyst and patient, in what Jung has called "participation mystique" and Winnicott has termed metaphorical space or potential space (1953), an intermediate state between fantasy and reality. This shared experience facilitates the activation of the transcendent function and results in an opportunity for healing and growth on the part of both patient and analyst. The transcendent function furthers the process of individuation by creating a transition from one attitude to another, or one stage of development to another, by the utilization of symbols. It is through the use of symbols that one can transcend inner experience by bridging pairs of opposites. The transcendent function is able to unite the opposing trends of several systems, and in doing so works toward the achievement of potential wholeness.

The processes of projection and introjection permeate all interpersonal relationships, and as such are important components of the countertransference/transference. The introjective response of the analyst allows for the identification that is the basis of the countertransference reaction of empathy. Countertransference includes not only the analyst's capacity for empathy, antipathy, sympathy, and other affects, but the analyst's total mental functioning. The analyst needs to be aware of being an instrument that furthers a process. While there is talk of the analyst's need for genuineness, warmth, patience, and humility, along with accurate empathy, additional qualities called forth in the countertransference are the ability to accept a patient's confusion, along with painful feelings, and not promote a positive attitude. Improvement takes place when the analyst can hold the attitude in the countertransference/transference that there is growth potential.

Since countertransference is more than the projection or introjection of unconscious contents, it represents "phenomena and processes" as well (Paulsen, p. 203). What starts out on an unconscious plane eventually gets translated into a conscious realization. It is this conscious realization of countertransference reactions that acts as a source of information and as a tool for understanding the patient's unconscious processes.

Newman notes that emphasis on the effects of consciousness as an aspect of the countertransference "continues to be skimped" (p. 119). While the ego and nonego of analyst and patient interact in a dynamic polarity, it is the ego function and consciousness of the analyst that allow for the separateness that enables the analyst to deal with countertransference reactions.

Hall provides us with a Jungian theoretical model that sums up the vectors and levels involved in the broad definition of the countertransference/transference interaction (p. 225):

1. The relationship between the ego of the analyst and that of the patient: the conscious relationship.
2. The relationship between the unconscious mind of the patient and the conscious personality of the analyst (and the reverse).
3. The relationship between the unconscious mind of the analyst and the unconscious mind of the patient.

The countertransference is not simply the projection of a momentary response on the part of the analyst. The art of psychotherapy is lived out in the interaction between analyst and patient. The analyst's countertransference activity plays a vital role in the search for wholeness: the more the analyst is in touch with the countertransference and his or her own reactions, the more the analysand will be aided in the healing process.

There is a delicate balance to be maintained within the countertransference/transference relationship, wherein the analyst provides the necessary structure while simultaneously remaining receptively attuned to the patient's emerging inner experience. It is the analyst's reaction in the countertransference that is the essential therapeutic factor in analysis. In the countertransference, the analyst uses his or her own reactions and dreams as a therapeutic tool. These indices are kept in mind all the time, and the countertransference reactions provide information about what is going on within the analytic process.

"Though it has been contested, and though many attempts have been made to diminish its importance, the transference, and its accompanying countertransference remain the central affective components in analytical psychotherapy" (Fordham 1978, p. 80). Patients introject the healing strength of the analyst and, by virtue of experiencing the archetypal image, are then able to activate their own capacity for self-healing. Countertransference is a constructive and desirable instrument of treatment when it is based on the healthy components in the analyst's psychology, as reflected in the individual's work style. When the countertransference reactions are due to the analyst's neurotic complexes and unconscious involvements, leading to unconscious identifications and projections, they have a negative effect.

THE ISSUE OF TECHNIQUE

In addition to the controversy surrounding the definition of the term itself, there is also a conflict regarding the relevance and applicability of countertransference to treatment. The dissension is between those analysts who view therapy as an art and the more clinically minded ones who emphasize its technical aspect. The dispute centers on whether to use methods and techniques within the analytic encounter. Some analysts with a strong intuitive bias have an antipathy toward the use of clinical methods and skills.

When categorizing countertransference as a technique, I am specifically referring to its use as a precise tool, and a valid instrument, for gaining an increasing understanding and broader conscious awareness of what is transpiring within the therapeutic field of the union between analyst and patient. Negative and positive countertransference reactions provide relevant therapeutic data.

A thorough elaboration of the therapeutic potential of countertransference has been undertaken by Fordham (1957, 1969, 1978, 1979), who is the leading spokesperson of the so-called London school of analytical psychology. Along with Moody, Lambert, Plaut (1955, 1956), Kraemer, and others, the members of this school have been at the center of the controversy surrounding the development and use of such phenomena as countertransference/transference as clinical methods. Having been influenced by the work of Klein, Winnicott, and other Freudians, this group is considered more psychoanalytically oriented than other analytical psychologists. They are more interested in questions of management, in the use of the couch, and in more frequent therapy sessions. This nucleus of the London school has made a major contribution to the clinical literature on countertransference/transference. Its members are predominantly concerned not only with theory, but with the practical application of clinical skills within the analytic process.

Zinkin has remarked that analytic psychologists as a group are more apt to be concerned with the content of analysis and less with the problems of technique. In their devotion to the archetypal and imaginal aspects of the psyche, they appear to glory in the notion of an analytic encounter that is not encumbered by an awareness of methods or a need to follow rules. To use countertransference/transference as a tool is perceived as obstructing the emergence of the patient's individuality. Fordham states that the criticism of technique can in itself be perceived as an impersonal and sustained countertransference reaction on the part of the analysts who hold this point of view (1979).

Edinger discusses the shortcomings of an approach that excludes the archetypal nature of the transference, but simultaneously cautions analytical psychologists who go to the other extreme of so emphasizing content to the exclusion of technique that, in their eagerness to amplify the archetypal material, they ''neglect the nature of the patient's interpersonal relations'' (p. 34).

While it is true that Jung was more interested in the content of the patient's material, and from time to time expressed ambivalent feelings about technique, he himself certainly emphasized the use of countertransference/transference and employed special analytical skills. These skills included the techniques of amplification, of dream interpretation, and of active imagination, as well as what Fordham refers to as the synthetic hermeneutic technique (1969). Jung also acknowledged the importance of the use of a reductive technique in some analyses.

In essence, Jung was trying to preserve the highly individual nature of the analytic process, to make sure that the whole person of the analyst was fully present and personally involved in the encounter with the patient. To be fully present and involved in this manner is to invoke countertransference whether we acknowledge it in these terms or not, since the ''analyst remains forever a patient as well as a healer'' (Guggenbühl-Craig 1971, p. 129). If the importance of the countertransference is not recognized, there is the danger that the analyst can become too intrusive and act out some of his or her unconscious needs. For example, an analyst's need to be loved can get in the way of the therapy. Or the analyst can live vicariously through the patient's life experiences. Groesbeck notes that the doctor can remain well at the expense of the patient, who remains ill, when both are blocked with respect to integrating their unconscious sides. According to Kraemer, an analyst's unrecognized shadow may well be at the root of an unrecognized countertransference.

Jung continues to address the issue of countertransference/transference when he says: "Even the most experienced psychotherapist will discover again and again that he is caught up in a bond, a combination resting on mutual unconsciousness" (1946, p. 179). Although Jung states that "the personalities of the doctor and patient are infinitely more important for the outcome of treatment than what the doctor says and does" (1931, p. 73), he was also very aware of the need for analysts to be constantly aware of their own primitive feelings, fantasies, anxieties, and biases. These elements could have a deleterious effect on the therapy by contaminating the therapist's field or by arousing negative feelings in the patient. In addition to these countertransference/transference concerns, he notes that the personal problems or situational pressures of the analyst can get in the way of the treatment.

While some of the resistance to the use of countertransference/transference techniques may be a manifestation of changing paradigms, these techniques are a fact of analytic work. Like every psychic reality, they have positive and negative potential. As such they need to be owned and used with skill.

THE ARCHETYPAL FOUNDATION OF THE COUNTERTRANSFERENCE

One reason for the dearth of material on the countertransference reactions of analysts is their almost phobic response to the revelation of what transpires in the countertransference or in the analysis itself. To discuss these matters is seen as a violation of the rule of *vas bene clausum*, the alchemical well-sealed vessel (cf. chapter by McCurdy, above). This point of view can possibly be justified during the course of an ongoing therapy. Leakage of affect and intrusion of foreign content can jeopardize the favorable outcome of treatment. However, this objection to submitting countertransference to scrutiny cannot be sustained. Indeed, Dieckmann and his group in Berlin have been studying the dreams and content of ongoing therapeutic sessions for years without reporting the need to jettison any of the analyses involved (1976).

Stein posits that the reluctance of analysts to reveal what transpires in their countertransference/transference reactions can be attributed to fear (p. 68). It is easier for the analysts to focus on the meaning of a symptom or a symbol than to consider "who they are at certain stages of the analysis."

Plaut states that the analyst is in the transference situation together with the patient, and that countertransference means just what it says—namely, against or "contra" the transference (1955). It implies that analysts resist accepting their share in the total transference situation. Although Plaut sees the countertransference as a result of the patient's transference, while Strauss and others speak of the countertransference as operative from the first interview onward, I would like to question these assumptions and share some speculations of my own. It seems to me that transference and countertransference begin even before the first meeting of analyst and patient.

We recognize that the patient can have burgeoning transference feelings before the first telephone call to set up an appointment with an analyst. Dim fantasies start to surface from the initial consideration of the possibility of starting analysis. The fantasies may include ideation about what sort of person the analyst is, and speculation about whether he or she will be able to understand.

Although the analyst's frame of reference is different in both content and intensity, the analyst has his or her own fantasies not only about the patient, but about the personal meaning of analytic practice itself. We analysts appear to have a need to delve into the unconscious fantasies of others, and, while doing so, to introject the patients' unconscious contents into ourselves. We may resist acknowledging that this countertransference/transference phenomenon emerges from the structure of our total personality, conscious and unconscious, in the interaction between patient and analyst.

In Jung's view, it is our own unconscious processes and projections that propel us into choosing the profession of analyst to begin with (1946, p. 177). In his study of the psychopathology of the analyst, Carotenuto puts forth some interesting thoughts along these lines (p. 57). He quotes Jung as follows:

> Presumably he [the doctor] had good reason for choosing the profession of psychiatrist and for being particularly interested in the treatment of psychoneuroses; and he cannot very well do that without gaining some insight into his own unconscious processes. Nor can his concern with the unconscious be explained entirely by free choice of interests, but rather by a fateful disposition which originally inclined him to the medical profession. The more one sees of human fate and the more one examines its secret springs of action, the more one is impressed by the strength of unconscious motives and by the limitations of free choice. (Jung 1946, p. 177)

In exploring this hypothesis, Carotenuto calls our attention to the similarities between the two-way encounter of analyst-analysand as it is experienced in the therapeutic relationship and the primal experience of the mother-child dyad. In each of these situations, one of the pair is experienced as the stronger and more powerful of the two, the other as the weaker.

While Carotenuto's main focus is on the choice of the profession of analyst as a reworking of aspects of the mother-child relationship, his thesis has important ramifications that can be extrapolated for the countertransference/transference relationship. Elements of countertransference seem to exist a priori. Countertransference can represent the maternal and matriarchal feelings that were involved in the analyst's choice of profession.

A similar hypothesis has been put forth by Olinick who, in his study on empathy and regression in the service of the other, also suggests that a powerful motivation for becoming a therapist is derived from a rescue fantasy involving a depressed mother. He emphasizes the importance of mastery of the underlying conflictual constellations if the psychotherapist is to function effectively.

While the actual choice of analyst as a profession can originate in a combination of genetic experiences, intrapsychic conflicts, and some degree of identification with a mother who may have given too much, or not enough, it is important to keep in mind that there is a positive aspect to all this. The motivations to do analytic work can be adaptive or maladaptive; pathological or nonpathological; well managed or poorly managed; openly expressed or defensively denied. The salient point is that all of the above are part of the countertransference. It is not enough for analysts to have knowledge of their own personal psychopathologies; they are constantly dealing with them in the countertransference/transference. It is only after analysts can make allowance for their psychopathologies that they can recognize their patients' difficulties in relating.

We know that even after a thorough training analysis and the acquisition of considerable analytic experience, countertransference reactions and attitudes are ever present in the treatment situation. The analyst must constantly deal with a barrage of feelings that include anxiety, frustration, rage, and omnipotence. But other feelings come to the fore as well: loving, caring, and tender feelings, elicited in the response of the analyst that is termed "holding"—in itself only an analogue of maternal care.

In addition to the activation of the maternal and matriarchal feelings of the mother-child archetype within the countertransference/transference, other complementary parts of total archetypes can become manifest. These complementary parts are the split aspects of the same archetype. When added together they comprise a totality. The split archetypes appear in the guise of polar opposites, such as guru-disciple, savior-sinner, master-slave, sorcerer-apprentice, healer-patient, and wise old man-fool. For example, in the transference, the patient can project the guru onto the analyst, while the analyst's countertransference projection onto the patient is that of the disciple. The psychic process remains blocked until the split polarity is unified.

The unification of the opposites transpires in the symbolic relationship of the countertransference/transference in which the analyst and patient interact in a dynamic polarity. The analyst's personality plays a vital role in this process of transformation.

Types of Countertransference

Adler (1970), Lambert, Fordham (1957), Dieckmann (1976), and Racker are some of the analysts who have made important differentiations between two distinct types of countertransference reactions. One type consists of countertransference reactions that are barely conscious, or unconscious, and that tend to be expressed via projection, introjection, or projective identification. The other category of reactions is characterized by a more conscious or cognitive awareness. More consolidated ego structures are involved that allow the analyst to maintain his or her own boundaries and to accept the projections without identifying with the patient.

As previously noted, the term *projection* has often been used inappropriately to describe the general phenomenon of countertransference. When used in this way, it frequently has a negative connotation, as it alludes to the displacement of unacceptable subjective psychic elements onto others. However, there is also a positive, creative aspect to projection, since it can afford access to potential growth. Langer takes note of this when she writes that by projecting knowledge into objective forms we recognize from the perceptible reality before us possibilities of subjective experience that we have not known in our personal life. According to Langer, "to project feelings into outer objects is the first way of symbolizing and conceiving those feelings" (p. 390).

Plaut describes two ways in which the analyst can handle these projected images (1956, p. 17). An educative procedure centered on the elucidation and differentiation of archetypal contents can be employed. Or the analyst can accept the projections of the archetypal constellation in a whole-hearted manner by allowing him- or herself to "incarnate" the image bodily for the patient. In this instance, no attempt is made to differentiate the contents that belong to the analyst from those that belong to the patient, or to neither of them, or to both of them. Plaut emphasizes that the analyst "needs to be able to incarnate the image in comparative safety without being swept away by identification with it'' (ibid.). These images need to be experienced by both the analyst and the patient.

When the identification with the archetypes does occur as a countertransference reaction, the analyst is rendered incapable of maintaining and sustaining that balance that facilitates the patient's disidentification from the archetypal image. Consequently, the prospects for unraveling the tangle via the transformation of the projected complexes are not too favorable. The analyst is too enmeshed in what Dieckmann terms the projective countertransference, in which the patient is experienced and treated as a familiar figure, such as mother, father, or sibling, in the analyst's personal history.

It is necessary for the blocked analyst to experience what Dieckmann designates as an objective countertransference reaction, with its conscious cognition of the shadow or other real existing aspect of the patient's psyche. In the objective countertransference, the analyst is identifying with aspects of the patient's inner life in what Lambert refers to as the countertransference proper. This type of countertransference corresponds to Racker's concordant countertransference, as well as, in part, to Fordham's syntonic countertransference (1957). In the objective countertransference, the analyst is able to carry and contain the patient's projections and be part of an enactment, while at the same time remaining disidentified with it.

Fordham distinguishes between two types of countertransference reactions, which he designates as the illusory countertransference and the syntonic countertransference (1957). In the illusory countertransference, there is an unconscious, or minimally conscious, reactivation of the analyst's own complexes in either a past relationship or in his or her current personal life. The presence of these problems makes analysis in the here-and-now practically impossible. Fordham states that the illusory countertransference demonstrates the fallibility of the analyst by placing him or her on the same level with the patient. Since such analysts are absorbed with their own life problems, there is the risk of an irrational involvement in which a patient carries the projections of figures in the analyst's unconscious. The analytic work reaches a standstill until such an analyst comes to an awareness of what is actually transpiring, and withdraws the projection from the patient and reintegrates it within his or her own person.

In essence, the analyst needs to be able to make the shift from the more symbiotic mode of relatedness that characterized the intermediate state of experience to a mode in which a bridge is activated linking the inner and outer reality of the two universes of inner feelings and introjections from the external world. When this is possible, the two universes harmonize and intermingle within the same experience. When it doesn't occur, the dyad gets stuck in an illusory countertransference or participation mystique, until such time as the analyst can extricate him- or herself from the shared psychic experience. Then, a new integration of the personality of the analyst and that of the patient can take place.

In a later work, Fordham reiterates that the illusory form of countertransference reaction obstructs the progression of the analytic treatment (1960). The patient, by being replaced by the analyst's projection of his or her inner situation and unintegrated parts, is conforming to the analyst's frame of reference in the subject-object relationship. The healing agent—that is, the analyst who can in some degree cope with his or her own psychic problems—is not available. When the analyst is able to confront the problems and resolve them, the patient will be able to do the same.

In Fordham's syntonic countertransference reaction, the patient makes the analyst play the emotional role of a partner in the relationship. It is an introjective type of experience in which there is conscious and unconscious communication between analyst and patient. The archetype remains in the background. By introjecting the aspects of the patient's psyche that pass unconsciously from the patient to the analyst, the analyst, in Fordham's view, is able to identify and experience the patient's psychic contents. Through affective understanding, these contents eventually become the basis for the analyst's interpretation. It is the conscious awareness of the countertransference/transference that allows the analyst to understand the interpersonal process and thereby make these interpretations. For interpretations are the end products of the inner processes of the analyst's syntonic countertransference reactions, which are located now in the shared metaphorical space or common ground. "They stand, as it were, on the basis of less definable affective preconscious experiences out of which they [the interpretations] are distilled" (Davidson, p. 138). For Fordham, "It can be just as valid for the analyst to know of the projection through registering its impact upon himself, as it is by listening to the patient and realizing it as an inference from what the patient says" (1957, p. 98). It is this impact that denotes a countertransference reaction.

Adler confirms Fordham's formulation of the syntonic and illusory countertransference reactions (1961a). However, he designates illusory countertransference as a counterprojection drawn from the analyst's personal background, which is to be differentiated from the creative, true countertransference that is syntonic.

Fordham's contributions provide us with an apperceptive basis for studying in greater detail the personal interactions involved in analytical work. They are aids to assessing the countertransference experience during the course of analysis. By providing us with an opportunity to acquire increased consciousness of the feelings evoked by the patient, these formulations help us to make critical observations of our own and the patient's states of mind.

There are instances in which it is difficult to differentiate between illusory and syntonic countertransference reactions. Moore describes an episode in the analysis of a regressed patient that occurred during a small change in the arrangements of the analytical environment. She found that during a period of regression, communication took place at an unconscious archetypal level, with joint reactions precluding the distinctions between the illusory and syntonic countertransferences. The shared reality of these joint reactions in the analytic interaction is also mentioned by Moody (p. 52), who notes that when his own unconscious was activated, he tended to be more subjectively involved in the therapy, to the point of expressing his own emotions more freely. Moody and the analysand lived out an enactment of the countertransference/transference "which in its reciprocal nature was the common creation of both."

In summary, analytical psychologists never believe themselves to be outside the sphere of influence of the archetypal and collective forces of the unconscious. Therefore, although countertransference may appear to be truly personal, in actuality it is conditioned by the presence of archetypal material (Plaut 1955).

Unless analysts consistently watch the countertransference reactions, through self-monitoring, they can be seduced into a positive state of inflation by narcissistically flattering and powerful projections. Analysts can also be provoked into the anger, frustration, and despair that are engendered by the demeaning and persecutory fantasies that lead to deflation. In the evocation of these powerful archetypes in the countertransference, there is the danger that analysts' shadow problems will get stirred up. Guggenbühl-Craig (1974) and Groesbeck emphasize the importance of analysts' staying in touch with their personal wounds, while confronting their own archetypal images in the countertransference.

Analysts are prone to identify, albeit partially, with the projected contents of the trickster-hero archetypes, which include the shaman, savior, wise old man, and guru, along with their shadow aspects. When this happens, analysts can get caught in states of inflation and deflation. At times, patients are searching for an idealized, omnipotent, and omniscient parent, one who has the magical powers to cure quickly and painlessly. When this constellation is projected onto analysts they have to maintain the delicate balance of accepting, carrying, and dealing with these projections psychologically, while at the same time not identifying with them. Analysts cannot reject the projections or process them rationally by explaining them away verbally. All projections need to be taken seriously. The personal projections are usually easier to deal with. When the projection is of an archetypal nature, the emotional investment makes it harder to carry and sustain. The consciousness of the analyst is the safeguard against identifying with archetypes such as the wise old man or savior.

One of Jung's basic premises was that the patient's illness needs to be met by the analyst's health. This interaction requires the confrontation and conscious interpretation of the conscious and unconscious countertransference/transference positions of both the analyst and the patient, and the subsequent integration of the contents. The patient cannot succeed at working through the process in his or her own psyche if the analyst is unable to do so first.

Countertransference and Management Issues

It is not quite good enough to say that the utilization of countertransference/transference phenomena as a clinical tool is now part of most major theories of depth psychology, without formulating clearer notions about how management issues influence the ongoing therapy.

For example, we know that issues such as the frequency of analytic sessions must have an effect on the therapy. With some patients, meeting once a week allows for an undesirable dissipation of affect between sessions, with a resultant feeling of discontinuity for analyst and patient. At the same time, less frequent meetings mean that less genetic material is shared, simply because there is less time to do so. Less intensive therapy may differ experientially, with respect to countertransference/transference reactions, from situations in which there are more frequent meetings. In the latter instance, particularly where the approach of the analyst calls for meeting four or five times a week, there is more reporting of intense countertransference/transference experiences, as well as more discussion of genetic material. Just what the implications of the frequency of sessions are for the countertransference/transference is not clear, as no data have been reported. What seems to be the case is that the analysts who meet with their patients more frequently are the ones who are more concerned with questions of technique and management, and the analysts who meet less frequently are the ones who talk about the art of psychotherapy. Whether this difference in interests is a reflection of the different types of countertransference/transference experiences remains to be investigated.

Another variable of similar import for the study of countertransference/transference implications is the question of the armchair versus the couch.

Although Jackson concludes that the personality of the analyst may be more important than whether the armchair or the couch arrangement is used, he concedes that with the use of the armchair the analyst is prone to have stronger countertransference reactions, since the analyst and the patient are facing each other. "The armchair can be traumatic for the analyst," as the visual confrontation puts him or her in a more vulnerable situation. Jackson reports as follows:

> The patient's staring evoked mild anxious irritation in me, accompanied from time to time by a sense of frustration, hostility, and guilt, with a recurrent doubting of my capacity as an analyst. I often imagined that if I were a more skilled analyst I could, by means of appropriate interpretations help resolve our mutual anxiety, and put an end to a tedious situation. (P. 39)

The various elements of the analytic setting have to be evaluated in terms of their implications for the countertransference. Analytic work is not simply a matter of personal style; management issues are a significant part of our professional orientation.

SPECIFIC COUNTERTRANSFERENCE RESPONSES

In many instances, an analyst is not consciously aware of responding to a particular patient in a defensive fashion. Forgetting appointments and failing to return a patient's call need to be acknowledged as countertransference reactions. A female analyst-in-training twice forgot to meet with a female patient with strong homosexual tendencies. Investigation corroborated that the analyst had fears centering around these issues and her ability to deal with them in the patient.

Sometimes an analyst experiences repeated difficulty in either starting or ending a session on time with certain patients. While negative countertransference reactions of a persecutory or angry nature can cause difficulty in starting on time, it is usually positive countertransference feelings of nurturing, or the analyst's own limitations in areas of self-worth or assertion, that habitually interfere with ending a session on time.

Another kind of countertransference reaction results in the analyst's inability to identify or empathize with a particular patient. It is true that Jung recommended that we work only with patients who have some quality that we like. There are times in the professional life of an analyst when it must be acknowledged that certain types of personalities, or certain types of psychotic or antisocial behavior, evoke countertransference reactions of defensiveness. When analysts find themselves using distancing behavior in therapy, it behooves them to examine their countertransference feelings in depth. Sometimes the countertransference reactions are due to difficulty in dealing with problems that are beyond their scope professionally or personally. In either of these instances, it may become necessary to refer the patient to another analyst.

At some level, the notion that patient and analyst must like each other can be in itself a common countertransference feeling. Its origins may be in the analyst's need for acceptance or approval. We need to disentangle this feeling from reactions of greater magnitude. Stein describes his countertransference reactions during some rather turbulent analyses of ''hag women'' or loathsome women patients who are difficult to like. ''There can be no doubt that an analyst who is faced with a loathsome hag is liable to become possessed by his own witch-like soul'' (p. 68). Murderous feelings can come to the fore with this witch-anima constellation.

In contrast to distancing countertransference reactions are instances in which the analyst overreacts emotionally to a patient's problems. This overreaction can take the form of being caught in an argument, being defensive, or becoming too sympathetic. Analysts may even discover that they are daydreaming profusely and having fantasies about particular patients. Careful scrutiny of the fantasies can reveal overevaluation or underevaluation of the patient, and can call the analyst's attention to the necessity for forming a better attitude toward the patient.

Jung considered the presence of sexual fantasies about a patient to be an indication of a disturbance of rapport within the analytic relationship, due to inadequate human contact. The fantasies are an attempt to compensate by covering the distance with a sexual bridge. Although there are instances in which this can be a valid deduction, there are also many other situations that can lead to sexual or erotic countertransference reactions. Among them is an unsatisfactory personal life on the part of the analyst: analysts may project their unmet needs onto the patients.

Another manifestation of a countertransference reaction may be a need to prescribe psychotropic medication, or to refer the patient elsewhere for it. This may be a manifestation of the analyst's unconscious motivation to avoid performance of a specific therapeutic task, or to blunt the patient's affects. While medication can be a necessary adjunct to analytic work, its use can also reflect a countertransference reaction.

At times, analysts' own needs and interests may lead them to be selective about the material that their patients reflect on. Through voice tone, facial expression, or body language, or through focusing on a specific segment of a patient's material, analysts may superimpose their needs on their patients. By encouraging some types of material, analysts are directing the interaction rather than waiting to see what emerges from patients. Analysts need to withstand the impulse to control the therapy by imposing their frames of reference or theoretical orientations onto patients. At times it is exceedingly difficult for analysts to struggle with their own countertransference reactions and to wait for patients to do the analytic work at their own pace.

Gratuitous advice giving, when it goes beyond providing educational information, may be a way of controlling, depreciating, or punishing the patient by assuming a dominating stance, and may thus have countertransference implications. Fordham considers the analyst's need to make personal confessions to patients early in an analysis, or on unsuitable occasions, to be indicative of an illusory countertransference reaction. Zinkin calls for flexibility: "At times I have found myself arguing with a patient, answering questions directly, giving advice, supporting the patient and expressing my feelings openly" (p. 130).

It is important to confirm that judicious advice giving can be appropriate if it is not motivated by the analyst's needs but reflects the needs of the patient. There are instances when information and opinions can be shared in a conscious manner.

Additional common feelings that can be construed as indications of countertransference reactions with the potential for deleterious effects on the analytic work are evidenced in such physical manifestations as bodily tension, drowsiness, or inattentiveness to the patient's material. Dieckmann notes that yawning, scratching, and other somatic reactions on the part of the analyst correlated highly with areas of unconsciousness common to both analyst and patient, in what can be perceived as a state of unconscious reciprocity (1974).

Sometimes physical illness in an analyst is a countertransference reaction affecting the sympathetic system. An analyst responded with a skin rash to a very demanding, regressed patient who was literally getting under his skin. This patient required great patience and understanding. The rash surfaced at a time when the analyst was dreaming that the patient was insisting on moving into his house. In the dream, he told her that she could move in for a limited period of time, namely three months, but after that she would be turned over to a social worker.

Somatic countertransference reactions may also result from the analyst's unrecognized frustration or anger, either with the patient or the unconscious contents. In the latter instance, the analyst needs to be in a relationship to the unconscious at those points where the patient is unable to be. The resistance of the analyst is based on the defensive measures of the personal unconscious and ego complex.

COUNTERTRANSFERENCE REACTIONS TO PARTICULAR
TYPES OF PATIENTS

Particular types of patients commonly evoke countertransference responses that are fairly characteristic and not simply idiosyncratic to a particular analyst. Countertransference reactions of frustration and indignation can be a response to a paranoid patient's awareness of subtle negative nuances in the analyst's attitude. Some patients are actually unable to take note of and experience any positive attitudes on the part of the analyst. They constantly need to attack the analyst in safety, and they come in and complain at each session about the shortcomings of the previous one. The analyst is informed that he or she is incompetent, derisive, and prone to misinterpret whatever the patient says. Every caring response on the part of the analyst is ignored. The analyst feels attacked, which is of course the goal of the patient's unconscious fantasies and wishes.

Campbell discusses her management of countertransference reactions in treating an adolescent with persecutory fears. "Considering my feelings of involvement with T evoked by his need for it, it certainly seems to me that parts of the transference were introjected by me, to emerge as . . . the parts of me that T wanted, through the spontaneous activity of the self in the countertransference" (p. 171).

Depressive patients are very adept at homing in on any sign of weakness, emotional or physical exhaustion, illness, or preoccupation on the part of the analyst. In their concern about inflicting damage on the analyst and their consequent need to make reparation, they continually want to rescue the analyst. Wanting to be taken care of could well be a countertransference reaction.

Hypomanic patients can bring excitement and color into a depressed analyst's life and often seem to be living out the sides of life that the analyst is unable to experience. Redfearn speaks of the infectiousness of manic patients and the analyst's susceptibility to getting caught up in their mood as a countertransference reaction.

An analyst may have a countertransference reaction of anxiety when dealing with a patient who has a history of psychosis or suicidal ideation. Redfearn reports on the countertransference feelings he has experienced with psychotic patients: dismay and sadness when the patient slips away from their interaction, anger and indignation when the patient seems to represent everything good and he becomes the repository of bad feelings. Schizoid callousness evokes cold horror, and patients on the brink of psychosis overwhelm him with a flood of unconscious material (pp. 208–17).

All of these countertransference feelings are accurate guides for the therapist's understanding of the patient's unconscious fantasies and wishes. Such patients may be splitting off feelings and making the therapist feel them for them. Positive countertransference feelings can surface in response to the neediness of deprived patients. There may be fantasies of holding, stroking, or feeding the patients.

What disturbs one analyst may not perturb another. The countertransference feelings, positive or negative, that cannot be explained in terms of the analyst's own neurotic preoccupations are a source of insight into the patient's problems, because they allow for identification with the patient. In the process, the analyst's self-knowledge grows as well. The assets and limitations of the analyst are important determinants for the outcome of treatment.

Sharing Countertransference Reactions

There is a difference of opinion about whether to share countertransference reactions with the patient. Some analysts feel that it is inappropriate to do so at any time. Others share them selectively. There is some consensus that one is more apt to share the feelings with borderline or psychotic patients who have difficulty with reality (see Bird; Little 1957; Rosenfeld; Searles; Spotnitz 1969, 1976; Winnicott 1945, 1965).

The phenomena of projective identification and counteridentification occur more frequently in the analysis of borderline patients than in the analysis of other types of disorders. The patient's projective identification can bring about the specific reaction in the analyst that Racker terms the complementary countertransference, and that Grinberg (1962) calls projective counteridentification. At those times, the analyst experiences affects such as anger, depression, anxiety, or boredom, as responses to the patient's projective identification. Verbalization of these reactions may lessen the persistence of undifferentiated states and allow greater distinction between self and not-self.

Whether to share countertransference dreams with patients is also called into question. Some analysts, such as Hall, are of the opinion that it is rarely of value to share a countertransference dream with the patient. The importance of the dream lies in its calling the analyst's attention to countertransference implications for the therapy. Hall cites the example of an analyst-in-training who had reached a therapeutic impasse. In the transference, the analyst was carrying the projection of a positive parent figure, while in the countertransference, the patient represented a favorite child.

The analyst had the following dream, which was not shared with the patient:

> [Dream:] *The patient and analyst were about to enter an arena or courtroom in which their confrontation was to be resolved. Just as they started up the stairs, it seemed that they mutually agreed not to go through the process of deciding who was right and who was wrong. Instead, they sat by a lake on the grass and talked in a friendly manner. As they sat there, both were aware of a dangerous white rhinoceros grazing nearby. They knew it might attack, but both decided it would be safe to stay together, since if the animal attacked it would be possible to knock it into the lake and escape the beast. (P. 226)*

By working on a problem that confronted both parties in the analytic relationship, and by dealing with the threat of an autonomous complex of impressive affective strength, the analyst was able to bring the analysis through the impasse.

Kraemer writes of the dangers of an unrecognized countertransference in an analytical relationship in which a dream was shared. A young female doctor articulated her positive countertransference feelings to her depressed male patient. Additionally, she embellished a countertransference dream as she related it to him. She dreamed that ''she saw herself standing hand-in-hand with this patient near the entrance of a big cave. She knew that she had to enter and to lead him through its labyrinthine maze. She felt that she would be able to do so successfully, and that they would both come out together at the other end'' (p. 36). The embellishment was that she and the patient were really lovers from then on. The patient did not appear for the next appointment, and the therapy came to a disastrous end shortly thereafter.

Jung, however, did share dreams with patients. He believed that the analyst, in using the countertransference, ''must at all times keep watch over himself, over the way he is reacting to his patient. For we do not react only with our consciousness'' (1961, p. 133). After being perturbed at a stalemate in the analysis of a highly intelligent woman, Jung decided to discuss the state of affairs with her the very next day. That night he had the following dream:

> [Dream:] *I was walking down a highway through a valley in late-afternoon sunlight. To my right was a steep hill. At its top stood a castle, and on the highest tower there was a woman sitting on a kind of balustrade. In order to see her properly, I had to bend my*

head far back. I awoke with a crick in the back of my neck. Even in the dream I had recognized the woman as my patient. (Ibid.)

Jung viewed this dream as a compensation for his conscious attitude of condescension toward her. The dream content enabled him to resolve the countertransference problem. When the dream was shared with the patient, the stalemate was removed.

THE NEED FOR A NEW CONCEPTUAL FRAMEWORK

Until fairly recently, analysts were largely, or completely, unaware of the importance of the countertransference for the outcome of therapy. It was only after the term was broadened, from its initial meaning of idiosyncratic or pathological contaminants on the part of the analyst, to include a wide range of positive and negative feelings toward the patient, that the countertransference became an instrument of research into the unconscious of analyst and patient alike. This utilization of the countertransference/transference is gaining wider acceptance among analysts of differing theoretical orientations.

Further investigation into the phenomenon of the countertransference, in its interaction with the transference, can be pursued only if analysts are able to overcome the arrogant, "holier-than-thou" attitude that allows them to ignore their own countertransference reactions and remove themselves somewhat from full participation in the dialectical process. Studying the phenomenon of countertransference/transference—and this can be done without sharing the content—can provide additional insight into the enigma of the psychic processes of both analyst and patient.

Objections to the use of clinical tools such as countertransference may not in fact be grounded in issues of a professional nature. Although the choice of therapeutic stance depends upon what a particular analyst finds comfortable, our main concern is not limited to matters of style. When we speak of countertransference/transference, we are not speaking of temporary, technical, situational adjustments; we are calling for a far-reaching change in the analyst's basic metapsychological patterns and attitudes, in which intrapsychic and interpersonal field orientations not only are more integrated, but evoke the exploration of new material as well.

REFERENCES

Adler, G. 1954. The archetypal content of transference. In *International congress of psychotherapy,* ed. M. Boss, pp. 285–92. Zurich: Karger.
———. 1961a. *Current trends in analytical psychology.* London: Tavistock.
———. 1961b. *The living symbol.* London: Routledge and Kegan Paul.
———. 1970. Analytical psychology and the principle of complementarity. *Harvest* 16:1–11.
———. 1978. A note on the analyst and the numinous. *Harvest* 24:1–4.
———, ed. 1974. *Success and failure in analysis.* New York: Putnam.
Bird, B. 1972. Notes on transference. *Journal of the American Psychoanalytic Association* 20:267–301.
Blomeyer, R. 1974. Constellation of the countertransference in relation to the presentation of archetypal dreams. In *Success and failure in analysis,* ed. G. Adler, pp. 97–108. New York: Putnam.
Campbell, R. 1967. The management of the countertransference evoked by violence in the delusional transference. *Journal of Analytical Psychology* 12/2: 161–73.
Carotenuto, A. 1977. The psychopathology of the analyst. *Annual of Italian Analytical Psychologists* 1:53–74.
Davidson, D. 1966. Transference as a form of active imagination. *Journal of Analytical Psychology* 11/2:135–46.
Dieckmann, H. 1974. The constellation of the countertransference in relation to the presentation of archetypal dreams. In *Success and failure in analysis,* ed. G. Adler, pp. 69–83. New York: Putnam.
———. 1976. Transference and countertransference. *Journal of Analytical Psychology* 21/1:25–36.
Edinger, E. 1957. *Some manifestations of the transference phenomenon.* New York: Spring Publications.
Fordham, M. 1957. *New developments in analytical psychology.* London: Routledge and Kegan Paul.
———. 1960. Countertransference. *British Journal of Medical Psychology* 33/1.
———. 1969. Technique and countertransference. *Journal of Analytical Psychology* 14/2:95–118.
———. 1978. *Jungian psychotherapy.* New York: Wiley.
———. 1979. Analytical psychology and countertransference. In *Countertransference,* ed. L. Epstein and H. Feiner, pp. 193–212. New York: Jason Aronson.
Freud, S. 1910. The future prospects of psychoanalytic therapy. In *Standard edition,* vol. 11, pp. 139–52. London: Hogarth, 1955.
Grinberg, L. 1962. On a specific aspect of countertransference due to the patient's projective identification. *International Journal of Psychoanalysis* 43:436–40.
———. 1979. Countertransference and projective counteridentification. In *Countertransference,* ed. L. Epstein and H. Feiner, pp. 169–92. New York: Jason Aronson.
Groesbeck, J. 1975. The archetypal image of the wounded healer. *Journal of Analytical Psychology* 20/2:122–45.
Guggenbühl-Craig, A. 1971. *Power in the helping professions.* New York: Spring Publications.
———. 1974. Has analysis failed as a therapeutic instrument? In *Success and failure in analysis,* ed. G. Adler, pp. 22–30. New York: Putnam.

Hall, J. 1977. *Clinical uses of dreams*. New York: Grune and Stratton.

Heimann, P. 1950. On countertransference. *International Journal of Psychoanalysis* 31/1:81–84.

Jackson, M. 1961. Chair, couch and countertransference. *Journal of Analytical Psychology* 6/1:35–44.

Jung, C. G. 1928. On psychic energy. In *Collected works*, vol. 8, pp. 3–61. 2d ed. Princeton: Princeton University Press, 1969.

———. 1931. Problems of modern psychotherapy. In *Collected works*, vol. 16, pp. 29–35. 2d ed., rev. Princeton: Princeton University Press, 1966.

———. 1933. The real and the surreal. In *Collected works*, vol. 8, pp. 382–84. 2d ed. Princeton: Princeton University Press, 1969.

———. 1935. What is psychotherapy? In *Collected works*, vol. 16, pp. 21–28. 2d ed., rev. Princeton: Princeton University Press, 1966.

———. 1937. The realities of practical psychotherapy. In *Collected works*, vol. 16, pp. 327–38. 2d ed., rev. Princeton: Princeton University Press, 1966.

———. 1946. Psychology of the transference. In *Collected works*, vol. 16, pp. 162–203. 2d ed., rev. Princeton: Princeton University Press, 1966.

———. 1951. Fundamental questions of psychotherapy. In *Collected works*, vol. 16, pp. 111–25. 2d ed., rev. Princeton: Princeton University Press, 1966.

———. 1961. *Memories, dreams, reflections*. New York: Random House.

———. 1968. *Analytical psychology, its theory and practice*. New York: Pantheon.

Kadinsky, D. 1970. The meaning of technique. *Journal of Analytical Psychology* 15/2:163–76.

Kraemer, W. 1958. The dangers of unrecognized countertransference. *Journal of Analytical Psychology* 3/1:29–42.

Kuhn, T. 1962. *The structure of scientific revolutions*. Chicago: University of Chicago Press.

Lambert, K. 1972. Transference/countertransference: talion law and gratitude. *Journal of Analytical Psychology* 17/1:31–50.

Langer, S. 1953. *Feeling and form*. Baltimore: Johns Hopkins University Press.

Little, M. 1951. Countertransference and the patient's response to it. *International Journal of Psychoanalysis* 32:32–40.

———. 1957. 'R'—the analyst's response to his patient's needs. *International Journal of Psychoanalysis* 38/3:240–54.

Meier, C. 1959. Projection, transference and the subject-object relation in psychology. *Journal of Analytical Psychology* 4/1:21–34.

Moody, R. 1955. On the function of the countertransference. *Journal of Analytical Psychology* 1/1:49–58.

Moore, N. 1972. Countertransference. *Journal of Analytical Psychology* 17/1: 51–65.

Newman, K. 1980. *Countertransference and consciousness*. New York: Spring Publications.

Olinick, S. 1969. On empathy and regression in the service of the other. *British Journal of Medical Psychology* 42/1:41–49.

Paulsen, L. 1956. Transference and projection. *Journal of Analytical Psychology* 1/2:203–6.

Plaut, A. 1955. Research into transference phenomena. In *Acta Psychotherapeutica*, vol. 2, ed. M. Boss, pp. 557–62. Zurich: Karger.

———. 1956. Symposium III. The transference in analytical psychology. *British Journal of Medical Psychology* 29/1:15–19.

———. 1970. Comment on not incarnating the archetype. *Journal of Analytical Psychology* 15/1:88–94.

———. 1973. Reflections on not being able to imagine. In *Analytical psychology: a modern science,* ed. M. Fordham; R. Gordon; J. Hubback; and K. Lambert, pp. 127–49. London: Heinemann.

Racker, H. 1968. *Transference and countertransference.* London: Hogarth.

Redfearn, J. 1980. The energy of warring and combining opposites: problems for the psychotic patient and the therapist in achieving the symbolic situation. In *Methods of treatment in analytical psychology,* ed. I. F. Baker, pp. 206–18. Fellbach: Verlag Adolf Bonz.

Rosenfeld, H. 1965. *Psychotic states.* London: Hogarth.

Searles, H. 1965. *Collected papers on schizophrenia and related subjects.* New York: International Universities Press.

Spotnitz, H. 1969. *Modern psychoanalysis of the schizophrenic patient.* New York: Grune and Stratton.

———. 1976. *Psychotherapy of pre-Oedipal conditions.* New York: Jason Aronson.

Stein, L. 1955. Loathsome women. *Journal of Analytical Psychology* 1/1:59–77.

Strauss, R. 1959. Countertransference. *British Journal of Medical Psychology* 33/1:23–31.

Whitmont, E. 1961. Magical dimensions in transference/countertransference. In *Current trends in analytical psychology,* ed. G. Adler, pp. 176–97. London: Tavistock.

Winnicott, D. 1945. Hate in the countertransference. *International Journal of Psychoanalysis* 30:69–75.

———. 1953. Transitional objects and transitional phenomena. *International Journal of Psychoanalysis* 34:89–97.

———. 1965. *Maturational processes and the facilitating environment.* New York: International Universities Press.

Zinkin, L. 1969. Flexibility in analytic technique. *Journal of Analytical Psychology* 14/2:119–32.

[6]

TERMINATION

Joseph B. Wheelwright

ONE must grant at the outset that termination is affected, or even determined, by the factors that brought the individual to analysis in the first place. When those aims have been met, it is usually time to terminate. With that understanding, I shall discuss various aspects of termination as I have experienced them in my clinical practice.

Very frequently there occur what might be called accidental terminations. My own termination with Jung is an example. When I was working with Jung in Zurich I would have stayed longer than I did, but the Nazis invaded Poland in 1939 and that made it impossible for me to continue. This was a termination caused by external events.

Michael Fordham, a close friend of mine and the founder of the Society for Analytical Psychology in London, has written on reasons for termination. He feels that an analysand should stay with his or her first analyst no matter how many years the process may take. Until the time comes for termination by mutual consent, he interprets initiatives from the analysand to work with another analyst, or simply to stop, as resistance. Thomas Kirsch has a different view. He proposes multiple analysts, either concurrent or in series. Here the initiative to change analysts is not automatically interpreted as resistance. I agree with Dr. Kirsch. I have worked with people who have thought they had gotten all they could from me.

Joseph Wheelwright, M.D., is Professor of Clinical Psychology, University of California Medical School, San Francisco, and has maintained a private practice of analytical psychology in San Francisco since 1940. A student and analysand of C. G. Jung during the 1930s, he is a former president of the International Association for Analytical Psychology, as well as a life fellow of the American Psychiatric Association and of the American Academy of Psychoanalysis. He is a graduate of Harvard College and St. Bartholomew's Hospital Medical College, and received his training in psychiatry at the University of California Medical School. Dr. Wheelwright is the author of "Jungian Type Survey," *Sex and the College Student*, "Marriage in the Second Half of Life," "A Personal Experience of Jung," and *St. George and the Dandelion*.

However, there have been indications—too numerous to record, but coming often in dreams—suggesting that they continue with another analyst, someone younger, older, female, or different in some other way. I have accepted this as a valid reason for termination.

Sometimes I have not terminated when a patient has, for example, also gone to a woman analyst. We have worked concurrently. In my own case, as a matter of fact, I had concurrent analyses. I worked with Toni Wolff and Jung at the same time. I saw her two or three times a week, and I saw him twice a week. This frequency, let it be said, is unusual in Jungian circles.

Parenthetically, I have a strong conviction that it is desirable for everyone to work with at least one female analyst and one male analyst. I do not propose this only because of the difference between the kinds of transference projections involved. I believe that the reality-based issues that are activated between a man and a woman are different from those that are activated between two men or two women.

My general opinion about termination can be put in what is perhaps a rather flippant way: I think the desirable thing is to have the analysand fire me! I will give an example. I was working with a woman, and it became apparent that she had gotten all she could from me; she had really come to the end of her work with me. (Of course, I never actually think people have come to the end of their work until their hearts stop beating. I do believe, however, that people come to the end of their analyst. I also believe that analysands cannot go beyond what their analysts have achieved in their own psychological development.) For about two months it had seemed clear to me that this woman was through with me but did not know it yet. And I wasn't going to push her out. One day she came in and said: ''I woke up this morning, and I turned to my husband and said, 'You know, I'm all through. I don't need Joe Wheelwright anymore. I've been through quite a long while, and I suppose he knows it, so I'll just go in today and thank him very much and say good-bye.' '' So she came and told me and asked for my reaction. I replied that I had had a moral dilemma, that really she could have said good-bye two months ago, but I had thought I'd better wait so she could be the one to deliver the *coup de grâce,* not me. I much preferred to have her fire me, rather than my firing her. And I told her that.

There is a difference, of course, between termination of short-term therapy and termination of long-term analysis. I distinguish between them, even though I do not think they are different in kind. One simply works differently in short-term therapy. I worked for many years at the Student Health Service in Berkeley, at Cowell Hospital, where we were forced by the number of applicants to limit treatment to a maximum of twelve sessions. We thought we should keep the doors open, so by accident we got into short-term therapy. What we found was that short-term therapy was more suitable for many young people, and it often became the treatment of choice, not a mere second best.

With regard to termination, I used to say within the first few minutes: "Look, just so you don't get your feelings hurt or feel that you are being rejected, we're under pressure here and so we have a policy: we don't see people for more than twelve times—maybe less. So what we can do is perhaps not get any answers, but we may be able to find a few of the right questions. And then you will have to take it from there." I was much more active than I would be in long-term analysis.

I have been asked if this technique was like Rank's early work. The answer is, not really. We were not trying to force the unconscious. I was trying to spare these young people from suddenly hearing me say, out of the blue, "We've only got one more time," or "This is our last session." I wanted them to know from the outset, before they began to have any transference to me, that our time was limited. I was very active with them, though not directive. Jungians, in contrast to Freudians, do not try to remain anonymous. They don't structure their consulting rooms as Freudians do, nor do they sit behind their patients nor use the couch very often. Although I did have a couch in my consulting room—I was probably the only Jungian in the United States who had one—I did not use it very much because it seemed to me to infantilize the patient and to sexualize the material to a great degree.

Regarding termination of short-term therapy, at one time everybody used to sneer at what they called a "transference cure." We made no apologies for transference cures in short-term therapy at Cowell. And my pixilated way of envisioning the transference therapy was that after ten or twelve sessions the young man or woman would walk away and have the therapist as an introject. They needed that introject because they were trying to work things out for themselves. Maybe they had found some of the right questions; they did surprisingly well. Our record was very good, and it was amazing what even very sick young people could do with ten sessions. If they were in trouble, they would always have the introject; they could take their analyst out and have a dialogue. The analyst would say, "That's all right," and pat them on the head. They would weather the crisis. But there would come a time, maybe in a month or six months or a year, when those young people no longer needed that introject. Then, as they went by an ash can, they would take the analyst and dump him or her in the can, saying, "Thanks very much, but I don't need you any more."

So we used this disgraceful thing, the transference cure, and it worked very well.

In long-term Jungian analysis, there is the transference and counter-transference relationship, as well as the reality-based relationship, to deal with. When work is done vis-à-vis, the two exist concurrently—the reality-based interaction and the projections going both ways in the transference-countertransference. Usually the analyst projects less onto the patient than the patient projects onto the analyst, but I am sorry to say that this is not always true. If analysts are in trouble with too much countertransference, the only responsible thing to do is either to terminate the analysis or to hurry off to an analyst of their own and start working on it as patients themselves. Then such an analyst might talk it over with the analysand, saying, "Now look. I'm going to go to an analyst myself because obviously I'm hung up with you on this. If you want to quit, that's okay with me; if you want to struggle along, I'll see if I can clarify my end of it." I have done this several times. It works sometimes, but a few times the patient has said, "Well, I think I'll quit." And I reply, "That's probably very sensible of you, and I'm sorry about this." Such a problem could be the result of a positive or a negative countertransference.

Larry Kubie, a Freudian analyst and a friend, used to say that the progress of an analysis could be measured by the movement from the couch to the vis-à-vis position. At the end, when he was terminating, it became more and more a real relationship and less and less a projection, a transference relationship. I find the same to be true in my experience. Even when vis-à-vis, patients will project upon the analyst what they need to project, even though the setting is not structured to encourage these projections. Projections come anyway. But as the analysis progresses, the amount of transference diminishes until it is fairly minimal. I do not think it is ever all gone; that it should be wholly gone is a pious hope. What I try to do, essentially, as time goes on, is to establish a reality-based relationship. I have a well-developed feeling function, which is unusual for a man. (My thinking function, on the other hand, is nothing to write home about, though I can struggle along in thinking without being too embarrassed.) So many patients will project their own inferior feeling function onto me. Somewhere in all of it, I am able to say: "Look here, I am over here, you know. What you are endowing me with is really yours—it is your feeling. It's all pink and white and infantile, and it's very awkward and all that stuff. You take it back into your own psyche, don't park it on me. Take it home, but this time get it into your consciousness so it can differentiate; don't shove it down into your liver again, or you'll have to go through this damn thing all over again." This kind of statement would be part of the preparation for termination, and it would occur in most analyses. So in that way one gets to termination. It comes by a mutual realization that now it is time; or, better yet, the patient says, "I'm through, we've done our stint." It may be a resistance, as Fordham might point out, but with experience, the analyst can differentiate between when it is resistance and when it is really the end.

A vignette will illustrate the move out of the transference into a predominantly reality-based relationship, as a preparation for termination. During World War II, I worked with a young man who was very *"Muttergebunden"* (tied to his mother) and had had an extremely negative relation to his father. The young man was an aesthete, and the father wanted an athlete—clearly an untenable and unresolvable opposition. In our work together, I was the father he had never had, and he got what Franz Alexander called the "corrective emotional experience." After a few years, there was very little of the negative father transference left, and we were approaching the end of our work. Then a dramatic thing happened. At that time there was a dearth of analysts in the Bay Area, most of them being in the armed forces, so those of us who were left at home were under great pressure. There was no fifty-minute hour then, and punctuality was a major problem for me. By late afternoon, I am ashamed to say, I would be a full hour late. My patients were tolerant and would not laugh or get angry when I said, "I will see you next Friday at five o'clock." They simply nodded and showed up at six.

One day this young man arrived at five for his five o'clock appointment, though he knew better. At about six, I went out to bring him into my consulting room. He was shaking with anger. "I hope you are satisfied," he shouted. I replied, "Harassed, yes. Guilty, yes. But satisfied?" "Well," he said, "you obviously wanted to humiliate me and you've succeeded. Your wife's patient came after I did, and your wife fetched him from the waiting room half an hour ago. I'm sure that he was inwardly laughing at your scurvy treatment of me. It must give you great pleasure to hear this." I replied, "On the contrary, it increases my chronic burden of guilt, because I can't stick to my schedule. Perhaps some day one of my galaxy of analysts will help me to learn to read a clock." There was a pause and he began to laugh. He said, "Isn't that funny. The old feeling—when I would see my father depreciating and rejecting me—took over. Now I see you again as a friend and mentor, and I know that you can't tell the difference between time and a hollyhock. I have the feeling that I will not be taken over again by that negative father thing for a long time, if ever. I guess we have just about finished our business—for now at any rate.'' Shortly after this incident, we wound up our work, by mutual consent.

In Freudian analysis, there are criteria that should be met by the end of treatment. Freudian analysis has a beginning, a middle, and an end. Jungian analysis does not. From the Jungian point of view, there is no such thing as termination. We interrupt, very often, rather than terminate. People get all they can from one analyst and then need someone else, someone who is more developed in other areas and with whom they will be able to move along further. But it would never occur to me that I didn't need more analysis, and I feel the same about my analysands. This is the Jungian point of view—that, all things being equal, the analysand will probably be back again for more analysis in four or five years. The pro tem termination occurs when the analysand has more or less caught up, not only on pathology but on what he or she was working on—that is, growth and development issues.

When analyst and analysand agree that the analysand is more or less up-to-date, it's time to say good-bye. Sometimes, of course, the infantile part of the analysand wants to stay with ''daddy'' or ''mommy'' forever and ever, and the analyst may have to do some nudging. But, in general, both analyst and analysand make the decision to terminate pro tem.

I do not differentiate between terminating with a neurotic and terminating with someone who suffers from severe psychopathology, because I do not see psychosis as different in kind from neurosis, or neurosis as different in kind from normality—whatever that is. I see them in a continuum. There is a difference in quantity but not in quality. Neurosis and psychosis are nature's attempt to initiate growth and development (cf. Perry 1970, 1974, 1976).

I do not set a date for termination. I usually work with analysands for an average of three to five years. In our field, one often hears the phrase *termination phase*. My experience with each person is so different that it is difficult for me to generalize and distinguish or describe a termination phase. Some people might have all the analysis they need quite quickly, and others might not have all they need for five years. Whatever the situation, I do not change my stance when interruption is approaching.

When I work with somebody, we get to know each other better and better; we become better and better friends. In a personal communication, Jung once formulated a statement about analysis to the effect that the analytic relationship is an intensely personal one in an impersonal framework. Very often analysands know things about me that my other friends do not know, simply because they have activated something in me. I consider all the people I work with friends, to a greater or lesser degree. The longer I work with them, naturally, the more intimate we become, and the better we get to know each other. I don't conceal myself. I frequently use myself as a therapeutic instrument, and I don't try to be anonymous.

Often I share my feelings with analysands—if the feelings are relevant. I have had many brisk arguments with my psychoanalytic friends over this policy, even though many of them are now beginning to do the same thing. Erik Erikson, for example, has, at some times, shared his feelings to a fair degree. I think an analysand is entitled to reactivity from his analyst. Of course, I may temper my reactions. It may be that the ego of the person I am working with is fragile, and if I get angry, for instance, I will hold back. But I would surely sooner or later be able to say, "You know, ten minutes ago I was terribly angry at you, and the reason was . . ." But if the patient is not too fragile, I might say, "The hell you say, you goddamn fool." Or I might laugh, or cry—any of these reactions is possible.

Quite often the question arises whether to meet one's patients socially after analysis is over. I see some, but not all, of my patients after termination. The older I get, the more I have cut down on friends anyway. By now, my energy is at such a low level that I can only maintain a handful of friends. I never did, of course, become social friends with all of my patients, although I could have with most of them, if I had had the time and energy. I have had quite a few things in common with some of my analysands. Many were trainees in the Jung Institute; they were social workers or psychologists or M.D.'s, so we were all in the same field. Of course, it is possible to become too friendly with patients, or to become friendly too early. Some analysts have dinner with their patients even before the analysis is over, for example. I think this is a mistake, because the analysands get confused, and sometimes the analysts do too. While I am working with a person, I prefer to keep the interaction in the impersonal framework, but afterwards, if there are reasons and I have the time and energy, and the analysand has the time and energy and inclination, we might very well become friends socially.

One other issue arises at this point. Usually one is not supposed to work with one's friends. However, I have been an analysand quite a few times in the last thirty-five years with Joseph Henderson, a dear friend, with the proviso that we would suspend our social relationship while we were in a professional relationship. Afterwards, we pick it up again.

I do follow-ups as often as I possibly can. I'm not a theorist, and I'm not interested in statistics. I want to know how the people I've worked with are doing. I'm interested in them as people, not as objects of research. I do follow-ups because I never work with anybody that I do not care a great deal about.

Toward the end of my work with an analysand, I often struggle with countertransference. Termination brings to the surface countertransference feelings that I might not have picked up before in my dreams or my fantasies. I try, of course, to keep up with these feelings, because they are a source of information about where I am with my patients. But toward the end, when a patient is going to go away, and I'm no longer going to see him or her once or twice a week as I have for a long time, I begin to feel sad. There's a lot of saying good-bye in this business. When you've been working together terribly hard and respect each other and care about each other, ending is not an occasion for joy. On the other hand, you may be very pleased at how much the other has accomplished, and be proud to have participated. Some of my feelings are, of course, reality-based, not projections. I may share these feelings with my analysand.

I should like at this point to state my emphatic objection to the loose use of the term countertransference, imputing to that phenomenon all positive feelings the analyst may have for his or her analysand. I prefer to stick to the literal meaning of the term, namely, the projection of unconscious contents onto the analysand. This usage leaves room for reality-based feelings. To deny the validity of these feelings is to deny the validity of normal relationship. Contrary to the opinion of many analysts, I consider these reality-based feelings to constitute friendship. The objection that the friendship is bought strikes me as false. The fact that we pay our architects, lawyers, stock brokers, teachers, does not preclude friendship or relatedness. In my opinion, relatedness is the heart of the analytic process, the *sine qua non*.

The way analysts have been terminated in their own analyses has a lot to do with how they handle termination with their analysands. During my last appointment with Jung in 1939, as I was being forced out by the impending war, he said: "Now, Wheelwright, we have obviously not analyzed your transference completely. As a matter of fact, despite one's best efforts, I do not believe *all* transference projections are ever withdrawn— especially the archetypal ones. There is some real legitimacy in your continuing to think of me as father, especially at the deepest level. So if you feel inclined to write me about yourself from time to time, do so. I shall be interested, though I may not reply. However, don't start bombarding me with trans-Atlantic telephone calls or asking me to intercede on your behalf. You're on your own now, which, after all, is what we have both been working toward." I guess that I have had very much the same attitude toward the people I have worked with.

REFERENCES

Fordham, M. 1978. *Jungian psychotherapy*. New York: Wiley.

Kirsch, T. 1976. The practice of multiple analyses in analytical psychology. *Contemporary Psychoanalysis* 12:159–67.

Perry, J. W. 1970. *Lord of the four quarters*. New York: Collier.

––––––. 1974. *The far side of madness*. Englewood Cliffs, N. J.: Prentice-Hall.

––––––. 1976. *Roots of renewal in myth and madness*. San Francisco: Jossey-Bass.

METHODS
OF
ANALYSIS

PART THREE

[7]

THE USE OF DREAMS AND
DREAM INTERPRETATION IN ANALYSIS

James A. Hall

DREAMS and dream interpretation are among the oldest concerns of humanity, far antedating the advent of psychoanalysis, which was born and nurtured only in the infancy of the twentieth century. The oldest dream report is recorded in Sumerian texts dating from the end of the third millenium B.C., followed by records of the neo-Assyrian king Ashurbanipal dating from the seventh century B.C., which include the Assyrian Dream-Book, translated by Oppenheim. Dating from the same era is the epic of Gilgamesh (see Heidel, p. 1). The earliest recorded dream from Egypt, that of Thutmose IV, dates from the end of the fifteenth century B.C. (Oppenheim, p. 187). These ancient dreams were classified by Oppenheim into three groupings (pp. 179–244): the "message" dream, usually sent by a "god" and requiring no interpretation; the "symbolic" dream that had to be interpreted to be understood; and the mantic dream, which we would refer to as a dream with parapsychological meaning, involving, for example, clairvoyance or telepathy or both.

The epic of Gilgamesh contains several descriptions of dreams and dream interpretations that leave a surprisingly modern impression.[1] Gilgamesh has two dreams in series that are metaphorical statements about the undiscovered parts of himself. They are not disguised versions of an un-

James Hall, M.D., is Clinical Associate Professor of Psychiatry, University of Texas Health Science Center, Dallas. He is a founding member and former president of the Inter-Regional Society of Jungian Analysts. He is a fellow of the American Psychiatric Association and of the American Academy of Psychoanalysis, as well as a former president of the North Texas Psychiatric Society. Dr. Hall is a graduate of the University of Texas at Austin, Southwestern Medical School at Dallas, and the C. G. Jung Institute of Zurich. He is the author of *Clinical Uses of Dreams: Jungian Interpretations and Enactments* (1977) and coauthor of *Clinical Hypnosis* (1975).

acceptable wish, as they might be considered in Freud's classical theory of dreams. The two dreams are similar in structure but different in content: both refer to something that is equal to Gilgamesh—his dark brother, Enkidu—but in one, Enkidu is symbolized as an ax, and in the other, as a star fallen from heaven. This suggests the way that dreams in series may refer to the same content expressed in different images. Furthermore, the dreams of Gilgamesh can be taken to refer to important events in his own life and development, in contrast to the way that the dreams of Pharaoh are taken to refer to Egypt rather than to Pharaoh himself (Genesis 40:5–19; 41:1–32). There are three ways, then, in which the epic dreams of Gilgamesh show a similarity to modern uses of dream interpretation: (1) they are not disguised statements, but they do use symbolic and metaphorical language; (2) dreams in series seem to be different metaphorical expressions of the same underlying meaning; and (3) dreams refer to the personal individuation of the dreamer, indicating a developmental task that must also be faced in waking life.

Biblical references to dream interpretation occur in both the Old Testament and the New Testament. As mentioned above, the dreams of Pharaoh are taken to refer to the land of Egypt, which he rules, rather than to the personal development of Pharaoh himself. This is an instance of an almost entirely objective understanding of dreams—that is, finding in dreams guides to the conduct of practical affairs in the everyday world. Jung cites a similar example in a primitive African culture where dreams had become less important as guides when political control was taken from the medicine men and chieftains (1930, p. 556). The prophet Daniel in the Old Testament understands dreams that refer to the objective state of present or future events (Daniel 2), as well as those that refer more to the fate of King Nebuchadnezzar himself (Daniel 4). In the New Testament, it is stated in the Gospel of Matthew that dreams tell Joseph that Mary is pregnant by God, that Herod plans the slaughter of the infants and the family must flee, and finally that it is safe to return with Mary and Jesus from Egypt to Palestine (Matthew 1:20–21, 24; 2:12–13, 19–22).

In these examples, as throughout antiquity, dreams are taken as revelations from gods or as visions of future events. Such an understanding implies a division of the world that is now foreign to our usual practice of dream interpretation. We no longer tend to think of the human world as existing within an encompassing divine order, whose ordination of future human destiny can at times be seen in revelatory dreams. In the modern world since Freud, dreams have lost the role of messenger between gods and humanity and have become messages between the ego and the unconscious, if indeed they are not reduced to the function of disguising unacceptable thoughts in order to preserve sleep.

Even outside such epic and religious dreams as those of Gilgamesh and biblical figures, dreams in antiquity had a useful place that was culturally defined and integrated. In ancient Greece, dreams were used in the healing cult of Asclepius, which spread to an estimated 410 temples from the original sanctuary at Epidaurus. The ill person slept in the Asclepian temple enclosure until a dream revealed the origin of the illness, as well as a suggested treatment. This personal and practical use of dreams continued well into the Christian era, as evidenced by manuals of dream interpretation (White, pp. 6–7). One of these manuals survives intact, the *Oneirocritica* by Artemidorus of Ephesus and Daldis, written to pass on the rules of dream interpretation to the author's son (ibid., pp. 8–9).

Artemidorus placed primary emphasis on reading dreams as portents of the future, rather than as movements within the dreamer's individuation process. His approach was empirical and practical, even moving toward a scientific attitude by comparing the dream interpretation with the future events that actually transpired. He criticizes the dream interpretation of Antipater of Tarsus, for example, for using the same interpretation for two different dreamers without giving sufficient attention to the differences in their situations (ibid., p. 212). Artemidorus does not commit himself to a theoretical position about the origin of dreams, but maintains a thoroughly practical, almost modern, empirical stance, comparing various opinions and examples of dreams. He exhibits a developed sense of the symbolic and contextual nature of dream images. The image of dung, for example, is taken by Artemidorus to be a positive one for a farmer, who uses manure as fertilizer, but a negative one for a city dweller. Tattoos are positive dream images in a culture where children are tattooed, but negative in another area where only slaves are tattooed. If the god Serapis says in a dream that one is going to live, it may instead mean death, since Serapis, like the Greek Pluto, was a god of the underworld. The *Oneirocritica*, therefore, was a mixture of fixed and contextual interpretative maxims.

During the Middle Ages, dreams were often considered to be either sent by God to reveal truth, or sent by other forces to deceive (Thorndike, pp. 290–302), reflecting in many ways the distinction in Homer's Odyssey between true dreams, which were said to enter the mind through gates of horn, and false dreams, which came through gates of ivory.

By the time Freud wrote his masterwork, *The Interpretation of Dreams,* in 1900, both the scientific and religious communities had lost all sense that dreams might be meaningful. In the first chapter of *The Interpretation of Dreams,* Freud reviewed some contemporary literature on dreaming. He cited studies that conceived of dreams as breakdown products of consciousness, or as attempts of consciousness to function when it lacked sufficient energy to synthesize fully the waking sense of reality.

Dreams were seen as an inferior form of consciousness; there was no sense of their having significance, nor any recognition that they sometimes contain more knowledge than consciousness itself, a commonplace belief in antiquity.

Surveying this wasteland of dream theory and research, Freud virtually carved out a new theory of the meaning of dreams based on his own observations and theoretical speculations. He considered the dream to be a guardian of sleep, presenting repressed infantile wishes (often sexual or aggressive in nature) in a disguised form, so as not to arouse the unpleasant affect that their undisguised appearance would presumably produce. This disguise of the "latent" dream thoughts in the remembered, "manifest," dream was the work of such psychic mechanisms as displacement, condensation, substitution, and symbolization. Thus altered, the repressed latent dream was then put into a dramatic and acceptable form by secondary elaboration, Freud believed, and the manifest dream was experienced by the dream-ego. In the process of analyzing a dream, Freud used the dream as a starting point for free associations, allowing each dream motif to suggest a series of associations. The process of free association ended, according to the theory, in the discovery of the supposed original, undisguised, latent dream. Theoretically, this content would be a repressed infantile wish that was at the core of an adult neurotic problem. Jung later called this type of analysis of a present dream into its roots in the past *reductionistic*.

The publication of Freud's book on dreams attracted the attention of Jung, who was nineteen years his junior. While practicing psychiatry at the Burghölzli, the University of Zurich Psychiatric Hospital, Jung was already working on studies on word association. In the word-association experiment, the subject was asked to give the first association that came to mind in response to each word on a list of stimulus words. Sometimes the subject blocked and was unable to give a response; sometimes a response was excessively delayed in time. Jung thought that such interferences in the association process indicated the activity of an unconscious psychological complex. The psychological complex, as defined by Jung (1913, p. 599), consists of a group of related ideas held together by a common emotional tone. The idea of "mother,". for example, might be connected to a complex containing many other images, memories, and fantasies, all having a common emotional tone. Other images in such a complex might be the grandmother, the Virgin, the queen, the female teacher, the mother country, and so on. Any of these images, when evoked during the word-association experiment, might activate the larger complex, which in turn would interfere with the normal functioning of consciousness by producing an affect-ego (Jung 1907, pp. 41–42). An affect-ego is an ego state in which the normal ego is modified by the arousal of affect from the complex. The affect-ego brings into prominence the ideas associated with the complex, and it thereby weakens the structures associated with the normal waking-ego. Defenses of the ego also interfere with word-association responses.

Reading *The Interpretation of Dreams*, Jung recognized that Freud was describing from observations of patients the same type of unconscious activity that he himself was studying in subjects with his word-association experiments. The two pioneering psychoanalysts began a correspondence (see McGuire), and in 1907 they met for the first time. Their initial conversation lasted thirteen hours (Jung 1961, p. 149) and foreshadowed what was to become their intense personal interaction and professional cooperation at the beginning of the psychoanalytic movement, a relationship that was to continue until 1913 (McGuire, pp. 550–51). In the early years of their association, Freud pictured Jung as his "crown prince" and potential successor (ibid., p. 218). With Freud's blessing, Jung was elected first president of the International Psychoanalytic Association and was the first editor of its *Jahrbuch*.

The reasons for Freud and Jung's parting were complex. The official reason was a disagreement about the nature of libido, Freud insisting on a basic sexual meaning, and Jung using the term in a more general sense. Jung described his principal reason for their separation as his growing sense that Freud was not dedicated to a dispassionate, scientific investigation of the unconscious, but wished rather to further a movement, psychoanalysis, over which he wanted to possess principal authority (Jung 1961, p. 158).

After his break with Freud, Jung endured a period of intense introversion and professional isolation (ibid., pp. 170–99). Searching for a path of his own, he turned to his dreams, fantasies, and childhood memories. He found that building a miniature village from stones—an activity he had loved as a boy—released a flood of emotions and fantasies (ibid., pp. 173–75). He began actively to confront the figures of his unconscious, engaging them in inner dialogue. Out of this period of exploration, Jung developed the central thrust of his own branch of psychoanalysis, which he called *analytical psychology*. Jung experienced the imagery of his dreams and fantasies as representing part-personalities having purposes of their own and only partially submitting to the control of his conscious ego. This insight related to his earlier doctoral dissertation, in which he described a case of mediumistic "controls" as prefigurations of the young medium's own future personality (Jung 1902). Out of this experience of isolation and self-study, Jung developed his unique technique of *active imagination* (cf. chapter by Dallett, below), and his understanding of dreams as autonomous self-representations of the psyche that stand in a compensatory relationship to the conscious ego (Jung 1916, pp. 250–51).

THE DREAM-EGO AND THE WAKING-EGO

The ego in Jungian theory is the psychological complex whose unique attribute is what we experience as waking consciousness, although all complexes have some quality of consciousness (Jung 1935, p. 73). While the ego feels itself to be the center of the entire psyche, it lives in a house more complex than it realizes: the ego is only the center of consciousness. The true center of the psyche as a whole is the Self, the central archetype (Jung 1961, p. 386). The relativity of the ego is experienced most notably in dreaming, where the ego involuntarily experiences dramatic episodes not under its own control, but with all the verisimilitude of the everyday world of waking consciousness.

While in the dream, the dream-ego can feel that it faces dangers and fears, or joys and opportunities, that cannot *in the dream* be qualitatively differentiated from similar experiences in waking life. Not until the dreamer awakens can the dream events be seen as having occurred "only in a dream." Like the waking-ego, the dream-ego experiences a sense of subjective choice and affective meaning. And yet the dream is a product of the same psyche that the waking-ego mistakenly thinks that it rules. The dream is to the psyche as an x-ray is to the body: it truthfully pictures the actual state of a portion of the whole organism/psyche. Just as x-ray images are not the body itself—although skillful understanding of them may give invaluable knowledge about the state of health of the actual body—so dreams are not the actual psyche, but offer rich images of its structure and dynamic movement. The dreamer may deny or misunderstand his dreams, but he cannot disown them.

It is the relationship of the dream-ego to the waking-ego that allows dream interpretation (and other uses of dreams) to play a primary role in the practice of Jungian analysis. Both the dream-ego and the waking-ego are felt to be "I," but it is not usually recognized by the analysand that the "I" of the waking state and the "I" of the dream may refer to vastly different contents. The dream-ego may sometimes behave in a manner similar to that of the waking-ego, but at other times it may behave very differently. This contrast may be seen as the dream-ego *compensating* for the ego-image of the waking-ego, bringing to the attention of waking consciousness ego-images that differ from the usual dominant ego-image of ordinary waking consciousness.

Both the dream-ego and the waking-ego are constrained by the worlds in which they find themselves. Both interact with a world outside themselves, even though the entire world of the dream-ego may be contained within the world of the waking-ego. The world of the waking-ego is a more or less constant world of time, place, and person, however, while the dream-ego experiences a world of shifting scenes and characters, only rarely having the constant qualities of the waking world. (Recurrent dreams may occur, of course, but they are often a symptom of traumatic neurosis.)

DREAM-EGO AND COMPLEXES

The relationship of the dream-ego to the waking-ego can be seen in the language of Jung's theory of complexes, which derived from his initial scientific work on the word-association experiment. In the theory of psychic complexes, a group or *complex of ideas* is held together by a feeling-tone common to all the individual ideas (Jung 1913). The feeling-toned complex produces a particular constellation of consciousness that can cause such disturbances in response as Jung found in the word-association task. It is useful to consider that the complexes that are associated with the waking-ego as part of its tacit structure may or may not be the same complexes that are associated with the structure of the dream-ego. For example, if the waking-ego has an image of itself that is too grandiose and inflated, the dream-ego may find that it has been given a compensatory role that is excessively deflated and weak. The Self, as dream-maker, has dissociated the ego from the inflated complex that it clings to in waking life, and causes it to experience a complex of a very different sort in the dream, as compensation for its inflated dominant ego-image.

The basic quality that the waking-ego and the dream-ego have in common is a sense of being the center of subjectivity in their respective worlds. The waking-ego feels itself to be the center of waking consciousness in the waking state, and the dream-ego feels itself to be the center of ego-awareness in the dreaming state. To avoid confusion, it is possible to differentiate waking consciousness and dream consciousness, rather than use the unmodified word consciousness, which implies the waking state. Rather than differentiate two types of consciousness, it is helpful to consider that both the waking-ego and the dream-ego share this experience of subjectivity.

OBJECTIVE AND SUBJECTIVE INTERPRETATIONS

In the waking state, the ego synthesizes all the contents of the psyche, both integrated and unintegrated, conscious and unconscious, into some constellation that permits interaction with the outer world. The apparently independent and objective attitude of the waking-ego actually contains, through projection, contaminations from the inner world that are directly experienced by the dream-ego in the dream.

These distortions are not usually very apparent in cases of normality or neurosis, but they become clearly evident in persons with psychotic delusional systems of belief. The ego has many images of itself, some very specific to certain states of mind—that is, the ego may fall into one particular image of itself in relating to most people in the world, but into another, neurotic image when in the emotional state associated with dealing with close personal relationships. Often the neurotic ego-image is based upon some early family role that has been unconsciously preserved and becomes a dominant ego-image that determines feelings of competency and self-worth. It is usually resistant to change since it is felt to be the "real" identity. Partly through defensive maneuvers designed to maintain its own dominant ego-image, the waking-ego always deals with the world from a somewhat distorted point of view. Dreams actively compensate this distorted view held by the ego of itself and of the outer world (Jung 1916, pp. 250–57).

When dreams refer to persons or events in the outer world, compensating our conscious view of them, the interpretation is considered *objective*. When they are interpreted as referring to the inner structure of the psyche, to the anima or shadow, for example, the interpretation is called *subjective*. Objective interpretation in this sense does not mean "actual" as opposed to a subjective, "imaginary" interpretation. Both objective and subjective interpretations refer to the state of the psyche, objective interpretation emphasizing outer relationships and subjective interpretation emphasizing the intrapsychic structure of the personality.

In maintaining that dreams can be interpreted from both the objective and the subjective points of view (Jung 1916, p. 276), Jung retained the valuable personal reference of Freudian dream theory but avoided the reductionistic position that dreams were simply disguised, unacceptable parts of everyday consciousness that had been previously repressed. Jung's view equally avoids the idealist or solipsistic error that dreams can be only personified or imaged parts of the dreamer's own psyche.

Dreams should be considered from both the objective and the subjective points of view. If figures in the dream are known to the dreamer, particularly in times of conflict, objective interpretation may be more valuable. Unknown persons or clearly mythological or archetypal dream motifs favor a subjective interpretation. It is best, however, always to consider a dream from both viewpoints.

DREAM IMAGES AND COMPLEXES

In the subjective interpretation of dreams, the images and motifs of the dream are seen as personified or imaged complexes. Any number of images or themes can represent the same psychological complex, which itself consists of a group of images with a common feeling-tone. In following a series of dreams, it is often possible to discriminate various figures or themes that are related to a single underlying complex, to a pattern of complexes, and to psychological development within the intrapsychic matrix. For example, a neurotic person has dreams of civil war early in analysis. The civil war motif indicates a unity divided against itself, a psychic split (cf. chapter by Sandner and Beebe, below). As the neurotic conflict lessens, this split is represented by two teams engaged in an athletic contest, such as a football game. Unlike the image of civil war, the athletic contest portrays a conflict that is contained within a safe boundary, and obeys the rules of the game. These dream motifs show a progression toward conscious integration of the conflict and suggest its future resolution in the service of a more comprehensive personality.

DREAMS IN SERIES

Because the dream life is an ongoing dialogue between the ego and the unconscious mind, single dreams must be interpreted in the context of the series of dreams in which they are embedded. In a series of dreams, it is possible to follow the maturation of a complex, as illustrated by the progression *war, civil war, athletic contest*. When a series of dreams is followed in analysis, misunderstandings and misinterpretations at an earlier stage can be corrected by later dreams (Jung 1935, p. 78). For example, a young man who had difficulty dating and making sexual contact dreamed that he was shyly watching a mermaid swimming in a lake beside his maternal grandmother's isolated resort cabin in the mountains. A male friend who was more outgoing and emotional stepped on the dock on which the dream-ego was crouching, upsetting the dock and "accidentally" throwing the dream-ego into the water with the mermaid. When the dream-ego quickly got back to shore and resumed his passive observation, he noticed that the number of mermaids in the water had increased. Within two weeks, the dreams began to contain more ordinary women, some of whom he knew.

At the time of the original mermaid image, there was no clear context in the dream to indicate whether the mermaid represented a regressive pull of the ego toward the unconscious, or whether it showed that the waking-ego's passivity had constellated an archetypal feminine image, the mermaid, as an attempt to compensate the analysand's conscious reticence in initiating appropriate and desired heterosexual contacts. The apparent movement of the mermaid image toward that of more ordinary women in later dreams shows that the original dream image of the mermaid was an image that would move him into life experience rather than away from life.[2] In retrospect, the personal grandmother, at whose cabin the first dream was set, may have been associated with the image of the great mother. This example also shows how the contact of the dream-ego with an archetypal image accelerates the developmental process, provided the ego is strong enough to integrate the conflict.

Analysis is clearly an ongoing process, with no privileged point at which one can say what a dream finally means. The willingness to tolerate this continuous ambiguity and uncertainty is a hallmark of Jungian analysis. The underlying reality is the individuation process itself, while any particular ego-image in relation to any particular constellated complex is only an aspect of the ongoing movement.

At times, dreams recapitulate earlier motifs. Some analysands may take this to mean that no psychological change has taken place and no progress has been made in analysis or in the individuation process. Careful comparison of dream motifs, however, usually shows that although similarities of motif and structure exist, important differences are also apparent, as in the change from civil war to athletics cited above. The movement in a long dream series can be seen as a spiral process, returning to a similar place but on higher or more integrated levels of the spiral.

DREAMS AS DRAMA

Jung suggested looking at the structure of dreams as dramatic forms (Jung 1916, p. 266), identifying the characters, the initial problem, developments in the plot, the climax of the action, and the result or solution (the *lysis*). It is important to pay particular attention to the actions and attitudes of the dream-ego. It may be a protagonist, taking active part in the primary action of the dream drama, or it may be a "floating eye" that watches the dream action or perhaps even watches "itself" acting in the dream from a viewpoint of detached observation (Marjasch).

The dramatic structure of the dream permits observations of the potential results of particular attitudes of the dream-ego.[3] A man in middle life, for example, dreamed that his college-age son found him in bed with a woman with whom he was having a casual sexual affair. Although the son took no notice of the situation in the dream, the dream-ego felt embarrassment. In the next scene of the dream, the dream-ego appeared as high-school age, explaining to a teacher that he was late to take an important examination because of having been involved in the same casual affair. Although his teacher was willing to let him take the exam late, a further regression in age occurred and he was with a baseball team. The coach told him that although he was an important player on the team, he would not be furnished with a uniform. The dream-ego thought to himself that this was because of the sexual involvement and became angry. When the coach remained passive, his anger increased to such a degree that he hit one of the other boys on the team. The dream-ego felt it was strange that the other team members were afraid of his temper when he was himself afraid.

The dream shows (1) a punitive and disapproving attitude about his sexual affair, for which he feels no conscious anxiety; (2) a regression, shown in the dream by regression to earlier ages; (3) the noninteraction of the coach, which parallels the waking-ego's withdrawal from ordinary confrontations with his wife; and (4) a potential model for his irrational and impulsive angry acts, which erupt at times in his waking life.

An understanding of the structure of the dream permitted insight into a recent incident in which he had suddenly become angry at his wife and had kicked her leg, causing severe bruising. The dream clearly outlined the sequence: disapproving attitude—regression—anger at the other person's passivity—eruption of anger—resulting fear and remorse. A similar sequence could be seen in the incident with his wife when it was examined in comparison with the dream sequence.

In some dreams it is possible to note distinct shifts of the dream-ego from one identity to another. The dream-within-a-dream is an example of this. One patient, a person who has to wear leg braces permanently, dreamed of walking across a room without the braces, only to awaken (within the dream) and realize it was "a dream"—and then awaken into the actual state of waking consciousness. Analysis of the structure of this unusual dream suggested that the dream was actually showing that "walking without braces is only a dream." Conceptualization of the dream-within-a-dream raises many of the same issues of figure/ground raised in Gestalt psychology; it also suggests the focal/tacit shifts of perception and intuition described by Polanyi. Hofstadter has discussed this problem of boundaries in *Gödel, Escher, Bach,* his "metaphorical fugue on minds and machines in the spirit of Lewis Carroll."

Another patient reported a recurrent dream in which he was watching a boy who was in turn watching a river; suddenly he became the boy watching the river, which now became turbulent and frightening. At the point of greatest fear, the process reversed, and he was again watching the boy who was watching the river, now smooth. The dream seemed to show a shift of ego-identity within the dream as a defense against anxiety. The fact that the dream has been recurrent over a number of years indicated a persistent problem of facing anxiety, as well as regression (becoming the boy) when he attempted to get closer to the "river" of life.

A commonly occurring dream motif that shows the relativity and alter-ability of the dream-ego is a dream that one is watching a movie, only to become an actor in the movie as the movie becomes reality in the dream. These changes in the dream-ego can be understood as alterations in the complexes with which the dream-ego identifies itself. In some dream se-ries, the dream-ego can appear at first as a detached spectator of action that seems to take place "outside" of the ego (as in a movie), while in later dreams it is an involved participant in similar actions. When the dream-ego becomes an active character in the dream, the analysand may think that the dream indicates a worsening of his or her psychological condition, since the dream appears at first glance to show greater stress and danger. But the opposite meaning is more likely true: the complex represented by the conflict has been assimilated by the ego-structure to such a degree that the dream-ego can be engaged in an interaction with forces that were previously too removed from the ego for resolution to be approached. Jung described the ego under the affective pull of a complex as an affect-ego (Jung 1907, p. 41); the dream-ego that is engaged in conflict would be an affect-ego in the dream. The activity of the dream-ego has an impact on the complexes of the unconscious and can alter their structural arrangement. Since the waking-ego relies in a tacit fashion on the structure of complexes in the unconscious, changes in the structure of complexes in reaction to the activity of the dream-ego may be reflected in changes in the waking-ego. Often such changes are recognized by the wak-ing-ego only as alterations in mood (Hall 1977, pp. 172–77). This process may be a significant factor in effecting therapeutic changes in the person-ality (ibid., pp. 141–62).

INITIAL DREAMS

In Jungian analysis, it is considered essential to note the initial dream or dreams that occur in analysis, often between the time the first appointment is made and the time that it actually occurs. Such initial dreams often have prognostic significance. For example, one man entering analysis first dreamed that he was walking down a steep slope, at the bottom of which was a large, godlike man toward whom he felt drawn. The godlike person anticipated the dreamer's own need to meet with transcendent masculine qualities, both in and beyond himself. The figure was partly an assimilable positive masculine shadow and partly an image of the archetypal wise man that lay deeper in the psyche than the image of the personal father. There were also implications for a later positive transference to the male analyst, and an implication that meeting with such a projection could be handled with relative ease.

Another man dreamed that he killed an evil woman who was the mistress of an abattoir, after which slaughtered animals were returned to life. This initial dream anticipated that this patient's instinctual life, which felt dead, would return again when the negative mother complex was faced and conquered. It was significant that the evil woman in the dream, in trying to kill the dream-ego with a trident, actually gave the dream-ego a weapon with which to oppose her. This showed the ambivalent nature of the maternal archetype, which both produces the ego and opposes it. Another man, middle-aged, who had made many false starts at analysis, dreamed that he was led into a square room where a respected scholar showed him an adjacent "treasure room" that could not be seen from his usual point of view. The dream indicated a need for consistent and dedicated "scholarly" work, a contrast to this man's usual adolescent style of quick interest and rapid abandonment of quests. He did not continue in the analytic process and accumulated another false start in his long series. All these dreams suggest an auspicious beginning for analytical work.

In addition to initial dreams, attention should also be directed toward dreams that occur on significant dates, such as birthdays, anniversaries, New Year's Day, Christmas, and so on. The inner psychic life often responds to archetypal seasonal images—for example, the meanings associated with Easter—and dreams should be noted at such times.

SYMBOLIC DREAMS

The Jungian approach clearly recognizes that dreams vary in their depth of symbolic meaning. Some dreams seem to deal with everyday events, as if they were a commentary on daily life. Other dreams may be "big" dreams, touching upon the characterological structure of the personality and having a valid meaning over months or years (Jung 1945, p. 290). All such dreams can be considered symbolic statements, but some reach even the archetypal level of symbolization, using images that are meaningful in mythological or religious systems that may not even be known to the dreamer's waking mind.

Archetypal dream images carry a transforming and healing power. It is as if the dream-ego has touched a basic dynamic power in the psyche and is transformed. A woman whose husband had committed suicide, leaving her alone to care for two small children, dreamed that she saw an image of Diana of Ephesus (to which she had no conscious associations); then she was in a house with the Virgin Mary (she had converted to Catholicism because it was her husband's church). The tears of the Virgin turned to blood, and when she touched the blood, she was able to see the spirit of her deceased husband. He comforted her and instructed her to give up wanting to be with him and to care for the children instead. Other dreams in a long series carried the same message in less dramatic form, but the archetypal image of the great mother, shown in both the Virgin and in Diana, was a turning point in her extended mourning process. Her dream can also be seen as carrying religious meanings (Hall 1981).

THE PURPOSE OF DREAMS: COMPENSATION

Freud believed that the basic purpose of the dream was to disguise a repressed infantile wish, often sexual, in order to avoid arousing anxiety and thereby to preserve sleep. Jung developed a much more psychological theory of the purpose of dreams. He saw them as producing a point of view in essential counterpoint to the stance of the conscious ego. Jung called this process *compensation*. If the conscious attitude of the waking-ego is significantly distorted, dreams strongly present the opposite position. For example, a person who in conscious life has an excessive inhibition of sexual feelings might have frankly sexual dreams. A person whose conscious personality is excessively inhibited and shy might dream of great activity and aggression. One patient who had given up an initial desire to become a minister and had become quite sexually active with a number of women dreamed that he was in church taking communion, experiencing in the dream the important part of his personality that he had consciously abandoned.

Compensation describes the manner in which the dream presents an alternative vision of the ego and its images, bringing to consciousness, in the dream, aspects of the situation that have been unknown or insufficiently emphasized by the waking-ego.[4] The dream is in a dialectical relationship with the ego and does not necessarily present a truer picture than the waking-ego does; rather, the dream presents a view in compensation to the view of the waking-ego. The compensation presented by the dream may be severe, and appear to oppose the position of the waking-ego, as in the case of a man who dreamed that an objective but authoritative voice said to him, "You are not leading your true life!" Dreams may compensate in a mild fashion, which might be called *complementation*. If the conscious attitude is essentially correct and appropriate, the dream may even emphasize the conscious attitude.

There are three ways in which dreams may be seen as operating in a compensatory fashion: (1) by adding information from the interpreted dream to the knowledge of the waking-ego; (2) by showing a self-representation of the state of the psyche, which may vary from the view of the waking-ego; and (3) by a direct alteration of the structure of the waking-ego itself.

Adding Knowledge to the Waking-Ego

When the dream is remembered and analyzed, the waking-ego can recognize in the actions of the dream-ego certain traits of its own that have been unconscious or not sufficiently noted in the waking life. A woman who consciously thought that she was being very caring and scrupulous about the needs of others dreamed that she had three dogs to divide between two people and was about to cut one dog in two to make the division equal. She loved animals and was horrified at what she was doing in the dream, which helped her to feel the difference between following exact rules of conduct and living with empathy for the needs of others.

Self-Representation of the Psyche

The dream may be viewed as a self-representation of the psyche (Jung 1916, p. 263) that shows the movement and change in the complexes at various levels, some in the personal sphere and some at a more archetypal depth. When the dream is seen as a self-representation of the psychic state, that representation can be viewed by the waking-ego as a contrast to its own view of the psychic state. At times, the dream can be seen as a self-representation of the psyche that is focused upon concerns other than immediate compensation of the state of the waking-ego (Jung 1945, p. 294). For example, it may illustrate family interactions, the nature of psychic processes, the solution of problems, or other matters. The dreams of children sometimes seem to compensate the family situation, in which the child's ego is contained, more than they compensate the child's ego itself. Even when dreams are seen as self-representations of the psyche, however, they offer the possibility of a compensatory function, depending upon the ego's attitude toward them. If the waking-ego compares the self-representation in the dream with its own views, the dream functions in a compensatory manner.

Alteration of the Structure of the Ego

The movements of images within dreams show the movement, connection, and separation of psychological complexes with archetypal cores, which in themselves cannot be otherwise observed except by inference from waking experience. Since the ego depends upon the structure of the complexes, changes in these complexes can affect the structure of the waking-ego, whether the change takes place in waking life or in a dream through the action of the dream-ego. When dreaming, the dream-ego deals directly with complexes that in waking life would be constituents of the waking-ego. The dream-ego sees these complexes in a focal way, personified as events or as persons in the dream. The waking-ego, which is focused on the outer world, relies upon the same complexes in a tacit fashion while giving focal attention to events and persons in the outer world. When the dream-ego effects a change in the structure of the complexes, that change is inherited by the waking-ego even though it may have no focal awareness of the change. This constitutes a third form of compensation: the direct action of the Self, through the dream, upon the tacit structure of the ego.

A man with a compulsive pattern of behavior based upon a father complex awoke from a dream of the father with a radically altered feeling about the conflict situation, even though the dream had not at that time been interpreted so as to add knowledge to the waking-ego (Hall 1977, pp. 172–77). The later interpretation qf the dream added conscious awareness to what was already a tacit change.

RECORDING DREAMS

All persons dream, but not all persons remember dreaming. An initial concern in analysis is to collect accurate dream reports. In most instances, it is sufficient simply to inquire of the analysand about the occurrence of dreams. Even those who never remembered dreams before are often able to begin recalling dreams after entering analysis. The analysand is instructed to lie awake with eyes closed for a few minutes each morning upon awakening, allowing time for dream recall before the day's activities begin to erase the memory of dreams. A dream or dream fragment that is remembered should immediately be noted in writing (or in a voice recording), since memory of dreams fades quickly. Dream reports should be dated to allow consideration of their relevance to situations occurring in waking life at the time of the dream. Associations may be written on the dream report, either in the body of the report (in brackets or parentheses) or appended to the dream report.

The most serious error made in reporting dreams is to record less detail than exists in the actual memory of the dream. The analyst should therefore make certain that the analysand presents as detailed a picture of the actual dream as possible. This description should be completed before the process of association, amplification, and analysis is begun.

A verbal or written dream report might be: *I was in a house with some people having dinner*. There are several obvious omissions in this report: What kind of house was it? Was it an actual house from the past experience of the dreamer? What was served for dinner? Who was present? What was the emotional tone of the dream? Asking such questions often stimulates the analysand's memory, and sometimes large segments of the dream that had been forgotten come into waking consciousness. After the details of the dream are established in as complete a form as possible, analyst and analysand can move to association and amplification of the motifs and images of the dream and then begin interpretation.

AMPLIFICATION OF DREAM IMAGES

To understand the remembered dream, it is important to establish the context in which the images of the dream occur. The context consists not only of the outer situation of life in which the dream occurs, but also of the images of the psyche that are closely related to particular images in the dream. To establish this inner context, amplification of the dream images is undertaken. It is accomplished by noting the images immediately associated with the dream images, both in the mind of the analysand and in cultural or archetypal material that may be known or unknown to the conscious mind of the analysand. Unlike free association, which consists of moving from one association to another association, to another association, and so on, amplification is concerned with images that always stay in proximity to the original image.

Amplification can be divided into three levels or stages. First, personal associations are made to the images of the dream. If someone with whom the dreamer has no immediate connection appears in a dream, it can be useful to ask, "What sort of person is that?" Unknown persons or persons not currently related to the dreamer in actual life situations are more likely to be personified parts of the dreamer's own psyche. This gathering of personal associations differs from the Freudian technique of free association, as noted above, in that it stays in the vicinity of the dream image rather than moving from the original image to a chain of associations. In amplification, one returns again and again to the image itself.

Because the dream is a self-representation of the psyche, constellated in compensation to a waking-ego attitude, it is not a disguised form of a repressed waking thought that must be investigated in detective fashion to pierce the disguise. The dream is a truly symbolic statement, the most appropriate representation at that time of a psychic content of importance to the ego. By keeping amplifications, whether personal, cultural, or archetypal, close to the images of the dream, one tends to amplify with images that are attached to the same group of complexes as are represented in the dream. When several dreams in a series seem to refer to the same context, although using different images, the different particular images usually express nuances within the complex or in the relationship of that complex to other complexes. It is important to remember that the dream shows not only what complexes are activated in the patient's psyche, but what the unconscious is doing with the activated complexes (Jung 1935, p. 84).

After the gathering of personal associations has been completed (or if none can be elicited), one may move to the next step, which consists of using cultural associations, common cultural meanings that are presumably present in the psyches of both analyst and analysand. Often the analysand will spontaneously confirm the accuracy of a cultural association offered by the analyst. One analysand who was given to having fits of jealous rage toward his wife reported a dream that occurred at a time when he would typically have experienced such an episode of rage but did not. In the dream he was watching a city that was about to be bombed by an airplane flying high overhead. At the very last moment, however, a smaller aircraft flew up from the city and shot down the bomber before the city could be destroyed. The dream-ego observed the small plane landing and the pilot getting out. This was the analysand's entire spontaneous dream report, but when engaged in the process of giving a clear description of the elements of the dream, he added a surprising fact: the small plane that had saved the city was perfectly round in shape, with a cockpit dome in the center. Furthermore, the pilot who stepped out of it looked like the dreamer himself!

Even with this more detailed account, however, the analysand offered no spontaneous personal associations to the strange round plane. He did, however, readily accept a cultural association: the plane resembled a flying saucer. This is an image rich with modern mythological meanings. It happens that Jung was so intrigued with flying saucer reports that he published a lengthy study of their psychological meaning (1958). Observations of flying saucers have some psychological similarity to observations made in alchemy: in both instances the objects studied are assumed to be physical, although there is no understanding of their physical nature. This intense straining to understand a mysterious phenomenon, presumed to be physical, causes a projection of symbolic images from the objective psyche. Jung considered the appearance of a flying saucer to be a projected mandala, a symbol of the Self.

The round plane in the dream, then, can be seen to carry meanings generally attached to the appearance of flying saucers. These include the fantasy of humanlike visitors from space, sometimes seen as unfriendly invaders, but more often as superior, saving intelligences. The flying saucer image can be amplified by archetypal material, as a mandala, as well as by cultural associations. *Mandala* means "circle" in Sanskrit. At times it is seen as the representation of a symmetrical city with four gates at the cardinal points. Bodhisattva figures are shown in various positions within the mandala for different meditative practices. Jung found many mandala images in the dream and fantasy material of his patients, images that bring attention to a center and a periphery. He understood them to be images of order, often appearing when the ego structure needed support from the archetypal level of the psyche. If the flying saucer is taken to be an image of the mandala, the round fighter plane of the man's dream represents an alliance between the Self (imaged as a mandala) and the ego (who pilots the craft). Together the two are able to defeat a potentially destructive autonomous complex, the bomber, that had repeatedly reduced the dreamer's marital relationship to rubbish.

Archetypal amplification is generally reserved until after the personal and cultural associations have been established. Archetypal amplifications are found in folklore, religion, and mythology. They represent archetypal images that have been accepted into collective conscious lore and have been sufficiently powerful to appeal to a large number of people over an extended period of time. There are likely many more archetypal images in dreams than are usually recognized. Such recognition depends upon the extent of knowledge of cultural and religious systems possessed by the interpreter. On some occasions, the dream material contains an archetypal image that is not known to the conscious mind of the dreamer and is unlikely to be an instance of cryptomnesia. Jung described the instance of this that first sensitized him to the presence of an archetype (McGuire and Hull, pp. 434–35; Jung 1952, pp. 99–103), and such observations are made by most analysts at some time during their work (Hall 1977, pp. 266–71). The psyche can, then, produce archetypal dream images that, when amplified, carry an appropriate contextual meaning previously unknown to the waking mind of the dreamer. This suggests that the Self has access to organizations of images that are similar to, but more archetypal than, the clusters of complexes in the personal unconscious to which the waking-ego relates in a tacit fashion. This structure at the archetypal level of the psyche is reflected in the recurrent archetypal images of myth and folklore. Edinger has discussed alchemical symbolism from this viewpoint of archetypal structure, carrying on a major interest of Jung's later years (Jung 1955–56).

AVOIDANCE OF REDUCTIONISM

A certain clinical skill is necessary in the elicitation and use of associations from the personal, cultural, and archetypal levels. It is possible to exaggerate any one of the three levels, thus leading to subtle forms of reductionism that may impede the process of analysis and individuation. Excessive emphasis on the personal associations can create the impression that all unconscious material is derived from personal events in the past, leading to a personal reductionism, which is a danger in classical Freudian psychoanalysis (Jung 1916, pp. 240–41). The primary danger of reduction to the personal is that the analysand will think that avoiding the repetition of past mistakes is all that is needed, whereas he or she may actually be faced with an entirely new archetypal constellation at the present stage of life. Personal reductionism also invites an inflation of the ego, which may come to consider that it is both guide and master of its own fate, without realizing that in fact it is in dialogue with the Self and the objective psyche, as well as the outer world. Such personal reductionism can also result from an overemphasis on objective interpretations of dream images: if all dream events are related to current interpersonal situations, the depth of intrapsychic process is lost. Everything may seem to be a question of furthering good interpersonal adaptation. Some of Jung's distrust of group psychotherapy (Jung 1959, pp. 471–72) seems to stem from his concern about aborting the process of individuation through the individual's assimilation of group norms, thus losing sight of what Jung felt was the more profound individual struggle with the opposites in one's own psyche.

Excessive use of cultural amplifications, to pursue this theme, can lead to the one-sided view that fitting into the world of collective consciousness is the primary goal. Dreams may mistakenly be seen as relating only to career goals, for example, or to "personal development" in a collective sense. A common error in this direction is to "explain" that the analysand dreamed of a particular person or situation because of a recent experience regarding that person or situation. This method reduces the intricate structure of the dream to a mere reference to what Freud called *day residue,* the persistent impressions of daily events that were not sufficiently attended to during the day and (in Freud's view) then developed connections with repressed material in the unconscious.

In Jungian analysis, there is also a peculiar danger of what might be called archetypal reductionism. Archetypal images are enduring forms of meaning, and almost any complex can be amplified toward an archetypal core of meaning. In a sense, Freud fell into this error by discovering beneath all kinds of different images only a few core meanings, invariably sexual. All images can be seen, if one insists upon it, as either phallic and piercing or womblike and containing. If climbing stairs and riding a horse are both Freudian symbols of sexual congress, what does one say about dreams of undisguised copulation? In some religious traditions, such as tantric Buddhism, frankly sexual imagery is intentionally used to symbolize nonsexual meanings. Jungians must be careful to avoid excessive archetypal amplification, particularly since there are many more archetypal patterns to consider than the few sexual ones Freud described. The images of alchemy, for example, are so profound and ubiquitous that once an analyst is aware of them, they may begin to appear everywhere, even in the most chemically innocent of images. To cite one of the less far-fetched examples of this, a coffee pot can be associated to the alchemical pelican vessel, in which the *prima materia* was subjected to a *circulatio* of distillation and condensation. Any system of mythology can be misused in this way if overamplified. The corrective to the danger of excessive archetypal amplification is to insist on closely following the actual dream images. It is helpful here to heed Jung's advice: the correct attitude with which to approach a dream is to remind oneself at the start that one does not know its meaning. This prevents reading into the dream thoughts that are already present about the analysand's problems.

Another form of interpersonal reductionism that should be avoided is the practice of invariably referring all dreams to the transference-countertransference relationship between analysand and analyst. At times dreams

do speak directly to this question. A young man who had an idealizing
transference to the analyst, coupled with the self-abasing idea that he himself could do nothing worthwhile, dreamed that he and the analyst were
looking for a mysterious "source," somehow metaphysical and at the same
time the source of an actual river. At times he was leading the analyst in
this quest, and at times the analyst was leading him. Finally they arrived
at the fountainhead. It was like an artesian well, and produced both water
and light. The dream illustrates graphically that the attitude of putting one
or the other of them ahead was a false approach; both must be engaged in
the quest for a transpersonal source of energy and vitality. In another case,
a woman with an erotic transference to her male analyst, behind which she
often hid from her other neurotic problems, dreamed that while in group
psychotherapy the analyst was lying on top of her on the floor. This, however, had no sexual meaning for her, and she realized that sexual feelings
were not the real issue. When dreams are this direct in pointing to a transference, they must naturally be considered as such. To overuse transference interpretation, however, may strengthen a transference neurosis.
While it may be a useful interpretation, it can cause the analyst and analysand to miss the course of the dreams themselves and lose their focus on
the material that is actually produced by the unconscious.

TYPOLOGY OF ANALYST/ANALYSAND

The analytic approach to a dream inevitably involves the typology of the
analyst. Most Jungian analysts seem to be introverted intuitive types (cf.
chapter by Quenk and Quenk, below). In my own training, I found it
particularly interesting to compare, from the typological point of view, the
approaches of the different analysts with whom I worked on my dreams.
For a year in Zurich, I was simultaneously in analysis with a woman who
was an introverted intuitive thinking type and a man who was an introverted feeling sensation type. The intuitive female analyst could take two
weeks of dreams and follow motifs in their changing form in various
dreams, then add archetypal amplifications and help me see a direction in
the movement of my entire dream life. The male analyst, on the other
hand, might spend two full sessions on one dream, looking meticulously
at the different motifs, weighing amplifications for them, and extracting
unsuspected nuances of feeling from the various images. Both approaches
were valuable. The experience served to teach me the open quality of
dreams and their ability to carry many different meanings, all of which
may further the analysis. Bradway and Wheelwright, among others, have

studied the psychological type of the analyst and its relation to analytical practice.

THE DREAM IN CONTEXT

Once the dream is elicited, clarified as to exactness of detail, and amplified through personal, cultural, and archetypal levels, it must be placed in the context of the dreamer's life, including the analytical context and the transference. It is by no means necessary or even desirable to interpret every dream that an analysand brings to a session. It is important for both analyst and analysand to decide when to work with dreams and when to use the analytic hour for other purposes. The analysand must not assume that simply producing a dream will trump any bid for discussing other material. If that is permitted to happen, dreams can be used defensively. An analysand may say (to himself if not to the analyst), "I didn't dream about it, so I don't have to discuss it," and thus neglect to bring up crucial material from other areas of life experience. In a training seminar for the Inter-Regional Society of Jungian Analysts, Stein has presented a discussion of how to avoid letting the use of dreams become a means of resistance rather than a furthering of analysis. Most often, however, dreams present an opportunity to delve more quickly and efficiently into the relevant psychological material than do other approaches.

The setting and context of the dream alone may serve as clues to the complexes activated in the dream. A woman who thought obsessively about sinfulness dreamed at least a third of the time about events that either were set in her hometown high school or involved persons from that era of her life. In associating to that time, she recalled how nuns in her Catholic school had given her a very black-and-white view of purity and sinfulness. In high school she had worried about how often she could kiss a boyfriend without committing a "mortal sin." Two dreams, selected almost randomly from her material, show how the unconscious confronts her with the inappropriateness of trying to use a standpoint not her own (dramatized as shoes and a borrowed car), which may cause her to lose her own sense of purpose:

Dream: *A girlfriend from my hometown and I were going shopping, trying on shoes, but when we were to leave the store, my own shoes weren't there and I couldn't find them.*

Dream: *I was driving a borrowed car and I was having difficulty driving it.*

Ego Activity/Passivity

Activity (or inactivity) of the dream-ego should be noted by the analyst. At times the activity of the dream-ego produces an immediate change in the action and structure of the dream; at other times its effect is more subtle. Even though the dream-ego often shows a narrower range of emotion and feeling than does the waking-ego, the feeling responses of the dream-ego should be given attention, because they constitute one effect of the dream upon ego structure and a reciprocal impact of the ego upon the complexes.

I have found it useful to consider a change of scene in the dream, occurring just after a feeling change in the dream-ego, to be a response on the part of the dream to that feeling change. For example, a professional man in his thirties dreamed that he and his girlfriend were in a house that was under attack by Mongol horsemen:

Dream: *One of the horsemen stopped at a window that was open and threw a spear at me. It missed, but I thought if I picked it up and handed it back to him he might leave us alone. But when I gave it back to him, it made him angry.*

In associating to the dream, he became aware of how his mollifying attitude would sometimes lead to increased tension in a situation, as in some recent events with his girlfriend and his ex-wife. A similar dream motif occurred in an early dream, previously mentioned in this chapter, of another professional person at whom a trident spear was thrown (see Hall 1977, p. 142). The spear was thrown back at the aggressing figure and this was followed by animal carcasses turning into live animals again. In both instances, the choice of the dream-ego in handling a weapon that has been used against it evoked a significant change in the action immediately following.

Sometimes the activity of the dream-ego produces a change of scene or action rather than a response within the same dream scene. Dreams of the same night will occasionally carry a motif of action and response through several dreams in sequence. A woman whose creativity was blocked dreamed these two dreams in succession in the same night:

Dream: *I am playing with four other women in a gymnasium in a prison. There are big doors at the end of the gym, but they only lead back to the prison. We boost two of the women up to some high windows. Then they lift me up, and I help pull up the last two. We escape from the prison.*

Dream: *I see an airplane on its back on the ground and bound up with barbed wire. Then I am in the airplane and I too am bound. I find that there is so much energy in my mind that by simply using my mind I am able to cause the airplane to right itself.*

Even without considering her associations, these dreams clearly show a problem of constriction and escape from it, or a change in its effect. Escape is accomplished in the first dream, but the problem returns in the second dream, where it is beginning to be worked through again. The second dream, in particular, strikingly illustrates how a change in the mental and emotional attitude of the dream-ego leads to a profound change in the nonego parts of the dream (the plane turning right side up again). Both of these dreams, reported early in analysis, suggested a good prognosis for analytical work.

DREAM SYMBOLS IN ANALYSIS

In practice a dream will often serve as a sign for other aspects of the patient's life. The man who dreamed of handing back the spear to his Mongol attacker, for example, was able to identify similar attitudes in waking experience, referring to them as examples of his "Mongol spear" attitude. Analysands will often use dream images as shorthand statements for entire patterns of behavior. Such use of the patient's own material stays close to the images that the unconscious itself has furnished and is a corrective to overintellectualization and the use of foreign or technical terms in the treatment process.

When dreams are understood as statements of important patterns in a person's psyche, one may be able to use them to identify other actions that reflect the same or similar processes at work: in the relationship with the analyst, in other current relationships, in the past, or in group psychotherapy. The practical advantage for analysis of finding the pattern first in a dream lies in understanding it as an inner subjective pattern of the analysand him- or herself. It is more difficult to "blame" friends, family, or others. If a complex is seen in group therapy, for example, the patient may well be less willing to accept it as his or her own pattern, since the interaction with other persons in the group can be cited as an important factor as well, and thus obscure the complex. The dream, however, comes directly from the psyche of the analysand and cannot be explained away or attributed to others. Things learned about oneself from a dream must be accepted just as one accepts one's own blood pressure or pulse.

Noninterpretative Uses of Dreams

The formal interpretation of a dream, using amplifications and relating the dream to the waking-ego as a compensatory view from the unconscious, is only one way of utilizing dreams within the analytical situation. Since dreams can show the structure of parts of the unconscious psyche, they can be of help to the analyst whether or not they are interpreted or understood by the dreamer. A dream may give the analyst a sense of favorable prognosis even when there seems to be little progress in the clinical state of the analysand. One man, an executive, came to weekly analytic sessions for over a year, often utilizing hypnotherapy as well. He suffered extreme anxiety about flying, and this had greatly restricted his personal and professional activities. Although he seemed to understand possible symbolic meanings of his symptom, and responded well to the induction of hypnosis, for more than a year he could not bring himself actually to fly. There was therefore no objective evidence that the treatment was being effective. During this long period, however, his dreams offered a continual suggestion of good prognosis. Below are all the consecutive dreams of flying from his dream material recorded over a ten-month period:

Dreams:

I dreamed of an airplane crash, with Henry Kissinger in it.

I dreamed of an airplane and was not comfortable.

A buddy flew into Dallas and flew back in a day.

I sat in the cockpit of a 707 or 747 plane and knew that everything was okay. Later I had a little apprehension about flying.

My wife was taking me to the airport to leave on our company jet. I was nervous but realized it was an irrational fear.

A plane was landing at Love Field. I am at an airport, concerned about flying.

Women pilots in a combination of old-time and four-engined planes. They take off without an instructor, and one of them is hanging onto a wheel, but all are safe.

I flew in a DC-3 from Canada to Louisiana to fish, then flew back and landed on a street and took off safely again.

I was going to an airport to fly on a 747; I felt fine. I am in the waiting room of an airport. Comfortable.

> *I am coming back from Houston on a commuter airline with people from the company and with you (the analyst).*

> *I seem to remember dreaming of a struggle about whether to fly. I went to the airport. I was on an older plane, maybe a DC-6, and concerned. I took off and made a safe trip and was comfortable. Glad I made the trip.*

> *I was supposed to go somewhere, but didn't want to go. I did fly and felt comfortable.*

> *I dreamed of an airlines flight. It was fine. I also dreamed of being ridiculed by an unknown man for not flying.*

These dreams of flying are presented in their chronological order, with other nonflying dreams omitted. They not only show a progression from fear to a sense of safety about flying, but also indicate that the dream-ego was less afraid of flying than was the waking-ego. The analysand was eventually able to fly comfortably.

Dreams may also be used noninterpretively in determining a diagnosis and in understanding changes that take place in the clinical condition of the analysand. If the dreams show less depression than the patient shows clinically, the diagnosis and prognosis are somewhat better, since there already exists in the unconscious a different pattern of ego functioning, a compensation to the depressed waking-ego. The reverse is also true: dream material may suggest that a patient is hiding depression or anxiety behind a cheerful persona.

It is difficult to use dream material as an indicator of changes in physical health (Hall 1977, pp. 196–98), but it is quite likely that some dreams do reflect the physical state of the organism. Jung mentioned two such dreams that aided in determining whether a condition was organic or hysterical (1934, pp. 158–60).

Dreams can serve a useful noninterpretive function, too, by indicating where the attention of the analyst should be directed. Since dreams compensate the attitude of the conscious personality, from the counterpoint of the Self, they can be thought of as working toward future solutions to present difficulties, or as further developments in the process of individuation (Jung 1945, p. 289). These solutions and developments may transcend rather than solve the current problems. When the analyst is aware of where the dreams are directed, he or she is better able to focus on an exploration of the past, or of present relationships, or of archetypal and symbolic material presented in the dreams.

DREAMS AND THE PRINCIPLES OF ENACTMENT

In psychoanalytic parlance, *acting out* means acting upon unconscious impulses and images rather than analyzing them and raising them to the level of conscious understanding. I have used the word *enactment* (in contrast to *acting out*) to mean the intentional utilization of various techniques to amplify further and understand symbols from the unconscious. Any intentional activity that puts further energy into dream images can be considered an enactment of that dream.

The well-known Gestalt technique of "being" one image in a dream, and talking about the image as if one were it, is an enactment of that image, but not of the dream. A psychologist had a dream in which, among other things, water ran up against a curb. Under the direction of his Gestalt therapist, he enacted the curb and was put in touch with character traits that he ordinarily experienced only vaguely: he felt his rigidity and immobility, and the way unpleasant people and situations flowed over him while he felt constrained not to move or respond; he also experienced some positive sense of his usefulness and reliability. The Gestalt enactment clearly made him aware of unconscious complexes in his characterological structure. When these were brought into focal awareness, he could take an attitude towards them and influence their activity. From a Jungian point of view, however, the enactment of the curb had nothing to do with an interpretation of the dream. However useful the process of identifying and understanding complexes may be, it does not create the same kind of compensatory dialogue between the ego and the unconscious that is achieved by a successful dream interpretation. A careful interpretative approach to a dream not only shows what complexes are activated in the dream, but also indicates the attitude of the Self, the dream-maker, toward the constellated complexes.

If this distinction between enactment and dream interpretation is kept clearly in mind, various forms of enactment of dream symbols can be a useful part of Jungian analysis. The Jungian technique of active imagination is perhaps the only form of enactment that fosters the same dynamic relationship between the ego and the unconscious as does the interpretation of dreams in a series (cf. chapter by Dallett, below). Sandplay is another enactment technique that offers great freedom of response to the unconscious symbolic process (cf. chapter by Stewart, below). Dance, writing prose or poetry, painting, and modeling in clay can be usefully employed to give substance and body to symbolic forms. It is necessary, however, to approach the forms created by these methods as one would approach dreams, as symbolic statements of the process of individuation, not as aesthetic objects. Guided imagination, sometimes used as a hypnoanalytic technique, is an intermediate form between waking fantasy and active imagination.

OUTLINE OF JUNGIAN DREAM INTERPRETATION

Dream interpretation is a skill and an art, and no formal description of it can do full justice to an authentic experience of its use in the hands of a skilled practitioner of Jungian analysis. The following outline is offered only for general information and education. It should always be kept in mind that any technique, including dream interpretation, can interfere with the dialectical interaction between analysand and analyst if misused in the analytical process.

I. The dream report should be as clear and as complete as possible.
   A. Analysands can be encouraged to remember dreams and given useful suggestions for remembering and recording them.
   B. The dream report may be verbal, written, or a tape recording of the patient's memory of the dream.
   C. The report should be clarified by asking questions about any points that are unclear from the analysand's report.

II. The dream should be placed in the context in which it occurs.
   A. The conscious situation of the dreamer at the time of the dream must be understood.
   B. The dream should be considered in the ongoing series of dreams that the analysand is reporting. Similarities to other dream motifs should be noted, as well as significant differences, in order to clarify different views of the underlying complex or structure of complexes.
   C. The dream should be considered in terms of transference-countertransference, but not forced into that mode of interpretation unless clearly referring to a problem that requires attention.

III. Motifs in the dream should be amplified on three levels:
   A. Personal associations from the dreamer.
   B. Cultural associations from the dreamer or the analyst.
   C. Archetypal amplifications from the dreamer or the analyst. As a general rule, personal associations take precedence over cultural meanings. To avoid the danger of archetypal reductionism, archetypal amplifications should not be allowed to overshadow personal associations.

IV. The dream should be examined to see if it fits into a dramatic structure with setting, cast, problem, development, and outcome or *lysis*. Not all dreams fit a dramatic form, but many do. Those that can be examined from a dramatic viewpoint should be carefully observed for actions by the dream-ego (including feeling changes) and responses from other figures in the dream, or changes in the dream structure itself, such as a sudden change of scene.

V. The state of the dream-ego should be particularly noted, together with any responses to actions (including feeling changes and emotion) of the dream-ego.

VI. The amplified and examined dream can then be related to the context of the waking-ego and the larger developmental process of the analysand. The principle of compensation is generally valid for this purpose, but it must be realized that the compensation may not refer simply to current personality problems. It can refer to the ongoing process of individuation or even to cultural or scientific questions beyond the limitations of individual ego development.

VII. The analyst should make a specific decision as to whether the dream(s) is to be interpreted, used in other ways, or omitted from any particular analytical session. Dreams should not be permitted to take precedence over more pressing analytical work, nor should the analysand be permitted to use them defensively. Dreams should further the analysis.

VIII. It does not seem possible to know the ''final'' meaning of a dream, even when it is examined in a series of dreams. The analyst should maintain an open attitude concerning the deeper meaning of dreams. Dreams, like consciousness itself, are ultimately a mysterious process between the personal conscious mind and the depths of the objective psyche.

SUMMARY

In Jungian theory, the dream is seen as a self-representation of the psyche, produced by the Self as part of the self-regulation of psychological processes.[5] When viewed from the point of view of the waking-ego, the dream is usually taken to be compensatory. Compensation is a useful clinical hypothesis for understanding the relations between dreams and the analytical process. Amplification at three levels (personal, cultural, and archetypal) helps to establish the context of the complexes that appear in the dream. The dream is a symbolic statement that carries meanings as yet unspecified, but it is not a disguised version of unacceptable repressed material.

To avoid the danger of various forms of reductionism, the dream must not be applied *simply* to past events in the life of the person, nor to current interpersonal relationships, including the transference situation, nor to the archetypal patterns that can be discerned, through excessive amplification, to be lying behind any particular dream image. Like other contents of analysis, dreams can be used defensively; they must be kept in perspective as a useful, but not completely sufficient, part of the analytical process. Dreams are ultimately mysterious, like consciousness itself, a fact that should be continuously remembered to avoid an inflated view in either the analyst or analysand: no dream is ever completely "understood."

NOTES

1. Rivkah Scharf Kluger has contributed a scholarly study of the Gilgamesh material from a Jungian view, presenting seminars in both Los Angeles and Zurich. I am indebted to her for indicating the profound psychological meanings in the ancient epic.

2. Hillman has emphasized the differences in the dayworld and the nightworld (terms borrowed from Gustav Fechner), claiming that the dream pulls the psyche away from the everyday world of reality into the "underworld," where all apparent forms are relative and can be "seen through." This is an extreme statement that seems to reify unnecessarily both the waking-ego and the dream-ego, leading to exactly the danger that Hillman seems to want to prevent. The more traditional (and I believe correct) view of the dream world is to see it as standing in a compensatory relationship to the experiences and belief systems of the waking-ego. As the attitude and understanding of the waking-ego change, so do those aspects that are compensated by dreams.

3. Berry has suggested that one can look at the images of a dream in a nondramatic way, observing what images occur in the presence of other images, and ignoring the dramatic sequence and the fashion in which a later scene may reflect a response to the attitude or action of the dream-ego in an earlier scene. She seems to be moving in the direction of interpreting dreams as patterns of complexes, but she goes too far in denying the value of a dream's dramatic structure (e.g., p. 63). The dramatic structure of a dream can yield important meanings that are lost if the dream is seen only as a constellation of complexes.

4. Mattoon believes that several types of dreams do not fall within the principle of compensation: prospective dreams, traumatic dreams, extrasensory dreams (those that are telepathic and precognitive), and prophetic dreams (pp. 142–45). In my own experience, however, extrasensory dreams refer to material that has psychodynamic relevance to the dreamer's present ego position (cf. Hall 1977, p. 322). Prospective, extrasensory, and prophetic dreams all seem compensatory to

the ego's usual waking state of being firmly bound in present time and place. Traumatic dreams are actually compensatory to the ego's sense of helplessness, representing the overwhelming (past) situation until mastery can be achieved by the dream-ego (cf. Hall 1977, pp. 302–3). In some rare cases, the traumatic dream does not occur immediately after the traumatic event, but rather begins after some later event that produces the same sense of helplessness. In such instances, the traumatic dream uses the previous trauma to symbolize a present state of trauma that is different in origin.

5. References to dreams and dream interpretation are spread throughout the *Collected Works* of Jung. Titles of particular interest (given with volume number and numbered paragraph designations) are:

The analysis of dreams, CW 4: 64–94.
Association, dream, and hysterical symptoms, CW 2: 793–862.
General aspects of dream psychology, CW 8: 443–529.
Individual dream symbolism in relation to alchemy, CW 12: 44–331.
The language of dreams, CW 18: 461–94.
The method of dream interpretation, CW 4: 326–34.
On the nature of dreams, CW 8: 530–69.
The practical use of dream analysis, CW 16: 294–352.
The problem of types in dream interpretation, CW 18: 495–559.
The significance of dreams, CW 18: 416–43.
On the significance of number dreams, CW 18: 416–607.
Symbolism and the interpretation of dreams, CW 18: 416–607.
UFOs in dreams, CW 10: 626–723.

REFERENCES

Berry, P. 1974. An approach to the dream. *Spring* 1974:58–79.
Bradway, K., and Wheelwright, J. 1978. The psychological type of the analyst and its relation to analytical practice. *Journal of Analytical Psychology* 23/3:211–25.
Edinger, D. 1978. Psychotherapy and alchemy. *Quadrant* 11/1:4–37.
Freud, S. *The interpretation of dreams*. New York: Basic Books.
Hall, J. A. 1977. *Clinical uses of dreams: Jungian interpretations and enactments*. New York: Grune and Stratton.
_____. 1981. Religious symbols in dreams of analytical patients. *Journal of the American Academy of Psychoanalysis* 9/2:237–49.
Heidel, A. 1946. *The Gilgamesh epic and Old Testament: parallels*. Chicago: University of Chicago Press.
Hillman, J. 1979. *The dream and the underworld*. New York: Harper & Row.
Hofstadter, D. 1980. *Gödel, Escher, Bach: an eternal golden braid*. New York: Vintage Books.
Jung, C. G. 1902. On the psychology and pathology of so-called occult phenomena. In *Collected works*, vol. 1, pp. 3–88. New York: Pantheon, 1957.
_____. 1907. The psychology of dementia praecox. In *Collected works*, vol. 3, pp.1–151. London: Routledge and Kegan Paul, 1960.

————. 1913. On the doctrine of complexes. In *Collected works,* vol. 2, pp. 598–604. Princeton: Princeton University Press, 1973.

————. 1916. General aspects of dream psychology. In *Collected works,* vol. 8, pp. 237–80. New York: Pantheon, 1960.

————. 1930. A radio talk in Munich. In *Collected works,* vol. 18, pp. 553–57. Princeton: Princeton University Press, 1977.

————. 1934. The practical use of dream-analysis. In *Collected works,* vol. 16, pp. 139–61. New York: Pantheon, 1954.

————. 1935. The Tavistock lectures: on the theory and practice of analytical psychology. In *Collected works,* vol. 18, pp. 5–167. London: Routledge and Kegan Paul, 1977.

————. 1945. On the nature of dreams. In *Collected works,* vol. 8, pp. 281–97. New York: Pantheon, 1960.

————. 1952. *Symbols of transformation. Collected works,* vol. 5. London: Routledge and Kegan Paul, 1956.

————. 1955–56. *Mysterium coniunctionis. Collected works,* vol. 14. London: Routledge and Kegan Paul, 1963.

————. 1958. Flying saucers: a modern myth of things seen in the sky. In *Collected works,* vol. 10, pp. 307–433. London: Routledge and Kegan Paul, 1964.

————. 1959. Introduction to Toni Wolff's "Studies in Jungian psychology." In *Collected works,* vol. 10, pp. 469–76. London: Routledge and Kegan Paul, 1964.

————. 1961. *Memories, dreams, reflections.* New York: Pantheon.

McGuire, W., ed. 1974. *The Freud/Jung letters.* Princeton: Princeton University Press.

McGuire, W., and Hull, R. F. C., eds. 1977. *C. G. Jung speaking.* Princeton: Princeton University Press.

Maduro, U. F. 1978. The clinical usefulness of an initial dream. In *The shaman from Elko,* ed. G. Hill, pp. 251–72. San Francisco: C. G. Jung Institute of San Francisco.

Marjasch, S. 1966. The "I" in dreams. *Spring* 1966:60–75.

Mattoon, M. A. 1978. *Applied dream analysis: a Jungian approach.* New York: Wiley.

Meier, C. A. 1967. *Ancient incubation and modern psychotherapy.* Evanston: Northwestern University Press.

Oppenheim, A. L. 1956. *The interpretation of dreams in the ancient Near East, with a translation of an Assyrian dream-book. Transactions of the American Philosophical Society* 46/3:179–373.

Polanyi, M. 1958. *Personal knowledge: toward a post-critical philosophy.* Chicago: University of Chicago Press.

Rhine, L. E. 1961. *Hidden channels of the mind.* New York: William Sloan.

Sanford, J. 1968. *Dreams: God's forgotten language.* Philadelphia: Lippincott.

Stein, M. 1978. The use of dreams. Lecture given at Inter-Regional Society of Jungian Analysts, Fall Conference, 25–28 October 1978, Wimberly, Texas. Privately circulated.

Thorndike, L. 1923. *A history of magic and experimental science.* Vol. 2. New York: Columbia University Press.

Ullman, M.; Krippner, S.; and Vaughn, A. 1973. *Dream telepathy.* New York: Macmillan.

White, R. J. 1975. *The interpretation of dreams: Oneirocritica by Artemidorus*. Park Ridge, N. J.: Noyes Press.

Williams, M. 1963. The indivisibility of the personal and collective unconscious. *Journal of Analytical Psychology* 8/1:45–50.

[8]

THE USE OF PSYCHOLOGICAL
TYPOLOGY IN ANALYSIS

Alex T. Quenk and Naomi L. Quenk

INTRODUCTION

THE importance of the theory of psychological types in the practice of Jungian analysis can best be introduced with two statements by Jung himself:

> When one begins as a young doctor, one's head is still full of clinical pictures and diagnoses. In the course of the years, impressions of quite another kind accumulate. One is struck by the enormous diversity of human individuals, by the chaotic profusion of individual cases, the special circumstances of whose lives and whose special characters produce clinical pictures that, even supposing one still felt any desire to do so, can be squeezed into the straitjacket of a diagnosis only by force. . . . The pathological problem upon which everything turns has virtually nothing to do with the clinical picture, but is essentially an expression of character. Even the complexes, the "nuclear elements" of a neurosis, are beside the point, being mere concomitants of a certain characterological disposition. (Jung 1936, p. 548)

Alex Quenk, Ph.D., is in private practice in Albuquerque, New Mexico, and is Associate Clinical Professor in Psychiatry, University of New Mexico. He is a graduate of the University of Connecticut, the University of Michigan, and the University of California, Berkeley, where he earned his doctorate in clinical psychology. He received his diploma from the Inter-Regional Society of Jungian Analysts, of which he is a member.

Naomi Quenk, Ph.D., is in private practice in Albuquerque, New Mexico. She is a member of the board of the Association for Psychological Type and a candidate-in-training with the Inter-Regional Society of Jungian Analysts. A graduate of Brooklyn College and the University of California, Berkeley, she was formerly associate director of the Longitudinal Study of Medical Students and assistant professor in Psychiatry and Community Medicine at the University of New Mexico. Her published monographs include *Types of Family Practice Teachers and Residents* (1975), *A Taxonomy of Physician Work Settings* (1975), and *On Empirical Studies of Jungian Typology* (1979).

> The opposition between types is not merely an external conflict between men, it is the source of endless inner conflicts; the cause not only of external disputes and dislikes, but of nervous ills and psychic suffering. (Jung 1923, p. 523)

Jung was, above all, an empiricist. His critical and discriminating empiricism enabled him to recognize, value, and account for individual regularities within the context of differences among people. In order to provide himself with an orientation to people by establishing what he called "average truths," Jung developed his theory of psychological types. He described it as "a phenomenology of the psyche, which enables us to formulate a corresponding theory about its structure" (1931, p. 527).

Typology, then, is a structural theory used to account for individual differences, as well as to help us understand "the manifestations of the psyche as expressions of its intrinsic being" (1936, p. 548).

The empirical basis for the average truths was the "emanations of the psyche"—attitudes, reactions, tendencies— that Jung observed in his patients, and that reflected the patients' conscious attitudes towards themselves and the world. Jung defined this kind of view as a *Weltanschauung* (1923, p. 523), comprising one's total conscious cognitions and values in regard to the world and oneself. Typological theory "thus constitutes a psychology of consciousness regarded from what might be called a clinical angle" (Jung 1961, p. 207). It is through one's consciousness that the psyche attempts to bring into balance the dynamic polarities within it, the moral expectations of collective society, and the contextual imperatives of outer reality. Insofar as one's consciousness contains habitual preferences, responses, and behavior patterns, typology is also a psychology of character.

Typological theory not only accounts for individual differences, but also indicates the source of what in modern terminology can be called character disorders. It is the differences among types, and the failure to recognize and appreciate such differences, that underlie the development of these disorders. As Jung stated above, the opposition between types creates not only interpersonal difficulties, but intrapsychic problems as well. The practical importance of typology in analytic work becomes apparent when type conflict is subsumed under the self-regulating principle of the psyche. This principle postulates that the psyche is an inherently self-regulating system containing within it a tendency toward balance and wholeness. When this balance is disrupted and an imbalance occurs, through either an overemphasis or an underemphasis on consciousness, unconscious complexes become autonomous and may gain energic amplitude. When this occurs, a neurosis or psychosis may ensue.

Jung assumes that one's type is a constitutional given, each type having its own natural pattern of growth. A child's type can often be recognized at an early age. Failure to appreciate a child's type as different from his or her parents' can interfere with or disrupt the self-regulating aspect of the child's psyche as it strives for balance, wholeness, or individuation. Hypothetically, individuation could occur if a child were completely accepted and were not the target of parental expectations that might impede or block the child's innate striving for wholeness. It is the task of analysis, within the context of the analytic relationship, to enable the patient to become aware of and remove such impediments. Since type differences or similarities, or both, that are not valued create difficulties, it is important in analytic work that analysts be aware of their own types, so that they do not unintentionally create additional impediments in the individuation process.

THE STRUCTURE OF TYPOLOGY

Jung's empirical research in the phenomenology of the psyche led him to formulate a structural theory of character, in which he posited two energic attitudes called *extraversion* and *introversion,* and four functions termed *sensation* and *intuition* (the irrational functions of perception) and *thinking* and *feeling* (the rational functions of judgment).

When the extraverted attitude predominates, energy is directed outward toward objects, people, and the environment. Extraverted individuals are thus drawn to the external world, are responsive to it, and seek out stimulation from the environment. The introverted attitude, by contrast, directs energy inward, toward the subject. Introverted individuals attend to ideas, concepts, impressions, feelings, or images. In contrast to extraverts, introverts find their orientation in their inner lives.

Jung called sensation and intuition, as modes of perception, *irrational*; they function as receivers of information, but do not evaluate, interpret, or judge that information. The sensation function operates through the five senses, so that the focus is on concrete, tangible reality in the present. Individuals in whose character structure sensation predominates tend to distrust any information or ideas for which they cannot clearly perceive a concrete basis; they demand that things "make sense." Intuition, on the other hand, is defined by Jung as perception via the unconscious, which means that a person using intuition can arrive at a perception without being aware of the concrete basis for that perception. Thus, intuitive individuals make leaps from the concrete present to future possibilities or to abstract and complex interrelationships of events, whereas sensation types focus their energy on the here-and-now.

The judging functions, thinking and feeling, are both *rational;* they are methods of evaluating the information acquired through one or the other mode of perception. Evaluation using thinking entails an impersonal, logical appraisal of perceptions. The criteria for the thinking person are whether or not something is valid or invalid, reasonable or unreasonable. Individuals who favor thinking appear to others as impersonal, analytical, and lacking in concern for others. Feeling judgments, by contrast, have as their criteria not whether something is valid or invalid, but whether it is important or unimportant, valuable or worthless, particularly in relation to human values and how they affect people. The difference between a thinking and feeling judgment is aptly characterized by the following statement, typical of a feeling judgment: There are many things in the world that are valid but unimportant, and many things in the world that are invalid yet extremely important. Thus a feeling judgment is made with concern not for logic and truth, but for consequences, especially those that benefit or cause misfortune for humanity. The term *feeling* is used here in the technical sense, indicating a value judgment rather than an emotion. For example, a thinking type may become very emotional about a mathematical equation, just as a feeling type may become very emotional about a personal value.

The attitudes and functions are bipolar in nature. Each member of a pair is in essential opposition to the other, and therefore they cannot be used simultaneously. Thus, for example, the use of sensation rules out the concurrent use of intuition, and one cannot have an introverted and an extraverted attitude at the same time. The attitudes and functions can, however, be exercised consecutively. Thus, one can arrive at a logical conclusion about something, and then consider its good and bad consequences before deciding what action to take.

Central to character is the habitual and favored use of one of the attitudes, as well as of one of the irrational and rational functions. When extraversion is the habitual mode, we speak of an *extraverted type;* when introversion is favored, an *introverted type.* Whichever of the four functions is best developed and differentiated is considered to be the *dominant function.* If the dominant function is one of the irrational pair—that is, sensation or intuition—the *auxiliary function*, which is less developed and differentiated than the dominant, will be one of the rational pair, thinking or feeling. If the dominant is a rational function, the auxiliary will be an irrational function, sensation or intuition. The *inferior function* is the opposite of the dominant function, and takes the opposite attitude. For example, if the dominant function is extraverted thinking, the inferior will be introverted feeling.

Finally, an important and often undervalued aspect of the functions is their relative differentiation or strength. The differentiation and strength of thinking as an auxiliary or secondary function is less than it would be if it were a dominant function. Similarly, tertiary thinking is less differentiated than auxiliary thinking. When it is an inferior function, it is even less differentiated. Such is the case for the other functions as well. For example, if a person with auxiliary thinking wants someone to review a paper he or she has written, it would be advisable for the person to seek out a colleague who has thinking as his or her dominant function, for the colleague's thinking would be superior in this context.

Furthermore, use of a function that is not dominant requires a greater expenditure of energy than does use of the dominant function. For example, a young woman whose dominant function was intuition was working as a laboratory technician. Her hours on the job were devoted to careful examination of specimens under a microscope. She became chronically fatigued and irritable. Medical examination revealed no physical cause for her symptoms. Her fatigue was probably due in large part to the fact that she was required to use her inferior sensation. Because it was considerably less differentiated than her dominant intuition, she had to expend a greater amount of energy in order to perform competently.

ASSESSMENT OF TYPE

Analysis begins with an appraisal of the patient's consciousness and character, for, as Jung has stated, character is at the core of any neurosis.[1] Determination of type enables the analyst to do the following: establish an operational appraisal of the patient's individual response to his or her inner and outer world, and determine the locus of the patient's failures at adaptation; (2) assess the strength and differentiation of the patient's conscious attitude and functions; (3) determine through the patient's family history the type mix of the family, noting the strengths and failures at adaptation; (4) infer the inferior function that "possesses" the patient in times of stress, after determining the dominant function and attitude; and (5) have available "an essential means for determining the 'personal equation' of the practicing psychologist, who, armed with an exact knowledge of his differentiated and inferior functions, can avoid many serious blunders in dealing with his patients" (Jung 1936, p. 555).

Through the initial interviews, the patient's dominant and auxiliary functions can be assessed to determine their degree of consciousness and differentiation. If the person is a *perceptive type,* with sensation or intuition dominant, the development of his or her functions can be determined within the context of the interview by noting the kinds of information to which a response is made. Does the person present global statements, or are facts and incidents presented in the form of dialogues between people? If the patient is a *judging type,* are conclusions supported by objective facts or internal states? Are value judgments—statements of like-dislike, meaningful-meaningless—expressed in the interview? Does the patient appear to be logical, valuing reasonableness? Does he or she appear cold or warm, personable or impersonal in presentation?

Attitude type can also be inferred during early interviews. Does the person exercise his or her preferred functions in the outer environment, focusing on people and activities? Or is there more of an emphasis on inner reflection and subjective factors? It has been clinically observed that tempo of speech may also be a sign of type. Perceptive types, especially intuitives, both extraverts and introverts, have a quick tempo in their speech, often to the point that their speech appears pressured. By comparison, judging types are slower in tempo, the introverted thinker being perhaps the slowest of all.

These signs may be considered the melody in which the content or lyrics of the interview are communicated. Occupation and its enjoyment or the lack thereof can be an indicator of type. A laboratory technician and an entrepreneur require quite different character structures. The laboratory technician would most likely be an introverted sensation type, whereas the entrepreneur might be an extraverted intuitive (Williams).

The familial history of the patient can often reveal the typological mix within the family, and this may shed light on the patient's responses to interpersonal typological differences that have influenced, if not caused, the neurotic behavior. For example, a young woman who was an extraverted intuitive thinking type reported that when she was a child her parents, especially her father, were very perturbed with her ineptitude in performing simple arithmetic calculations and similar tasks. Private tutors were employed to help correct her errant and at times recalcitrant ways. The child was the only daughter in a family of four. Her younger brother showed an easy mastery of the mysteries of arithmetic calculations and rote memory. Upon inquiry, it was surmised that both parents and her younger brother were sensation types. The father was an engineer and the brother is now an accountant. From her description, the other three members of the family were introverts as well. Being an extraverted intuitive, with sensation as her inferior function, she failed to live up to her father's standards. Her general untidiness was also an aberration from family values. Consequently, this young woman developed a negative father complex that interfered with her relationships with men and with figures of authority. Her unkemptness was exacerbated as an adult, so that it became a mark of her individuality. Had she been characterologically an introverted sensation type, the development of the negative father complex would probably not have occurred. This is the sense of what Jung meant when he stated that character is more basic to a neurosis than the complex.

Another patient, a man in his early forties, initiated analysis with the statement: "I am a forty-two-year-old failure." He proved to be an introverted feeling type. His occupational failures consisted of work in sales and business. His familial structure indicated that his father was an extraverted thinking type who professionally and personally had the reputation of an autocrat. His mother was most likely an extraverted intuitive who was socially quite visible, with active memberships in civic and social groups. His older brother, also an extravert, was a successful corporate lawyer and prominent as a functionary in local politics. Unfortunately, this self-proclaimed failure was a characterological deviant within his family. He recalled that as a child he was chided and then ridiculed for his preference for and joy in reading. He was encouraged, at times forcefully, to be more active in school affairs. His character was demeaned and invalidated. He had fantasies of getting a doctorate in English literature or becoming a professional in human services. Had he been extraverted, or had his parents appreciated his character differences, his life would have taken a different path, and his complexes would perhaps have been less damaging to his adaptation.

Once the attitude type and dominant function are assessed, determination can be made of the inferior function, which provides clues into the nature of the personal unconscious. Alternatively, if the patient is experiencing acute stress and is therefore in the grip of the inferior function, the dominant function can be inferred. Thus, if the conscious attitude has the attributes of strength, reliability, stability, and adaptiveness, the inferior (dissociated) function will be characterized by weakness, instability, capriciousness, and maladaptiveness. These archaic attributes of the inferior function would erupt when an *abaissement du niveau mental* (lowering of consciousness) occurs, whether it is due to stress, fatigue, or illness. When some form of stress is chronic, the influence of the inferior function can take on a pervasive aspect, affecting many parts of the person's life. Depending upon the nature of the dominant and inferior functions, the person may be plagued by doubt, obsessional fears, hypochondriacal concerns, general unhappiness, and even acting-out behavior.

For example, a young man in his early thirties gave as his presenting complaint his concern about his obsessional fears of his wife's infidelity. He had a concomitant fear of being unmasculine. He was an introverted feeling type; his extraverted thinking, which had a negative valence, had erupted into notions that he was a cuckold, not a man. Ensuing sessions revealed that he was plagued with fears about his competence both personally and professionally; he was despairing and unhappy.

His history revealed that his father was most likely a thinking type who frequently criticized him, although from the father's thinking point of view he may have simply been providing his son with constructive criticism. For an introverted feeling type, however, the father's criticism was devastating. His adolescence was aimed at seeking approval from his father; he became an excellent student and later obtained a professional degree. However, he was plagued with feelings that he was a sham. He married a woman whom he regarded as a "free spirit," a woman who was fun-loving, enjoyed people, and eschewed the trappings of middle-class life. He attempted to be an extravert and in his social milieu strove to affirm his manhood with hard living and drinking. As the stress of maintaining a one-sided existence continued, he became the chronic victim of his inferior function. He was obsessed with fears that others, his wife included, viewed him as incompetent and inadequate. His inferior function erupted in the form, "I am stupid, incompetent, etc." His father complex added this affective statement: "I am regarded as stupid, just as my father regarded me as stupid."

In this example, the type differences between father and son were such that the father's type fed into and activated his son's inferior function. For an introverted thinking type, by contrast, the inferior function would emerge in the form, "I am unloved or disliked." Depending on history, the complex would be given its specificity by the further affect, "You do not love me, as my father/mother did not love me." Both the introverted feeling and thinking types would seek approval, but of different kinds. At first glance, both might appear paranoid, when, in fact, this might not be the case. An extraverted intuitive's inferior function, introverted sensation, appears as obsessional ideation, in which negative facts or instances in the present confirm similar negative occurrences in the person's history. Under stress, extraverted intuitives may also be plagued with hypochondriacal concerns regarding their body sensations. Thus, the determination of a patient's dominant attitude and function can suggest important hypotheses about the compensatory aspect of the patient's unconscious. In this sense, typology can become, if not the "royal road to the unconscious," then at least a "royal signpost" on the way to understanding the unconscious.

TYPOLOGY AND THE ANALYTIC RELATIONSHIP

The conscious relationship between analyst and patient is very important in Jungian analysis; the analyst does not serve the role of a blank screen, but interacts with the patient in an atmosphere of trust. An analyst who has an awareness of his own dominant, auxiliary, and inferior functions, and who is skilled and experienced in typology, has at his disposal an important tool in establishing "rapport." The importance of rapport is often cited, but rarely is information given about how to achieve it. With a practical knowledge of typology, the analyst can "rotate" his typology in order to obtain a congruence with the patient's type. The effect is to establish and communicate an understanding and appreciation of the patient's view of himself and his world—in short, to speak the language of the patient and establish a good conscious relationship.

For example, extraverts of any function type direct their energies upon the object. Consequently, relative to the introvert, they require more interaction with the analyst and more feedback. For the introvert, a quiet, receptive atmosphere is important. Thus, in the beginning of analysis, a knowledge of type can serve to reduce the tension between analyst and patient and help to establish rapport. This becomes especially important when the patient is severely neurotic.

Maintaining rapport is important in establishing trust, which may take different forms for different types. The following examples are generalizations based on clinically observed differences among the types. Sensation types tend to appreciate and respect an analyst who is able to remember the details of the patient's life and the content of previous sessions, and who has an ability to appraise life events pragmatically. In so doing, the analyst does not go beyond what the patient presents. Intuitives, by contrast, respond to the analyst's ability to bring disparate information into a new and complex whole, or to present the patient with a new way of viewing him- or herself. The analyst must be insightful. Thinking types respect an analyst who is at least as "smart" as they. The analyst should be able to maintain a logical rhetoric and come to logical conclusions. A thinking type patient once described his feeling therapist: "He's a nice guy, very helpful, but he's not very bright.'' Feeling types often want to be appreciated and approved as being unique.

The above examples illustrate some of the ways a good conscious relationship can be established and maintained, so that the patient may later be able to tolerate and accept increased tension within the analytic session. The importance of typological awareness throughout the entire course of analysis is emphasized by Meier, who states:

> We must assume that whatever the analyst's system looks like to begin with, he should always be able to change altogether every single moment of the process, so as to produce a tension of opposites with regard to the system of the analysant [sic], so that something really can happen and things can really be constellated and the problem can really come to a head. (P. 282)

Thus, for Meier, it is through shifts in the analyst's attitude and function type that growth is induced.

The clinical judgment of when to use the intrusion of intuition, or the pragmatic fact-finding of sensation, or the impersonal probing of thinking, or the empathic understanding of feeling, in addition to attending to the patient's inner and outer life, is at the core of analytic technique. Any rotation can serve to increase or decrease the dynamic tension not only between the analyst and patient, but within the patient as well, leading to the integration, and at times the painful emergence, of the unconscious.

Whereas tension between the analyst and patient can be decreased by the analyst's rotating his or her typology so that congruence with the patient is achieved, tension can be increased by the analyst's taking a compensatory or polar function in opposition to the patient. For example, a schizoid young man who was very intuitive but lacking in judgment spent many of his waking hours writing in his journal and recording his dreams. These activities served his avoidance of living in the world. The initial sessions supported his flights of imagination, and new insights were given to him. After many months, the clinical judgment was to direct his concern to the mundane, sensation aspects of living. He was asked such simple questions as, ''What did you have for breakfast this morning?'' These questions served to create some tension in order to direct his attention to his inferior function. The ensuing sessions gradually became more focused on his lack of friends, his fear of people, and his career choices.

When tension should be increased is a clinical judgment, but Jung has provided a general rule:

> The general rule should be that the weakness of the conscious attitude is proportional to the strength of the resistance. When, therefore, there are strong

resistances, the conscious rapport with the patient must be carefully watched, and—in certain cases—his conscious attitude must be supported to such a degree that, in view of later developments, one would be bound to charge oneself with the grossest inconsistency. That is inevitable, because one can never be too sure that the weak state of the patient's conscious mind will prove equal to the subsequent assault of the unconscious. In fact, one must go on supporting his conscious (or, as Freud thinks, "repressive") attitude until the patient can let the "repressed" contents rise up spontaneously. Should there by any chance be a latent psychosis which cannot be detected beforehand, the cautious procedure may prevent the devastating invasion of the unconscious or at least catch it in time. (1946, p. 186)

Jung's general rule contains an admonition against unduly evoking the contents of the unconscious. The conscious relationship can be attended to when the analyst can rotate his typological compass so that it is congruent with the patient. This is especially important when the evaluative initial sessions show any signs of a borderline condition or severe character disorder.

Neglect in accommodating one's own typology to that of the patient can lead to several unfortunate consequences when strong resistances are present. On the one hand, a strong transference can be induced; and on the other, an assault of unconscious contents can erupt. Both of these may have a deleterious effect upon the progress of analysis.

Awareness of typology is also important with regard to the phenomenon of transference. The concept of transference has several meanings and uses in analytical psychology. Transference is used, at times, almost as a synonym for the analytic relationship, for it is through the relationship with the analyst that the individuation process occurs. As such, transference is the sum total of conscious attitudes towards the analyst, the myriad unconscious projections that have occurred during the analysis, and the unconscious relationship that has existed between analyst and patient.

A more specific use of the term *transference* involves a projection onto the analyst of a significant person in the patient's past. An important attribute of this phenomenon is that the projection thereby defines the relationship with the analyst. An example will illustrate this. In the case presented above of the introverted feeling man who was in the grip of his inferior function, the man's analytic work was essentially a repetition of his attempt to be the dutiful son to his father. In analysis, he became the "good analytic patient"; he brought in dreams, responded well to interpretations, began reading Jungian literature, and even expressed an interest in becoming a Jungian analyst. Just as he had sought his father's approval, he was seeking the analyst's approval. This projection onto the analyst defined his relationship to the analyst and thus was a transference in the second meaning of the term.

Such transference projections must be distinguished from other kinds of projections that occur in analytic work. Jung stated that the unconscious first appears in projected form. Thus the analyst may be the recipient of many projections during the course of an analysis, as precursors to emerging unconscious contents, which, in fact, do not define the relationship. For example, a patient who has difficulty expressing anger may project his or her anger onto the analyst, so that the analyst is viewed as being angry with the patient. This projection may not define the relationship, and to regard it as a transference would be an error. Continued focus on the so-called transference might only serve to inhibit further projections—that is, other contents of the unconscious.

Extraverted perceptive type analysts—those with sensation or intuition as their superior function—are more likely to view projections of their patients as indicators of the relationship—that is, as a transference projection. If this occurs, and if the analyst focuses on the reductive-regressive aspect of the patient's projections, the ground is laid for an analysis in which the patient gets stuck in a regressive complex. This would only occur if a projection is taken to be the sole relationship with the analyst. An error of this kind is frequent with analysts-in-training, especially those who have a reductive bias.

Thus, for the extraverted analyst, the transference may be an impediment resulting from failure to recognize the analyst's own typological concerns, as well as a misjudgment of the nature and pervasiveness of the patient's projections, especially if the patient happens to be an introvert. The error of the introverted analyst would be a failure to recognize a transference projection, so that his or her conduct would result in a blind concern for the patient's inner life, without noting that the crucible of integration for the patient is the relationship, albeit distorted, with the analyst.

Another error in not following Jung's general rule is that the premature evocation of unconscious contents, through the creation of tension, may result in an eruption of these contents, resulting in acting out or psychosis. Here the emphasis on eliciting the unconscious may have unfortunate results. As Jung has stated:

> It would be a dangerous prejudice to imagine that analysis of the unconscious is the one and only panacea which should therefore be employed in every case. It is rather like a surgical operation and we should only resort to the knife when other methods have failed. So long as it does not obtrude itself the unconscious is best left alone. (1946, p. 186)

TYPOLOGY AND COUPLES

In 1931, Jung indicated the importance of typology in marriage when he stated:

> My profession has always obliged me to take account of the peculiarities of individuals, and the special circumstance that in the course of I don't know how many years I have had to treat innumerable married couples and have been faced with the task of making husband and wife plausible to each other has emphasized the need to establish certain average truths. How many times, for instance, have I not had to say: "Look here, your wife has a very active nature, and it cannot be expected that her whole life should centre on house-keeping." (1931, pp. 532–33)

One's *Weltanschauung* is embedded in one's typology and character, and it therefore contains attributes that are not, by virtue of their subtlety, available in the fashionable and faddist publications of popular psychology. Whereas an emphasis on similarity is implicit in many of the current panaceas for marriage, typology, especially in the analysis of couples, underlines the understanding and tolerance of differences. For most of us, our typology is the standard by which everyone else is judged. Just as systems and theories of psychology are often partially a reflection of the author's psychology, so too one's expectations of one's spouse or partner are a projection of one's own psychology. It is usually the failure to recognize and appreciate a partner's typological differences that leads to the misunderstanding of a spouse.

Failure to appreciate differences can lead to serious consequences. This is aptly illustrated by a couple whose presenting complaint was that their disagreements, though in retrospect trivial, resulted in battles that at times led to reciprocal physical abuse. The husband complained that his wife was disorganized, untidy, and, worst of all, illogical. His wife perceived her husband to be organized to the point of rigidity, hypercritical, and rarely complimentary toward her. These perceptions of each other were the ground for their projections of malevolent motives. When they came into therapy, they were at an impasse and desperate. Within the framework of their respective typologies, each judged the other by a personal, though unarticulated, standard.

The husband's typological character was extraverted thinking with sensation, and the wife's was extraverted intuition with feeling. Each appeared fairly well developed and although complexes were evident from their respective histories, it was judged that the primary difficulty between them was a consequence of their failure to respect each other's differences. In the ensuing sessions, their differences were presented. They were both very receptive, and affirmed each other; after ten hours, the sessions were terminated with a mutual recognition that their relationship was much improved. About six months later, the wife called to say that the marriage was good and their relationship enhanced.

The above example is a somewhat dramatic instance of the ameliorative effects of an awareness of typology in marriage. Often the debilitating effects are more subtle, especially when the marital type-mix difficulties are intertwined with personal neurosis.

An example of this is a couple who misperceived each other's typology. The man and woman were both in their late thirties and had been married for nineteen years. They entered treatment because the wife had announced her intention of getting a divorce. Both stated that they doubted whether they loved each other when they married. They agreed that their early marriage was, for both of them, a way to escape from oppressive family situations dominated by rigid and demanding fathers. The Myers-Briggs Type Indicator was administered, and they were asked to fill it out for themselves, as well as the way each thought the other would answer it. The results would enable them to have an objective indicator of the accuracy of their mutual perceptions. The husband turned out to be an extraverted feeling type with intuition as auxiliary function, and the wife an extraverted sensation type with thinking as auxiliary function. Each perceived the other, however, as an introverted sensation type with thinking. This type matched the typology of both of their fathers! This result indicated that they projected onto each other their negative father complexes. Their projections prevented them from having any awareness of each other's true natures. It was no wonder that they were literally strangers and felt lonely and inhibited. The couple mutually agreed to a divorce and subsequently entered individual analysis.

Awareness and practical knowledge of the analyst's own typology is perhaps more essential for the couples therapist because of the addition of a third person, the partner. In couples therapy, the analyst must rotate his or her typological compass twice, so that there can be effective communication with both partners. To speak the language of only one partner means that the analyst runs the risk of being regarded as the champion of one of them. By effectively speaking both languages, the analyst can also perform the role of translator for the couple, which is an essential role for the analyst.

CONCLUSION

Typology is important throughout the duration of analysis. It is especially important in the second half of life, when the striving for wholeness and balance becomes a major task. Whether analysands are directed towards the outer extraverted world or the inner introverted world, they must obtain a balance between the two that does not violate their basic characterological trends. Psychological typology as a psychology of consciousness and character can also be a psychology of individuation, insofar as strengthening ego-consciousness where it is needed can allow the ego to permit unconscious contents to emerge purposively, leading to increased integration and wholeness. Individuation is not necessarily a goal, but a process through which the individual integrates the contents of the unconscious, leading to adaptation to the world and to the Self, in a highly individual manner. The psychology of types becomes the means through which the unconscious is manifested.

Finally, the importance of typology for the process of analysis is aptly stated by Jung:

> But one thing I must confess: I would not for anything dispense with this compass on my psychological voyages of discovery. This is not merely for the obvious, all-too-human reason that everyone is in love with his own ideas. I value type theory for the objective reason that it provides a system of comparison and orientation which makes possible something that has long been lacking, a critical psychology. (1931, p. 541)

NOTE

1. Two major instruments for assessing type are the Gray-Wheelwright Test, available through the C. G. Jung Institute of San Francisco, Inc., and the Myers-Briggs Type Indicator, published by Consulting Psychologists Press. Both these instruments reflect "classical" Jungian typological theory. A third, recently developed instrument is the Singer-Loomis Inventory of Personality. Rather than reflect classical theory as presented in this paper, it uses Jung's type concept within the tradition of trait theory, according to which scales can independently co-vary. This instrument is in its early validation-research phase, and therefore its clinical use lacks the research foundation that the other instruments have. For information on the Singer-Loomis inventory, contact the Psychology Department, Wayne State University.

REFERENCES

Bradway, K., and Detloff, W. 1975. Psychological types and their relationship to the practice of analytical psychology. *Professional Reports*. San Francisco: C. G. Jung Institute of San Francisco.

Fordham, M. 1972. Note on psychological types. *Journal of Analytical Psychology* 17/2:111–15.

Franz, M.-L. von, and Hillman, J. 1971. *Lectures on Jung's typology*. New York: Spring Publications.

Groesbeck, C. J. 1976. Psychological types in the analysis of the transference. *Professional Reports*. San Francisco: C. G. Jung Institute of San Francisco.

Jung, C. G. 1923. Psychological types. In *Collected works,* vol. 6, pp. 510–23. Princeton: Princeton University Press, 1971.

––––––. 1931. A psychological theory of types. In *Collected works,* vol. 6, pp. 524–41. Princeton: Princeton University Press, 1971.

––––––. 1936. Psychological typology. In *Collected works,* vol. 6, pp. 542–55. Princeton: Princeton University Press, 1971.

––––––. 1946. Psychology of the transference. In *Collected works,* vol. 16, pp. 163–321. Princeton: Princeton University Press, 1954.

––––––. 1961. *Memories, dreams, reflections*. New York: Pantheon.

McCaulley, M. H. 1974. Psychological types and career preferences. Paper presented at Career Development of Physicians, A Colloquium, at the meeting of the Association of American Medical Colleges, Washington, D.C.

––––––. 1976. *Sample set of type tables*. Gainesville, Fla.: Center for Applications of Psychological Type.

––––––. 1977. *The Myers longitudinal study*. Monograph II, U.S. Department of Health, Education and Welfare, Health Resources Administration, Contract No. 231–76–0051. Gainesville, Fla.: Center for Applications of Psychological Type.

Meier, C. A. 1974. Psychological types and individuation: a plea for a more scientific approach in Jungian psychology. In *The analytic process,* ed. J. B. Wheelwright, pp. 276–89. New York: Putnam.

Myers, I. B. 1980. *Gifts differing*. Palo Alto: Consulting Psychologists Press.

Plaut, A. 1970. "What do you actually do?" Problems in communicating. *Journal of Analytical Psychology* 15/1:13–22.

––––––. 1972. Analytical psychologists and psychological types: comment on replies to survey. *Journal of Analytical Psychology* 17:137–49.

Quenk, A. T. 1978. Psychological types: the auxiliary function and the analytic process. Unpublished thesis, Inter-Regional Society of Jungian Analysts.

van der Hoop, J. H. 1970. *Character and the unconscious*. College Park, Md.: McGrath.

Wheelwright, J. 1972. Critical notice: *Psychological Types, Collected works* 6 (C. G. Jung). *Journal of Analytical Psychology* 17:212–14.

Williams, M. R. 1976. The relationships among the personality types, job satisfactions, and job specialties of a selected group of medical technologists. Ph.D. dissertation, Florida State University. *Dissertation Abstracts International* 37:3342B.

[9]

ACTIVE IMAGINATION IN PRACTICE

Janet Dallett

A long-range goal of Jungian analysis is the establishment of a consistent and continuing dialogue with the unconscious, a living relationship that does not come to an end simply because an analyst no longer mediates it. Work with dreams and with manifestations of the unconscious that come up in everyday life tends gradually to set this relationship in motion. A patient may not think of what he or she is doing as a dialogue until, at some point, it becomes necessary to make it conscious and to continue it in a more effortful and responsible way. Then the process called active imagination can be indispensable. Active imagination is the most direct way of relating to the unconscious, although its very directness brings unique complications and difficulties.

It is neither necessary nor desirable for everyone who works analytically to reach the depth of connection to the unconscious at which active imagination is required. These pages should not be used as a "how-to-do-it" course, for deep involvement with the unconscious requires guidance from an analyst. Like all relationships, this one is entirely individual and follows its own, partly irrational direction. From a certain perspective, everything I write here will be completely incorrect. That is because anyone who reads it too rigidly, without taking into account that the opposite of any statement is always also true, will do violence to the individuality of the psyche.

Janet Dallett, Ph.D., a poet, practices Jungian analysis in Los Angeles, California. A member of the Society of Jungian Analysts of Southern California, she is a former director of training of the C. G. Jung Institute of Los Angeles and has taught in its analyst training program. A graduate of Kalamazoo College, she received her Ph.D. in psychology from UCLA and the diploma in analytical psychology from the C. G. Jung Institute of Los Angeles. She edited *The Dream: The Vision of the Night,* by Max Zeller, and has published several papers, including "Theories of Dream Function" and "Looking for Jung: The Man in the Myth."

A relationship with the unconscious as it expresses itself in active imagination is a symbolic process. That is, it will forever remain at least partly irrational. A living symbol expresses something that is not fully conscious, nor able yet to become fully conscious. As soon as a symbol is completely understood, it dies and becomes a sign. Something else can be substituted for a sign, as its equivalent. If, for instance, I say that a rose means love, and if the word love fully expresses the meaning of a rose, then the rose is a sign rather than a symbol.

The images of the unconscious are not signs; their nature cannot be expressed by a simple equation like $A = B$. They are true symbols, deeply rooted in the irrational ground of being. To relate to them, it is necessary to accept paradoxes unacceptable to the rational mind and be ready to set aside all the rules at any moment. It takes a certain instinct and experience to know when to do that or when, on the contrary, to insist upon the rules. That is why an analyst's help is well advised when active imagination is undertaken.

Rather than "how to do it," I want to give the flavor of this kind of work and bring out some questions that my use of this process has raised. I do not intend to answer my own questions so much as to circumambulate them—that is, to wander among them in order to illuminate some facets of each. If the reader were to find my exposition too clear, it would be disappointing. That would give the illusion of understanding, whereas real understanding can only be attained through emotional involvement and through grappling with the thing itself. As Jung has pointed out in *Aion,* the difference between merely intellectual and real understanding "amounts roughly to that between a severe illness which one reads about in a text-book and the real illness which one has" (1951, p. 33). Bearing this in mind, let us cautiously approach the subject.

WHAT IS ACTIVE IMAGINATION?

In one of the very few papers published about active imagination, Hannah writes:

> Whenever man has tried to come to terms with an invisible, supernatural and apparently eternal reality . . . he has instinctively evolved . . . some form of meditation or dialogue that corresponds in a greater or lesser degree with what Jung has called active imagination. (1953, p. 38)

Her treatment of the subject in spiritual terms resonates with my own sense that active imagination is most meaningfully defined as a *dialogue with the gods.* If this definition were understood fully, with all the meaning implicit in it, no more would have to be said. The rest of this chapter can be seen simply as an amplification of it.

There are some immediate implications of seeing active imagination as a dialogue with the gods. First of all, there must be at least two partici- pants, separate from each other. One of the participants in active imagi- nation is the conscious ego, rooted in external reality. It is impossible to relate to the world of imagination if you are simply caught and floating in it. Jung emphasizes this point in his autobiography, writing about a period when he was deeply immersed in the unconscious:

> Particularly at this time, when I was working on the fantasies, I needed a point of support in "this world," and I may say that my family and my profes- sional work were that to me. It was most essential for me to have a normal life in the real world as a counterpoise to that strange inner world. My family and my profession remained the base to which I could always return, assuring me that I was an actually existing, ordinary person. (1961, p. 189)

In addition to the ego, whose importance is indisputable, the other partners in the dialogue of active imagination consist of the gods as they express themselves through the psyche. Gods include also what religion has traditionally called devils. It is possible to say that the other parties in the dialogue are the archetypes of the collective unconscious. That sounds more scientific than "the gods." It would be quite correct then to go on to define "collective unconscious" and "archetypes" as I did in a paper pub- lished some years ago:

> The collective unconscious constitutes all those aspects of the psyche that are basic to the human condition, those psychological characteristics that be- long to us by virtue of our biological structure. It is part of being human that most of us are born with two legs, two arms, a cerebral cortex, and the capac- ity to walk upright. These and all other aspects of our biology have certain psychological consequences and lead to typical modes of functioning and pat- terns of behavior that are reflected in the affects and images of the collective unconscious. Underlying the images are nuclei of energy which give impulse and direction to thought, perception, and at the instinctual level, behavior. These energic nuclei are called archetypes, which are [quoting Jung] "the nec- essary *a priori* determinants of all psychic processes. Just as his instincts com- pel man to a specifically human mode of existence, so the archetypes force his way of perception and apprehension into specifically human patterns." (P. 412)

This statement demonstrates clearly why I have come to prefer talking about the gods! It is all too easy to relate to the term *archetype* intellec- tually, without any sense of what that means as an experience. The word *gods* gives an emotional jolt, conveying something of the reality of a dia- logue with the unconscious. The gods (and demons) are autonomous fac- tors, rooted in a different reality (the reality of spirit, not necessarily the material world), that can express themselves through the imagination. As William Blake has said, imagination is the "divine body" in all of us.

Once the partners in the dialogue have been identified, the definition next implies that in active imagination there is a *relationship* between them. Some of the same considerations apply to this inner relationship as to relationships between people in the outside world. For example, full regard for the other's separateness and idiosyncracies is essential. In the inner relationship, the unconscious must be permitted to be what it is, and not forced into ego or external reality notions of how it ought to behave. At the same time, the ego must hold firmly to its own reality. This is as difficult in inner as in outer relationships.

Another similarity to outer relationships is that many aspects of the inner relationship are personal and private, not to be discussed indiscriminately with others. It can be very important to discover when to keep to yourself what is going on between you and yourself, and when to talk about it.

Furthermore, if you make a promise, it is as much a violation to break it in the inner world as in the outer; if you try to control or to have power over your partner, inner or outer, it is no longer possible to relate; and an inner relationship can no more be forced to obey rational considerations than can an outer one.

The word *active* in active imagination is crucial. As in any relationship, if one partner (the ego) does not participate actively, the other (the unconscious) simply fills the vacuum by running on its own way, unchecked and unchanged, possibly taking over completely. Then there is no relationship. This is the case, for example, when a person is passively obsessed by fantasies.

There are many examples in literature and drama of the kind of relationship to divinity that expresses itself in active imagination. One of my favorites has long been the scenes in *Fiddler on the Roof* in which the father, Tevya, carries on down-to-earth, no-nonsense discussions with God. These provide a most authentic example of the actively participating relationship between God and man.

More recently, the film *Close Encounters of the Third Kind* impressively expresses both the emotional intensity of active imagination when it is fully engaged and some very specific aspects of it. In this film, visitors from another planet fill their human contacts with a sense of urgent necessity to paint or sculpt a specific image, a picture of the mountain where they land on earth and can be met. Others experience the same compelling drive to work out the mathematical-musical-color language that the aliens speak. These means of expression constitute the only way in which communication with the "others" can be established. Similarly, the voice of the unconscious in the dialogue of active imagination often pushes to be given form in some quite specific way, whether it be sculpture, painting, dance, music, or some other medium besides words.

One last direct implication of our definition of active imagination is the requirement for consciousness of the power and vastness of one of the partners in the dialogue, the gods, with whom a relationship is not to be undertaken lightly. Caution and religious respect for the other is a prerequisite of this encounter.

THE COMPONENTS OF ACTIVE IMAGINATION

Von Franz has spoken about four steps into which the process of active imagination can be divided (p. 88). These steps offer a conceptually convenient way to break up the process in order to look at it more closely, although it is unlikely that anyone ever actually does active imagination in such an orderly fashion.

1. The first step is what von Franz calls "stopping the mad mind." The thoughts of ego-consciousness must first be set aside in order to give the unconscious a chance to enter.
2. The unconscious begins to come in, usually in the form of fantasies, images, or emotions. These are written down or given some other external form at this point.
3. The ego reacts. There is a confrontation with the unconscious material that has come up.
4. Conclusions are drawn and put to work in life.

The First Step

In *The Visions Seminars,* Jung speaks of the condition of the human being that is the starting point for active imagination:

> [You have] two different standpoints inside. One is your conscious standpoint. You say: I like this. But then a voice says: I don't like it. Make that experiment, try it, it is a sort of dialectical method of finding out about your partner, your own differences. Choose a somewhat controversial object, a modern art exhibition, or the standpoint of one's wife, or of one's husband, and ask yourself what you think or feel about it. . . . It is not necessary that anybody listens to this experiment, you can do it for yourself in the quiet of your room. Say: I think so and so—and then listen, just cock your ears to hear whether you hear another opinion. Instantly up it comes: Oh no, not at all, I think otherwise. . . . This possibility of a dialectical method or a contradictory process is given by the fact that you never can get rid of the other point of view . . . which simply expresses . . . the opposites which are always in

yourself. We hate it, but it is nevertheless true. You cannot get rid of the opposites by saying the other thing does not exist. It does exist, it exists first of all in yourself, you are split from the beginning, because the hermaphroditic image of man . . . was split when you were born. You are outside, but inside you still have the recollection of the two, . . . this side and that, the opposites. (1976, p. 498)

To permit that other point of view to come up, most people must find a way to set aside the critical, judging mode of the ego. At this stage the ego must simply observe, uncritically, what comes up, remaining alert but not filtering out anything. Something akin to the alpha state of unfocused attention is cultivated. About this Jung comments:

We must be able to let things happen in the psyche. . . . Consciousness is forever interfering, helping, correcting, and negating, never leaving the psychic processes to grow in peace. . . . To begin with, the task consists solely in observing objectively how a fragment of fantasy develops. (1929, p. 16)

I once had a dream that expresses nicely what not to do. In the dream I planted some young trees, and right away, the next day, got worried that not enough nutrients would reach their roots. So I dug up the trees in order to see how the roots were doing! That is the kind of thing the ego does to interfere with the very growth process it intends to nurture.

A number of things can facilitate the first step of active imagination and help the interfering ego to stand aside. Naturally occurring situations of unfocused attention like tooth brushing, shaving, washing dishes, ironing, or jogging can be used to good advantage. Long before a patient is ready to engage the process fully, he or she can carry around a small notebook or tape recorder to catch the fragments of fantasy that impinge upon consciousness. The first thing is simply to notice the psyche's activity.

A ritual can help one to get into active imagination. When I first began to do active imagination, I would light a candle, turn down the lights, and sit in a particular way in a particular chair. Now, after many years, the act of sitting down at a typewriter is sufficient ritual.

Often a dream ends at a moment when it might easily be continued in imagination, or there may be a particularly powerful dream image to relate to. Then, getting back into the imagery and mood of the dream facilitates the beginning of active imagination.

Finally, working with graphic or plastic material rather than words may help reduce ego interference. The hands can do what they want without help from the head.

What is really required at this first stage is the attitude of the child at play. The hardest thing for adults to learn about play is to take it seriously.

They usually feel they can indulge in play only after having taken care of serious business. Yet play is a serious matter for the child, who continually creates, destroys, and re-creates new worlds. Recognizing the importance of this kind of play is essential for active imagination, as well as for many other endeavors.

When, at the age of thirty-five, I returned to graduate school, I dreamed that I had to go to my childhood home and bring back with me a set of children's building blocks. At the time I did not fully appreciate how vital it was going to be to recapture the playful-serious creative perspective symbolized by the blocks, to help my spirit survive the deadly earnest, overrational atmosphere of graduate school.

Jung's meeting with the deeper reaches of the psyche began when he realized that he would have to play with stones, like a little child:

> . . . as a grown man it seemed impossible to me that I should be able to bridge the distance from the present back to my eleventh year. Yet if I wanted to re-establish contact with that period, I had no choice but to return to it and take up once more that child's life with his childish games. This moment was a turning point in my fate, but I gave in only after endless resistances and with a sense of resignation. For it was a painfully humiliating experience to realize that there was nothing to be done except play childish games.
>
> Nevertheless, I began accumulating suitable stones, gathering them partly from the lake shore and partly from the water. And I started building: cottages, a castle, a whole village. (1961, p. 174)

Much later, after he had integrated this experience, Jung wrote: "The creative activity of imagination frees man from his bondage to the 'nothing but' and *raises him to the status of one who plays"* (1931, p. 46; italics added). This is the status that must be gained before active imagination can begin, with the play that so often initiates the process.

The Second Step

As the voice of the unconscious emerges, it is given expression. Whether in writing or some other medium, it is essential to give outer form to the material. Otherwise it is too easy simply not to hear (or see) what passes through, to be just a little dishonest about what the voice really said, or what the image really was, or how you truly felt at that moment. There is nothing more damaging to the psyche than self-deception. You can deceive your neighbor, your spouse, even your analyst, and get away with it; but when you deceive yourself, you simply become the victim of your unacknowledged inferiorities.

Active imagination is defined by the relationship between ego and unconscious, not by the particular medium employed. The unconscious can be expressed in an infinite number of ways, including poetry, stories, direct dialogue, verbal description of images, clay, painting, dance, photographs, movies, music, and collage. Doing these things does not in itself constitute active imagination. The ego must react to what has been expressed, draw conclusions, and put them to work in life before the process can be said to be complete.

Deciding what medium to use is an individual matter, and I can offer only a few hints from my experience. In general, whatever is comfortable or feels right at a given moment is fine. If someone is skilled in one medium (for example, a painter or a writer), it is usually better to begin active imagination in a different medium. Skill too easily serves ego control rather than expression of the unconscious. As Freud observed, mistakes usually express the unconscious and interfere with the ego's intentions. Skill interferes with mistakes! On the other hand, someone who is particularly afraid of the unconscious may be able to ease into the work by using a medium over which some personal control is possible.

Clay has the advantage of being down-to-earth and far from the head. It makes the process very concrete and real. Writing, on the other hand, may facilitate more cognitive understanding.

In my own active imagination, the medium I use depends partly on the state of the content. When I am in an emotional state, or when the content is deeply unconscious and newly emergent, or both, I prefer some graphic or plastic material. When I have come closer to understanding a message from the unconscious, writing works best for me.

The Third Step

Once the voice of the unconscious has been given form, the ego can confront it. It is only from this moment that we can legitimately speak of the process as active imagination, and it is only now that the personality can be deeply changed by it. Now is the time for the ego's questions, reservations, doubts, and judgments, as well as its emotions and its understanding. Now the ego must react to what has come.

At this stage it becomes essential to come to know the reality of the psyche. In its responses, the ego must recognize the inner event as being just as real as any outer event, even though it is in a different realm. If, in outer reality, a strange man appears and says, "Follow me," it is not a good idea to do so without knowing something about him; it is no wiser in inner reality. If a rattlesnake bites someone in the outer world, pretending it did not happen will not undo it. The same is true in the inner world. Inner events have real effects.

The figures of the unconscious express the reality of their own realm, but they are often unaware of human reality until the ego informs them about it. The ego has to confront the unconscious with the limitations and conditions of its human world. Once, when considerably greater inner demands were being made upon me than I had the strength to meet, I was startled to hear my analyst say, "Sometimes you have to say no to the Self." It was a revelation to discover that I could talk back and inform the inner figures about my limitations. It was still more startling to find that when I did talk back, enormously important changes came out of the clash between the yes and the no of the conflict.

Here, at the third step, it is necessary to take an ethical attitude toward what comes from the unconscious. It is difficult to move from watching the images like a movie to responding emotionally and making judgments about the contents. Part of the change is that now it is necessary to try to understand what the contents mean, in addition to appreciating their form.

Jung gives an interesting example of a passive patient who failed to move into an ethical attitude in a piece of active imagination:

One of my patients had the following fantasy: *He sees his fiancée running down the road towards the river. It is winter, and the river is frozen. She runs out on the ice, and he follows her. She goes right out, and then the ice breaks, a dark fissure appears, and he is afraid she is going to jump in. And this is what happens: she jumps into the crack and he watches her sadly.*

This fragment, although torn out of its context, clearly shows the attitude of the conscious mind: it perceives and passively endures, the fantasy-image is merely seen and felt, it is two-dimensional, as it were, because he himself is not sufficiently involved. Therefore the fantasy remains a flat image, concrete and agitating perhaps, but unreal, like a dream. This unreality comes from the fact that he himself is not playing an active part. If the fantasy happened in reality, he would not be at a loss for some means to prevent his fiancée from committing suicide. He could, for instance, easily overtake her and restrain her bodily from jumping into the crack. . . . The fact that he remains passive in the fantasy merely expresses his attitude to the activity of the unconscious in general: he is fascinated and stupefied by it. (1928, pp. 211–12)

The individual's ethical participation in active imagination protects him from inflation by the archetypes of the collective unconscious—that is, from identifying with the gods. Without the commitment of confrontation, it is all too easy to become seized by the power principle, to use the unconscious for ego purposes rather than forming a relationship with it. This can have terrible consequences, as the following example shows.

A young professional writer had for many months repressed the painful emotions connected with a tragedy in his life. Suddenly one day he began to write, day and night, and in the space of a few weeks had written a complete novel consisting of unconscious fantasies that played about the experience he had not faced. He became completely possessed by this material, but even now, in writing about it, he did not face it. It took him over and poured out of him, but it was as if he were not there.

He then had a dream clearly indicating that he must acknowledge and experience the painful emotion connected with what he had written. Still he steadfastly turned away from it. Instead of meeting his pain, he became identified with the book and possessed by fantasies of the wealth and power he expected to result from its publication. His inflation culminated in a long and destructive psychotic episode that might have been avoided had he been able to hear and act upon the dream's message.

The Fourth Step

Once the ego has confronted the voice of the unconscious, the final step— drawing conclusions and putting them to work in life—requires full acceptance of the responsibility for oneself. It means that one can no longer live unconsciously, as if one did not know what one has learned from working with the unconscious. What began as the play of a child leads now to the most profound ethical consequences in terms of how an individual life is lived. This is the hardest part, and the step that is too often not taken.

People often ask how a dialogue with images and emotions of the unconscious can lead to an ethical demand in life. A simple illustration follows. Because this did happen simply and rapidly, it is easier to describe than most pieces of active imagination, which are usually slower, deeper, and harder to grasp.

At a certain time in my life I had become profoundly exhausted, physically and emotionally, from doing more than my introverted nature could tolerate. I was at the end of my rope but did not know it. In this condition I made a collage. Getting to the first step of active imagination was no problem. I was already walking around in a half-conscious state that permitted unconscious contents to come through easily. From a large selection of pictures I rapidly chose some that appealed to a certain spot in my stomach, and pasted them to cardboard without thinking about what I was doing. Then I stood back and looked at it.

The central image was a young woman asleep in a hammock. The surrounding images were predominantly sad, dark, primitive women, children, animals, and people in introverted, prayerful, and self-reflective postures. As I looked at the collage, I descended into profound sadness and realized for the first time that I was exhausted. I saw that I had been ignoring my instincts, my femininity, my inner children, and my introverted nature. I knew that I should take time off from work and other obligations. Then the protests of the ego came in: I couldn't possibly do that, I was needed by my patients, I had many commitments for which I felt indispensable, and so on.

The depth at which these images touched me convinced me that I truly needed time in which to renew myself, but I did not take it. Within a few days I had developed a severe cold, which forced me to spend several days in bed, meeting the obligation to myself that I had not met voluntarily. In this case I had had the insight to draw the right ethical conclusion, but had failed to carry it out. Then life took care of the fourth step for me.

WHAT ACTIVE IMAGINATION IS NOT

A number of processes are often confused with active imagination, but are in fact different in important respects. To understand fully what active imagination is requires differentiating it from what it is not.

Although it can be seen as a form of *prayer,* active imagination differs significantly from most traditional approaches to prayer. In the latter, the ego is instructed to give up its own requirements in submission to the gods. That is, the ideal of prayer is acceptance of whatever the gods say, without the "yes but's" of ego-consciousness and human reality. In active imagination, on the other hand, the "yes but's" are expressed fully.

In traditional prayer, then, the ego is valued less than the gods. This valuation can be dangerous because it fails to recognize the dark side of the gods, the demonic. Religious dogma is a response to and recognition of the power of darkness and the dangers that come from giving up ego considerations. Dogma serves as a protection, attributing anything too disruptive to demons and thereby repudiating it. In active imagination, everything that comes up must be heard. There is no dogma to say that one thing is right and another wrong. The reaction of the ego then becomes a most crucial part of the relationship.

Active imagination can be seen as a form of *meditation,* too, but it also differs from traditional meditation. Traditional forms of meditation usually prescribe the outcome (for example, nirvana, or the union of Shiva and Shakti), and the path for arriving at that outcome is predetermined. The spontaneous contents of the psyche are seen as nuisances at best, to be gotten out of the way in order to proceed along the path. In active imagination, these spontaneous contents are themselves the path. Whereas in prayer the ego is asked to step aside, in meditation it is the unconscious that is asked to get out of the way, while the ego (or, more accurately, dogma) exerts a kind of control over the process. From the perspective of active imagination, traditional forms of meditation undervalue the role of the unconscious as a partner in the dialogue.

Active imagination is not *guided fantasy*. Guided fantasy offers particular images for the person to use or routes upon which to proceed, or both, and in this respect it is more like traditional meditation. In guided fantasy, the analyst's images are added to the patient's inner equation, muddying the relationship between ego and unconscious. This increases the patient's ever-present temptation to put him- or herself totally in the analyst's hands, and give up personal responsibility. It is easy for the analyst then to be seduced into what von Franz calls "the pride of the shaman"—that is, taking on the position of power that has been offered and accepting the whole responsibility for another person.

In learning to do active imagination, one needs guidance from an analyst in the process, but not in the content. At best, the analyst helps patients to open up to their own images and to respond to them in a way that is consistent with their own human reality.

Active imagination is different from Gestalt ways of working with dreams. For example, one Gestalt technique is to try to "get into the skin" of a dream image in order to understand the image in the internal psychology of the dreamer. Active imagination stresses that one must remain clearly anchored and in one's own skin, precisely not identifying with other figures. While pieces of the psyche can only speak through the voice or hand of the individual, still the point is to differentiate from inner figures rather than to identify with them. Only when differentiation has occurred is it possible to relate to the archetypes in a meaningful way.

Active imagination is not necessarily *art,* although some art is active imagination. That is, some artists grow and change through a confrontation with their work, but many do not, nor is this a necessary function of art.

Hannah speaks of active imagination as a "creative function" (1953). All people have this creative possibility if they can tap it, but not everyone is a potential artist. It can be a serious mistake to confuse the products of active imagination with art, for several reasons.

First, to be seduced into thinking that active imagination is art when it is not can lead one away from one's real tasks in life. In his autobiography, Jung speaks of a moment when he encountered this temptation, offered by the woman within him, the anima:

> When I was writing down these fantasies, I once asked myself, "What am I really doing? Certainly this has nothing to do with science. But then what is it?" Whereupon a voice within me said, "It is art." . . .

. . . I caught her and said, "No, it is not art! On the contrary, it is nature," and prepared myself for an argument. . . .

. . . If I had taken these fantasies of the unconscious as art, they would have carried no more conviction than visual perceptions, as if I were watching a movie. I would have felt no moral obligation toward them. The anima might then have easily seduced me into believing that I was a misunderstood artist, and that my so-called artistic nature gave me the right to neglect reality. . . . Thus the insinuations of the anima, the mouthpiece of the unconscious, can utterly destroy a man. In the final analysis the decisive factor is always consciousness, which can understand the manifestations of the unconscious and take up a position toward them. (1961, pp. 185–87)

Further, if active imagination is mistaken for art, the product of work on the unconscious may become more highly valued than the process. Then the meaning and value of active imagination easily become lost. Finally, if active imagination and art are confused with one another, the individual who has no particular artistic talent will think there is no point in doing active imagination.

The question remains whether there is any connection at all between active imagination and the work of an artist. A number of factors enter into the making of an artist. At a minimum he or she must have talent, developed skills, and a factor I think of as the inner necessity to give expression to certain contents. It is as if the gods insist that a talent be put to work. The artist carries something for all of us, giving public form to emergent changes in the collective unconscious. Active imagination gives private form to similar changes that are often, however, more idiosyncratically personal than the artist's expressions.

There are people whom I have come to think of as creative personalities. They may or may not be artists, but are characterized by an absolute necessity to give form to inner images. Expression is therapeutic for them even if they never engage the complete process of dialogue that is active imagination. If they do not express, they become ill: physically, emotionally, or both. The unexpressed images act like a poison in them. These people usually find themselves crucified in a conflict between the requirements of everyday outer reality and the inner demands of the spirit. Classically this is seen as the artist's conflict, as shown, for example, in the film *The Turning Point*. It is also manifest in the frequently expressed fear on the part of artists that they will prostitute themselves if they create to sell, rather than out of the purity of their vision. However, the same conflict occurs in the creative person who is not an artist, illustrating the fact that creative vision is usually incompatible with existing collective values. Creativity brings images of new gods that challenge or destroy the old, while an established collective necessarily holds to the old gods. It is easy

to glorify creativity, perhaps without sufficient appreciation of its destruc-
tiveness to existing values.

Dangers of Active Imagination

The enormous power of the unconscious can be devastatingly destructive
if it is released naïvely. Dreams express this power in such images as
atomic bombs, tidal waves, or earthquakes. Since, in its first step, active
imagination encourages reduced ego control and issues an uncritical invitation to the unconscious, it is potentially more dangerous than working
with the images that come spontaneously through dreams. As Hannah
points out (1953), active imagination is not dangerous when it is done
right, but it is hard to do right and easy to do wrong. For people who find
it especially easy to do, this very ease may be a sign that they are doing it
in a way that leaves them dangerously vulnerable.

There are a number of things the guiding analyst watches for in order
to ground the adventurer in the psychic wilderness. Most danger spots
involve loss of a firm standpoint in human reality. These things do happen.
For the most part, it makes no sense to try to prevent them, but only to
recognize them in order to bring in the antidote of consciousness before
they reach serious proportions. For example, psychological inflation is an
inevitable consequence of contact with an archetype. The only way to
avoid inflation would be to stay away from archetypes, an absurd notion
even in the usual, unanalyzed life. However, it is possible to become conscious of the symptoms of an inflated state, to suffer it, and to learn how
to get out of it at the first opportunity.

The most serious danger of this work is the possibility of becoming
overwhelmed by the unconscious. Sometimes unconscious contents take
over completely, in a psychotic interval. It is most likely to happen when
no way is available for separating from, confronting, and working with
emergent contents—that is, when the person does not know how to do
active imagination. A number of patients have first come to me in this
condition, having fallen into the unconscious by using drugs, for example,
or by practicing some form of meditation. They have been able to come
out of it when given active imagination as a tool for relating to the overwhelming contents. However, it is possible for even the most experienced
journeyer to venture further into the depths than he or she is able to handle
and to become overwhelmed.

A second danger lies in ego ambition and power. In extreme form, the
attempt to exploit the power of the unconscious for ego purposes is black

magic. How nice it is to discover a personal atomic reactor in one's own back yard, with the possibility of using that power to control others! This attitude fails to recognize the unconscious as a separate, autonomous "other," a divine power. The unconscious responds badly to such ego-mania and in one way or another may take its revenge. The least damaging outcome of a power attitude is that the ego may try to push development faster than the psyche is ready to go, and it simply does not work. More seriously, I have seen people become terribly destructive, even fall into paranoid psychosis, when driven by a desire to dominate the unconscious. The only real protection from the dark side of the gods is a religious attitude—that is, full recognition and respect for the gods' autonomy and power.

A third danger is that emergent fantasies may be acted out in a literal way when their meaning is actually symbolic. To relate seriously to a fantasy of doing something is not necessarily the same as doing it. A sophisticated sense of paradox is required to take the unconscious fully seriously, as something totally real in its own realm, and at the same time not to take it literally or act it out. To live out a fantasy concretely in the human realm, failing to recognize that it may concern spiritual (symbolic) reality, can on occasion be a disastrous error. Charles Manson is one of the best examples I know of someone who received and acted out unconscious contents concretely and uncritically. He said, "God told me to kill those people," and he did it without ever questioning whether what he heard might have a symbolic meaning.

On the other hand, things may come up that do need to be lived concretely in the outside world and not be taken only as inner symbolic contents. Discerning the difference is rarely simple, and only becomes possible at all in a careful confrontation between an emergent content and human reality, judgment, and ethical values.

Another serious danger lies in the potential for inflation by, or identification with, or possession by, unconscious contents. An instance of this kind of inflation is identifying with the product when a content has been given a beautiful form. It is important to realize that such products come largely from a divine creative power within, shaped with the ego's help. Most real artists and writers know this instinctively. Robert Louis Stevenson, for example, spoke of the little men inside his head who did his writing. Identifying with creative products is a little like identifying with one's children, without fully appreciating that, after birth, they are separate and have their own identity.

Hitler was someone who became totally identified with contents of the unconscious. He became a living myth. Someone in such an inflated state can be extremely charismatic, as he was, because the content that possesses the person has the magnetic attractiveness of divinity.

The fact that unpleasant, unattractive contents are as common as beautiful ones makes it easier to disidentify. It is tempting to lay claim to the beautiful poem one has written, but easy to think that the black witch who reared her ugly head is either accidental or came from somewhere else. An ounce of honesty will restore the humbling insight that both arose from the same source.

Active imagination does not create dangerous contents, although by focusing on them, it can give them added power. The contents exist in any case, and they have an effect whether or not they are seen. Often it is more dangerous to remain unconscious of them than to meet them in active imagination.

Valid Resistances and "Lousy Excuses"

Resistance to doing active imagination should always be taken seriously, particularly when there is a feeling of real fear. The healthy personality's natural protection against dangerous aspects of the unconscious is resistance, and it should not be pushed aside lightly. However, the person who really needs the process must eventually overcome what Jung is said to have called "the damnedest lousy excuses" for not engaging in active imagination. After many years of doing active imagination regularly, I still suffer from the form of resistance that generates lousy excuses. It is sometimes hard to distinguish between valid resistance and a lousy excuse. The same words can express either: "I have no time"; "I have no talent"; "I'm just making it up."

Valid resistances stem from at least two possible sources: There may be some perception of the dangers involved, including a fear of acting out if the fantasies are permitted to become conscious. It may take a lot of work to become aware of the fact that admitting the existence of a fantasy is not the same as doing the imagined thing.

A second source of valid resistance is the sense that something may be destroyed that one is not yet ready to live without. When the new is created the old must give way. Something new emerging from the unconscious may be perceived as demonic because everything outside the conscious perspective threatens its existence. Active imagination inevitably moves people out of their old boundaries, and they may or may not be ready for it.

Lousy excuses stem from different sources. Probably most often they come from the realization that active imagination is incredibly hard work; or there may be some misunderstanding about what it is, or a mistaken attitude or expectation about it. For example, maybe there is the idea that it is art, or that what comes out should be beautiful; or perhaps there is the attitude that it is "nothing but" play, for which there is no time. Possibly there is insufficient realization that the process is what counts, not the product; or maybe there is too much identification with what comes out, a failure to realize the "otherness" of the unconscious. Then, of course, anything embarrassing or unacceptable to consciousness has to be shut out.

In most people, there exists a healthy separation between consciousness and the unconscious. Tension comes up quite naturally at the prospect of reducing the separation. This very tension is what permits a true confrontation between conscious and unconscious perspectives, rather than simply drowning in the unconscious, but it does generate lousy excuses that have to be overcome.

When I first began doing active imagination, my own experience with resistance was instructive. I was under a considerable amount of pressure to get into it at that time, but would sit unproductively in front of my typewriter for long periods of time. I could not do it. One day as I sat there, I suddenly saw an image of another "me" sit down at my left. She was talking and talking, so I listened and wrote down what she was saying. She had a great deal to say indeed, about how absurd this whole business of active imagination was. She *was* the resistance, personified as a very rational side of myself that wanted nothing to do with this most nonrational process. Until that moment I had been identical with her, with no possibility of hearing what she was saying, confronting it, and going beyond it. I had to work hard to come to terms with her before I could go further.

WHY DO IT?

So much has been said by now about how hard it is to do active imagination right, and how dangerous it can be when it is done wrong, that the reader could be forgiven for asking, "Why bother? What's the point in doing active imagination at all?" There are some excellent reasons.

Active imagination contains the very essence of psychological transformation. The relationship between conscious and unconscious is what leads to a new center and synthesis of the personality. Work with dreams also brings about change, but the more profound changes that can occur later in life and in analysis usually require the additional help of active imagination.

In the long run, active imagination brings psychological independence of the analyst. Dreams always fall directly into the dreamer's blind spots, making them singularly difficult to understand without help. Active imagination provides an Archimedean point from which to work on oneself directly. Until then the perspective of the unconscious is mediated by the analyst, but with active imagination it is met face-to-face, bringing a new autonomy. Jung said that in the use of active imagination it becomes apparent whether someone truly wants to become independent through analysis (Hannah 1953).

Finally, active imagination reduces the psychological contamination of the environment to which we all contribute with unconscious projections. Through active imagination we become aware of our own images and begin to take responsibility for what belongs to us, rather than forcing spouses, children, neighbors, "the Blacks," "the Arabs," "the Jews," or "the WASPs" to carry fragments of the psyche that we fail to recognize as our own. Upon the possibility of all individuals bearing their own weight the very fate of humanity may depend.

REFERENCES

Dallett, J. 1973. Theories of dream function. *Psychological Bulletin* 79:408–16.
Davidson, D. 1966. Transference as a form of active imagination. *Journal of Analytical Psychology* 11/2:135–46.
Franz, M.-L. von. 1980. On active imagination. In *Methods of treatment in analytical psychology,* ed. I. F. Baker, pp. 88–99. Fellbach: Verlag Adolf Bonz.
Hannah, B. 1953. Some remarks on active imagination. *Spring* 1953:38–58.
_____. 1967. Active imagination. Paper read at a lecture series for the C. G. Jung Educational Center of Houston, Texas, September 1967, Zurich.
_____. 1981. *Encounters with the soul: active imagination as developed by C. G. Jung.* Santa Monica: Sigo Press.
Humbert, E. 1971. Active imagination: theory and practice. *Spring* 1971:101–14.
Jung, C. G. 1928. The relations between the ego and the unconscious. In *Collected works,* vol. 7, pp. 121–239. New York: Pantheon, 1953.
_____. 1929. Commentary on "The secret of the golden flower." In *Collected works,* vol. 13, pp. 1–56. Princeton: Princeton University Press, 1967.
_____. 1931. The aims of psychotherapy. In *Collected works,* vol. 16, pp. 36–52. New York: Pantheon, 1954.
_____. 1938–1940. *Modern psychology.* Vols. 3 and 4. Lectures at the Eidgenössische Technische Hochschule. Zurich: C. G. Jung Institute.
_____. 1944. The conjunction. In *Collected works,* vol. 14, pp. 457–553. New York: Pantheon, 1963.
_____. 1951. *Aion. Collected works,* vol. 9, part 2. New York: Pantheon, 1959.

_____. 1958. The transcendent function. In *Collected works,* vol. 8, pp. 67–91. New York: Pantheon, 1960.

_____. 1961. *Memories, dreams, reflections*. New York: Random House.

_____. 1976. *The visions seminars*. Vol. 2. Zurich: Spring Publications.

Plaut, A. 1966. Reflections about not being able to imagine. *Journal of Analytical Psychology* 11/2:113–33.

Watkins, M. M. 1977. *Waking dreams*. New York: Harper Colophon Books.

10

DANCE/MOVEMENT AND BODY EXPERIENCE IN ANALYSIS

Joan Chodorow

INTRODUCTION

THE role of dance/movement and body experience in Jungian thought and practice has remained largely undeveloped. This neglect is despite Jung's own relationship to his body and his love of dancing (Jaffé); his purposeful practice of specific movement exercises to calm and center himself (Jung 1961, p. 177); his references to body movement as a form of active imagination (1916, pp. 83–84; 1929, p. 23; 1935, p. 173; 1947, p. 202; 1976, p. 374); and his dance/movement interactions with certain patients (Fay 1977, p. 183; Van der Post 1977, pp. 57–58; 1979).

From his earliest work in the Burghölzli Psychiatric Clinic in Zurich, Jung was fascinated by the mysterious, perseverative gestures made by some of the most regressed patients (1961, pp. 124–25). Fay (1977) and Van der Post (1979) describe one of his cases. While working with a woman patient who had not been known to speak for many years, he noticed that she continually made certain odd movements with her hands and head. Going on instinct, he shut his eyes and repeated her movements in order to sense what she might be feeling. He then spoke out loud the first words that came to him. The woman responded immediately by saying,

Joan Chodorow, M.A., is a registered dance therapist and a licensed marriage, family, and child therapist, with a private practice in Santa Barbara, California. She serves as Dance Therapist, Psychiatric Unit, Santa Barbara Cottage Hospital, and as consultant to clinical and professional education programs in the United States and abroad. She is currently an analyst-in-training with the C. G. Jung Institute of Los Angeles. She received her dance/movement therapy training from Trudi Schoop and Mary Whitehouse, and is a past president of the American Dance Therapy Association. Her work is described in a documentary film entitled *Dance Therapy: The Power of Movement.*

"How did you know?" From that moment, a connection was made. The woman, previously regarded as incurable, was soon able to talk with him about her dreams and was ultimately able to be discharged. After this experience, he frequently relied on the body experience as a communicative bridge to reach patients who were completely withdrawn (Fay 1977, p. 183; Van der Post 1979).

In discussing ritual, Jung said that the gesture is the most archaic manifestation of culture and spiritual life. In the beginning was the symbolic gesture, not the word (von Franz 1978, p. 25; 1979). Although he had an instinctive grasp of movement as our primal means of expression and communication, Jung seems to have given it relatively little attention in the development of analytical psychology. But his comments on the body-mind relationship are of interest for our topic. Psyche and matter are "two different aspects of one and the same thing" (1947, p. 215). "The symbols of the self arise in the depths of the body . . ." (1940, p. 173). What we call psychic includes both physical and spiritual dimensions (1929, p. 51). Jung envisioned the analogy to the color spectrum with two poles, ranging from "the 'psychic infra-red,' the biological instinctual psyche" to "the 'psychic ultra-violet,' the archetype . . ." (1947, p. 215). As with much of his other work, he offered here a vast foundation from which others have built and may continue to build.

THE JUNGIAN LITERATURE

An awareness of the need for body experience and movement seems to be emerging in the Jungian literature. Kalff (1971) and Kreinheder address the importance of the body in the development of spiritual life. Sullwold presents a powerful case study of her analytical work with a child, which includes her description of the two of them becoming immersed in a dance the child taught her. Singer explores psychological androgyny as experienced and expressed through the dances of gods and humans. Hall differentiates between enacting and acting out and suggests dance as a form through which dreams may be enacted (pp. 331–43). Whitmont traces the historical tradition that produced our separation of body-mind and states that we can no longer operate with this schism: ". . . our emotions and problems are not merely in our souls, they are also in our bodies . . ." (p. 16). He explores the use of techniques involving body-level awareness and symbolic enactments to deepen and broaden the Jungian analytic process. Bosanquet suggests that "touching can, in certain circumstances, promote the analytical process and . . . prohibition of touching can delay or inhibit this'' (p. 42). She discusses the role of tactile contact in a case history, in early development, in regression, and in the larger society.

In his discussion of Pan/Echo, Lopez-Pedraza weaves wonderfully rich images around a therapy based on Echo-like reflections.

> The happening of Pan's echo in psychotherapy can constellate a true epiphany of Pan, which is one of the most vivid expressions of the psychotherapeutic relationship. Like cures like . . .   this is where the real symmetry happens, where the dance is, where the psychotherapy of Pan is. It is the expression of two bodies dancing in unison, a psychotherapy of the body. Are we in the psychoid realm of the psyche? Perhaps—but for sure we are in the realm where Pan appears in a psychotherapy within a sort of dance and through body movements, constellating the transference which belongs to him. (Pp. 84–85)

Hillman contrasts the medical/diagnostic approach to the body, which emphasizes definition, with the dialectical approach in analysis, which seeks amplification:

> Analysis too pays meticulous attention to the body. It observes and listens to the *body as experience*. The body is the vessel in which the transformation process takes place. The analyst knows that there are no lasting changes unless the body is affected. Emotion always tears at the body, and the light of consciousness requires the heat of emotion. These affections of the body during an analysis are symptomatic—not in the diagnostic sense—of stages in the dialectic. To take them diagnostically and treat them medically might harm the process. The outbreak of skin rashes, circulation disorders, internal organ complaints, aches and pains, all reflect new areas of body experience, which must often first come about in the guise of ailments until the body can be heard without having to scream for recognition. The analyst also pays the same careful attention to his own body, listening to cues in his own flesh to aid his dialectic. He tries to sense during the hour when he is tired and hungry, sexually excited, slumped in passivity, irritatedly fidgeting, or developing symptoms and illness. His body is a sounding board. This sensitivity is appropriate to the body as experience and fits the analytical work. (Pp. 145–46)

Woodman addresses issues of body and psyche throughout a beautifully written psychological study of obesity, anorexia nervosa, and the repressed feminine. She suggests dance as a powerful, practical way women may learn to listen to their bodies. It is terrifying for modern women

> to give themselves up to their emotions and the music and thus experience their own corresponding depths. . . . That leap into the unconscious, however, is the very link that could connect them to the life force. . . . This is not to recommend that women return to primal dance. Rather it is to suggest that the medium of music and creative dance is one of the surest ways to bring consciousness into the forgotten muscles. The dialogue with one's own body is a form of active imagination. (P. 113)

DANCE/MOVEMENT THERAPY

While the use of dance as a healing ritual goes back to the dawn of history, dance therapy is a relatively new profession. The American Dance Therapy Association, founded in 1966, defines dance therapy as the psychotherapeutic use of movement as a process that furthers the physical and psychic integration of an individual (Smallwood 1974*b*, p. 115). Dance therapy is based upon the assumption that mind and body are in constant reciprocal interaction (Schoop 1974, p. 44). It is built on psychological and physiological concepts, with an emphasis on the relationship of body and psyche. To use movement in therapy is to work directly with the most basic and primitive aspects of human experience. "Differences in theoretical conceptualizations may alter the style or technique, but the underlying movement theories are inclusive. Dance therapy offers an alternative method for working within the context of any systematized theory of human behavior" (Chaiklin, pp. 701–3).

One approach to dance therapy is based on Jungian psychology. Jungian movement therapy utilizes the technique of active imagination in movement to contact directly the individual's symbolic world (Bernstein 1980, p. 45). The therapist most often suggests a structure for self-directed movement that will enable discovery and development of themes from the unconscious. The movement process may produce an overall impression, a repetitive gesture, a certain body state or image that invites further exploration. Dreams, fantasies, life relationships and situations, early body memories, art, and issues of transference and countertransference may also be explored through movement. The experience and reflections on it may lead toward reduction of the theme to a personal early memory, or it may unfold toward mythological motifs and other universal experiences; often both occur. Whether the therapist watches or enters into the patient's enactments, the therapeutic relationship is the vital container. This aspect of the work is closely related to Kalff's description of the "free and sheltered space," the temenos, the receptive container that enables constellation of the self (1980, pp. 29–30).

Active imagination through movement offers an individual the opportunity to develop a deep, self-sensing awareness—an attitude of inner listening (cf. chapter by Dallett, above). Out of this receptive state, a movement response may emerge that is unplanned, authentic. Powerful images, feelings, and memories often arise out of a self-directed movement process and out of the relationship that contains it. The experiences of both mover and observer become intricately interwoven. With a deepening, mutual sense of involvement, mover and observer approach the synchronistic moment that transcends conscious-unconscious, inner-outer, self-other.

Verbalization is an important part of the process. There is usually some verbal expression and exchange before, after, and occasionally during the movement. Self-directed movement may go on for twenty to thirty minutes or more. At other times, a movement experience of a few minutes may serve as material for much subsequent reflection and processing, with or without words. Whether long or short in duration, movement is often followed by a period of natural stillness and continuing inner attentiveness. At this point, verbal exchange may be premature. Art expression is sometimes a helpful bridge, or poetic metaphor, or simply sitting together in silent, mutual reverberation. General rules are impractical for this transition because the links connecting movement/body experience, imagery, reflection, and verbal processes between two individuals are subtle and complex. At times, conscious psychological connections, insights, or interpretations are immediately available. At other times, it may take longer. Sometimes, a transformative experience simply cannot be expressed in words.

Rather than attempting to evoke specific behavioral change, this approach to dance therapy relies on the natural development of internally generated cues. It sees the body as the primary guide to the unconscious (Adler-Boettiger). This approach represents an important part of the dance therapy literature and its developing body of knowledge. It is a major focus of studies in some of the graduate-level training programs in dance therapy and an area of specialization for postgraduate studies.

MARY WHITEHOUSE

Mary Whitehouse made a profound contribution in the field of dance therapy, and her work offers rich resources to Jungian psychology. From her roots in dance, she was drawn into the experience of personal analysis with Hilde Kirsch in Los Angeles and into studies at the Jung Institute in Zurich. She became a major pioneer in the field of dance/movement therapy, linking her understanding of movement to the principles of depth psychology.

In a paper entitled "C. G. Jung and Dance Therapy" (1979), Whitehouse delineates two major principles—active imagination and polarity—and explores them from the perspective of dance/movement. Polarity is built into the physical body. We are organized via pairs of opposites, physically and psychologically. No human action can be accomplished without the operation of two sets of muscles, one contracting, one extending. As three-dimensional beings, each body axis contains a pair of opposites: up-down, left-right, backward-forward. One-sided psychological attitudes manifest themselves and can be explored at the body level. To sense consciously the simplest body movement is to experience an interrelationship of the opposites.

An example of this may be helpful. The following is meant to be read as if you are listening and responding to the voice of someone you trust. As you read, give some attention to the rhythm of your breathing. Give yourself time simply to notice the taking in and giving out of each breath cycle. Can you find not only inhalation and exhalation, but also the two subtle moments of reversal in-between? Feel how the inhalation pauses before it reverses itself. And feel that suspended space at the bottom of the breath cycle, where the wonder of renewal continually emerges out of emptiness. You may find that your body has shifted, or wants to shift, towards an alignment that allows air to come in and out more easily. Yawning may occur, or some other transition toward deepening the breath cycle. But give primary attention to awareness. Don't direct, don't inhibit, just let it happen. No praise, no blame. As you continue to attend to your breathing, notice where you feel it. Is it in your throat? Chest? Rib cage? Abdomen? Lower back? Pelvic floor? Do you feel the transformation from coolness to warmth as air enters and leaves you? Notice the tendency to grow, to take up more space with each inhalation. You may feel yourself lengthening (up-down), widening (left-right), deepening or bulging (front-back). There is usually shrinking with exhalation: shortening, narrowing, compressing. With each breath cycle, sense the fullness of your three-dimensionality, the length, width, and depth of your body. Sense how breath and body, spirit and matter, have effect upon each other. Then, when you finish reading this paragraph, close your eyes and let your body remember what you've just experienced.

Whitehouse describes another form of the polarity principle: "The core of the movement experience is the sensation of moving and being moved" (1958, p. 3). To feel "I am moving" is to be directed by the ego. To experience "I am moved" is to know the reality of the unconscious. "Ideally, both are present in the same instant . . . it is a moment of total awareness, the coming together of what I am doing and what is happening to me" (ibid., p. 7–8).

In a 1963 lecture, Whitehouse described the origin of movement as

a specific inner impulse having the quality of sensation. This impulse leads outward into space so that movement becomes visible as physical action. Following the inner sensation, allowing the impulse to take the form of physical action, is active imagination in movement, just as following the visual image is active imagination in fantasy. It is here that the most dramatic psychophysical connections are made available to consciousness. (P. 3)

Whitehouse encouraged people to embody their images from dreams and fantasies and emphasized the importance of staying with the image: '' 'When the image is truly connected in certain people then the movement is authentic. There is no padding of movement just for the sake of moving. There is an ability to stand the inner tension until the next image moves them. They don't simply dance around' '' (Frantz, p. 41).

SENSATION AND IMAGE

The question of whether internally generated movement cues are perceived by the mover as having the quality of sensation or image, or both, is most likely related to individual typology. Some people move with depth and authenticity but initially report either no images or only the constantly changing image of their own bodies and/or body parts in motion. It may be that such persons perceive the inner world predominantly through felt body sensations. They may have a powerful emotional response and even a sense of resolution, yet what it is about or where it comes from remains a mystery.

Those whose movements follow and reflect an ongoing stream of inner imagery often move through journeys of mythic proportion. These people usually make intuitive connections between the movement experience and their lives. Following the image alone may lead to some sense of its meaning, but without attention to the instinctive body (through felt body sensations), a movement experience lacks emotional spontaneity.

Although one's basic inclination may remain one or the other, self-directed movement tends to develop a relationship to both sensory and imaginal realms. When felt body sensation emerges as physical action, an image may appear that will give the movement meaning. Or, when an inner image emerges as physical action, the proprioceptive, kinesthetic experience may lead the mover toward connection to his or her instinctive body. The richest movement experiences seem to involve both sensation and image, fluctuating back and forth or occurring simultaneously.

EXPRESSION AND IMPRESSION

Dance/movement may fulfill two basic psychological objectives. We have been discussing how it arises out of an internal state; this is movement as a means of expression. Yet it may also be employed to produce emotion, to subdue it, or otherwise to have an effect upon internal states; this is movement as a means of impression. Although the latter is a behavioral approach to psychic change, it sometimes has a place in the individuation process. An example is Jung's occasional use of certain Yoga exercises to control an emotional response that might have otherwise been overwhelming (1961, p. 177).

Some of us are familiar with the planned and unplanned effects of rhythmic movement. It can take possession of groups. It can incite passions or subdue them. People can be motivated to work, disciplined to march into battle, energized, or lulled into passivity: ". . . rhythm is a classic device for impressing certain ideas or activities on the mind" (Jung 1912, pp. 154–55). Like any primal force, movement, particularly rhythmic movement, is powerful, and this power must be respected. It merits increasing recognition and study by those who are concerned with depth psychology.

An emphasis on movement as expression or movement as impression may produce two distinct ways of working. Attention to both, however, creates fluctuation and constant interchange. The movement process serves as a bridge between inner and outer worlds, each having an impact on the other. Expression and impression may form an ongoing two-way flow that builds toward new integration.

CASE ILLUSTRATION

Anna, a talented professional woman in her early thirties, has been in analysis for nearly three years. Although most of the process is verbal, she also utilizes movement, sandplay, and art expression. The following movement sequence will illustrate some of the concepts discussed in this article.

Recently married, Anna is struggling with the tension between her career and potential motherhood. In movement exploration, she finds two opposite attitudes. When her right side leads, she finds quick movements that emphasize extension, definition, firmness. When her left side leads, she finds sustained softness: her body gathers inward, her arms gently overlap and envelop a small unseen shape.

After enacting each of these attitudes, she pauses and begins to experience tension between the two. She attempts to find a way of moving that simultaneously embodies both sides, but instead she is gradually pulled apart into the shape of a twisted, hanging crucifix. As her right arm reaches outward, it is rigid and ineffective. Her left side is awkward as she attempts to encircle a baby with one arm. She begins to cry, yet is able to remain with the symbolic action.

Watching her, the therapist notices that her own body is becoming tense with restricted, shallow breathing. In Anna's pain, she recognizes her own. She now finds herself drawn into the enactment and reflects Anna's body state. Almost as if mirror images of each other, they hang together, twisted by a seemingly unresolvable tension. It is a timeless experience that moves through and beyond personal pain. They remain suspended together, moving only slightly, crying silently until both know that something has shifted. Although the issue is not resolved, there is a feeling of completion and relief. A struggle known by each of them individually, and by many women, has been seen and touched. A synchronistic moment has occurred. When they are ready to talk, the sense of mutuality remains strong. Rather than interpreting, they each tell about their own experience of the movement.

Here, simultaneous work on physical and psychological levels has activated the archetype of the wounded healer. As both analyst and patient contact a profound sense of individual and collective woundedness, the depth of their experience constellates the other side of the archetype. As the wound is felt and recognized, it brings some experience of healing.

Like many modern women, Anna expected herself to fulfill all professional and family needs simultaneously. Her ego's attempt to integrate the polarities, soft-firm, gather-extend, slow-quick—all in the same instant—was ineffective. In subsequent work, she discovered that sequential, fluctuating rhythms can encompass many pairs of opposites. Her life now includes both motherhood and career. As in the movement sequence, the struggle is not resolved, but there is some feeling of completion.

Conclusion

It seems that as the Jungian collective turns its attention to the neglected feminine and to the shadow, it cannot avoid attending to the third aspect of this rejected trinity: the body. Jung pointed the way to this in 1928 when he wrote:

> . . . if we can reconcile ourselves to the mysterious truth that the spirit is the life of the body seen from within, and the body is the outward manifestation of the life of the spirit—the two being really one—then we can understand why the striving to transcend the present level of consciousness must give the body its due. (Pp. 93–94)

REFERENCES

Adler-Boettiger, J. 1973. Integrity of body and psyche: some notes on work in process. In *What is dance therapy really?*, eds. B. F. Govine and J. C. Smallwood, pp. 42–53. Columbia, Md.: American Dance Therapy Association.

Bernstein, P. L. 1980. A mythologic quest: Jungian movement therapy with the psychosomatic client. *American Journal of Dance Therapy* 3/2:44–55.

———. 1981. *Theory and methods in dance-movement therapy*. 3rd ed. Dubuque, Iowa: Kendall/Hunt.

Bosanquet, C. 1970. Getting in touch. *Journal of Analytical Psychology* 15/1:42–58.

Chaiklin, S. 1975. Dance therapy. In *American handbook of psychiatry*, vol. 5, ed. S. Arieti, pp. 701–20. 2d ed. New York: Basic Books.

Chodorow, J. See Smallwood, J. C.

Fay, C. G. 1977. Movement and fantasy: a dance therapy model based on the psychology of Carl G. Jung. Master's thesis, Goddard College.

———. 1978. Five dance therapists whose life and work have been influenced by the psychology of C. G. Jung. *American Journal of Dance Therapy* 2/2:17–18.

Frantz, G. 1972. An approach to the center: an interview with Mary Whitehouse. *Psychological Perspectives* 3:37–46.

Franz, M.-L. von. 1978. *Interpretation of fairy tales*. Irving, Tex.: Spring Publications.

———. 1979. Comments made during a panel discussion, Panarion Conference, 21–27 July 1979, Los Angeles.

Guggenbühl-Craig, A. 1971. *Power in the helping professions*. New York: Spring Publications.

Hall, J. 1977. *Clinical uses of dreams: Jungian interpretations and enactments*. New York: Grune and Stratton.

Hayes, D. 1959. Consideration of the dance from a Jungian viewpoint. *Journal of Analytical Psychology* 4/2:169–81.

Hillman, J. 1976. *Suicide and the soul*. Zurich: Spring Publications.

Jaffé, A., ed. 1979. *C. G. Jung: word and image*. Princeton: Princeton University Press.

Jung, C. G. 1912. The transformation of libido. In *Collected works*, vol. 5, pp. 143–70. Princeton: Princeton University Press, 1956.

———. 1916. The transcendent function. In *Collected works*, vol. 8, pp. 67–91. 2d ed. Princeton: Princeton University Press, 1969.

———. 1928. The spiritual problem of modern man. In *Collected works*, vol. 10, pp. 74–94. 2d ed. Princeton: Princeton University Press, 1970.

———. 1929. Commentary on "The secret of the golden flower." In *Collected works*, vol. 13, pp. 1–56. Princeton: Princeton University Press, 1967.

———. 1935. The Tavistock lectures: on the theory and practice of analytical psychology. In *Collected works*, vol. 18, pp. 5–182. Princeton: Princeton University Press, 1976.

———. 1940. The psychology of the child archetype. In *Collected works*, vol. 9/part 1, pp. 151–81. 2d ed. Princeton: Princeton University Press, 1969.

_____. 1947. On the nature of the psyche. In *Collected works,* vol. 8, pp. 159–234. 2d ed. Princeton: Princeton University Press, 1969.

_____. 1961. *Memories, dreams, reflections.* New York: Random House, Vintage Books.

_____. 1976. *The visions seminars.* Vol. 2. New York: Spring Publications.

Kalff, D. 1971. Experiences with far eastern philosophers. In *The analytic process,* ed. J. B. Wheelwright, pp. 56–67. New York: Putnam.

_____. 1980. *Sandplay: a psychotherapeutic approach to the psyche.* Santa Monica: Sigo Press.

Kreinheder, A. 1979. The call to individuation. *Psychological Perspectives* 10/1: 58–65.

Lefco, H. 1974. *Dance therapy: narrative case histories of therapy sessions with six patients.* Chicago: Nelson Hall.

Lopez-Pedraza, R. 1977. *Hermes and his children.* Zurich: Spring Publications.

Mindell, A. 1982. *Dreambody.* Los Angeles: Sigo Press.

North, M. 1974. The language of bodily gesture. *Main Currents* 31:23–26.

Robbins, A., with contributors. 1980. *Expressive therapy.* New York: Human Sciences Press.

Schoop, T. 1974. *Won't you join the dance?* Palo Alto: National Press Books.

_____. 1978. A way of working. In *Motion and emotion symposium proceedings,* eds. B. Lynch and J. Nicholson, pp. 9–10. Los Angeles: Southern California Chapter of the American Dance Therapy Association.

Singer, J. 1976. *Androgyny.* Garden City, N.Y.: Anchor Press/Doubleday.

Smallwood, J. C. 1974a. Philosophy and methods of individual work. In *Dance therapy: focus on dance VII,* ed. K. Mason, pp. 24–26. Washington, D.C.: American Association for Health, Physical Education and Recreation.

_____. 1974b. Dance-movement therapy. In *Current psychiatric therapies,* ed. J. H. Masserman, vol. 14, pp. 115–21. New York: Grune and Stratton.

_____. 1978. Dance therapy and the transcendent function. *American Journal of Dance Therapy* 2/1:16–23.

Sullwold, E. 1971. Eagle eye. In *The well tended tree,* ed. H. Kirsch, pp. 235–52. New York: Putnam.

Van der Post, L. 1977. *Jung and the story of our time.* New York: Random House, Vintage Books.

_____. 1979. World unrest as a loss of meaning. C. G. Jung Cassette Library. Los Angeles: C. G. Jung Institute.

Whitehouse, M. 1958. The tao of the body. Paper presented to the Analytical Psychology Club of Los Angeles, 11 April 1958.

_____. 1963. Physical movement and personality. Paper presented to the Analytical Psychology Club of Los Angeles, May 1963.

_____. 1968. Introduction of videotape: individual dance and verbal therapy session. In *Workshop in dance therapy: its research potentials,* ed. B. Bird, pp. 20–22. New York: Committee on Research in Dance.

_____. 1977. The transference and dance therapy. *American Journal of Dance Therapy* 1/1:3–7.

_____. 1978a. Reflections on a metamorphosis. In *A well of living waters: festschrift for Hilde Kirsch,* ed. R. Head; R. E. Rothenberg; and D. Wesley. Los Angeles: C. G. Jung Institute.

————. 1978*b*. Conversation with Mary Whitehouse and Frieda Sherman. *American Journal of Dance Therapy* 2/2:3–4.

————. 1979. C. G. Jung and dance therapy. In *Eight theoretical approaches in dance-movement therapy*, ed. P. L. Bernstein, pp. 51–70. Dubuque, Iowa: Kendall/Hunt.

————. n.d. Creative expression in physical movement is language without words. Unpublished manuscript.

————. n.d. Some thoughts on movement, dance and the integration of the personality. Unpublished notes.

Whitmont, E. 1972. Body experience and psychological awareness. *Quadrant* 12:5–16.

Woodman, M. 1980. *The owl was a baker's daughter*. Toronto: Inner City Books.

11

SANDPLAY AND JUNGIAN ANALYSIS

Louis H. Stewart

I

S ANDPLAY is an activity in which a shallow tray of sand and a collection of miniature figures are used by patients, both adults and children, to play out fantasies in the sand. It is a natural addition to Jung's various techniques of active imagination (cf. chapter by Dallett, above), which foreshadowed today's art therapies. Sandplay clearly satisfies the fundamental criterion of permitting a person to elaborate and develop themes "by giving free rein to his fantasy" (Jung 1946, p. 202)—as, perhaps, guided fantasy and psychodrama do too. Still, for all the similarity to other techniques of active imagination, sandplay is set apart from them by virtue of its roots in the symbolic play of childhood.

From time immemorial, children have found in their native soil, and in the miniature objects in the world around them, the basic tools for the structuring of their imagination. Such play is timeless and universal. Just how essential and effective private rituals may be for the psychic equilibrium of an individual child is evident in this example from Jung's own childhood:

> My disunion with myself and uncertainty in the world at large led me to an action which at the time was quite incomprehensible to me. I had in those days a yellow, varnished pencil case of the kind commonly used by primary-school pupils, with a little lock and the customary ruler. At the end of this ruler I now carved a little manikin, about two inches long, with frock coat, top hat, and

Louis Stewart, Ph.D., is Professor of Psychology, San Francisco State University, and Clinical Professor of Medical Psychology, University of California, San Francisco; he maintains a private practice in Berkeley. A founding member and former president of the C. G. Jung Institute of San Francisco, he is currently a training analyst and lecturer at the Institute. Some recently published papers are "Kinship Libido: Towards an Archetype of the Family" (1976), "Sandplay Therapy: Jungian Technique" (1977), and "Play to Sandplay" (1981).

shiny black boots. I colored him black with ink, sawed him off the ruler, and put him in the pencil case, where I made him a little bed. I even made a coat for him out of a bit of wool. In the case I also placed a smooth, oblong blackish stone from the Rhine, which I painted with water colors to look as though it were divided into an upper and lower half, and had long carried around in my trouser pocket. This was *his* stone. All this was a great secret. Secretly I took the case to the forbidden attic at the top of the house . . . and hid it with great satisfaction on one of the beams under the roof—for no one must ever see it! . . . I felt safe, and the tormenting sense of being at odds with myself was gone. In all difficult situations, whenever I had done something wrong or my feelings had been hurt, or when my father's irritability or my mother's invalidism oppressed me, I thought of my carefully bedded-down and wrapped-up manikin and his smooth, prettily colored stone. From time to time—often at intervals of weeks—I secretly stole up to the attic when I could be certain that no one would see me. Then I clambered up on the beam, opened the case, and looked at my manikin and his stone. Each time I did this I placed in the case a little scroll of paper on which I had previously written something during school hours in a secret language of my own invention. The addition of a new scroll always had the character of a solemn ceremonial act. (1961, p. 21)

This type of play is clearly ritualistic and carries religious overtones. In such play, children are responding to the same dim impulses that have moved humanity from time immemorial to seek communication with the spirit world, the realm of the ancestors. Late in his life, Jung had this to say of his childhood ritual:

The meaning of these actions, or how I might explain them, never worried me. I contented myself with the feeling of newly won security, and was satisfied to possess something that no one knew and no one could get at. It was an inviolable secret which must never be betrayed, for the safety of my life depended on it. Why that was so I did not ask myself. It simply was so. . . .

The episode with the carved manikin formed the climax and the conclusion of my childhood. It lasted about a year. Thereafter I completely forgot the whole affair until I was thirty-five. Then this fragment of memory rose up again from the mists of childhood with pristine clarity. While I was engaged on the preliminary studies for my book *Wandlungen und Symbole der Libido* [now called *Symbols of Transformation*], I read about the cache of soul-stones near Arlesheim, and the Australian *churingas*. I suddenly discovered that I had a quite definite image of such a stone, though I had never seen any reproductions. It was oblong, blackish, and painted into an upper and lower half. This image was joined by that of the pencil box and the manikin. The manikin was a little cloaked god of the ancient world, a Telesphoros such as stands on the monuments of Asklepios and reads to him from a scroll. Along with this recollection there came to me, for the first time, the conviction that there are archaic psychic components which have entered the individual psyche without any direct line of tradition. (1961, pp. 22–23)

In considering examples like this, it is of great importance to realize that children, without question or doubt, simply proceed to play out their fantasies as they occur to them. While it is evident that there is a collaboration between the unconscious fantasy images and the child's developing ego-consciousness, it is also clear that the lead in the process is taken by the unconscious images. The question of the relationship between unconscious fantasy images and ego-consciousness in active imagination was something Jung pondered for many years. His most considered opinion on the process, as it takes place in adults, is expressed in the following quotation:

> . . . a dark impulse is the ultimate arbiter of the pattern, an unconscious *a priori* precipitates itself into plastic form, and one has no inkling that another person's consciousness is being guided by these same principles at the very point where one feels utterly exposed to the boundless subjective vagaries of chance. Over the whole procedure there seems to reign a dim foreknowledge not only of the pattern but of its meaning. Image and meaning are identical; and as the first takes shape, so the latter becomes clear. Actually, the pattern needs no interpretation: it portrays its own meaning. There are cases where I can let interpretation go as a therapeutic requirement. (1946, p. 204)

For the child, then, it would appear that symbolic play is a direct analogue to adult active imagination, and, as a spontaneous activity of the psyche, serves the purposes of "individuation" in childhood.

II

The metamorphosis of the child's private, symbolic play into a technique for use in Jungian analysis seems to have required that first it be domesticated to home and family. From thence it was removed to clinics for children, and finally to the offices of Jungian analysts working with adults. The first stage in this transition appears as a long-term consequence of the rediscovery of the child and of childhood following the awakening of humanist values during the Renaissance (de Mause). One of the tangible results of this renewed interest in the child was a burgeoning toy market, which, in the late nineteenth century, began to provide miniature figures particularly suited to play in a restricted area that could, nevertheless, represent a world. The incipient origins of sandplay can actually be traced to this development, through the fortuitous publication in 1911 of a book by H. G. Wells entitled *Floor Games,* in which the author describes the exciting games he played on the floor with his two young sons. This book influenced Margaret Lowenfeld and led directly to the creation of the World Technique, the immediate precursor of sandplay.

Wells wrote his book to edify other parents and to stimulate the manufacture of more adequate toys for children. But he had a more comprehensive agenda as well, one that was consistent with his general aims of goading humanity into creating more imaginative goals for future living: "Upon such a floor may be made an infinitude of imaginative games, not only keeping boys and girls happy for days together, but building up a framework of spacious and inspiring ideas for them for after life. The men of to-morrow will gain new strength from nursery floors" (p. 10).

Railing against the inadequacies of toy manufacturers, he wrote:

> We see rich people, rich people out of motor cars, rich people beyond the dreams of avarice, going into toyshops and buying these skimpy, sickly, ridiculous pseudo-boxes of bricklets, because they do not know what to ask for, and the toy shops are just the merciless mercenary enemies of youth and happiness—so far, that is, as bricks are concerned. Their unfortunate under-parented offspring mess about with these gifts, and don't make very much of them, and put them away; and you see their consequences in after life in the weakly-conceived villas and silly suburbs that people have built all round big cities. (Pp. 20–21)

When Wells talks of toys, we hear the same dissatisfactions that every sandplay enthusiast still experiences today:

> . . . we want civilians very badly. We found a box of German civilians once in a shop, the right size but rather heavy, and running to nearly five cents apiece (which is too dear), gentlemen in tweed suits carrying bags, a top-hatted gentleman, ladies in gray and white, two children, and a dog, and so on, but we have never been able to find any more. They do not seem to be made at all—will toy manufacturers please note? I write now as if I were Consul-General in Toyland, noting new opportunities for trade. Consequent upon this dearth, our little world suffers from an exaggerated curse of militarism, and even the grocer wears epaulettes. . . . (P. 25)

It is evident in the foregoing that Wells, in his twofold endorsement of the parental pleasures of imaginative play with children and the beneficial influences of such play on future citizens and their creations, had a well-formed idea of the role of play in childhood. Moreover, in his own enthusiasm for the games that he played with his sons, he showed that the spirit of play was alive and well in him. His unique little book, then, owes its existence to the lively presence of the "eternal child."

Lowenfeld read Wells' book in her youth, and it left a lasting impression. Many years later, when she turned from pediatrics to establish her Institute of Child Psychology in London, it occurred to her to provide such materials for the children. Then, in that natural and spontaneous way that reveals the quality of genius, she had some shallow trays built in which sand and water were made available. The children took it from there. Here they found ready at hand the basic tools of their creative life. Lowenfeld notes that the children in her clinic came to call the box of toys the "world," and soon they spontaneously combined the toys and the sand trays (1979, p. 4). It may be said in all seriousness that the technique was created by children. What was also required for it to become a vehicle of psychotherapy, however, was the lively presence of the "eternal child" in two creative adults.

From another perspective, it might appear that children did not so much create the World Technique, as Lowenfeld has suggested, but rather simply reintroduced the adults around them to their natural mode of symbolic play. As we noted earlier, children, quite on their own, have always played in this way, and with the very same materials.

It is apparent that we are in the purview of the archetype of the child, defined by Jung as the "childhood aspect of the collective psyche," whose function, Jung reminds us, is not confined to childhood but exists at all stages of life:

> The child motif represents not only something that existed in the distant past, but also something that exists *now:* that is to say it is not just a vestige but a system functioning in the present whose purpose is to compensate or correct, in a meaningful manner, the inevitable one-sidednesses and extravagances of the conscious mind. (1940, p. 162)

In an illuminating commentary on Jung's thesis, Hillman encourages recognition of the implication that, for the adult, "freedom comes from the imaginal redeemed from the amnesia of childhood" (p. 46). In the resolution of his own midlife crisis, Jung provided a model for this process (Jung 1961, pp. 170–99).

III

For all the brilliance of Lowenfeld's contribution to child psychotherapy, it was many years before the full potential of her World Technique was realized with adults, through the application of Jung's theories of active imagination and the individuation process. Of course, the hand-in-glove fit that then occurred was no matter of chance, for Jung had arrived at his theories through a long period of personal "confrontation with the unconscious," during which he prefigured sandplay. In his memoirs, *Memories, Dreams, Reflections,* Jung for the first time revealed publicly the personal source of his conviction about the value of fantasy and play. He describes in moving terms the malaise that followed his "parting of the ways with Freud." The state of disorientation in which he found himself led him to a realization that he himself lacked a myth by which he could live. He sought relief through analysis of his dreams and through a reexamination of his entire life, with the emphasis on his early memories and childhood, but to no avail. With no conscious solution at hand, he decided to do whatever might be suggested to him by the unconscious:

> The first thing that came to the surface was a childhood memory from perhaps my tenth or eleventh year. At that time I had a spell of playing passionately with building blocks. I distinctly recalled how I built little houses and castles, using bottles to form the sides of gates and vaults. Somewhat later I had used ordinary stones, with mud for mortar. . . . To my astonishment, this memory was accompanied by a good deal of emotion. . . . The small boy is still around, and possesses a creative life which I lack. (Pp. 173–174)

Jung took this hint from the unconscious: he would seek to recover the creative life, which he had possessed as a boy and which his new experience suggested was still alive. But how was he to return to that boy, to become again like a child? His solution was to do what that boy had done, to play, and moreover, to play exactly what he remembered that boy to have played, a game of "building houses, castles, a whole village." So he began playing by the side of the lake near his home. He played for some time until he came to the altar of his church, which gave him pause. The church was

> a square building with a hexagonal drum on top of it, and a dome. A church also requires an altar, but I hesitated to build that. Preoccupied with the question of how I could approach this task, I was walking along the lake as usual one day, picking stones out of the gravel on the shore. Suddenly I caught sight of a red stone, a four-sided pyramid about an inch and a half high. It was a fragment of stone which had been polished into this shape by the action of the water—a pure product of chance. I knew at once: this was the altar. I placed it in the middle under the dome, and as I did so, I recalled the underground phallus of my childhood dream. This connection gave me a feeling of satisfaction. (P. 174)

The significance of this memory for Jung can be appreciated only in reference to the experiences of his early childhood, which are related in the first chapter of his memoirs. There one learns that perhaps the most important experience of his childhood was this dream of the "chthonian God," to which, in retrospect, he attributed the first stirrings of his intellectual life. Buoyed up then by the satisfaction of recalling the dream, Jung went on with his building game every day that weather permitted. In the course of this play, he began to acquire a new understanding of what his goal was:

> . . . my thoughts clarified, and I was able to grasp the fantasies whose presence in myself I dimly felt.
>
> Naturally, I thought about the significance of what I was doing, and asked myself, "Now really, what are you about? You are building a small town, and

doing it as if it were a rite!'' I had no answer to my question, only the inner certainty that I was on the way to discovering my own myth. For the building game was only a beginning. It released a stream of fantasies which later I carefully wrote down.

This sort of thing has been consistent with me, and at any time in my later life when I came up against a blank wall, I painted a picture or hewed stone. Each such experience proved to be a *rite d'entrée* for the ideas and works that followed hard upon it. (Pp. 174–175)

What Jung had discovered in his "building game" was that play did not necessarily lead down the slope of memory to childishness, but rather led directly to the unfinished business of childhood, represented in his early dream of the underground phallus. This connected him once again with the theme that had preoccupied him throughout his childhood. Following that discovery, as he says, he found that his continued playing unleashed a flood of fantasies that he religiously wrote down, sometimes drew and painted, and always sought to understand.

The ultimate discovery that Jung made in this long period of self-exploration was that he had set in motion an ongoing process of psychological development, first through his "building game," and then through his active engagement with the constellated fantasies. His conclusion from his own experience, and his observations of his patients, was that this process had aim and purpose:

It is in the first place a purely natural process, which may in some cases pursue its course without the knowledge or assistance of the individual, and can sometimes forcibly accomplish itself in the face of opposition. The meaning and purpose of the process is the realization, in all its aspects, of the personality originally hidden away in the embryonic germ-plasm; the production and unfolding of the original, potential wholeness. The symbols used by the unconscious to this end are the same as those which mankind has always used to express wholeness, completeness, and perfection: symbols, as a rule, of the quaternity and the circle. For these reasons I have termed this the *individuation process*. (1917, p. 108)

We have reviewed Jung's "confrontation with the unconscious" at some length in order to present clearly the development of the technique of active imagination, with its beginnings in child's play, and, secondarily, to emphasize the paradigm it offers of the process of constellating the child archetype and redeeming the imaginal.

IV

The adaptation of Lowenfeld's World Technique to use in Jungian analysis was the accomplishment of Dora Kalff, who had been encouraged by Jung to become a child psychotherapist. In view of Jung's use of play in his building game, coupled with the fact that he had actually become acquainted with Lowenfeld and her technique at an international conference in Paris in 1937, and, it is reported, even interpreted the "worlds" presented by Lowenfeld (Bowyer), one might have supposed that he passed this information on to Kalff. But apparently this was not the case. Instead, Kalff encountered Lowenfeld and her World Technique at another international conference, this one in the late 1950s. Later she visited Lowenfeld's Institute of Child Psychology in London to observe the use of the technique, and then promptly adopted it for her own work with children.

Kalff first presented her work at the Second International Congress of Analytical Psychologists in 1962. This paper was subsequently incorporated into her book *Sandspiel,* which was published in Europe in 1966 and in an English translation, *Sandplay,* in the United States in 1971; this is the extent of her publications to date. She has, however, produced a superb documentary film that shows her in the studio of her centuries-old house, engaged in psychotherapy with several children and surrounded by the materials of her art: crowded shelves of miniature figures, sand trays, and an array of other expressive media. The film consists of segments in which Kalff narrates the essentials of her theoretical orientation and the nature of her practice, interspersed with "live" interactions with several children using sandplay. Included is the case of an imaginative young boy whose lengthy course of treatment is followed from beginning to end with representative sandplay constructions, some actually produced in the course of the film. Next to having personal contact with Kalff herself, this film is, without a doubt, the best possible introduction to her method of sandplay.

Kalff's book and her film are the seminal documents of sandplay. Yet her impact on Jungian analysts and other psychotherapists has come in large measure from the countless lectures, seminars, and individual training sessions that she has undertaken over the past twenty years in Europe, the United States, and Japan. Through this person-to-person contact, she has single-handedly created a community of sandplay therapists around the world. The effectiveness of her presentations is greatly enhanced by the sand worlds themselves. Even when frozen in the static images of photographic slides projected upon a screen, they still retain some of the magical quality of the living worlds, which spring to life once again for all who can see them with the inner vision of imagination.

Kalff's theoretical orientation, as expressed in her book and film, comes from the convergence of an early interest in Eastern thought with Jung's theory of the individuation process. She finds a model for her understanding of a child's therapeutic progress in Neumann's theory of the stages of ego development in early childhood (Neumann, p. 24). In practice, she focuses on the period of development when the integral ego is established and the Self is constellated, between two and three years of age. It is her experience that the children she sees have not successfully negotiated this stage. Her goal is to create, through the transference, a "free and sheltered space" (1971, p. 18) within which the child may reexperience the primary relationship with the mother and thereby successfully constellate the Self anew. When this happens, familiar symbols of a fourfold structure, centering, the circle, and the like, appear in the child's sandplay, and this development is followed by progression through the subsequent stages of ego development. In her book, Kalff presents seven case histories of children, and two of young adults, in support of her view. Additional cases can be seen in her film. Kalff's more recent work has been largely with adults, but she has yet to publish anything on this experience.

Few published works exist by other Jungian analysts on the use of sandplay. There are a pair of introductory articles written for the larger community of psychotherapists (Bradway 1979; L. H. Stewart 1977); a discussion of recurrent themes in work with adult patients (Aite); and a collection of articles written for a book entitled *Sandplay Studies: Origins, Theory and Practice,* published by the C. G. Jung Institute of San Francisco.

Aite, in his work with adults, describes an early phase of sandplay in which the ego seems relatively passive and in which consciousness appears fragmented. Gradually, as consciousness becomes more integrated, the play shows evidence of a more active collaboration of the ego with the fantasies being played out. In this latter phase, Aite sees sandplay taking on the characteristics of active imagination. At the same time, all aspects of the analysis—dreams, transference, and sandplay—begin to coalesce into an integral experience for the patient. New attitudes, and their expression in behavior outside analysis, become more evident. In general, Aite's observations are confirmed in my own experience with both children and adults, and they would appear to be consonant with Jung's distinction between the *rite d'entrée* to memories and unconscious fantasies and the succeeding stages of active imagination per se.

Sandplay Studies is perhaps the most comprehensive publication on the subject to date (Bradway et al.). It contains an extensive bibliography, and a thorough review of the non-Jungian, as well as the Jungian, literature (Thompson); detailed case studies of male and female adult patients (Signell; Bradway); an extensive exploration of the nagging questions and problems that may arise in the use of sandplay (Spare); two papers on stages of development in children, one illustrating Neumann's stages of ego development (Bradway), and one aimed at facilitating research, as well as clinical work, through an integration of Neumann's theories with those of Erikson and Piaget (C. T. Stewart); and a theoretical article (L. H. Stewart). A characteristic of this collection of papers, seen as a whole, is the expression of individuality in such matters as preference for particular miniatures, when and how patients are to be introduced to sandplay in the course of analysis, and the like; yet all are contained within the framework of Jungian theory.

V

To illustrate the use of sandplay, I shall present some material from the case of a young boy on the threshold of puberty and adolescence. His sandplay was particularly instructive because of the clarity with which major themes were depicted in the first sand worlds and subsequently worked through to resolution. The boy, nearly twelve years of age, whom I shall call Tom, was brought for treatment by his mother, who was worried about his lack of interest in school and friends and about his general malaise, which found expression at home in hypersensitivity, sadness, and moody withdrawal. Although some of these symptoms were of long standing, they were intensified by the parents' recent divorce. When I first met Tom, he struck me as introverted, intelligent, and curious, a bit shy and reticent, yet quietly cooperative. After a brief period of getting acquainted, I drew his attention to the sandplay materials and indicated that he was free to use them if he liked. At that, he went to the sand trays, and, after briefly examining the toys, played for the rest of the session, producing his first sand world. This session set the pattern for the following six months of therapy: a brief initial period discussing whatever Tom had on his mind would be followed by thirty to forty minutes of intense involvement in sandplay.

During sandplay, I ordinarily sit close enough to the sand tray so that I can follow what transpires, but not close enough to seem intrusive. When the sandplay is completed, I may inquire about some feature of the dramatic action, ask the identity of a figure, or pose some other question. Any further discussion of the sand world, if it occurs at all, tends to arise spontaneously, from a shared interest in a theme or its amplification. With active imagination, one is in the presence of the creative process, and analytic understanding assumes greater importance than interpretation. The attitude one seeks to realize has been aptly described by Henderson as fluctuating between that of a friend sharing the experience and that of "a commentator whose knowledge of mythology may help to provide some amplification of the archetypal background from which the visionary images arise" (p. 201). With children, of course, comments are couched in the imagery and discourse appropriate to the child's world.

The dominant theme of Tom's first sand world was war; a pitched battle between Romans and Vikings was represented. Significant details included: (1) Roman generals in one corner directing the battle from their observation post, a square of colored tiles; (2) a mound near the center of the tray marked with a black stone at one end and a white stone at the other; (3) black stones used as an escarpment protecting a Viking warrior; and (4) a rather incongruous piece of pink coral being used as a protective barrier by another Viking.

What can we say about the symbolic meaning of these images? Taken at face value, conflict is evident, specifically, conflict between an ancient civilization and a vigorous society of seafarers. Is this the conflict of the generations, of father and son, that inevitable struggle that the adolescent boy must undertake in order to avoid stultification by outmoded customs and expectations and to win through to his own true values? Are the black stones depression, and is the mound with its marker stones a burial mound, a presage of the heroic ego's rite of passage in which death itself is transformed into a "death of what I am now in order to become what I want to be"? (Vitale, p. 27). The pink coral is a puzzling element, for though the Vikings are seafarers, they come from the North, whereas coral accretes in the depths of warm, southern waters. Is this a deeply unconscious symbol of the feminine and Eros? Finally there are the Roman generals at their command station, a square of colored tiles, with a blue border enclosing diagonals of red, yellow, green, and white. Is this an image of self-reflective consciousness that is now dominated by logical thought, leaving the ego isolated from instinct and life? Yet the colorful tiles and the square structure may also foreshadow a constellation of the Self and a new structuring of the ego and the unconscious, the ego-Self axis.

In light of the two sand worlds constructed during the second visit, some of the foregoing speculations seemed to be supported. The first world was a battle scene, this time between contemporary military units of Asians opposing American, British, and French troops. Is the internal conflict between conscious and unconscious more clearly represented here as ego and shadow? The second world, described as "the changing of the guard," alluded perhaps to the parental divorce, but, at a more collective level, it suggested a symbol for the continuity in change that is a value carried by the masculine spirit, an encouraging prognostic sign. But there was also an incongruous intrusion of fan-shaped sea shells lining a corridor into the regimental yard. Like the coral of the first sand world, this suggested a deeply unconscious symbol of the realm of Aphrodite. Finally, the symmetrical structuring of the guards and the stone-lined yard were perhaps another indication of the centering process.

The four themes that were to be followed through the next six months of therapy can be summarized as follows: (1) the conflict of the generations, of father and son, the *puer-senex* archetypal configuration, as represented in the Viking-Roman battles; (2) the conflict of consciousness and unconsciousness, ego and shadow, represented in the theme of war; (3) the centering process, the constellation of the ego-Self axis, and the strengthening of the ego; and (4) the feminine and Eros, as represented in the deep-sea images of coral and sea shells.

The Viking-Roman battles, the conflict of the generations, recurred in three subsequent sessions, the third, ninth and nineteenth. In the third and ninth sand worlds, the battles became more articulated: a river and bridge appeared, and the fighting seemed somewhat more heated, but the outcome of the struggle remained undecided. In the nineteenth session, however, a dramatic change took place. The Romans appeared to have been ambushed on one of their tiled roads, and were surrounded by Vikings, who seemed in command of the situation. Two Viking warriors stood at the edge of the tray, watching the battle, perhaps representing the "continuity in change" that had been foreshadowed in the earlier "changing of the guard." Did this show a new development in self-reflective consciousness indicating less intellectual isolation from life's struggle?

The second theme, the ego-shadow conflict, which anticipated the symbolic death and ceremonial burial, was fought out in a majority of the sessions with increasing ferocity, along with increasingly realistic articulation of the details of warfare and a gradual encroachment upon civilian habitation. One significant detail of these battles was a pair of soldiers carrying a stretcher. They were present throughout some fourteen battle scenes, always with an empty stretcher. In the fifteenth session they appeared at the very center of a huge circular fort. Did this suggest that the healing function was becoming more central in the process? Subsequent sand worlds would seem to bear this out. Throughout the series of battles up to this point, the fighting had surged back and forth without any clear victory or apparent resolution. In the eighteenth session, however, something new occurred: near-total destruction. Most, if not all of the soldiers appeared wounded or dead, and the surrounding forest was decimated. During this same session, another sand world was constructed, in which, at long last, the medics seemed to have found their purpose, and a ritual burial appeared to have taken place.

Looking next at the theme of centering, we gain some new perspectives on the issues we have been discussing, as well as indications of events to come. In the ninth visit, a dramatic change in both image and structure of the sand worlds occurred, with the appearance of the theme of pirates burying treasure on a desert island. Some of the significant features of this world were: (1) a mountain island in the center of the tray; (2) a pirate digging a hole at the very top of the mountain; (3) the rather surprising touch of flowers on the island; and (4) the theme of conflict continuing here between two bands of pirates. This sand world represented that constellation of the Self that Kalff has discussed at length (1971). Both the theme, a fairy tale-myth motif, and the structure of this world, centered on a vertical axis, suggested the development of a more harmonious and collaborative relationship between ego and Self. Such a development in the imaginal realm was accompanied by changes in feelings and behavior, evident during the sessions and at home and school, as reported by mother and son. In Tom's case, depression began to lift, a new spontaneity was evident, and I heard about a new friend. These changes for the better did not mean, however, that there were no more struggles ahead, for there were. But the influx of energy, and the easing of internal conflict, made possible a further strengthening of the ego, which in turn encouraged an ever deepening involvement with central conflicts.

This process became apparent in subsequent sand worlds. For example, in the thirteenth session, a new theme of collaborative work appeared, with two miners using a railroad cart to bring up huge pieces of salt from a mine shaft deep in the earth. The sandplay of the following session began as a battle, but that scene was replaced by a large pool of water in the center of the tray in which four aquanauts were swimming, and then by a sculptured pool. These sand worlds were the prelude to resolution of the fourth theme, the deep-sea realm of the feminine and Eros.

The next indication of the theme appeared in the midst of a battle scene when a sea shell was used to screen the entrance to a dugout. Then in the twentieth session, a bottom-of-the-sea scene was created in which Tom used the pink coral of sand world one, a fan sea shell from "the changing of the guard," and other shells and a sea horse. The action involved four aquanauts whose relatively small size in relation to the sea shells and the sea horse made formidable antagonists of those denizens of the deep. In fact, one of the aquanauts was apparently caught and was shown emerging from a giant shell, with the assistance of his companion, who held the shell open with a huge pair of shears. On the other side of the scene, another aquanaut, holding a knife before him, was in an apparent stand-off with the sea horse. The overall impression was that the aquanauts were in command of the situation. Tom constructed another sand world the same day. He began with some preliminary working of the damp sand and then, using a block, made a square hole near the center of the tray. He then reached over to the dry sand tray and scooped up two handfuls of sand, which he slowly drifted through his fingers, filling the square hole and producing a four-sided pyramid. Was this the goal of the work, the alchemical *sal sapientiae,* the bitter salt of wisdom, which, in *Mysterium Coniunctionis,* Jung suggests, "represents the feminine principle of Eros, which brings everything into relationship, in an almost perfect way" (1955–56, p. 241)?

At this juncture, one naturally wishes for some further correlation of the images and symbols of the sandplay, with personal life history and the experience of the transference. Desirable and valuable as such an endeavor might be, it is beyond the scope of this presentation, and not appropriate to this context. For those readers, however, who may be interested in references directly pertinent to the material presented, I suggest the collection of essays in *Fathers and Mothers* (Berry et al.) and Henderson's *Thresholds of Initiation.* As for Tom's therapy, a lengthy period ensued in which dreams and life experiences replaced sandplay as the focus, and during which the accomplishments of the six months of sandplay were confirmed and consolidated.

In conclusion, I must emphasize that the interpretations suggested in this presentation are by no means to be taken as "explanations" of the sand worlds or the sandplay process. My efforts have been directed toward increasing our appreciation for sandplay as a form of active imagination, and our knowledge of those aspects of the process and of the sand worlds that may help us to understand better the psyche and psychotherapy. The individual who creates a sand world is the only one who knows what the experience was like, or what may have been intended. As a psychotherapist, one feels privileged to have been a participant-observer.

REFERENCES

Aite, P. 1978. Ego and image: some observations on the theme of 'sandplay.' *Journal of Analytical Psychology* 23:332–38.
Berry, P., ed. 1973. *Fathers and mothers.* Zurich: Spring Publications.
Bowyer, L. R. 1959. *The Lowenfeld world technique.* Oxford: Pergamon Press.
Bradway, K. 1979. Sandplay in psychotherapy. *Art Psychotherapy* 6:85–93.
Bradway, K.; Signell, K.; Spare, G.; Stewart, C. T.; Stewart, L. H.; and Thompson, C. 1981. *Sandplay studies: origins, theory, and practice.* San Francisco: C. G. Jung Institute of San Francisco.

Henderson, J. L. 1967. *Thresholds of initiation*. Middletown, Conn.: Wesleyan University Press.

Hillman, J. 1978. *Loose ends*. Irving, Tex.: Spring Publications.

Huizinga, J. 1955. *Homo ludens: a study of the play element in culture*. Boston: Beacon Press.

Jung, C. G. 1917. The psychology of the unconscious. In *Collected works*, vol. 7, pp. 3–117. New York: Pantheon, 1953.

––––––. 1940. The psychology of the child archetype. In *Collected works*, vol. 9, part 1, pp. 151–81. Princeton: Princeton University Press, 1959.

––––––. 1946. On the nature of the psyche. In *Collected works*, vol. 8, pp. 159–234. 2d ed. Princeton: Princeton University Press, 1969.

––––––. 1955–56. *Mysterium coniunctionis*. *Collected works*, vol. 14. 2d ed. Princeton: Princeton University Press, 1970.

––––––. 1961. *Memories, dreams, reflections*. New York: Randon House, Vintage Books.

Kalff, D. M. 1966. *Sandspiel*. Zurich: Rascher Verlag.

––––––. 1971. *Sandplay: mirror of a child's psyche*. San Francisco: Browser Press.

––––––. 1981. *Sandplay: a psychotherapeutic approach to the psyche*. Los Angeles: Sigo Press.

Lowenfeld, M. 1967. *Play in childhood*. New York: Wiley.

––––––. 1979. *The world technique*. London: George Allen & Unwin.

Mause, L. de. 1974. *The history of childhood*. New York: Harper & Row.

Neumann, E. 1973. *The child*. New York: Putnam.

Stewart, L. H. 1977. Sand play therapy: Jungian technique. In *Encyclopedia of psychiatry, psychology, psychoanalysis, and neurology*, ed. B. Wolman, pp. 9–11. New York: Aesculapius.

Stewart, L. H., and Stewart, C. T. 1981. Play, games and affects. In *Play as context*, ed. A. T. Cheska, pp. 42–52. West Point, N.Y.: Leisure Press.

Vitale, A. 1973. Saturn: the transformation of the father. In *Fathers and mothers*, ed. P. Berry, pp. 5–39. Zurich: Spring Publications.

Wells, H. G. 1911. *Floor games*. New York: Arno Press, 1976.

[12]

GROUP THERAPY AND ANALYSIS

Thayer A. Greene

G ROUP psychotherapy with a Jungian orientation is designed to provide both interpersonal and intrapersonal experience of the psyche
within a group setting. In Jungian theory and practice, the priority of individual analytic therapy is explicitly affirmed. In no sense, therefore, is
group therapy seen as a substitute for or alternative to the central work of
individual analysis, but rather as a valuable adjunct and aid to it. The
varied psychic composition of a group constellates unconscious projections, affective reactions, and struggles for individual autonomy. The concreteness and experiential immediacy of group interaction provide an arena
in which individuals can encounter their psychological reality in ways that
individual analysis, by its very nature, may be unable to offer.

Jung himself was skeptical about the value of group therapy and did
not include this form of treatment in his own practice. Many of his immediate followers continue to share his skepticism. Their concern and appreciation for the value and uniqueness of the intrapsychic experience of
the individual has made them wary of the intrusiveness and categorizing so
typical of much group behavior. It was not until the early 1960s, at about
the time of Jung's death, that a few Jungian analysts began to experiment
with group process as an adjunct to individual analysis. Group therapy as
a treatment modality has become increasingly accepted by Jungians, but
even now it is practiced by only a minority. Only in the New York training

Thayer Greene, B.D., S.T.M., a former president of the New York Association for Analytical Psychology, is a board and faculty member of the C. G. Jung Training Center of New
York and maintains a private practice in New York City. A graduate of Amherst College, he
received an S.T.M. from Union Theological Seminary in Psychiatry and Religion and graduated from the C. G. Jung Training Center of New York. He is the author of *Modern Man
in Search of Manhood* (1967) and several articles or chapters, including "Confessions of an
Extravert" (1975), "America's Loss of Innocence: Bicentennial Reflections" (1976), and
"C. G. Jung's Theory of Dreams" in *Handbook of Dreams* (1979).

center is group therapy included as a required element in the training experience of prospective analysts. Similarly, except for a few articles, little or nothing has been published by Jungians concerning either theory or practice of group therapy.

THEORETICAL FOUNDATIONS

In spite of the skeptics, the Jungian analysts who practice group therapy do so on the basis of theoretical formulations to be found in Jung's own writings. The archetype, for example, was considered by Jung to have an underlying bipolar character. We see this in such primary differentiations of human experience as light-dark, male-female, weak-strong, life-death. Individual and group represent opposite poles of a single, unified archetype. One finds a strong emphasis in Jung and his followers on the value of individual consciousness as opposed to group consciousness, so the underlying unity of group and individual is often neglected or undervalued. The creative influence of family and social milieu in shaping the individual is appreciated much less than their destructive effects. Nevertheless, Jung's theoretical approach to polarities was a holistic one; the encounter between, and reconciliation of, opposites was seen as the pathway to growth and greater consciousness. To allow energy to remain fixed at one end of a bipolarity is to invite its opposite to react destructively from the unconscious.

In light of these principles, familiar to any Jungian, it seems curious that the value of an encounter with group process would not be clearly recognized. Whatever element of psychic life we refuse to deal with is most liable to haunt us. Whatever we are willing to confront is most likely to become more conscious and creative. It may well be that the introverted bias of both Jung and the great majority of Jungian analysts has left its mark on the issue of group therapy. According to various studies, 72 to 85 percent of those analysts tested are introverted (Mattoon, p. 20). The instinctive withdrawal of energy away from objects into subjective reactions predisposes introverts to approach any group encounter with suspicion and anxiety. There is a natural and genuine fear that the unique values of subjective experience will be somehow violated by exposure to the group.

Yet those who practice group therapy have found their work to be validated by the empirical products of the unconscious itself. The dreams of group participants, for example, do not invariably reveal the experience to be destructive. On the contrary, the response of the unconscious seems most often to indicate that a damaged connection is being healed. One introverted woman who participated in a group consisting of trainees, in which a great deal of very personal material was shared, had the following dream: "I am urinating in an enclosed bathroom, surrounded by group members who can hear me. I have the feeling that I need not be embarrassed." She felt that the dream indicated her basic feeling that she was accepted in the group, that her "pourings out" were listened to and not rejected. She reported, "I could be me and at the same time my own sense of privacy was not violated."

Such evidence, which repeats itself regularly, argues against the assumption that a small group of six to nine people *by its very nature* prohibits the evolution of an ethos of differentiated acceptance within which genuine individuality may be expressed. Within a group atmosphere, silent introverts can learn to risk sharing their subjective reactions and can discover, through expressing their inner contents, a more immediate and genuine relation to the object. Likewise, extraverts learn to be still and to wait until a response that is truly their own wishes to be expressed.

Another major theoretical issue that group process opens up is the nature and function of the persona. In rereading the material on the persona in Jung's writings, one cannot help but note the double message Jung himself seems to convey concerning it. On the one hand, he contends that the persona and the anima/animus have essentially equivalent functions in relation to the ego. The former provides the potential for differentiated adaptation to the outer world, the latter for adaptation to the inner world. These functional structures of personality have different directions of attention and energy but their value is similar. On the other hand, Jung sometimes writes of the persona in depreciatory and reductionistic terms: "Fundamentally, the persona is nothing real . . . a compromise between individual and society as to what a man should appear to be . . . in relation to the individuality of the person concerned, only a secondary reality, a product of compromise" (1966, p. 158). "As its name shows, it is only a mask for the collective psyche, a mask that *feigns individuality* and tries to make others believe that one is individual, whereas one is simply playing a part in which the collective psyche speaks" (p. 157).

Such a disparaging view seems to contradict Jung's more substantial insight that the persona is an inherent—that is, archetypal—function of human personality that provides a bridge to the many "others" of the outer world in a manner similar to the guiding or bridging function of the anima/animus in relation to the inner "others." Holt evaluates Jung's view of the persona as follows: "More stress is placed on the persona as a rigid and deceitful mask, identification with which inhibits the process of individuation, than as a function of relationship through which the individual can experience the differentiating process of education and social life'' (p. 89).

The view one holds of the persona has direct implications for group process. If one believes that its function is to conceal and protect, to ''feign individuality,'' then one's reaction to group encounter will be defensive. There will be little willingness to risk revelation of genuine selfhood, nor will there be much capacity for allowing and receiving the unique reality of other group members. Conversely, if one understands group process as being centrally concerned with the therapy of a damaged, distorted, or overly rigid adaptive capacity in the individual, then one can regard the persona itself not only as a source of pathology but also as a potential area for psychic transformation. Much of the recent literature about narcissistic wounds and disorders suggests that true relatedness with an ''other,'' what Buber calls the I-Thou experience, calls for a gradual dissolution of the ''false self''—that is, a pathological persona—in favor of an adaptation through which authentic interiority can be shared with others (see Kalsched). Such an understanding and approach to the persona indicates the value and validity of group process as a therapeutic modality.

DYNAMIC AND THERAPEUTIC ISSUES

The leadership styles of group therapists are as varied as the therapeutic styles of individual analysts. Jung contended that the personality of the therapist was an essential element in the healing process and therefore should not be concealed. In this, he departed from the psychoanalytic model, in which the analyst presents a neutral screen for projection and makes rational, objective interpretations of the patient's material and behavior. Jung rejected the couch in favor of a face-to-face encounter with the patient, and often revealed his own psychic reactions, and even his dreams, when he felt they would contribute to the analytic process.

The personal style of an analyst is likely to be emphasized by the group process. So many variables are present, so many different energies are activated, so many perceptions of and reactions to the therapist are available, that it is more difficult for the analyst to play a role and to control the flow of the process than it is in individual analytic sessions. Some analysts lead groups in a relatively directive and formal manner, centering the interactions around their own interpretations and responses to individual group members. While the rest of the group provides support and additional feedback, the main focus of the therapy is on interactions between a group member and the therapist. When practiced to the extreme, such a focus obviously blocks the free flow of group interaction and the sense of a group's cohesiveness. Nonetheless, in the hands of a perceptive and skilled analyst, such an approach can provide many of the values of individual analysis, with the added dimension of group exposure and experience.

In contrast to this model, some analysts function as enablers or catalysts in the group. They attend to the group process itself, and they seek to activate and release the therapeutic potential within and between group members. Such an approach assumes that it is the group or its members, rather than the group leader, that supply the primary resources and skills for raising consciousness and stimulating change.

Leadership style may also be profoundly affected by the composition of the group. A group composed largely of professional therapists and other experienced helpers may call for a very different style than a group made up of persons with very limited educational, psychological, or emotional resources. Regardless of group composition, analysts beginning the practice of group therapy will need to explore the spectrum of leadership styles to find the place that feels most comfortable and congruent with their own personal preferences. Authenticity is the key here, as it is in individual analysis.

When analysands enter groups conducted by their personal analysts, the transference is often significantly affected. The power that the analyst has held, due to projections evoked in the privacy of personal work, may shift partially to the group. For some patients, this partial transfer of power to the group can reduce the intensity of the transference bond prematurely and hence limit the therapeutic potential of individual analysis. In other cases, an analytic relationship that is stuck and shows no significant movement may be reawakened by the energy and insight drawn from common participation in group process. The group container can supply the necessary psychic support for an analysand to work out difficult transference issues with the analyst that had not been touched in years of individual treatment. Such a solution may not represent the ideal, but it does in fact occur and is often creative. In general, however, analysands' participation in their analysts' groups provides parallel experiences, one of the group, one of individual treatment, each of which has a separate existence and does not intrude significantly upon the other.

Sitting in a room with seven or eight other people who also have a relationship with the therapist sets in motion any number of effects. Issues of sibling rivalry, which are not constellated in individual work, are almost sure to emerge. New sides of the analyst's personality are revealed; his or her shadow problems are much more evident in a group. The group container may also provide a vital protection and support for the expression of strong reactions to the analyst.

The analyst's experience of the patient is also significantly enlarged. Interpersonal and typological behaviors of the patient can be observed in concrete forms, providing the analyst with a fuller and more realistic experience of the analysand. The perceptions and judgments of the analyst, which have been limited and distorted by his or her own typology and personal complexes, can be modified.

Historically, healing has been associated much more with groups and communities than with isolated, one-to-one relationships. Studies of primitive healing, for example, indicate its dependence upon the corporate energy of the family or tribe. Rarely does the primitive healer attempt transformation of physical or psychic ills without the supportive libido of a community. In most religious traditions, the relation of healing to worship and to sacramental action implies its essentially corporate character. The congregation, the church, the "people of God" are seen as mediating instruments of healing power. Even the privacy of the confessional in Catholic practice is only meaningful within the context of the corporate celebration of the Eucharist. The bond of individuals to their communal roots is an integral part of the healing process. In our own time, such approaches as family therapy indicate that the healing of individuals must take account of their involvement in the social matrix.

The psychic energy activated in a group process is often more intense than that between two individuals. This intensity may manifest itself as powerful affective expression, as vigorous physical behaviors, or as a concentration of silent, introverted, meditative libido. Particularly in cases in which the problem has to do with a person's sense of social acceptance of individual identity, the group can effect rapid and dramatic change. A very introverted and vulnerable young woman had a dream just prior to her first group meeting. Consciously, she was afraid she would not be able to reveal herself in the group process for fear of rejection, an experience she had had over and over again in her own family.

Dream: *Our group meets at A's house. We are sitting in a circle observing a candle. Simultaneously we all rise and walk single-file into a one-room shower. We remove our clothes. I remain standing while the group sits around me. They begin to chant as they wash me. Everyone is rubbing my body with soap and then splashing me with water. It ends with all the people embracing.*

As the dream indicated, this woman's experience in the group was to be extremely positive, providing her with her first opportunity to reveal her true feelings and to feel known and accepted by others. The images of the dream are rich with both personal and archetypal meaning. They indicate how powerfully the group experience can constellate therapeutic change in the damaged adaptation of an individual.

Genuine adaptation includes another and more difficult experience. Sooner or later, all group members find themselves at odds with the group majority. Such a situation demands that the individual take a stand in the face of the collective, a circumstance that often activates an archetypal reaction from the unconscious. Knowing the freedom and courage to dissent from the majority viewpoint can be extremely valuable. Whitmont writes:

> This experience of positive dissent is one of the most vital, important, and unique aspects of therapeutic group experience. It teaches the analysand to have the courage of his or her convictions and still to function as a relating, participating member of a community—opposites which many Jungians have found difficult to reconcile. . . . Instead of being swayed by anonymous currents, a more conscious relationship is established to the group archetype. By having to defend one's own position against the group's opposition, members learn to relate individually to individuals in what was sensed at first as a shapeless, threatening mass, and thus they acquire a degree of immunity against mass compulsiveness. (1974, p. 14)

It should be noted that when a group member is under pressure or attack from the group, the well-timed intervention of the therapist may be a crucial factor in the birth of greater autonomy for the individual. In contrast with group experiences that take place for an "intensive weekend" or a weeklong "workshop," valuable as those may be, the ongoing, week-by-week continuity of group therapy provides a structure within which strong and painful psychic reactions may be brought back to subsequent group sessions until there is some resolution.

The model that most adequately corresponds to the dynamic of group process is the family. Every person entering the group is in some sense reopening the repressed and unconscious memories of early family experience. In one form or another, the family has been for everyone the primary and primal group. The group may activate needs and hungers never adequately met or satisfied, or it may reembody the warm womb of security from which genuine separation has never been ventured and achieved. One meets brother, sister, father, mother, in disguised form, and relives, unwittingly, the patterns of perception and reaction that have shaped memory. Childhood trauma and buried affect are stirred to consciousness by the reenactment of universal human patterns that were first encountered within the family.

One young psychiatrist, in commenting on his experience as a member of a group, said: "Group is not a theory. It's a family. Mary here is my mother. She intimidates me and makes me feel all the awful feelings of childhood, but I am also jealous of her strength and honesty. I have issues with Mary that I can work out here and nowhere else in my life. When I feel a longing to curl up in Susan's lap and cry and cry and just be held until there are no more tears, I know it can happen here if it needs to happen." For Susan, "the group, at least this group, is not only a family; it is the family I never had and always needed." Such expressions are reflective of the archetypal basis of the group experience and the potential it offers for reexperiencing and healing early relational wounds. Therapists' thorough awareness of this dimension of the process will aid their responses and interpretations of particular interactions.

METHOD AND PRACTICE

Starting a group for the first time raises many practical questions. What is the optimum number of people? What is the best length of time for a session? How should fees be handled? Does the group need ground rules to be effective? What criteria does one follow in selecting people for a particular group? There are no absolute answers to these questions, but experience shows certain basic tendencies. When the number of group members exceeds nine persons, excluding the therapist, the cohesive quality of group process is affected. In this writer's experience, eight persons is ideal. Anything more begins to stretch the limit of effective interaction. The longer a group session, of course, the more possible it becomes to enlarge the number beyond eight. Most Jungian group sessions meet for an hour and a half, a relatively short period for such a process. For groups meeting two to three hours, some modest increase in number may be possible without losing qualitative involvement.

Time and number are related, naturally, to the professional fee. The longer the session, or the smaller the group, the more it is liable to cost. Therapists make up a fee schedule and contract with group members individually as they enter the group. Unlike individual therapy, where a sliding scale can be used to take into account differing financial capacities, group therapy should have a standard fee for all members, with as few exceptions as possible. Most group therapists charge not by the session but by the month, since group members cannot be replaced when they are absent. Participation in a group offers an economic advantage for people with limited funds, since it provides another hour and a half of therapy at roughly one-third the cost of an individual session. Where an individual's psychological process needs more than one therapy session per week, the group can be a help.

Absolutely crucial to the effectiveness of group process is the confidentiality of what happens within the group. Members are free to reveal, or not to reveal, whatever they choose within the group, but there must be trust that other group members will maintain confidentiality. Issues of shame, doubt, privacy, and psychic intrusion are inevitably constellated for every person who enters a group, and the leaking of confidential material destroys the basis of the group process. Another rule that occasionally must be invoked in the heat of powerful affective confrontation is the unacceptability of physical violence. Expressions of violent feelings, fantasies, and language can be allowed within the group container, but the physical enactment of these impulses must be channeled in ways that do not injure other persons.

Unless the group therapist feels otherwise, group participants are free to relate and socialize as they choose outside the group session. Some group members prefer anonymity and separateness, while others may develop considerable interaction at postgroup meals together, or in significant friendships or erotic relationships that emerge between group members. Many analysts regard such involvements as a complicating but inevitable aspect of human freedom and the life process. Other therapists may try to control such outside interaction for the sake of a less contaminated therapeutic container. In my own practice, I do not discourage such involvements, since that feels inappropriately intrusive and controlling. But the integrity of the group process, I feel, demands that these involvements be discussed within the group; otherwise the psychic energy of the group can be secretly or unconsciously dissipated.

Careful selection of group members by the therapist is a significant factor in the quality of the group. In general, a balance between males and females is needed, unless the group composition is specifically intended to be all men or all women. (Such one-gender groups can be helpful in exploring issues of personal and sexual identity in depth, but by their very nature they lack a fundamental bipolarity of human experience, and this limits them in areas of significant psychic interaction.) A variety of typology is also welcome. A room full of introverted intuitives cries out for the presence of an extraverted sensation type, just as two thinkers ensnared in theory need the incisive reaction of a feeling type to provide compensation and access to other values. Typological variety makes for a laboratory of human relations. In it, the participants can explore problems of marriage, work, friendship, and love as they occur in daily life. Reactions similar to those of one's husband, wife, child, parent, boss, or lover are almost always available through one or another member of the group.

The most delicate selection problem, for the therapist, involves the relative ego capacity of applicants for group therapy. With one's own analysands, presumably, there has been ample opportunity to assess this factor. But a problem can arise when other therapists refer their patients for group therapy. A discussion with the other therapists may prove useful as background for careful interviews with the applicants. One should be able to verify that candidates for group therapy have sufficient ego strength to allow them to relate to unconscious contents and projective reactions. Where there is no sense of a symbolic dimension, or an absence of access to inner reality, or extremely rigid interpersonal defenses, the therapist is wise to encourage more individual analysis prior to group therapy. Severe narcissistic disorders do not lend themselves very well to group therapy, because the lack of an adequate ego-Self connection produces an extreme sensitivity to any negative feedback. The tyranny of the narcissistic need in such a person can consume the time and energy of the group to a disproportionate degree; such individuals usually need lengthy individual therapy before venturing into a group.

What happens, then, when the group gathers for a session? After the small talk has died away, there is frequently a period of silence. This is a waiting period, when energy and awareness gather and become ready to attend to the need that will press forward. Some group therapists encourage a defined period of group meditation before any other interactions take place, believing that this provides better access to psychic material. The spontaneity of the group process itself, however, can be the guiding spirit. When group members are wandering off into private fantasy, falling asleep, or looking bored, it may be a sign that contact has been lost with vital psychic energy. Often the simple recognition of this fact will release the flow again. The content of a particular group session may concern personal reactions between group members; a dream or several dreams about the group; the life crisis of a member who is now seeking support and insight from the others; a personal dream or fantasy that leads back into childhood memory and feelings. The methods employed to work with such material will depend upon the resources and skills available in the group and particularly in the therapist.

Group psychotherapy is such a recent development for Jungians that no distinctively Jungian technique has as yet developed. At this point, the particular personality and experience of the therapist are liable to determine technique more than any other factor. The lack of a substantial history or literature on group therapy among Jungians has led them to look outside their own school to find models and methods with which to work. Two methods used extensively in individual Jungian analysis, namely, dream analysis and active imagination, are also frequently employed within the group process. When, for example, a group member has had a dream about the group, this piece of unconscious material is considered appropriate for exploration within the group, even though it may also be the subject of analysis in an individual session. It frequently happens that several group members have similar dreams within the same week, and these may compensate for a blind spot in the group's awareness. A group dream may lead to a ritual of enactment, or to psychodramatic action, which incarnates its emotional reality. Similarly, a strong affective state or a fascinating or obsessive image brought into the group may become the starting point for active imagination. A vivid quality of psychic energy can be activated in a group when the participants focus their attentive and receptive awareness upon the imaginal journey of an individual. Silent and absorbed attention may last for an hour or more as some inner encounter and discovery is taking place, perhaps with the direct assistance of the therapist or of another member.

Other important methods of group work that have been incorporated into Jungian practice by some analysts are drawn from Gestalt and Bioenergetic therapies, encounter-group experience, and sensory-awareness techniques. In all cases, the purpose of the method is to aid individuals in exploring the intrapsychic dimensions of an interpersonal issue. Using a pillow or an empty chair, a significant figure from an individual's past or present life can be invited into the circle of the group and finally confronted or allowed to speak. Rage, love, guilt, and pain can be expressed to these figures of the past, who, though dead, continue to live as imagoes within our psychic depths. Some people are so frightened by their unexpressed potential for affective and physical discharge that it remains locked under tight controls in body, voice, and appearance. The freedom to scream, to pound, to rage, to sob within the safety of the group can bring about dramatic advances in emotional and psychological development. An understanding of bioenergetic methods is useful for releasing such repressed energies. And, frequently, a person's dreams will indicate when the time is right for risking such an effort. Then, too, a gentle sensory experience is often the key to dissolving an inner barrier. Members may sit in the center and stare into each other's eyes, or slowly explore each other's faces, until some genuine contact is made. On occasion, when a group member is feeling overwhelmed and without support, the experience of being lifted physically, held aloft, and rocked by the whole group provides a concrete experience of support.

Projection is a pervasive element in all human interaction. A great deal of time and energy in Jungian analysis is devoted to identifying and clarifying projective mechanisms and contents. This task is made difficult for analysts by the fact that the analysand's descriptions and reports of interactions with others are all they have to work with. Group therapy provides an added dimension. With eight other people in the room, a projection is unlikely to slip through. Group members will give clarifying feedback to an individual who is reacting out of distorted perceptions. The presence of an activated and energized personal complex will be sensed by group members and exposed to conscious examination. The group members act as reflective and reactive mirrors, so the group provides a composite image of each individual in it. This reflection is not something to be trusted implicitly, but it should be weighed carefully when offered with good will and compassion. The therapist who frequently requests the feedback and mirroring of the group will discover that this method not only yields benefits for the particular issue at hand, but also re-collects the attention and energy of all participants and keeps them actively involved.

Jung's passion for the individual journey has left its mark on all Jungians. Those who are skeptical of group psychotherapy remain faithful to Jung's deep concern for the individual psychic process. Those of us who practice group psychotherapy share that concern, but clearly we have a different attitude toward the potential of group therapy for increasing consciousness and promoting therapeutic change. Individuals do not lose their priority within the group. A Jungian group exists, actually, for the sake of each individual. This approach can raise problems in leading a group, because so much attention can be given to individual needs that the dynamics of the group as a whole are slighted. There needs to be an alternation of energy and attention between individual focus and communal interaction. The group therapist is wise to see that neither is ignored.

The training of Jungian analysts involves years of work: personal analysis with at least two training analysts, supervised work, and mastery of considerable theory. At this point, there is no comparable training for group therapists within the Jung Institutes in the United States. Certainly there is a need for Jungians to develop a theory of group interaction and therapy and to begin introducing the practice of group therapy into their own private work. Before beginning a group, however, it is advisable for analysts to be participants in a therapy group, just as they were analysands before sitting in the analyst's chair.

REFERENCES

Franz, M.-L. von. On group psychology. *Quadrant* Winter 1973:4–11.

Holt, D. 1965. Persona and actor. Unpublished typescript. Zurich: C. G. Jung Institute.

Jung, C. G. 1966. *Two essays on analytical psychology. Collected works,* vol. 7. New York: Pantheon.

Kalsched, D. 1980. Narcissism and the search for interiority. *Quadrant* Fall 1980: 46–74.

Mattoon, M. A. 1977. The neglected function in analytical psychology. *Journal of Analytical Psychology* 22/1:17–31.

Whitmont, E. 1964. Group therapy and analytical psychology. *Journal of Analytical Psychology* 9/1:1–22.

———. 1974. Analysis in a group setting. *Quadrant* Spring 1974: 5–25.

SPECIAL
TOPICS
IN
ANALYTICAL
PRACTICE

PART FOUR

[13]

TREATMENT OF CHILDREN IN ANALYTICAL PSYCHOLOGY

Edith Sullwold

THEORETICAL REMARKS

THE process for a child in Jungian therapy is similar to that for an adult in Jungian analysis. The therapist provides a container in which the shadows and monsters of the dark, often frightening and unknown, can be explored, where fears and angers can be revealed, and where the joys of life and fantasies for the future can be expressed.

The journey of the child is full of hazardous obstacles, hindrances, and heroic requirements, as well as happy, spontaneous moments of growth. However, in the case of a child, the primary task is the development of ego-strength and an independent personality. The emerging ego, not yet strengthened by years of life experience, can be overwhelmed by forces of the inner world or by circumstances of the outer world.

The therapist, armed with the shield of an adult ego, along with experience and knowledge of the tasks and struggles of life, can provide a protected space in which the child can strengthen itself. The therapist stands guard and helps the child search within for the creative energies needed to resolve the issues of its life.

Edith Sullwold, M.A., M.F.C.C., is founding Director of the Hilde Kirsch Children's Center, C. G. Jung Institute of Los Angeles, and maintains a private practice with children and adults. A graduate of the University of Chicago, she helped found the Center for the Healing Arts in Los Angeles and later became director of Turning Point, a professional group working with children with serious illnesses. A published paper, ''Eagle Eye'' (1970), illustrates the symbolic process as it is experienced by a child.

Although Jung himself worked almost exclusively with adults, the practice of child therapy using the insights of analytical psychology has developed over the last sixty years. The pioneers in this field have been Frances Wickes, Erich Neumann, Michael Fordham, Dora Kalff, and Dorothea Romankiw, all of whom built on Jung's work as well as on their own experiences and ideas. Wickes was an American whose *Inner World of Childhood* was honored by Jung in his introduction to the work. Fordham, working in London, presented his view of childhood development and analytic treatment in *Children as Individuals*. In Zurich, Kalff studied the child's psyche through sandplay and described her method in *Sandplay*. Her work is based in part on the study of the development of the child by Neumann set forth in his book *The Child*. Romankiw is the founder and director of St. George Homes, a pioneer residential treatment center for adolescents with severe emotional difficulties. At her center in Berkeley, California, an innovative and effective use is made of myth, ritual, and dream, with a focus on tasks directed from within.

For many years, the only training program in Jungian child analysis that existed was located in London, and was directed by Fordham. In the last few years, several other programs have been started, in addition to St. George Homes, indicating a growing interest in the work with children. The Jung Institutes in Berlin and in Küsnacht, Switzerland, have training programs for the treatment of children that are complete in themselves and distinct from the regular training for adult work. At the Jung Institute in Los Angeles, the Hilde Kirsch Children's Center was formed in 1978 as an integral part of the training program for analysts, requiring of all trainees both theoretical and clinical knowledge of child treatment in addition to the work with adults. The incorporation of the work with children has resulted in an increased awareness of the natural developmental processes of human life, as well as the difficulties that can occur in these processes. The work with children has also stimulated a greater sensitivity to the archetype of the child, the inner child that symbolizes the explorer of possibilities: the developing, creative spirit in the adult, whether analysand or analyst.

These training programs, and the analysts and scholars who have contributed to the field, base their work on a particular view of the psyche. The structure they use includes the developing ego and the emerging archetypes within the totality of the Self. The goal of human development is seen as the individuation of the person within a context of the collective, both inner and outer. The therapist assesses the stages of development of the child—physically, emotionally, mentally, and socially—in order to facilitate the full expression of the unique being of the child in its proper timing and context.

The infant is born into a state of unity, defined by Neumann as an experience of total, undifferentiated union with the mother. Fordham suggests this unity is a primary unity, within the original individual being of the child. It is a state of unity upon which the sense of personal identity can rest and individuation proceed.

During this time of primary identification, the child is fundamentally influenced by the parents. At the same time, it is affected by the deep level of the psyche that carries within it archetypal patterns. Beyond this is the actual state of unity in which the child resides, at one with laws of nature and the universe, albeit in the unconscious state.

Ego-consciousness begins when the child first experiences itself as a subject. It moves from the primary state of unity and develops a sense of the "me" that is distinct from the mother and other objects in the world. Separation takes place. The ego increases as it strengthens its ability to handle these objects and to master its world. The attention and energies of the child turn toward relationships, to the task of exploring likenesses and differences. Thus begins a spontaneous development toward maturity. The child starts to form its own personality. This personality is influenced by the family, by education, and by the culture.

There is always an underlying reality in the child from which to draw strength and courage for this development and separation. It is a remembrance, an imprint, a substratum of unity from which consciousness develops. Who has not seen a child spin around and around, trying to see all 360 degrees at once? Who has not noticed the child who sits in a magic circle drawn on the sand, or who scribbles circles and squares in first drawings? In *Analyzing Children's Art*, Kellogg describes these scribbles as the result of an innate impulse of the young child to create symbols of totality.

A Chippewa song of creation describes this memory of unity: "The Center of the Earth Is Where I'm From." The pictograph that accompanies the song is an individual point within a circle. I have seen spontaneous clay representations of this image made quite separately at different times by a girl of three and a boy of five. First, each created a round, hollowed-out container, carefully decorated with sand and colored stones. Then a little round ball of clay was formed, decorated with circular forms. This little round totality could be taken out and put back into the large round vessel at will. The five-year-old boy described this action by saying, "This is how it was, and this is how it is." This is the task of the developing child. It establishes itself through the increase of ego-consciousness as it separates from the unity it experienced with the mother. It comes to relate to the world without losing a relationship to the larger Self, which provides a container and a foundation for the awakening sense of the individual. The initial experience of totality helps the ego of the child face the challenges of maturation, including the collective pressures to conform to a standardized norm.

Sometimes this experience of inner totality is not firmly founded in the child. There may be a difficulty in the relationship between the mother and the child, so that the child does not feel securely connected to this early source of unity. There may have been an illness, a divorce, a major move, or violence within the home or in the outer world. An unstable environment may not have supported the child's first delicate explorations of life. The child may then begin to respond to its environment with fear, anxiety, aggression, or despair. Then the ego does not have enough strength to relate effectively, and it may lose its connection to the totality.

Although distortions and blocks in a child's natural development may be caused by the influences of the outer world, it is also essential to look at the individual nature of the child. There are qualitative differences in children. This fact is seen in families where children respond quite differently to the parental and social environment. One child may be strengthened by it and another weakened. Creative and gifted children, or those who have physical or mental limitations, are already outside normative standards. They can suffer from a parental or cultural attitude that requires adaptation to itself but that is contrary to inherent tendencies. The particular gifts or the "given" nature of each child must be clearly seen and supported. Then the child is not cheated of its right to contribute fully to life according to its capacities, such as they are.

In *The Inner World of Childhood*, Wickes describes the difficulty created for the child whose primary psychological typology is not accepted by its social environment. Jung's conception of typology, as described in *Psychological Types*, is based on the particular strengths and weaknesses of the four functions of sensation, thinking, feeling, and intuition. Each of these functions may be displayed in an extraverted or introverted manner. The child attempts to relate to the world through its strongest function or functions. If this happens not to be a generally acknowledged mode of adaptation, the child's sense of self-acceptance or even reality is placed in question. For example, an introverted child may be in a school that emphasizes extraversion, or an extraverted child may be in a family that is primarily introverted. Depending upon the child, this disparity can be seen as a challenge to define a strong sense of individuality, or it may lead to a sense of alienation. Sometimes a distortion in personality may be created by the child's attempt to make an adaptation contrary to its own nature.

In addition to outer forces and individual differences, the ego of the child may be overwhelmed by internal forces; it may be drowned or mired in contents of the unconscious. These contents may appear as factors of the unknown darkness, or as threatening figures such as monsters or dragons, but they are all qualities inherent in the child's own psyche. In addition, the child's unconscious may be deeply influenced by the unconscious material of the parents. Since the child is in a state of identity with the parents, there is little barrier of ego-discernment between the psychic life of the child and that of the parent.

It is the view of analytical psychology that the child has within itself a resource for strength that can aid in the development of individual personality and of the growing ego. This resource is the Self and the archetypal world of instincts, images, and spirit. These primary factors of the inner world, and the energies that reside in them, can help bring about a realignment of the child to its true and natural individual development, even when the circumstances of its life seem overwhelming.

The Child and the Self

In the process of child therapy, according to Jung's psychology, there are certain assumptions: The child is already born into its totality, the totality of the Self. The pattern of its being is already potentially defined, much as the acorn "contains" the oak or the caterpillar the butterfly. It is hoped that in the therapeutic process a connection to both the Self and the individual pattern will be established and that the unfolding of a strong personality will proceed.

The natural growth energies of children are often quite blocked when they arrive in therapy. In some cases it takes time to establish trust with the therapist before these energies can reemerge. Frequently, however, in the accepting atmosphere of therapy, they will burst through the dam. The experience of these energies and the imagery that accompanies it may be exuberant or full of fear or anger. If dark spaces and fires are opened up in the child, appearing either in action or expression, the therapist must be ready to enter these spaces with the child.

Often a struggle appears, either symbolically, with boats being pursued by sea monsters or knights killing dragons, or in outer action, with fights in school or anger at the parents. As the tensions and pains of the child begin to emerge into the open, the therapist provides a safe container through his or her own experience and understanding of struggle, and through the strength of his or her own ego.

As the process of sharing continues, the energies that have been blocked or distorted start to flow. The art of the therapist is to allow the flood to continue, including its aggressive qualities, until energies are ready to be used creatively. The hammer used to destroy old fences can be the same hammer used to construct a new go-cart.

Sometimes as the energy is released, the tension in the psyche increases. This tension can be the trigger for the emergence of the Self, frequently appearing suddenly and by surprise. It can appear symbolically (in images of centering or balancing, or as a circle or a square) in a dream, in a drawing, in a clay piece, or in song or dance.

This experience is a numinous moment in therapy. It can reenergize and direct the course of the growth process in true relation to the individual nature of the child. The harmonizing effect of this moment provides in itself a healing factor for a child.

Almost all activities of the therapeutic process lead to this moment in which the Self is constellated and then they continue by supporting the direction of these energies into life. A little girl of five was torn by pain and anger at being asked to decide which of her divorced parents she wished to live with. After being able to share the anguish of this choice with the therapist, she painted a many-petalled flower of all the colors of the rainbow. She entitled it simply, "Who I am." Her pain and anger seemed relieved by this image. A little later came another painting, divided into two sections, one red and the other black. In the red were black spots, in the black, red spots. She remarked, "It's like any person. There is good in the bad and bad in the good." With this insight she was able to make a stand for joint custody, desiring the experience of both good/bad parents. The connection to her many-petalled Self created strength to choose a path for her own development.

This connection to the Self can be so full of impact on the psyche that quite a lot of time needs to be given for its integration. As in any new birth, the first stages are vulnerable and sensitive. It is wise to be especially protective of the child during the next phase of therapy, suggesting to the parents or the teachers that the outside environment remain as stable as possible. Then the experience of contact with the Self can be integrated and a new direction for the developing personality can grow out of it.

Just as there is birth and renewal in this process, there can also be death and destruction, as old patterns of behavior that are inappropriate or damaging to the nature of the child are discarded. A young boy in therapy was able to burn down the fences in a sand tray that had surrounded all the animals, wild and domestic. Even the trees had been fenced in. The fire transformed the structure of inhibitions and released the animals to return to their proper and natural habitats, the farms and the jungles. He himself ran out and climbed the nearest tree. It was the first sign of exuberance that I had seen from this nine-year-old boy. The symbolic release of previously imprisoned animal energies simultaneously released his own physical energies.

The energy and strength and security provided by contact with the Self may allow a child to go more courageously into a deeper resolution of his conflicts. The same boy who burned his fences to release his physical animal vitality, after integrating this change, burned down the image of an old, tired-looking church. The church, as he had experienced it, had denied the fire of his emerging sexuality. He replaced this church with a temple built, as he said, all out of nature—of sand, stones, and flowers. It was a temple of mandalic form and was large enough to honor the exuberance of his spirit and his body—that is, to house his totality.

Contact with the Self in therapy provides the springboard for a new entry into the world with increased ego-strength and balance. When this nine-year-old began therapy, he was withdrawn, listless, and depressed, his body almost rigid. A month or so after his temple-Self was built, he was able to join his peers in athletic games, and he began a private scientific exploration of the planets and outer space. As he said, "If God is natural, I'd better know all about nature, here and in the Universe." Thus, he was able to enter the collective world of boys his own age, but without sacrificing his own particular development and interests.

In his book *The Child,* Neumann describes three stages in the development of the child after unity with the mother. The child first explores the surrounding world, experiencing its tastes, smells, sounds, textures. Neumann calls this first stage the animal-vegetative stage. It is a period of natural growth. The second stage is a stage of battle or defense, where the child becomes aware of potential dangers to itself, physically and psychically, and begins to learn how to protect itself from such dangers. The third state is the entry into the collective, where the task is to make an adaptation to group demands without sacrificing individual growth. Each time the Self reemerges, the child has an opportunity to go through these stages of development anew, strengthening ego and personality for their tasks.

A relevant description of the stages of natural growth for a child can be found in Pearce's *Magical Child.* His concept of development is that the child moves naturally, biologically, from one matrix to another, each matrix appropriate to a certain age. The child moves with success if the context is adequate. *Matrix* is the Latin word for "womb." He defines five matrix shifts, moving from concreteness to abstraction. In the first year of life, the matrix is the mother, moving then, until about age seven, to the matrix of the earth, as the child explores the world. The matrix of personal power in the world is experienced until about age eleven, and in the matrix of adolescence, the person becomes his or her own matrix. The full abstraction of mind itself is the matrix of adulthood.

The essential similarity of this description to the Jungian understanding is Pearce's sense that each matrix shift is natural, but is a birth into an unknown state. This movement is made possible by a firm foundation in the previous matrix and by a gradual preparation for and exploration of the new state. Each shift is seen as expanding and encompassing the last. In this way, also, when the Self emerges, a new birth is constellated, moving the child or the adult into a fuller experience of its totality, and providing increased possibilities for creative engagement with the world.

Jung's statement of this innate drive toward totality was expressed in his paper, "The Psychology of the Child Archetype." Although he is speaking of the child as an archetype or symbol, his view informs the perspective of the actual child as it develops toward maturing self-realization.

> The "child" is born out of the womb of the unconscious, begotten out of the depths of human nature, or rather out of living Nature herself. . . . It represents the strongest, the most ineluctable urge in every being, namely the urge to realize itself. It is, as it were, an incarnation of *the inability to do otherwise,* equipped with all the powers of nature and instinct, whereas the conscious mind is always getting caught up in its supposed ability to do otherwise. The urge and compulsion to self-realization is a law of nature and thus of invincible power, even though its effect, at the start, is insignificant and improbable. (1940, pp. 170–71)

The Child and the Archetypes

Images of archetypes other than the Self are commonly experienced by children. Emerging from the primal structure of the psyche, these images appear in dreams and fantasies and often in the description of outer reality. They help children to define their reality, and they carry with them powerful psychic energy that can be useful to the awakening personality. The child lives in this archetypal realm quite fundamentally at the beginning, since little conscious viewpoint of the personal world has been established.

A small boy of three was in the hospital for a tonsillectomy. He saw the nurse come into his room and he whispered, "Here comes the queen of the desert." The nurse-stranger in his world was understood through this inner image.

Observing the subtle play of a child's psyche, one often sees the overlay of archetypal figures onto the personal parents and other adults. The great mother or the queen is not distinguished by the child from the personal mother or the nurse, who are human personalities with limitations.

The archetypal mother and father contain both negative and positive characteristics that may or may not correspond to actual qualities of the personal parents. A child rejected by her mother, for example, may carry an internal image of a good and nourishing mother in an archetypal form: a good fairy godmother image. Or a child whose parents project only the nurturant qualities may carry an image of a stern, judgmental father whose rules and regulations are to be followed as strictly as if they were set by the personal father.

As these archetypal images emerge to compensate for life experiences, they can be very helpful to a child who needs a sustaining force to balance a one-sided, often devastating, outer experience. A girl of six in therapy had played for a long time with a favorite toy witch. The girl admired her for her magic but feared her potential to destroy children. One day an Oriental figure was also chosen from the toy shelves. Unknown to her, it was Kwan Yin, goddess of compassion and protector of children. She placed these in a balanced position with each other. In this play, she represented a balance of both the destructive and nurturant forces in her own psyche.

As the child matures, the characteristics of the personal parents become distinct from the archetypes. In adolescence, the difference between archetypal and personal parents can become clear, helping the ego in its task of freeing itself from distorted views of the personal parents. A fourteen-year-old boy, having just drawn an exceedingly ugly creature, said, ''This is the witch that was my mother.'' He had removed the projection of the negative feminine from his mother, a projection that had been useful as a balance for her overly nurturing attitude toward him.

The child's ego can be nurtured by its connection to the archetypal world, and through this connection the child's capacity for handling its personal world is increased. Later, when archetypal forms are released from this projection onto the parent, an individual can experience their power as spiritual, nonpersonal forces. They originate in the depths of the soul, connecting the individual personality to the universal forms in humanity.

However, there is a danger for some children of becoming lost in the archetypal world and of not developing their own egos. The archetypal world becomes a haven from pain or an escape from the necessary struggle to develop and survive in the personal world. Such children remain identified with the archetypes, playing Cinderella to the jealous stepmother or the prince to the royal father. The task of the therapist is to assist in the removal of these projections and identifications, not by the denial of their reality, but by helping the child to integrate these images into an ordinary human life. In her work at St. George Homes, Romankiw creates an environment in which highly disturbed adolescents can explore the archetypal myth with which they are identified. The children are helped to carry the myth to its completion, thereby making use of the dynamic of the myth but freeing themselves from its possession of them. In this way they are released to explore other imaginal options through which to live their lives.

The Child and Imagination

The images of witch and Kwan Yin, mandala flower and desert queen, may help reveal the power of symbols in the growth process. The energy behind such symbols, expressing itself in archetypal images, has transformative power.

Through a symbol, the imagination creates a vision of health or wholeness, focusing and channeling the images of life libido toward that end. In addition, the action needed to move toward that goal is stimulated by the energy of the symbol itself. Imagination is the source of symbols and images and is therefore a prime source of healing. For the child, imagination is innate, a natural realm of experience. Images appear spontaneously in fantasy, story, and play, and are expressed in painting, song, and dream.

At first, these images may present an opposition, or split, or blockage of energy, such as those caused by fear or anger—for example, monsters, or a fight between angels and devils. When these images are honored, and the tension behind them is accepted and made conscious, a healing symbol or action may appear that transcends the opposites or releases the energy that has been blocked. This can be so profound that physical as well as emotional releases take place.

A small boy had difficulty with fine motor coordination. He had trouble tying his shoes and became the target for teasing in kindergarten. He had the following dream:

> Dream: *I was in a Magic Castle in a black box, and my feet were locked in golden chains. I kicked and kicked my way out and got free. I knew it was a Magic Castle because I could tie my shoes that I kicked off.*

The action in the dream imagery was so intense and effective that, to everyone's amazement, he could indeed tie his shoes the next day!

Such helping images can come in dreams, but they also come in fantasy and through the use of creative media. An adolescent girl who had not menstruated by the age of sixteen did a series of drawings. The first showed a rigidity of conflict between sexuality and religion. The second was a stunning image of the sun radiating its full power to the earth. This series of pictures had the effect of releasing the menstrual flow in the girl.

A child's images may not be as powerful and dramatic as these, but they can be used as guideposts and helpful signs along the road of development. They may reflect the imagery of myth and fairy tale, with underground passageways leading to new worlds, talking animals that become totems, monsters and creatures from outer space, hurricanes and floods, long sea voyages in search of a special island, and so on. These images and imagined actions lead children forward into the unknowable adventures in their worlds, giving them practice in being heroes, princesses, or dragons, and supporting their ego development.

THE CHILD AND THERAPY

In therapy a child meets an adult with whom to share this imaginative journey. The therapist is an adult who can act as guide and protector: a Hermes of the healing process. How does it begin?

Parents

I meet with the parents first, to hear their reasons for wanting to place the child in therapy. I ask for some history of the child and its place within the family. I want to know about its birth, its health, its relationship to school and friends, and any particular view the parents have of the child's strengths and weaknesses. In this interview, I try to remain aware of the special ways in which the parents describe the child, giving evidence of their own value systems and expectations, and of their way of nurturing and disciplining. I also want to know about the state of the marriage and any personal psychological issues within the parents.

Some therapists prefer to see the child in this interview. I do not. Children may all too easily feel overwhelmed by the adult descriptions of their problems. I would rather make the first contact with the child alone. I try to set aside even the parents' description so that the vision and experience of this child is as fresh to me as possible.

It is of primary importance, however, to be as empathic with the parent as with the child. Only in this way is the whole world of the child properly sensed. It can also happen that a subtle polarization occurs between parents and therapists, and this must be guarded against. The therapist's task is to provide an atmosphere in which the Self of the child can be constellated. Although the transference is useful in this, it is quite different from simply being a better parent.

The parents need to support the process of therapy as much as possible, so as not to undercut it with jealousy or guilt. Since parents have taken the initiative to bring the child for therapy, their action needs to be respected and emphasized.

For this reason, I try to tell the parents as much as I can about the way I will be working with their child. I explain that while the child and I work together, the work will be private; that the process must be protected until some resolutions and strengths are gained. During therapy the parents will frequently request a consultation. These meetings can be useful if necessary for the child, or if the parents need assurance that the therapy is progressing. However, I have always talked this over with the child beforehand and have explained the content of the consultation afterward in such a manner that the child understands and feels included. In this way, the bond of therapist and child is kept intact.

This does not mean that the parents' world can be ignored by the therapist if the parents do not ask to be involved. Disturbances of growth can be created by the family system, either from harmful actions or distortions on the part of the parents. In some cases, the problems of the parents are of such intensity that it is wise to suggest that they also enter therapy, not only to free space for their child, but to resolve their own conflicts.

On the other hand, it should never be forgotten that the psyche of the child has great potential strength within it. As this strength is developed, the child experiences health and energetic involvement in life as coming from its own inner resources. It is not totally dependent upon an external arrangement of life circumstances. There is a sense of active participation in change, instead of the sense that life can only be improved if the external environment is changed by others. The ego of the child is vitalized by experiencing its own power and capacity for creating change. In addition, if the child begins to carry the energy of health, the dynamic of the family will be affected. I have seen many families whose overall well-being has been positively affected by the work of one child in establishing its own health.

In general, the issue of how to deal with parents in child therapy is, like every other issue, dependent on the individuality of the child, its particular gifts, limitations, and needs, as well as on the sensitivities of the therapist in providing and supporting the best possible environment for the development of the child's soul.

The Child

I am flooded with images of the many children coming into my work place for the first time. They come to a strange place, to a strange person, and for a strange event. Usually children have come not out of their own motivation or intent but out of that of parents, school, or doctor. They may be afraid, shy, resistant, or eager. It is a pleasure to invite them into a space we will share and to make them as comfortable as possible. I show them around, and then I visit with them as I would with any stranger that I welcomed into my place. I do not probe for problems or attempt a diagnosis, except as I intuitively feel the issues. Above all, I watch and listen and observe, with acceptance and love, this full human being that has come into my life. I begin listening to their stories in the many ways children tell them, sometimes in silence, sometimes sharing, through gesture and postures of the body, and through the quality and sound of the voice.

The first session always reminds me of a primitive ritual for meeting strangers who approach the village. It is customary in some places for strangers to circle the village three times, while the residents and visitors get a chance to know each other through careful observation. This is what I imagine as we share histories—my family and interests and theirs.

One of the reasons I find child therapy so challenging is that whatever the child brings, or is, must be faced directly. The child has very little overlay of developed personality and no accumulation of life experiences or problems to discuss. We are left face-to-face with immediate feelings, sensitivities, and emotions. These are displayed directly and through imagery and play, and they cannot be obscured as easily as with an adult by verbal analysis or intellectual discussion.

It is rare indeed that a child enters this process with a sense of having a problem. That is usually a perception of parents or the school. Children experience directly their pain, loneliness, fear, confusion, joy, excitement, boredom, wonder. These are the raw alchemical ingredients that they bring to their adventure with the therapist.

Not only do children present themselves directly, but their expectations are equally direct. The honesty of children with regard to the integrity and presence of the therapist can be unnerving. I once worked with a small boy whose grave seriousness was charming, and I found myself frequently smiling at this until he said one day, "This is a serious business. You are old enough to know that, and much too old to giggle."

The Therapist

One of the primary requisites of the child therapist is to be able to listen and observe on many levels of communication. Children are not always able to verbalize how they feel directly, and the fear, pain, frustration, or anger may be expressed in some highly imaginative way. A little girl, whose mother felt the child was overly concerned with death, told me the story of the "Monster of Love." The monster made a rose that smelled so sweet you could not resist it, but the minute you picked it you died. This is reminiscent of the poisoned apple the witch-mother offers to Snow White. In truth, the mother had not wanted this child, and as a compensation she overindulged the girl with too many material things. Through the story the child was communicating to me the pain of this ambiguity, the seduction of the love that was not truly nourishing to the heart, and even deadly. In receiving communications of this sort and understanding them, the therapist provides a sense of acceptance and shared reality for a child whose secret is either too painful or dangerous to share, or for which there are as yet no words.

It should be noted that it is not always necessary or even advisable to interpret these communications back to the child. It is an assumption of this mode of therapy that the child has already made a clear statement, either directly or indirectly through a symbolic form. This statement is in itself the beginning of a process, the initial ingredient. Therapists need only communicate their understanding and appreciation of statements like these in such a way that the process can continue. To do this therapists must create out of their own being what Kalff so beautifully describes as a "free and sheltered space." Enthusiasm for the child-spirit is helpful in this. It is also necessary for therapists to remember the processes of development they experienced as children. Without this memory, the necessary understanding and empathy are not operative. If the child-state remains unconscious in therapists, it is likely to be projected onto the child in therapy, and adult therapists will find it difficult to be totally and freely accepting of children as they are.

Therapists must also bring to their work an understanding of the process of maturation. Their sense of where the journey may lead subtly entices children onward to their own adulthood. It is of prime importance that therapists know of the healing power of the unconscious from their own personal experience, as well. In order to have this knowledge, they must have experienced the power of symbols to change the course of life.

It is essential that therapists be aware of any inhibitions they may have with regard to the direct work that children require. Fear of using creative media, of expressing emotions directly, or of being active physically should be acknowledged and worked through. All of these are forms used by children to experiment with life and to help the physical body, the emotions, the imagination, and the developing mind to mature. These modes must, therefore, be accepted as legitimate stages on which the psychological complexities of life are worked out. If not, the child's creative energies will be subtly stifled, as so often happens anyway in our society. This does not mean that therapists need to enter directly into such expressions of play and creativity, but they must feel comfortable in allowing children to use such expression. Otherwise, the inhibitions of the therapist become a restrictive fence for the child.

ENVIRONMENT AND MEDIA

In creating a therapeutic environment for children, it is important to keep in mind, again, that it be a "free and sheltered space." It should be a place in which the child feels protected, private, and safe. Within these bounds, children should feel free to move about, to make sounds, and to express themselves fully. Most children will identify a space as "their" workspace. Ideally, it is advisable to have access to the outside and to a source of water.

In the therapeutic setting, material should be readily available with which children can express their psychological processes. This material may include sandplay resources, clay, art materials, and craft materials, such as enamel kilns, woodworking tools, soldering irons, and so on. Puppets are very useful for storytelling, as are costumes. Musical instruments and a space to dance are important for many children. Games such as darts, chess, and ball games can be used at a particular stage, when competition and skill are being explored by the child.

Play and games can be used at many levels and for different purposes. A game of darts, for example, may allow for an expression of aggression and for practice in competition, but at the same time it can be used to develop skill in focusing and in hitting the mark.

There is no limit to the possibilities of equipment that can be used creatively by a child. Therapists can be on the alert for the special needs of a particular child and add to the stock of equipment as needed. I had a small piano in my office for years that was rarely used. One day a fourteen-year-old boy discovered it and began to play out two characters within himself on the piano, allowing the dialogue to continue in this musical form for weeks. The final harmonizing of these two characters resulted in a song that was inspiring to both of us.

Sandplay

Sandplay is a powerful therapeutic agent in work with both children and adults (cf. chapter by Stewart, above). The technique is simple in form. A box of standardized size is made, and two or three inches of fine sand are placed in it. Two trays are generally used in therapy, one with damp sand and one with dry. On shelves near the tray are miniature figures representing many aspects of the outer world—people, buildings, trees, plants, animals, vehicles—as well as figures representing the inner world of fantasy and spirit—gods, demons, witches, fairies, and so on. Children place these figures in a sand tray and make a miniature world scene. The sand itself may also, of course, be molded and shaped. The great value of this therapeutic tool lies in its ability to focus and contain the symbolic expressions of the psyche.

Sandplay provides an opportunity for changing the old structures of the world and creating new structures, as these are envisioned by the psyche. It provides the ego of the child, therefore, with greater power and effectiveness. In sandplay the Self is activated, and this activation creates the foundation for new psychological growth and movement. The communication of the drama played out in the sand tray, when received by the therapist with clear understanding of the symbolic meaning, affects the unconscious and induces a spontaneous movement toward growth in the child. It does this even if simply received, without discussion. Sometimes, however, the therapist may want to bridge the symbolic expression in the sand tray and the outer world of the child by a simple interpretation or suggestion, offering the child a different perspective or direction in its daily life.

Painting and Clay

Art forms such as painting, drawing, and sculpting can also be used as channels for transformative energies. Here again, as with sandplay, free expression provides a vessel for the manifestation of symbols that portray important influences in the personality. The energy of the unconscious process is contained within a work of art produced by a child. The child then in turn reacts to the energy that the product contains. Drawings or clay pieces thus begin to inform their consciousness. A dialogue begins between the expressed manifest form and the observer. As observers, children begin to gain acquaintance and make a bond of friendship with the expressions of the Self.

Archetypal images, such as monsters or angels, or expressions of strong affects, such as anger or fear or love, are experienced by the child.

Once drawn or sculpted, these take on a definite shape, and the child can recognize and handle them. This is similar to the mask-making activity of primitive peoples, who also can identify their honored and feared unconscious "figures" in these forms. When these forces are known, their energies can be usefully integrated into life. Monsters and angels can become familiar, even friendly. They can represent carriers of powerful energies, useful to the child as it moves into the world.

Story, Poetry, Dance, and Music

For many children, words and sounds are more natural creative tools than visual forms. Explorations of image and fantasy can be made through storytelling, plays, puppet shows, and poetry just as well as they can through visual media. What is important, as in the visual forms, is that the true individual creation of the child does, indeed, emerge, and not an imitation based on an idea of performance.

One little girl completed her therapy with a cycle of songs called, "The New Seasons." Writing songs was a very eloquent mode for her, since she was more facile with sound than with paint. Although such expressions as these may be only a temporary form of self-expression, stimulated by the work of therapy, one does occasionally uncover a gift that needs further support and development.

Movement or dance is another possible form of expression (cf. chapter by Chodorow, above). With an individual child, the therapist may have to join in the dance to create a free environment for movement. This experience can also be a joyous sharing for the therapist.

Poetry touches very important areas in the child, since it consists of metaphor and image. Topics that are very difficult to share, such as birth and death and pain, can often be expressed in the shaped container of a poem. Haiku is a simple form that can be used by children. As with any form, the goal is not performance but the containment and expression of images in forms that allow healing psychic forces to emerge in the child.

DREAMS

Children may bring dreams to the therapist, especially now that an interest in sharing dreams has taken hold in the larger society. When parents honor their own dreams and those of their children, children are more apt to share them in the intimacy of the therapeutic process. Although the usual analytical discussion of dream content is often inappropriate with a child, the contents can be indirectly explored for their meaning in the context of the child's life. Often this can be done through continuing the procession of images in painting, puppetry, or storytelling. This is what I often call "second chaptering." The child then brings itself actively into contact with the images, and this activity can help to integrate the material into life.

When children share dreams, they may be communicating to the therapist that there are overwhelming forces that need managing or intervention by the therapist. Sometimes these dreams have to do with confusion and fear created by misinformation about certain of life's mysteries, such as sex, birth, or death. On the other hand, dreams may reflect outer circumstances, such as family dynamics. The child's psyche is greatly influenced by the life of the parents, the school, and even larger events, such as disasters and celebrations. Since children still live largely in unconscious identification with their parents, they remain profoundly open to these influences.

The therapist has the opportunity to provide boundaries and a protected container for the child who shares dream material. Together, a plan can be drawn up for the use of the material. Specific tasks can be given to the child if a dream points to a need for ego-strengthening. Sometimes objective information needs to be given to clear up distortions. Sometimes intervention with parents or with the school is needed if these forces are too destructive.

The content of children's dreams is vast. There are, naturally, the nightmares. These often contain unknown, devouring figures and forces: ocean waves and hurricanes, monsters and snakes, lions and tigers, robots and machines—all of which may be overwhelming to the nascent ego. Some dreams picture the child's developing consciousness: an island, a candle, a new plant or animal, a star. Other dreams portray profound archetypal patterns and motifs from the realms of gods and demons. Others are clearly responses to daily life, involving fantasies, wishes, hurts. Others contain unconscious contents belonging to parents. This happens frequently, and in the sharing of a dream the child may be helped to release this psychic overload. For example, one boy whose father was experiencing great rage that was neither expressed nor transformed dreamed that every time he sat in his father's chair, it burst into flames. It was necessary to discuss then with the father the enormous burden and fear the boy was carrying. The father began to take responsibility for his anger, relieving the boy of this pressure and thereby freeing his son's energies for his own life. Whatever the contents, all dreams should be treated with honor as profound offerings of the child.

THE WORK

The work between the child and therapist begins at its own pace. It is the art of therapy to provide the means for sharing. Once allowed into the child's psychological world, the therapist must offer opportunities for healing to take place. Some children find it easier to work in therapy through imaginative play, others through sharing of dreams, others through games, and some through the relationship with the therapist alone. The therapist must be open to any option that will facilitate the flow of psychic life. The sensitivity to the child must be twofold: first, the child must be assisted in developing an ego that will be effective in the world; second, the particular pattern of this individual being must be recognized and nourished.

A sense of these two aspects of the work is essential, and is responsible for creating the exciting challenge of therapy with children. The individual uniqueness of a child will be displayed in the child's own pace and timing, through action, through dreams, and through fantasy and imaginative play. Diagnosis and objective description of a child's psyche, and a plan for the work that can lead to growth for the child, must be derived from the child's own expressions.

As the child leads the therapeutic process forward, the therapist must remain aware of the deeper dynamics that are being expressed. The gesture, action, emotion, artistic product, or play must be responded to with direct empathic understanding. The symbol-maker in the therapist must be able to receive directly the symbol-maker in the child. Often this means by-passing logical or verbal analysis. So often the gold mine of imagery for self-creation that emerges from a child can be overlooked if the emphasis is on "cure" or "solving the problem" or "normalcy." While adaptation to the collective is an essential ingredient in the maturation of a child, it should not be achieved at the expense of, but rather with the help of, the child's individual and creative response to life.

As this self-creation takes place in the "free and sheltered" place provided by the therapist, the healing process also emerges. The energies of the Self are constellated, and the ego is strengthened to take on the task of the world. The timing of this entry into the world usually coincides with termination. Exceptions occur, of course, with moves, vacations, illnesses, and the withdrawal of children from therapy by parents.

In almost all cases, the child knows the pace and extent of the therapy. Sometimes children will say directly that they need come only one or two times more. Sometimes the communication will be indirect, as when they prefer a party or a baseball game to the therapy session. So often, the attachment of the child to the process of life is greater than the attachment to the therapist. If the course of therapy has been successful, termination is anticipated symbolically or by an action that indicates the child's desire to try its own wings in the world. At this stage I have seen sandplay images or drawings of a car or bicycle that is moving in an arc out of the tray or drawing. It is as though the work of therapy is seen by the psyche as part of the totality of the life process, and the vehicle has been placed on course for the arc of the journey. It is the joy of the therapist, equally nonattached, to say, "Good journeying."

REFERENCES

Allan, J., and McDonald, P. 1975. The use of fantasy enactment in the treatment of an emerging autistic child. *Journal of Analytical Psychology* 20/1:57–68.

Axline, V. 1964. *Dibs, in search of self.* Boston: Houghton Mifflin.

Edinger, E. 1972. *Ego and archetype.* New York: Putnam.

Fordham, M. 1970. *Children as individuals.* New York: Putnam.

———. 1976. *The Self and autism.* The Library of Analytical Psychology, vol. 3. London: Heinemann.

Gardner, H. 1980. *Art scribbles: the significance of children's drawings.* New York: Basic Books.

Hayes, D. 1970. A child's fantasy. *Psychological Perspectives* 1/2:122–37.

Jung, C. G. 1921. *Psychological types.* Collected works, vol. 6. New York: Pantheon, 1971.

———. 1940. The psychology of the child archetype. In *Collected works,* vol. 9, part 1, pp. 151–82.

———. 1954. *The development of personality.* Collected works, vol. 17. New York: Pantheon.

Kalff, D. 1981. *Sandplay, a psychotherapeutic approach to the psyche.* Los Angeles: Sigo Press.

Kellogg, R. 1970. *Analyzing children's art.* Palo Alto: National Press Books.

———. 1979. *Children's drawings and children's minds.* New York: Avon.

Marshak, M. 1976. Observations of the treatment of adolescents. *Journal of Analytical Psychology* 15/2.

Neumann, E. 1973. *The child: structure and dynamics of the nascent psyche.* New York: Putnam.

Pearce, J. C. 1977. *Magical child.* New York: Dutton.

Stone, H. 1970. The problem of good and evil in the development of a child. *Psychological Perspectives* 1/1:43–56.

Sullwold, E. 1971. Eagle eye. In *The well tended tree,* ed. H. Kirsch, pp. 235–52. New York: Putnam.

West, K. L. 1978. *Crystallizing children's dreams.* Portland, Oreg.: Amata Graphics.

Wickes, F. 1972. *The inner world of childhood.* New York: Appleton-Century.

Winnicott, D. W. 1965. *The maturational process and the facilitating environment*. New York: International Universities Press.

———. 1971. *Therapeutic consultations in child psychiatry*. New York: Basic Books.

[14]

ANALYSIS WITH THE AGED

Bruce Baker and Jane Wheelwright

If at the end of life, you have only yourself,
it is much. Look, you will find.

—Scott-Maxwell

JUNGIAN theory suggests that the greatest potential for growth and self-realization exists in the second half of life. The demands of the ego lessen, much experience awaits examination, and time is short, making contact with the Self more likely, as well as more necessary. "For a young person it is almost a sin, or at least a danger, to be too preoccupied with himself," Jung wrote, "but for an aging person it is a duty and a necessity to devote serious attention to himself" (1930–31, p. 399). He also suggested that only a mature person, having a developed ego and plenty of experience, can face the Self, and thus individuate fully. Along the same lines, Joseph Wheelwright has pointed out (in a personal communication) that young people by nature focus on the goals of life, but older people, with less concrete goals to look forward to, tend to see life as an ever-changing process to be experienced. Fordham states that concern about

Bruce Baker, M.D., is a graduate of the C. G. Jung Institute of San Francisco and a member of the Society of Jungian Analysts of Northern California; he maintains a private practice in San Francisco. Educated at Bucknell University and Temple Medical School, he served his psychiatric residency at Langley Porter Neuropsychiatric Institute in San Francisco. Dr. Baker worked for several years as community consultant in geriatric psychiatry for the Northeast Mental Health Center in San Francisco.

Jane Wheelwright is in private practice in San Francisco. A former student and analysand of C. G. Jung, Toni Wolff, and Erna Rosenbaum, she is a founding member of the London Analytical Psychology Club, the San Francisco Analytical Psychology Club, the Northern California Society of Jungian Analysts, and the C. G. Jung Institute of Northern California. She is a former chairperson of the certifying board of the C. G. Jung Institute of Northern California and is the author of "Women and Men," *Death of a Woman*, and *Ranch Papers* (in progress).

individuation begins in the second half of life and necessitates maturity, although he also believes that the process of individuation starts unconsciously at birth.

The idea that the old as well as the young continue to grow psychologically toward fulfillment of their psychic potentials distinguishes the Jungian approach from many other therapies. Freudian theory, for example, suggests that analysis with older people is unlikely to effect much change because there is not enough libido in them for a strong transference. Moreover, Freud wrote that "near or about the age of fifty the elasticity of the mental processes on which treatment depends, is as a rule lacking—old people are no longer educable—and, on the other hand, the mass of material to be dealt with would prolong the duration of treatment indefinitely" (p. 264). King comments that Freud was forty-nine years old when he wrote this.

Although old age is supposed to be the psychological culmination of life for Jungians, very few old patients are written about in the Jungian journals. According to King, and from discussions with colleagues, it seems that most analysts do not work with them. In a recent survey of Jungian analysts (Bradway and Wheelwright), twenty-nine percent of the respondents stated that they try not to accept patients over seventy, and only twenty-three percent felt they worked well with this group. We talk and read a lot about midlife crises, but what about the people beyond middle age, who make up one of the largest sections of our population?

The paucity of old patients in psychotherapy may reflect the fact that, in general, older people do not know enough about psychotherapy, and so do not understand its healing potential. Many people who are old today were more concerned in their younger years with the Depression and with World War II than with their inner lives. In their youth, the only knowledge many people had about psychotherapy was associated with "asylums," where people were locked up for years on end. At the time that they were defining their values, furthermore, psychology was seen as a radical assault upon the established values of society. In addition, older people may think that analysis deals primarily with childhood, and they see little to be gained from examining that long-past stage of their lives. So it is little wonder that older people, except for those receiving inadequate help in geriatric wards in state and federal hospitals, today represent such a small proportion of voluntary patients in psychotherapy.

On the other hand, little organized effort is made to explain to older people the possibilities inherent in such treatment, or to counteract their shame in even needing such help. Perhaps some unconscious resistance inhibits therapists from seeking or accepting old patients. We are a youth-oriented culture, and we tend to overlook these older, "unproductive" people. This is reflected in the "economic argument" that analyzing older people is almost a waste of time because they have fewer years to live. Putting people's lives into such a quantitative frame of reference only reflects our society's present basic denial of the worth of wisdom and experience.

THE PRESENTING PROBLEMS OF OLDER PATIENTS

At the heart of many psychological problems in the troubled elderly lies an inability to adjust to the profound changes, both internal and external, that are inherent in aging. The only constant in life is change, but the changes that age brings are so basic and so numerous that sometimes old defenses and solutions no longer silence the new kinds of anxieties that come with them. Our society's emphasis on youth compounds these anxieties immeasurably. In older people, time and energy run out, independence lessens, long-cherished goals remain out of reach, lifelong relationships break off, unsolved problems grow urgent, unresolved past transgressions become ever more painful, and former paths to satisfaction appear less and less accessible. New adjustments are called for, but unfortunately the awkwardness that any old person inevitably feels when developing latent abilities and new attitudes usually makes the less conscious old person too uncomfortable even to think about them. And, as Jung said, "It is hard to see what other goal the second half of life can offer than the well-known aims of the first" (1930–31, p. 400).

To increase these difficulties, many old people with conflicts often feel constrained to be silent, in order to spare younger people their painful knowledge of old age. And so, often, the past seems the only comfortable place of refuge. Routine and habit rule the day, meaning flees, and despair instead of hope takes its place in the heart.

New adjustments and new attitudes can be developed, however. Jung believed that "the very frequent neurotic disturbances of adult years all have one thing in common: they want to carry the youthful phase over the threshold of the so-called years of discretion" (1930–31, p. 396). And, he went on, "whoever carries over into the afternoon the law of morning must pay for it with damage to his soul" (1930–31, p. 400). But, while he described the problem, he was also intimating a solution to it. He said, for instance, that the disturbances of the second half of life were due to an incapacity to be in touch with those unconscious feelings and images that, if fully experienced and examined, could insure a closer relationship to the

Self. Such a viewpoint implies the necessity of a more profound change within the psyche of the older person than in any prior time of life; this is a difficult, but not impossible, task.

' Major growth-oriented changes in the psyche are often temporarily or permanently blocked, however, or so slow in coming that symptoms emerge. These may include depression, tyrannical convictions of superiority, defensive dogmatism, cynicism, hypercriticalness, denial, quiet despair, suffering designed to guarantee guilt-generated concern, obsession with the past, boredom, exhaustion, stagnation, and all the physical and psychic woes arising from unacknowledged physical and psychic tension. Many patients are also debilitated to the point of illness by their bitterness over the fact that, having obeyed all of society's mandates, they still lack a sense of fulfillment.

This is a bleak picture, and it illustrates the worst that can happen. On the other hand, many older people show their unique strengths in their satisfactory adjustments to aging, especially those who are by nature more deeply and instinctively in touch with their inner selves, who are religiously oriented, or who have had some analysis. A greater percentage than we commonly suppose thus find in old age the best part of their lives. Even the isolation that some old people experience, while abhorrent to most younger people, is at times savored as an opportunity for reflection, rest, self-knowledge, and creativity, as well as a preparation for meeting death alone.

When analysis is undertaken by older people, they often bring to it richer, if not happier, remembrances of the past, with more obviously repetitive patterns of behavior, than younger people do. (Perhaps this is why Jung once said that a person without a past is hardly a complete person, and preferred working with patients in the second half of life.) For instance, if a woman has had seven divorces by the age of sixty-two, she is much less likely to argue that her failure at marriage is due to "bad luck" or a poor choice of partners. She is almost forced to admit that there is something unusual going on that bears self-examination.

Old people who have been coping with life over many years also often bring into analysis a strong and flexible ego, an indispensable asset if they are to relate to the Self during their analysis and avoid the pitfalls, enumerated by Edinger (p. 3), that occur when the ego is engulfed by the Self. Old patients, their childhood complexes now less affect-laden, do not worry so much about what others think about them. They feel they have "nothing to lose" by trying a new way of problem solving. Painful insight, once reached, can often be more easily integrated because of lessened resistance. In addition, many older people describe an increase of intensity in their feelings and in their connections to the world that makes them more reflective. And, as death draws closer, patients often feel the pressure to solve their problems and realize themselves. As one patient put it, "I just hope I can grow up before I die." With their ego-involving problems of "doing well and getting ahead" relegated to the past, their relationships often less idealized, and their lessened energies forcing them to be more selective, old people can face the profound questions that age poses. Thus old age, especially with the help of analysis, can be a fertile ground for growth.

WORKING WITH OLDER PATIENTS

There are many ways in which the process of analysis with older patients differs from analysis with younger ones. Older patients are more likely to have medical problems or to be taking medications that affect their mental state. These factors have to be taken into consideration and allowance made for them. A headache may be the result not of a marital disagreement but of high blood pressure; stabbing pains may be caused not by someone disappointing the patient and stabbing him or her in the back, but by arthritis or a gall bladder problem. A depression may be worse because the patient is now taking reserpine. Consultation with patients' physicians, or a referral to one, may be needed. Energy and attention can lag at times, and the pace of analysis, like the pace of everything else, can be slowed. Missed sessions are more common, as are tardy arrivals, because unexpected physical problems arise. It may even be necessary to terminate sessions early because of fatigue. Also, it can be harder for older patients to put their insights into words. In general, more patience is needed. Much life has to be relived. But results can be just as profound, if not more so, than with younger patients.

Resistances, however, can be quite strong, especially at the start, for they have been built up over a lifetime in a society that has turned its back on death and old age. Some older patients seem to want to echo the words of Scott-Maxwell, who said, "I know my faults so well that I pay them small heed." Another resistance is "At my age, what does it matter?" Often, too, an older patient has so much of his ego committed to a certain point of view, and so little faith in his ability to change, that an interpretation given too soon may induce categorical denial, even panic. A cherished point of view, however inapplicable, can be clung to like an old and trusted friend.

Independence is of paramount importance to most older patients because they see it, rightly, as the keystone of their existence; they also see their emotional, physical, and financial problems as a threat to this independence. They can thus view analysis, and the possibility of dependence on the analyst, as one more threat to their independence. The methodology of analysis in general needs to be discussed with the patient.

The process of transference may also be different with older patients. Hinton advises the analyst to be prepared for the transference to be focused on the actual process of searching for new meaning itself—that is, on the archetype of the way or quest—rather than on the analyst him- or herself (p. 538). The analyst, Hinton adds, may be seen as "a stern initiator into a new world, or as the ideal person . . . containing infinite knowledge and wisdom" (p. 539). The reverse, however, can also happen, and older patients may see the therapist as one of their less competent children, or, in a parallel way, as a beloved child who was somehow lost to them. The former type of transference, unless it is resolved, can inhibit progress in analysis; the latter, positive transference can aid it. It can be vital to the process that the analyst accept some of this positive transference and allow the projection to stand unchallenged, sometimes for a long time. Older people, especially if living alone and thus deprived of touching, may also find it helpful to make contact in a physical as well as an interpersonal sense. Actual physical contact, such as shaking hands or even holding hands while the patient reveals a particularly difficult thought, memory, or feeling, can be quite helpful. For most older patients, the sexual implications of touching are much less significant than the human meaning of such a gesture.

Older people who see the younger generation as brusque, impatient, and hurried, as well as lacking in experience and expertise, may find it hard to believe that a younger person actually wants to listen carefully to them. In a recent Hollywood movie, an old man commits a robbery and then hides the money. When apprehended, he chooses to go to jail rather than reveal where the money is hidden, because he knows that as long as he keeps his secret, some people besides salesmen will want to talk to him for the rest of his life.

Often older people find it humiliating to have to turn to a younger person for help, feeling they should have transcended their personal problems. They may feel they should not reveal their failures—especially to people younger than themselves. Later in analysis, extreme envy of the analyst's perceived competence in life can emerge, as well as the desire to frustrate the analyst and the process.

Many therapists tend to want to protect older people from harsh realities, either because they see them as "frail" or because they have guilt feelings themselves. In fact, as Castillejo points out, there is no such need to shelter older people: grief does not shatter them, because of the wisdom they have gained through the years. She goes on to point out that older people who are given too much not only become weakened but can constellate a poisonous bitterness in the young. Williams speaks about the analyst's unconscious assumptions about death as a cause of problems in analysis (p. 30). These assumptions protect either the analyst, the patient, or both. One such assumption is "Neither of us is going to die." Another is "You're going to die, but I'm not." The only helpful resolution to this problem obviously lies in making conscious the reality "We are both going to die, but much remains to be done."

Older patients can represent parental figures to therapists, and can thus evoke many unconscious feelings, including anger, idealization, and a wish to deny such clients' problems or to avoid older patients in general. Some therapists want to deny their own future selves as seen in older clients, or they are uncomfortable with such clients' proximity to what they see as the ultimate failure of therapy—that is, death. Some therapists, moreover, may not yet have faced the issue of their own inevitable death. Older people also represent in living form another coming crisis for the therapist—that is, finding the meaning of his or her own life. Often those older people who have gained a sense of meaning for themselves are seen by others, including some therapists, as unscientific and subjective. Their gift of seriousness is thus spurned, and some valuable, far-reaching insights are lost. When old and retired as an analyst, Scott-Maxwell wrote: "The purpose of life may be to clarify our essence, and everything else is the rich, dull, hard, absorbing chaos that allows the central transmutation. . . . I ask all those who like me seem to do nothing: Does the passion in our hearts somehow serve?" (p. 129).

When seen to be ill, weak, or helpless, old people make therapists feel similarly helpless and ineffectual. To regain their potency, therapists overprotect their patients, withhold painful insights, avoid conflictual interpretations, console too much, and are drawn into helping solve concrete problems in the outer world that are better left to the patients or others. The idea that older patients are weak and helpless, simply because of their age, fits into the collective modern prejudice that age itself is some kind of incurable disease rather than a natural, somewhat limiting, process that holds great potential for growth and happiness. This collective viewpoint that death must be resisted as a defeat and insult to our being puts us all in a hopeless struggle against the natural tides of life and death.

Old age is not a stage of life with many common characteristics, as most suppose. The only things all old people seem to have in common are a statistical closeness to death, a gradual reduction of physical energy, and more leisure. The many other supposed attributes that are projected onto old people arise out of stereotypic thinking that is in part a device used by younger people to protect themselves from the reality of their own advancing, individual old age. Since stereotypic thinking is usually applied to others, not to oneself, anxiety can be at least temporarily allayed by seeing everything bad as "old" (not me), and everything good as "young" (like me). Stereotypes are also used by old people to escape the demands of old age.

Extraverted patients are more easily seduced by our outward-oriented society and "get along in the world more easily in the first half of life" (Jacobi 1943, pp. 25–26). When faced with the isolation old age brings, they may have the hardest time. Many extraverts in our society have had little incentive during their lives to be contemplative. In analysis it becomes necessary for them to look inward, even to archetypal levels, and often this process produces great resistance in them. Old age may be easier for introverts, on the other hand, who are more naturally geared to the inward view. But the challenge of the archetypal level of the unconscious can be threatening to any person who has not had prior experience of the inner world.

Problems presented by the negative animus and anima (cf. chapter by Bradway, below) in all unanalyzed patients not only continue to be present, but also can become more urgent. Incidentally, those who have been in a creative connection with their contrasexual component feel that in old age the animus and anima are more and more integrated into the personality. But an older man who is possessed by his anima, and is moody, irritable, and depressed, is in greater trouble than a younger man with the same problem. Projecting his anima onto a much younger woman may help for a while, but sooner or later this projection becomes disastrous. And an animus-ridden, domineering, and harsh older woman becomes still more rigid and at odds with cultural and family expectations as she ages. Some of these old people actually identify with the contrasexual components and, more often than not, cannot be helped unless disaster strikes.

In a similar way, a serious shadow problem in an older person can also lead to painful ostracism, for the unconscious and denied aspects of the personality, such as hate, greed, and envy, begin to dictate a person's actions. But, as many therapists note, such shadow problems have often been tempered by experience or lack of energy. Fordham states that in old age the sharp distinctions among ego and shadow and anima can no longer be maintained so rigidly. Other analysts find the shadow, in the face of imminent death, the worst problem of all. Discomfort, fatigue, debilitation, and weakness let loose the shadow. An example of what can happen is given in Jane Wheelwright's account of a terminally ill patient (1981).

Psychological typology applies to old people, but in a different way than it applies to younger people. Young and middle-aged people tend to operate mostly through their superior functions. This is logical because they have to orient themselves to their conscious world and achieve success in their communities. During these stages, they become more and more aware of their third, less developed, function. When it surfaces from the unconscious, it becomes their best and most available channel to the unconscious and keeps them refreshed with new life, new ideas, new understanding, and more awareness of themselves (cf. chapter by Quenk and Quenk, above).

As old age sets in and the patient needs to turn inward for more and more insight, it is necessary to draw on the fourth, most undeveloped, function. Apparently nature intended this development, because if old people are sensitive to what is happening to them they will realize that their fourth function wants to surface naturally. They may have to be guided toward this development, even though nature favors it, because our society has not paid much attention to what goes on in old age. Old people tend to be afraid of their most unavailable (inferior) function because through their earlier years they have experienced it negatively. What breaks through prematurely from the unconscious tends to be negative. For example, a sensation type can, in early life, be seized and totally riveted by his or her inferior intuition's gloomy preoccupation with the inevitability of death, a problem best dealt with later. But if old people are patient, they will learn that the inferior function is potentially their most valuable channel to the unconscious and the royal road to the Self, the source of their creativity. If they heed the fact that the fourth function wants to be heard, they will be greatly rewarded. In fact, their individuation will also be enhanced because creative acts increase consciousness. At one time, Jung saw the process of making the functions conscious as equivalent to the individuation process in the second half of life.

One qualifying note has to be added. As the superior functions are superseded by the inferior ones, the former become less viable and less functional. There comes a time when it seems that the fourth function absorbs the other three, and the person lives more and more as a whole being.

One great difference between older patients and younger ones lies, as might be expected, in their dreams, which are less ego-related and reflect a more collective level of the psyche. Many dreams tend to be vague and unstructured, especially for those people who are stuck in neurotic patterns. The elements of space and time may even be missing. There is a shadowy underworld quality in others. Von Franz remarked in a private conversation that the dreams of old people are difficult to interpret because of this fact. It has been mentioned that the dying, at any age, have collective dreams. Jung speaks of older patients' dreams as dealing not only with death and the hereafter, but also, at times, with a final love affair or marriage, symbolizing the coming together of the opposites and indicating something new in the offing. Old people often dream of going home, going on a trip, packing, visiting with those who have died (Wheelwright 1979), or of a breakthrough of some sort, such as being led through a waterfall into some beautiful hidden world.

One apparently physically healthy American Jewish woman in her sixties, who had been estranged from her religion, described a dream in which a white ship with Israeli markings on it lay at anchor nearby to take her to Israel. She thought the dream might refer to her loss of faith, and she seriously investigated joining a synagogue and becoming involved in a Jewish discussion group. Her efforts, however, were so alienating and unsatisfying that she gave them up. Within a year she was dead from an unsuspected cancer. The white ship had come to take her home in a much more literal sense than she realized.

Sharp describes a dream that a very old woman had just before her death—so close to it, in fact, that there was no time to interpret it. In the dream, the woman said, "I saw all my sicknesses gathered together, and as I looked they were no longer sicknesses but roses, and I knew the roses would be planted and that they would grow" (p. 200). Perhaps, as Scott-Maxwell says, "We suffer as we change, that life may change in us" (p. 141).

The Tasks and Stages of Aging

"From the middle of life onward," Jung states, "only he remains vitally alive who is ready to *die with life*" (1934, p. 407). Or, as Jung said elsewhere, if you are lucky, you will live yourself out of life! In order to live fully as we age, we must meet and acknowledge, if not master, at least seven specific tasks. These tasks are more evident, more urgent, and perhaps more possible in the autumn of life. But it must be remembered that these tasks of aging are also the tasks of living, for old age is not separate from life. Old age is, rather, the time for finding one's essence. These tasks also reflect the basic demands of analysis. There is a saying that older people are the same in old age as they were in their youth, only more so. Perhaps analysis, too, is the same for old people, only more so.

The seven tasks of aging introduce themselves at different stages of life, and the work of completing them occurs to some degree in all the stages. The first task typically begins in the fifties, when the first half of life is definitely over and the certainty of death must be faced. Many people in their fifties, even those who have done well and had analysis, fall into a chronic state of panic as the startling reality of death sinks in. For some, it is the ultimate insult or betrayal by life. But as the fifties progress into the sixties, if the reality of death is accepted, further demands of life pull people onward. For when life is threatened, at any age, there is a need to live more deeply. (Terminally ill people, including the young, are challenged the most, but can, with interpretation of messages from the unconscious or with some kind of religious support, also find meaning in the time left to them.) Younger people almost always associate any age over sixty with death, but most of the less neurotic old seldom think about it, focusing instead on living and accepting death as a part of life. They might be aware, however, that death is always at their shoulder and can be a confidant, an advisor, even a friend and source of power. Death then becomes, as Goethe put it, "nature's expert advice to get plenty of life."

Jung spoke of the psyche at the end of life as seeming virtually to ignore death. He also said, however, that a person who cannot face death is often childishly greedy, fearful, defiant, and willful, much like a young man who refuses to embrace life (1930–31, p. 402). Jung spoke of death as both a focus of life—"man goes through analysis so he can die" (McGuire and Hull, p. 360)—and as a goal—"It is hygienic to discover in death a goal towards which one can strive. Shrinking away . . . robs the second half of life of its purpose" (1930–31, p. 402). He suggested that perhaps death is as pregnant with meaning as birth (1934, p. 408). It may be that life is a pregnancy, and death a birth. Simone de Beauvoir makes the point that if time stretched out indefinitely, there would be no measure and no meaning. Clinically, one of the best signs that the idea of death has been assimilated is that a patient makes arrangements for his or her funeral.

The old need to review, reflect upon, and sum up their lives, and this reflection is a second important task of aging. If people are alert, they will feel this urge, off and on, throughout their old age. Jung comments that neurosis in older patients can be secondary to the act of repressing the natural development of reflection (McGuire and Hull, p. 108). Reviewing his own life, Jung wrote: "In old age one begins to let memories unroll before the mind's eye and, musing, to recognize oneself in the inner and outer images of the past. This is like a preparation for an existence in the hereafter . . . " (1961, p. 320). He goes on to say: "I try to see the line which leads through my life into the world, and out of the world again.''

It is remarkable how many old people feel an urgent need to tell their story or state their case before they die. Many people have written their life stories and then died shortly thereafter. Jung himself died shortly after writing *Memories, Dreams, Reflections,* and Ernest Becker wrote his major work, *The Denial of Death,* unaware that he would shortly be dying. It is not hard to see the true value of the frequent reminiscing in the aged, for it is essentially an act of witnessing one's own life. ''A life needs to be seen for what it was before it can be laid reverently aside'' (Hine, p. 50). Butler and others have spoken of the therapeutic advantage of the life review. To paraphrase Santayana, one who can't remember an emotion is doomed to repeat it.

This process brings to light a third task of aging. As we witness our own lives, reviewing our goals and accomplishments, we come face-to-face with a fact that heretofore we have denied for the sake of extending our abilities and expanding our experiences—namely, the reality that our lives have finite limits. These limits have gradually become more obvious as life has gone along, but they now demand conscious acknowledgment. For time, in its relentless advance, makes certain experiences unattainable. Some children will never be born; some careers will never be followed; some relationships will never be resolved; desired achievements in one's chosen field become improbable, if not impossible. Cherished goals must be abandoned, perhaps with grace but most certainly with pain, for time and energy are ebbing and the noon of life has passed.

And so one must draw some conscious mental boundaries beyond which it is not reasonable to extend the remainder of one's time and energy. This feels at first like a painful constriction of potential, a loss of a part of life's promise. But seen from another perspective, it is an unloading of self-imposed burdens and a deliverance from exhausting efforts toward unlikely goals. Perhaps it is also a relinquishing of some only half-wanted rewards. Consciously letting go of these burdens and aspirations lets one focus total attention and energy not only on what is attainable, but on what is one's truest concern. A middle-aged patient once took to Jung a puzzling, numinous dream that consisted of just the image of a circular clearing in a forest. Jung spoke of this image as symbolizing the necessity of drawing limits in our lives, and of how even the Romans had to build walls in southern Germany and northern Britain to mark the outer limits of their hegemony; he mentioned also their ritual of plowing a furrow to mark the outer limits of a new city. If empires demand boundaries to thrive, then surely also do human lives.

Unless one at least begins to review and honor the past, acknowledging what has been left undone, one will find the subsequent, fourth, task of old age much more difficult. This next step consists of a letting go of the dominance of the ego, a process that already begins to occur naturally as one follows the thread of one's life and sees one's fate revealed. (Of course this assumes that the ego has already been well developed.) Jung spoke of this letting go process, which occurs after much of the unconscious is assimilated, as "an approximation of conscious and unconscious where the center of the personality no longer coincides with the ego, but with a point midway between the conscious and the unconscious" (1966, p. 221). In his own life, Jung's partial letting go of the dominance of his heroic, ego-bound thinking function illustrates the beginning of this process. As Fordham describes it, when the ego no longer needs to be so significant, as happens later in life, it gets drained of part of its energy and archetypal activity increases (p. 129). The Self then eliminates the ego's position of preeminence.

The process of letting go, if it happens at all, varies for different people. A successful, unretired business magnate may persevere in ego-dominated actions far too long, and then be laid low by depression or physical symptoms that are messages to let go and contact the Self. The more rewards such activities have afforded such persons, and the more society's esteem for productivity influences them, the harder and less likely it is for them to give up the ego's dominance without a struggle, because to them the process of looking inward seems self-indulgent, weak, and nonproductive. In all fairness, one has to admit that for such persons, it is indeed a discouraging, negative experience at first. Because of the prolonged emphasis on the outward "persona" life, the shadow within has become autonomous and powerful, and therefore frightening. To avoid facing this threat from the shadow, they hopelessly push on, in an effort to compensate for their growing sense of personal and social inferiority. At the other extreme, some people are only too willing to turn toward the inner world in order to escape what is for them a legitimately challenging life of external struggle and disappointment. Many others want to let go, but their friends and relatives insist they stay involved with the outer world, forcing them to turn inward defiantly if they are to meet themselves. Still others have a shattering life experience, such as the death of a loved one, that forces them to reassess their priorities and focus on their own inner reality. As Scott-Maxwell put it, "Life does not accommodate you, it shatters you. It is meant to, and couldn't do it better. Every seed destroys its container or there would be no fruition" (p. 65).

Once death is accepted, the past honored, limits drawn, and the ego allowed to become relative, there is the fifth task of aging: encountering and honoring the Self. This is, of course, the great goal of any Jungian analysis. As Jacobi points out, the ego, in the second half of life, turns back to the source, to the creative archetypal background, for a new rooting in the Self (1952, p. 101). Meanwhile, neglected potential forces in the unconscious are summoned to awareness. By bringing together the opposites, the Self creates a sense of wholeness, and the ego receives a growing ability to see all sides of issues (Wheelwright 1979). And, more and more, the ego's relationship to the cosmos is revealed. Jung saw the ego's relationship with the Self as a dialogue between the conscious personality and the all-inclusive voice from the depths, establishing an "ego-Self axis." He saw the Self as "God within us" (1966, p. 238), "our life's goal" (ibid., p. 240), the most complete expression of our wholeness, which is also our uniqueness. Fordham sees the realization of the Self in each individual's consciousness as the problem of our era and a manifestation of an ongoing historical process (p. 127).

Most Jungians would agree that one of the most vital tasks of life, especially of old age, and one that comes with the realization of the Self, of God within, is the articulation of our own raison d'être, and, through this process, of life in general. This is a sixth step in our development as we age. Jung believed that if people follow their fate, they find life meaningful, and he wrote that the "lack of meaning in life is a soul-sickness whose full extent and full import our age has not as yet begun to comprehend" (1934, p. 415). Finding meaning involves an honest attempt to examine and experience one's inner being, as well as the person one presents to the world, and this can result in an answer to the modern problem of meaninglessness for oneself and also, perhaps, for society. It is a contribution that differs from what talented younger people make because of its far greater scope. The growing interest in old age today may, in fact, reflect society's nascent awareness of the need to find meaning. Medicine's extension of life, moreover, which is increasing the number of old people in our population, may be accelerating society's interest as well.

Adler believes that "the synthesis of nature and consciousness is the key to the real meaning of human existence" (p. 152). This corresponds to Jung's statement that wisdom is the agreement of our thinking with the primordial images of the unconscious (1930–31, p. 403). In these images, too, there are messages about the future, and this gives life continuity. Old people need to trust them. By coordinating, in old age, one's important subjective memories, bit by bit, with important outer happenings, a sense of one's archetypal ground plan is revealed, and through it a reason for existence. This matching of outer and inner aspects of life can link us to our fate and connect us to historical and universal meaning. Fordham states, "A philosophy of life is a transpersonal manifestation of personality," and part of individuation (p. 118).

Jung wrote: "A human being would certainly not grow to be seventy or eighty years old if this longevity had no meaning for the species" (1930–31, p. 399). (Undoubtedly he was not thinking of those people who have to live many years to learn anything at all!) He went on to muse: "Could by any chance culture be the meaning and purpose of the second half of life" (p. 400)? Perhaps old age is important for our species because it is the period when this whole question can be addressed. The fruit of biological life is children, but the fruit of psychological life is meaning.

About his own life, Jung wrote: "The meaning of my existence is that life has addressed a question to me. Or, conversely, I myself am a question which is addressed to the world, and I must communicate my answer . . ." (1961, p. 318). Jung saw humanity's task as "to become conscious of the contents that press upward from the unconscious" and "to kindle a light in the darkness of mere being" (1961, p. 326), in the hope that this might influence the unconscious, just as the unconscious influences us. He believed that the meaning of life lay in cultivating and enlarging consciousness in the universe, perhaps as partners with God, in helping Him to realize and know Himself. He saw God becoming manifest in the human act of reflection, and the unconscious as God's link to us.

The most far-reaching, and most often uncompleted, aspect of aging is the engagement of unused potentials, a process that can make "dying with life" even more a reality. If courageously met, this seventh task can transform life into a highly creative process through contact with the archetype of the child, the symbol of rebirth. Those who age most successfully, in fact, emerge from this encounter with a playful approach to life, using all the possibilities that life has to offer, not in an ego-dominated way, but as a creative artist, or as a child at play. Through a no longer dominant ego, these old people make just enough order out of the profusion of life manifested by the Self to let this happen. Living itself becomes the point, and the unexpected becomes the raw material of its exploration. If one ages in this fashion, renewed by the archetype of the child and other life events, and recognizing and honoring one's most inferior function, old age becomes a time when one can be one's own authority and make a unique contribution. This process is well exemplified by Grandma Moses, whose art originated in her old age. Its childlike freshness appealed to the sophisticated art critic as well as to the average art lover. Her art shows that a certain quality of newness and vitality, a prerogative of the old, is conveyed by the fourth function, which is itself new and vital, having only recently surfaced. Many people would feel that Jung himself became more creative as he aged. His last and most widely read book, *Memories, Dreams, Reflections,* demonstrates his fourth function, feeling, through its human, personal quality.

Gordon has written extensively about the relationship of creativity to death. She believes that the imminence of death increases the tension of the opposites, especially the major pair, life and death, making us more conscious not only of the gift of life but also of what transcends and reconciles life and death—that is, creativity. She sees many similarities between the psychological constellation that favors a good and peaceful dying and the constellation that favors creative work. Rorschach tests taken by people who were dying, but who did not consciously know it, showed, when compared to others, a symbolic relationship to death, less importance of the ego function, a surrender to emotional and imaginal inner events, and more creativity. These productions were similar in some ways to the productions of psychotic patients, only more cohesive. The relationship to death was a mixture of resistance and surrender.

Gordon concluded that creativity can allow one to say yes to the finality of death, and in so doing, discover what transcends death. This creativity, it seems, can be expressed in subjective understanding—an increase in consciousness—as well as in actual achievement. She states that "those who would die well and those who would create well are people who must be capable of being open and available both to the life forces as well as the death forces" (p. 165). In other words, these are people who could strive for control but let go of it without panic or resentment.

Jung spoke of death in opposition to life as an essential energic component of libido and saw the creative potential lying in the tension between life and death. The final task of aging, creativity, is intimately connected with all the great tasks of aging, including facing death. In fact, all four stages of creativity that Gordon describes in her recent book, and that are also enumerated by Wallas, correspond closely to the tasks of aging detailed above. These four stages of creativity and the related tasks of aging are (1) immersion in the problem (facing death, reviewing the past, drawing limits); (2) incubation, or creative emptiness (letting go of the ego); (3) inspiration (contacting the Self); and (4) verification, in which inspiration is given relevant form and expression (finding meaning). Aging, analysis, and life itself, when entered upon fully, one could say, are all basically processes of creativity and of its counterpart, the increase of consciousness.

With Jung's phrase "dying in life" in mind, one might take Gordon's findings a step further and realize that a creative individual approach to death transcends both life and death. In the employment of unused potentials in old age, one might actually achieve, in words of wisdom, in relationships, in images or movement, or in insight into one's own being, a certain meaningfulness that goes beyond the life-death polarity. Through contacting our unused potential, much of which comes to us via our fourth, most undeveloped or unused, function, we can find that essence of ourselves that can create a bridge between the world of life and the world of death. To understand better what is meant by "essence," one might observe the behavior of certain unconscious people. Like undomesticated animals who fight to the death to preserve the species, some people, through certain archetypal identifications, do die creatively. The solder who dies as a hero for his country; the man who refuses to give up and dies with his boots on; the aging, still working farmer who unconsciously sees his land as the embodiment of his essence and continues to work it right up to his death—these are examples of people unconsciously seeking and living their essence.

Virginia Hine, an anthropologist, has written a beautiful account of a man dying of cancer, called *The Last Letter to the Pebble People*. It is the story of a man in his fifties, probably a feeling type in Jungian terms, who was able to choose death positively. Through the love and caring of his extended family, as well as through his love for them, he experienced a transformation such that his death became a positive choice. His was not a psychological approach of any specific persuasion. It was, instead, an individual, conscious effort to follow and articulate his own instinctive, spontaneous impulses. He followed these impulses all the way to his final struggle and confrontation with death, and his conscious acceptance of it. The life flow engaged in his creative transformation was what carried him over from his living to his dying. A conscious transcendence as described in this story is certainly more satisfying than the more unconscious variety, but it probably follows the same archetypal patterns that govern the behavior of more unconscious people. The latter are also "dying with life" and are unconsciously transcending the life-death polarity.

Jung's final years are an example of transcending death by "dying with life," and of living out one's creative essence to the very end. His final complete work, the autobiography, was a sharp departure from his prior work, and something he had always vowed he would not do. But a dream convinced him of the rightness of this project. The Self was demanding creative fulfillment. Acknowledging the imminence of his death, and the limits of his existence, he recalled in great detail and with great intensity his entire past, immersing himself in it thoroughly. He approached the project with characteristic courage, candor, and thoroughness, trusting in the rightness of this painful and tiring procedure. And by allowing his inferior function—that is, feeling—to come to the fore, he created a moving human document, a testimony to his own essence and to the value of the human soul in general. It is his most powerful, creative, and widely read book, a personal summary and living testament of his own theories. He transcended his death by relating creatively to the Self, thus finding the meaning of his own life. And, in doing so, he helped others to find the way to their own essences as well.

REFERENCES

Adler, G. 1969. The ego and the cycle of life. In *Studies in analytical psychology*, pp. 120–53. New York: Putnam.

Bradway, K., and Wheelwright, J. 1978. The psychological type of the analyst and its relation to analytical practice. *Journal of Analytical Psychology* 23/3:211–25.

Butler, R. 1963. The life review. *Journal of Psychiatry* 26:65–76.

Castillejo, I. 1961. *The older woman*. Lecture 115. London: The Guild of Pastoral Psychology.

Edinger, E. 1960. The ego-self paradox. *Journal of Analytical Psychology* 5/1:3–18.

Fordham, M. 1958. Individuation and ego development. *Journal of Analytical Psychology* 3/2:115–30.

Frankl, V. 1963. *Man's search for meaning*. New York: Washington Square Books.

Franz, M.-L. von. Archetypes surrounding death. *Quadrant* 12/1:5–13.

Freud, S. 1905. On psychotherapy. In *Standard edition*, vol. 7, pp. 255–68. London: Hogarth, 1953.

Gordon, R. 1978. *Dying and creating: a search for meaning*. London: Society for Analytical Psychology.

Hine, V. 1977. *The last letter to the pebble people*. Santa Cruz: Unity Press.

Hinton, L. 1979. Jung's approach to therapy with mid-life patients. *Journal of the American Academy of Psychoanalysis* 7/4:525–41.

Jacobi, J. 1943. *The psychology of Jung*. New Haven: Yale University Press.

———. 1958. The process of individuation. *Journal of Analytical Psychology* 3/2:95–114.

James, W. 1902. *The varieties of religious experience*. New York: Longmans, Green.

Jung, C. G. 1930–31. The stages of life. In *Collected works*, vol. 8, pp. 387–403. 2d ed. Princeton: Princeton University Press, 1969.

———. 1934. The soul and death. In *Collected works*, vol. 8, pp. 404–15. 2d ed. Princeton: Princeton University Press, 1969.

———. 1961. *Memories, dreams, reflections*. New York: Random House.

———. 1966. *Two essays on analytical psychology*. *Collected works*, vol. 7. 2d ed. New York: Pantheon.

King, P. 1974. Notes on the psychoanalysis of older patients. *Journal of Analytical Psychology* 19/1:22–37.

McGuire, W., and Hull, R. F. C., eds. 1977. *C. G. Jung speaking*. Princeton: Princeton University Press.

Maduro, R. 1974. Artistic creativity and aging in India. *International Journal of Aging and Human Development* 5/4:303–29.

Scott-Maxwell, F. 1968. *The measure of my days*. New York: Knopf.

Sharp, E. F. 1937. *Dream analysis*. London: Hogarth.

Wallas, G. 1926. *The art of thought*. New York: Harcourt Brace.

Williams, M. 1958. The fear of death (part 2). *Journal of Analytical Psychology* 3/2:20–40.

Wheelwright, J. 1979. Old age and death. Unpublished paper.

———. 1981. *The death of a woman*. New York: St. Martin's Press.

[15]

GENDER IDENTITY AND GENDER ROLES: THEIR PLACE IN ANALYTIC PRACTICE

Katherine Bradway

A businesswoman is fired from her job. A man is left by his wife. Both bring their pain of failure—she as an office administrator, he as a husband—into their analytic hour. For reasons that will be discussed later in this paper, it seems clear to them that their experience of failure in an outer role penetrates to the level of gender identity: Am I adequate as a woman? Am I adequate as a man? Many of the wounds brought to analysts for healing have been inflicted at points where people are vulnerable about being a male or a female and about the roles they take in the outer world. Before considering the healing of such wounds in analytic practice, and the place that gender holds in the individuation process, I would first like to offer some facts and reflections on male-female and masculine-feminine differences.

GENDER DIFFERENCES

Male-Female

It has been commonly observed that men are, in general, more aggressive than women, and that women tend to show more nurturance and concern for people; but the extent to which these differences are a consequence of

Katherine Bradway, Ph.D., maintains a private practice in the San Francisco Bay Area. Formerly an associate professor at Stanford University, she is a founding member and past president of the Society of Jungian Analysts of Northern California and a founding member of the C. G. Jung Institute of San Francisco. Dr. Bradway is the author of ''Hestia and Athena in the Analysis of Women'' (1978), ''The Psychological Type of the Analyst and Its Relation to Analytical Practice'' (1978), and ''Sandplay in Psychotherapy'' (1979); she is also a contributor to *Sandplay Studies: Origins, Theory and Practice* (1981).

what is expected of each sex, and to what extent they are linked to chromosomal and hormonal differences, is less obvious.

Studies of neonates give compelling evidence that potentials for some male-female behavioral differences are present at birth. A review of such studies shows that the differences can be grouped under muscle strength, sensory dissimilarities, and degree of affiliative behavior toward adults. In comparison with newborn females, for example, newborn males have been found to have greater gross muscular strength, to be able to lift their heads from the prone position earlier, and to have more flexible limbs. Newborn females, on the other hand, are more receptive to oral and cutaneous stimuli, as exemplified by their surpassing males in an early taste for sweets, in frequency of reflex smiles during irregular sleep, in oscillations of the tongue, and in mouth domination in hand-to-mouth approach behavior. The activity of male neonates involves the whole body, whereas that of the female is focused in the muscles and skin of the face. Moreover, it has been found that female infants look at, vocalize to, and maintain proximity to, their mothers more than do their twin brothers (Green; Korner; May).

Starting with these findings, one can surmise a course of development that would lead to some of the characteristic differences between men and women without bringing in stereotyping to explain them. As the infant-to-child boy experiences his muscular strength, one can imagine how using it would bring its own rewards, in addition to its being reinforced by the persons attending him. It could be conjectured, then, that he would work toward perfecting his strength, become competitive in mastering tasks requiring it, and develop aggressiveness in achieving recognition for it. As the infant girl's smiles elicit smiles from adults, and as her receptivity to cutaneous stimuli leads her to reach out for touch experiences, one can conceive how her "skill" in relating might be developed and, with it, an increasing interest in people. Stereotyping would reinforce these developments, but the roots of the differentiation between aggressiveness in the boy and affiliative behavior in the girl may exist at birth.

Additional findings pointing to inborn and/or psychobiological differences are provided by animal, cross-cultural, and hormonal studies (Green; May; Money and Ehrhardt; Stoller), as well as by Erikson's study of the play constructions of preadolescents. He found parallels between the constructions of boys and girls and the different structure and function of their sex organs. (Boys' involved height, the outdoors, motion; girls' were low, indoors, concerned with threats from outside.)

The demonstration in the early 1970s of a bimodal brain in humans has provided further evidence of a possible link between psychological and biological gender differences. Ornstein, who is responsible for some of the early research on bimodal consciousness, uses the words masculine and Yang in association with the left side of the brain, which is used predominantly for analyzing data, making logical deductions, and processing information sequentially, and the words feminine and Yin in association with the right side, which is related to artistic talent, body awareness, and diffuse as opposed to linear processing of information (pp. 50–72).

Recent research suggests that male brains are more lateralized than female brains. Males excel in tasks that do not involve shifts between the two sides of the brain, and females in tasks requiring flexible shifts between the two sides (McGuinness and Pribram). This is reminiscent of the associations that Neumann makes between focused consciousness and masculinity and between diffuse awareness and femininity (1954a).

Anima and Animus

The evidence supporting natal predisposition to gender-linked behavior is consistent with the opinion of Jung and most of his followers that there are basic psychological differences between men and women that should not be ignored. However, Jungian theory on contrasexual archetypes provides for the potential of each sex to behave like the other. In fact, the bringing to consciousness of one's opposite-sex components is important in one's approach to totality and wholeness. Jung was not the first to recognize that each sex carries the potential for being like the other, but he was the first to perceive the contrasexual parts as archetypal images and to name them anima and animus (Jung 1928a, pp. 186–209).

In Jung's early descriptions of these contrasexual archetypes, he emphasizes their disruptive qualities. He sees the anima, the feminine image within man, as producing obscure, undifferentiated emotional states he calls "moods," and the animus, the masculine image in woman, as the source of undeveloped reasoning capacities that lead to outbursts of "dogmatic opinions." The negative effects of the anima and animus are magnified by the fact that the man and woman are unaware of them, are not anticipating their appearance, are taken by surprise. Jung speaks of persons "being possessed" by the anima or animus, usually at times of challenge or threat. A man may react to a slighting remark or a disappointment by withdrawing into a dark mood. A woman may react in situations that threaten her self-confidence by a sudden burst of impersonal and unrelated opinions.

As is true with many other archetypes, the anima and animus tend to function in negative ways as long as they remain wholly in the unconscious and therefore function only autonomously. When a man becomes aware of and accepts his contrasexual part, he no longer has to deny it, and its disruptive aspects are diminished. Furthermore, as he discovers the positive quality of the anima—the principle of relatedness—he finds he can use it to understand himself better, as well as those around him. Likewise, as a woman familiarizes herself with her animus, she learns how to monitor its outbursts and let it help her focus (Harding), throw light as a torch does (Castillejo), and become a creative power (Jung).

Descriptions of the characteristics of the anima and animus appear throughout Jung's writings and a review of them shows the development in his ideas. There were no radical changes, however, from his early perception of the autonomous anima as being personal, emotional, and a producer of moods, and of the autonomous animus as being relatively impersonal, rational, and a producer of opinions. Moreover, there was continuity in his view that the conscious approach to and acknowledgment of the anima and animus provide experiences that carry one into contact with inner conflicts as well as with one's own vital resources. The anima and animus thus provide for consciousness a bridge or link with the unconscious and therefore contribute to the individuation process, which requires the bringing of unconscious components into consciousness.

Jung's observations on the contrasexual archetypes were made at a time when the standards of male and female behavior were more rigidly prescribed than they are today. Men were supposed to be "all male" and women to be "gentle ladies." Consequently, Jung's proposal that all men had an inner woman, and women an inner man, was a more revolutionary idea than it is today, when men have learned how to change a baby's diaper and women how to change a flat tire. Changes in cultural standards are both consequent to, and reflected in, a decrease in the polarity of the behavior of today's men and women.

Analysts who have responded to cultural changes by dissenting from Jung's major premise regarding the anima and animus include Hillman (1974) and Whitmont (1980), both of whom argue for the theoretical advantage of seeing both the masculine and feminine, or the anima and animus, in the unconscious of each sex. Hill suggests seeing the unconscious contrasexual as "the other," letting it be the opposite of whatever is conscious, which would seem to obviate the need for the terms *anima* and *animus*.

Masculinity-Femininity

There are times, in both my personal life and my analytic practice, when the precise fit between an immediate experience and Jung's definitions of anima or animus elicits the "aha" feeling that accompanies the bringing of an unconscious component into consciousness. At these moments, I find the ability to recognize the functioning of the contrasexual archetypes, as Jung conceived them, tremendously useful, and consequently I retain the terms *anima* and *animus* to represent exclusively the unconscious contrasexual sides of a man and of a woman respectively.

However, since most of the women and many of the men I see in analysis readily recognize two sides of themselves that are roughly identifiable as a "masculine" side and a "feminine" side—or perhaps as an achieving, assertive, or mastering side and a relating, nurturing, or affiliative side—I speak of masculine and feminine sides in both men and women without regard for the degree to which either side is conscious or unconscious. But the usage of the terms *masculine* and *feminine* presents problems. My easy use of these terms was called into question in the late 1960s by women students who felt that making the distinction between masculine and feminine was an implied put-down of women. It was easier to stop using the terms in my teaching than to try to change the feelings of women who needed to use this objection as one way of making a larger point worth making: linking traits to gender can perpetuate the stereotyping that women initially recognized, and that men have increasingly seen, as potentially limiting to the development of both sexes.

Male-female, referring to a biological classification, is not brought into question. Whether one is male or female— that is, has male or female genitalia—is determined at conception, except in the rare instances of pathological absence in males, or presence in females, of fetal androgens. These hormones may reverse the chromosomal fetal development and result in biological transsexualism or ambiguity of natal gender (Green; Money and Ehrhardt; Stoller). Although the terms *male* and *female* are used in a single sense that is readily understood, the terms *masculine* and *feminine* are used in two overlapping senses: to identify the psychological traits and the range of behavior associated with being a male or a female, and to denote principles or patterns that are experienced as opposing or complementary sides of individuals irrespective of their gender. If we can separate the terms *masculinity* and *femininity* from being male or female, we can reserve them for reference to principles that function in either sex. This usage would avoid the suggestion that maleness or femaleness is diminished or enhanced by the expression of masculinity or femininity and would also avoid implying that we support traditional stereotyping.

I think an appreciation of the functioning in *both* sexes of the complementary principles of masculinity and femininity is essential in Jungian work. Bernhardt and Hill, each taking off from some aspects of the work of Neumann, of Perry, and of Whitmont (1969), describe subclassifications of these principles based on a dynamic-static dimension. A distinction is made between the dynamic-masculine, which we associate with the hero archetype, and the static-masculine, which we associate with patriarchy. Similarly, both authors distinguish between the static-feminine, embodying the characteristics associated with the great mother archetype, and the dynamic-feminine, which yields characteristics associated with the archetypal image of the maiden.

Other Jungian writers, in corresponding recognition that the masculine and feminine principles function as archetypes, have drawn upon the gods and goddesses of Greece and India to depict aspects of these principles (see, for example, Bolen; Guggenbühl-Craig; Hillman 1973, 1974; Schmidt; Whitmont 1980; Zabriskie).

Other pairs of terms commonly used in connection with gender are *Logos-Eros, thinking-feeling,* and *Yin-Yang. Logos* and *Eros* refer to the principles of rational reasoning and of relatedness respectively; usage has often equated them with the masculine and feminine principles. Jung felt that the consciousness of men was guided by Logos and that of women by Eros. Whitmont has argued for freeing these principles from gender linkage (1980), so that they can be appreciated independently of whether they make their appearance in men or in women (just as has been argued for freeing the principles of masculine and feminine from gender linkage). Eros, of course, was a male god, so that linking Eros specifically with femininity and with women has a paradoxical element. Solar and lunar consciousness are sometimes used as alternatives for Logos and Eros.

Although not a pair of gender-linked terms, the *thinking-feeling* dichotomy is occasionally used as if it coincided with the Logos and Eros principles. There are similarities in the ways the two pairs are described. But thinking and feeling are evaluative functions in Jung's system of typology and refer to whether a person evaluates something more with his or her thinking function or more with the feeling function. In simplified formulation: Is something evaluated or judged after consideration of the facts (thinking) or from a subjective impression of the personal values involved (feeling)? Jung found the feeling function more highly developed in women and the thinking function more highly developed in men. The corroborative statistically significant differences shown in two studies of type frequency are numerically small (Gray; Schaefer).

The pair of terms *Yin-Yang* is represented by an ancient symbol that places the light Yang on the right and the dark Yin on the left. Although the cluster of traits associated with the masculine principle is assigned to Yang, and those associated with the feminine principle to Yin, the two terms encompass more than the masculine and feminine. The symbol portrays the relationship between opposites: together the two parts form a whole, and within each half the nucleus for the other half exists. The symbol could stand for any pair of opposites, such as light-dark, consciousness-unconsciousness, hot-cold. The symbol denotes this relationship in the abstract and has been assigned, or defined by, various clusters of opposite characteristics. The two parts symbolically portrayed have a spiritual or numinous aura to them, which is a quality to be honored with the masculine and feminine principles themselves.

It is clear that the use of gender terms is not precise, but neither is our differentiation between what we think of as masculine and feminine. Despite the imprecision in the use of gender terms by Jungians, there seems to be a general conviction that human beings are guided by archetypal principles that are separate and complementary to one another.

Cultural Expectations

To understand gender identity problems fully, it is important that we take into account the extent to which expectations of our culture affect the behavior of its members. In addition to the early stereotyping of boys and girls, which many of today's parents are trying to minimize, there is also the influence of society's expectations for adults, in which there have been noticeable shifts, more for women than for men, in the last several decades. In the 1930s, with its devastating economic depression, women were expected to limit the number of their pregnancies, and this resulted in the lowest birthrate on record in the United States for any one decade. In the 1940s, women were called upon to leave home and take up jobs left by men who went off to war. Then the 1950s brought the message that woman's place was in the home, and the record baby boom took off. In the 1960s, as the women's liberation movement got under way, women were told they must reject their roles as housewives, along with their financial dependence upon men. And in the 1970s, many women heard a voice that told them they must succeed both as wife/mothers and in careers. So within a few decades, women have been called on to respond to mixed, sometimes diametrically opposite, demands.

Society's expectations for men have remained more static: show courage, achieve, produce, provide for a family. The women's movement has, however, changed the expectations that women have of their husbands. Many husbands are now expected to share in household work to allow their wives more time and energy to continue their education or take up careers or both. The initial stage of this expectation involved men's merely accepting their wives' aspirations for careers, by *letting* them go to school or work outside the home. But many women, spurred on by such concepts as the Rapoports' "dual-career family," now expect their men to share the responsibility in the home, including both housework and childrearing.

The modification in expectations for men and women has been paralleled by a growing appreciation for androgyny. The word *androgyny* comes from the Greek *andro* ("male") and *gyn* ("female"), and thus represents a combination of male and female. Becoming androgynous means overcoming stereotypical attitudes about what is appropriate behavior for males and females, so that one develops more flexible behavior appropriate to a given situation: an assertive or aggressive behavior if that is required; a caring or nurturing attitude if that is required (Bem; Gelpi; Heilbrun; Rupprecht; Singer).

Singer observes that androgyny is an archetype that represents in human form the principle of wholeness. As a symbol, androgyny has been represented since ancient times as the hermaphrodite. Henderson has pointed out that Jung saw the symbol of the hermaphrodite as tending to break down into its components, thus turning into a symbol representing potential dissociation. Jung would have seen the symbol of *coniunctio* as offering a more stable symbol than the hermaphrodite or androgyne in the formation of wholeness.*

To me, androgyny represents dual attitudes and behavior at a conscious level, whereas the *coniunctio* represents the coming together—the "marriage"—of the masculine and feminine principles at an unconscious level. Androgyny seems to have to do with role, *coniunctio* with identity.

ANALYTIC PRACTICE

Analysts learn—in fact when we are patients ourselves—that the seeds of healing lie in the unconscious. The woman who had lost her job and the man who was losing his wife had dreams that provide examples of this truth. On the night that she was fired, the businesswoman dreamed that she was with her mother and daughter. She sensed this meeting to be a reconnecting with her feminine nature. If she had not made this observation herself, I might have suggested it to her, but her discovery of it herself facilitated the healing, and was in itself a moment of healing. The imaging in a dream or fantasy of three generations of women, either grandmother, mother, and the dreamer herself, or the dreamer as daughter to her mother

---

*J. Henderson 1980: personal communication.

and mother to her daughter, is frequently experienced as a thread of femininity. The dreamer reported at a subsequent session: "I realize that my animus has been living me. I am not going to look for a job right away. I am going to take time for my feminine side. I am going to look at my relation with Andy [her male friend] and at me."

The man whose wife had left him experienced a dream image of a kind of dagger that looked like an equilateral triangle with a handle. "It would be awkward to use," he said about it; so it was the shape of the dagger and not its cutting ability that was significant to him. He drew it with light rays emerging from the three sides. It was clear to both of us that this image represented masculinity, that it was a masculine symbol. I thought how different this was from the conventional male sign, the arrow pointing upward from a circle. The triangular symbol had a numinous quality for this man. He formed it with clay to show its three-dimensional aspects. During the following session, he outlined it in the sandtray and placed pieces of turquoise within it. He then told me: "Everytime I think 'This is it; I can't take it; I'll have to end it,' I think of this. It has become brass— layers of brass.'" So the image was becoming stronger.

For both of these persons who had suffered jolting blows, the unconscious provided symbols of their own gender. In some other instances, there might have been a connection with the contrasexual side, or with the Self as indicated by a mandala. But the wisdom of the unconscious determined that a same-sex symbol reaffirming their gender identity was needed for this man and for this woman at this time.

In addition to dream fragments and images such as these, there are several recurrent dream themes that alert the dreamer to a neglect of the anima or animus. A strange man trying to enter the house, which often occurs in dreams of women, for example, has been found to represent the attempt of the animus to gain the attention and acknowledgment of the dreamer (Marcus).

Experience in working with homosexual men and women has shown that the contrasexual "other" is still found in the unconscious. The female figures in a homosexual man's dreams, for example, had been confined to his mother until he dreamed of a girl standing in the rain playing music. Later he dreamed:

‖ Dream: *I find a woman who is ill. We climb some perilous stairs* ‖
‖ *and she loses her footing. I save her at the risk of my own life.* ‖

The first dream presents the image of the anima with no interaction with her. The second portrays the urgency of saving the feminine part of himself. This sequence is similar to those I find in dreams of heterosexual men: the activation of the anima, followed by the rescuing of the anima. And with this comes the possibility of relating to women, to the world, and to their own unconscious in a new way, free from the dominance of the great mother archetype.

Neglect of, or attempts to save or get help for, the feminine or masculine side are represented in dreams of both men and women. For example, a young lesbian dreamed:

> Dream: *I picked up the body of a little girl and realized it was me. I took it to the undertaker but he refused to take it. I went to two. I was still carrying it trying to find help when I awoke.*

At another time she dreamed of hurting, and then trying to save, a masculine figure:

> Dream: *I was driving with Jill [her lover] and we ran over a little boy. I went up to two officers asking for help but neither would help. I went back to the little boy and realized I could not save him without help.*

This young woman had suffered psychological damage from both her mother and father and was subject to suicidal depressions in which she thought nothing could help her. But she persisted, working at one time with both a male and a female analyst, and eventually saved herself.

When Jung saw that undeveloped contrasexual archetypes were erupting into men's behavior in the form of irritable moods, and into women's behavior as opinionated declarations, he advocated using a method he called active imagination. (This has some elements in common with techniques used by Gestaltists and others; it is given a separate discussion in this book in the chapter by Dallett, above.) Jung used as an example a man with an "honorable, flawless persona" whose tantrums and explosive moodiness were estranging him from his wife and children. When men have such episodes, they feel they are being weak and unmanly; their masculine ideal for themselves is threatened. "Clearly," writes Jung, "the anima is trying to enforce a separation." Before making assumptions as to why this is happening, one can, Jung continues, "investigate what is behind the tendencies of the anima. The first step is what I would call the objectification of the anima." By this, Jung meant to use one's imagination to experience the anima as a real woman. When this was done, one could face her with the question "Why do you want this separation?" Jung notes: "The more personally she is taken the better" (1928*a*, pp. 198–99).

In explaining the value of this process, Jung writes: "The purpose of the dialectical process is to bring these contents into the light; and only when this task has been completed, and the conscious mind has become sufficiently familiar with the unconscious processes reflected in the anima, will the anima be felt simply as a function'' (1928*a*, p. 209).

The technique of coming to terms with the animus is the same in principle as that used with the anima, but Jung felt that the animus was likely to be experienced as a plurality of persons rather than as a single figure. Often a woman perceives her animus as a jury passing judgment on her. A young married woman who had a punishing animus, for example, used sandplay, a variation of active imagination, to depict herself in a cage before a jury of twelve who were going to sentence her. Despite the fact that soldiers were placed ready to shoot her unless she repented or could find her way out of a maze, she maintained her innocence. Later her animus worked for her to cope with her mother's powerful animus, and eventually she made a sandplay scene of a royal father-daughter connection. It's as though she had been able to stand up successfully against her own and her mother's negative animus (the jury and the firing line), and then to let her feminine side relate to a positive archetypal father. The final scene after this one indicated the approach to wholeness in the form of two concentric circles (Bradway 1979).

There are other variations of active imagination in which an encounter with one's contrasexual side occurs. Shortly after starting analysis, a young professional woman reported an experience of spontaneous imagery that was like a waking dream. A male figure, whom she later drew as a hobo, was directing her to go and save a twin who had been in an automobile accident. She went to the accident and extricated her girl twin from the car and gently carried her to safety. She felt that the twin was still alive and would recover. Since this woman had been ignoring her feminine side in her challenge of patriarchal authority, the saving of a female twin at the direction of a male figure made her take notice of the relationship between the masculine and feminine sides of herself. The numinosity of the experience helped her to stay with it until she could understand that her masculine side was helping her to revitalize her feminine side. She had several subsequent spontaneous images involving benevolent male figures until she had one in which she had a daughter whom she was teaching to ride a horse. At about the same time, she made a sandplay world in which two female figures were riding horses. She made a connection among all of these fantasies or images. In her outer relationships she became less challenging toward men and more able to relate to them as friends.

The contrasexual side also makes itself known in projections. Falling in love includes the projection of the contrasexual side onto the loved one, the animus onto the man and the anima onto the woman, or, in the case in which the loved one is the same sex, onto the contrasexual side of the loved one. This latter kind of projection was experienced by one of my women analysands and I have since discovered that it holds for men also. The analyst helps the analysand to sort out what is projection and what is the real person, and then to look for and recognize in him- or herself the characteristics that had been erroneously perceived in the loved one. There is a mutual withdrawal of projections. That is, as a woman takes back her projections, the man on whom she has placed them is helped (forced) to withdraw his projections onto her. Increasingly, the sorting out of projections is being done through couple and family therapy. In a recent international survey, 60 percent of the responding members of the analytical societies indicated that they had either themselves used family therapy, or referred one or more patients to others for it (Bradway and Wheelwright, p. 220).

Most of the women who come to me for analysis identify two sides or parts of themselves, each having both positive and negative aspects. One side is experienced as the part that cares for people, for all life; it is the part that can enjoy the noncompetitive creation of things. In its less positive aspects, it is the part that feels overly dependent—one young woman described it as her "puppy dog" feeling. Then there is the side that relishes a challenge and is effective in getting things it wants in the way that Jung once defined masculinity: "Knowing what it wants and doing what is necessary to achieve it." But in the negative column is its tendency to block the relating side. Its quality of driving ahead may push others away. And one young poet complained that while trying to get her poems published utilized her masculine side, this effort blocked her poem-writing feminine side.

In an attempt to study these two sides, I looked at what had been happening in the women I had seen in analysis. I found that all but one of thirty-one women I had seen in a preceding five-year period could be identified as belonging to one of two groups that were characterized by the life style of the women; one group consisted of wife/mothers without outside jobs, and the other group of unmarried women who were actively engaged in the helping professions. I came to identify these two groups as the Hestia and Athena groups.

Women in both groups wanted what those in the other group had, not to replace what they had, but in addition to it. The married women wanted to "count" more outside their homes, and the women with careers wanted a husband and children, or at least a lasting intimate relationship. The analysis with both groups had the common element of finding an "inner core." This was expressed by members in both groups in a variety of ways: "I want to know who I am; no, that sounds too much like persona; I want to find my inner core." "You can sense when your core gets vitalized and growth can start." "It's like an inner flowing." "I am finding my focal point." The common quality of caring for or nurturing others—family or patients and clients—had sent members of both groups outside themselves. The resolution came in relating to, and later from, their inner core, through focusing on themselves, drawing or painting the inner place, developing body awareness, or providing themselves with more opportunities for relationships with other women who were also seeking an inner core.

After relating to this central place, a place not identified with either gender but a nearly sacred place of their own being, they were freed from subservience to the previously dominant archetype, be it masculine (the career group) or feminine (the family group), and the opposite archetype was constellated or strengthened. Furthermore, the functioning of the initially dominant side was typically enhanced rather than jeopardized. Symbols of centering and wholeness appeared in fantasy productions (Bradway 1978).

An example of the development toward wholeness through relating to a central inner place is contained in the sandplay worlds of one of the women in the Hestia group. Her initial sandplay portrayed a conflict between fear of patriarchal authority, represented in the sand tray by policemen, and respect for her instinctual feminine side, represented in the sand tray by domestic animals. A sequence of twenty-five sandplay productions in which a centered pool played the dominant part, with gradual shifts in the placement of female and male figures, was followed by a centered circle made up of all the significant figures from the preceding sandplay worlds. Placement of animal families in the four corners formed a "squared circle," which completed her sandplay journey. This sequence of sand trays was made in the last part of an interim between a D and C operation that was followed by a psychotic break and, four years later, an emergency hysterectomy that had no adverse psychological effects. Her feminine identity had become sufficiently secure during this interim to withstand the loss of her internal female organs (Bradway 1981).

More women coming for analysis today are both wife/mothers and career-oriented persons than was true when the women in the above study entered analysis ten to fifteen years ago. Many are having problems in their relationships with men. The double standard of sexuality that plagued the previous generation of women has been replaced by a double standard regarding availability. Women complain that their men expect them to be available at all times, to listen, comfort, and reassure, but then feel put upon if the woman expects a similar degree of availability. Swings between extremes of guilt and resentment rob the women of energy and further limit their availability in all outer roles—in relationships with their families and friends and in their careers. The animus function judges them inadequate at the same time that their femininity feels threatened. Of course they have too little time and energy for themselves. One of their tasks in analytic work is to search for an inner core, just as was true for the family and career groups of women described above. And as they find it, they are more able to say no and to reserve spaces for themselves where they can *be* and *become*.

The gender-identity problems of today's men who come for analysis are often expressed in their relationship with two types of women who are nearly polar opposites. Sometimes the two are differentiated from one another in their orientation to family and career. As one man put it, "If I could only mix them together and come out with one woman . . ." Recognition of what parts of themselves are projected onto each woman permits a gradual withdrawing of the projections and a consequent formation of a relationship with the real woman in one (or both) of them.

As they withdraw their projections, they often begin to own their feminine sides and become willing, sometimes eager, to take on "feminine" roles. When mother-child relations are being discussed, men in audiences are demanding, "Where does the father come in?" Male peer groups, which began appearing soon after women's consciousness-raising groups were started, are providing a means for men to explore and to share their feelings. Self-disclosure was a taboo for men not too many years ago. Articles and books on male psychology, although still not reaching the number of contributions on female psychology, are appearing in greater numbers. (See, for example, Goldberg; Johnson; Pleck and Sawyer; Steinmann and Fox.)

Since gender wounds are suffered within the relationship with one or both parents, an important ingredient for healing these wounds is found within the transference/countertransference relationship with the analyst. Whether male or female, Jungian analysts commonly use both their masculine and their feminine sides in relating to the analysand, thus providing means for the analysand to identify with the same sex and complement the opposite sex. This practice directs the healing process to the specific point at which early damage due to deprivation in parenting may have occurred.

A common fear among the women in both the Hestia and Athena groups was that of being like their mothers: feeling inadequate, being critical of self and others, being unable to give. One of the women with this complaint had lost her father when she was three years old. She needed to experience both my positive feminine and my positive masculine sides, not only as behavior models but also in a complementary relationship, since she had missed these in growing up. If the analyst and the analysand feel that the contrasexual side of the analyst is not sufficiently available for a particular task, a referral to an analyst of the other sex may be made, usually for a relatively brief period—for example, a few months—and usually in conjunction with the primary analysis—that is, the primary analysis continues, although perhaps at temporarily reduced frequency.

It is my impression that the initial stages of many analyses are marked by an acceptance of the analysand by the analyst in a way that might be likened to "mothering." Later, after the temenos is well established, the analyst, regardless of gender, diminishes the "mothering" and the interchange is more at a level that might be described as "fathering" (similar to Kohut's "mirroring" and "idealizing" stages). This is one way that analysts make use of both gender sides of themselves. Many years ago, a young woman whom I had been seeing in analysis for about a year voiced this distinction specifically: "I don't want you to love me any longer for being just me; I want you to love me for what I can do"—a good differentiation between the mothering and fathering stages. Many times the mothering has to go on for a long time to reestablish what Edinger calls the ego-Self axis. But the next stage is equally important, and is reflected in a shift in the attitude of both analyst and analysand.

In using both their masculine and feminine sides, Jungian analysts form a syzygy with the masculine and feminine parts of their analysands. During analysis, there is always a four-sided relationship going on among the masculine and feminine sides of each member of the dyad. One side is always conscious and the other side is typically unconscious. The awareness of the interpersonal and intrapersonal relationships among the various parts (ego and masculine and feminine parts—animus and anima) comes from the analyst at first, but then may come from either analyst or analysand, and thus helps in bringing about this syzygy. Jung wrote: "An emotionally charged content is lying ready in the unconscious and springs into projection at a certain moment. This content is the syzygy motif, and it expresses the fact that a masculine element is always paired with a feminine one" (1954, p. 65). "The male-female syzygy is only one among the possible pairs of opposites, albeit the most important one in practice and the commonest" (ibid., p. 70). I think it is this syzygy, whether experienced consciously or not, that is at the heart of Jungian analysis. "The touchstone of every analysis . . . is always this person-to-person relationship" (Jung 1928b, p. 137).

Often it is nonverbal interactions that best illustrate the functioning of the syzygy. A male analysand and I were modeling with clay as we talked, not consciously noting what either was making. When the time was up, we compared what we had done. He had formed a round ball; I had made a bowl. I offered him my bowl and he placed the ball into it—a perfect fit. He observed, "That feels good. I like that." The image of the ball in the bowl provided a reference point in subsequent sessions.

An example of my using my masculine side with a patient occurred in an initial session with a woman who had come for an exploratory therapy visit. She noted the miniatures that were on a table by her chair and placed a woman figure with a train going toward it. Without thinking, I turned the train away from the woman figure. Nothing was said at the time, but the young woman entered into analysis. Several years after termination of analysis, this woman came to see me for one visit. She reminded me of this incident and explained what it meant to her. She had been feeling unable to cope with authoritarian threats and needed someone to help her. She wanted to go to a woman for analysis but wanted a woman who was stronger than herself or her mother. My animus provided a kind of protection until hers became sufficiently strong to take over.

Another woman in analysis had been talking to me about her memories of being left in a crib while her mother was at work. In one session she drew vertical lines without at first recognizing that they resembled bars of a crib. When she did, she pounded the drawing and screamed out her anger. Then she sobbed in my arms. Many sessions later, she brought in a draft of a feminist article she was writing. It was her first such writing and she wanted to share it with me and get some feedback. We talked about it that hour. In the first instance, it was the feminine part of the analyst that was functioning; in the second, it was the masculine side that was being used. Women frequently bring what they are writing or have written to the analytic hour. They are often daughters of mothers who are weak and of fathers who are opposed to higher education for girls. Their masculine sides need the masculine side of the analyst to make up for what was lacking in their mothers and to defend against the put-down experienced with their fathers.

My preferred way of handling nonverbal interchanges such as the above is to let them do their work without interpreting. Connections among these interchanges and dreams, previous history, or other experiences may at some time be made, but I am reluctant to dilute the immediate experience with words. In subsequent sessions, there may be a collection of connectible items to which we jointly refer to increase our understanding of the process.

The examples I have used from my analytic practice cover a span of twenty-five years. As I was looking through my records, I began to wonder if the tremendous changes in attitudes and life styles that I see reflected in the content of the analytic hours might be producing discernible changes at a deeper level—at a dream level. I started to look for recurrent images or themes in dreams that might represent masculine or feminine status or function. But I soon realized that there were far too many variables to permit me to discover anything with such a casual approach.

As I went to sleep one night, I was trying to design a study to compare dream symbols over the years. And I had this dream: I was holding a box with black sides and a white lid that I removed to reveal a multitude of "symbolic" figures (royal, religious, mythological) like those I use in the sand tray. I tried to take them into a brighter light so that I could get a better look at them. I was holding out my skirt to carry them. But they kept falling out of my hands and my skirt so that by the time I reached the light, I had lost many of them. Perhaps this is what would happen if one were to apply a scientific method to the study of symbols. Perhaps we would lose more than we would gain. The numinosity of symbols makes their meaning elusive and requires that they remain somewhat in the dark, out of the light of rational understanding. In that way, they retain their ability to function as symbols and to connect us to the source of the Self's own mystery.

REFERENCES

Bem, S. L. 1974. The measurement of psychological androgyny. *Journal of Consulting and Clinical Psychology* 42:155–62.

Bernhardt, A. 1976. Synthesis of the developmental frameworks of Erik H. Erikson and analytical psychology: ego and self development. Ph.D. dissertation, California School of Professional Psychology.

Bolen, J. S. 1980. The goddesses in every woman. Public lecture sponsored by C. G. Jung Institute, 22 November 1980, California Historical Society, San Francisco.

Bradway, K. 1978. Hestia and Athena in the analysis of women. *Inward Light* 41:28–42.

————. 1979. Sandplay in psychotherapy. *Art Psychotherapy* 6:85–93.

————. 1981. A woman's individuation through sandplay. In *Sandplay studies: origins, theory and practice,* pp. 133–56. San Francisco: C. G. Jung Institute of San Francisco.

Bradway, K., and Wheelwright, J. 1978. The psychological type of the analyst and its relation to analytical practice. *Journal of Analytical Psychology* 23:211–25.

Castillejo, I. C. de. 1973. *Knowing woman.* New York: Putnam.

Dieckmann, U.; Bradway, K.; and Hill, G. 1974. *Male and female, feminine and masculine*. San Francisco: C. G. Jung Institute of San Francisco.

Edinger, E. F. 1972. *Ego and archetype*. New York: Putnam.

Erikson, E. 1951. Sex differences in the play constructions of preadolescents. *American Journal of Orthopsychiatry* 21:667–92.

Gelpi, B. C. 1974. The androgyne. In *Women and analysis: dialogues on psychoanalytical views of femininity*, ed. J. Strouse, pp. 227–38. New York: Grossman.

Goldberg, H. 1976. *The hazards of being male*. New York: Nash.

Gray, H. 1948. Jung's psychological types in men and women. *Stanford Medical Bulletin* 6:29–36.

Green, R. 1976. Human sexuality: research and treatment frontiers. In *American handbook of psychiatry*, ed. S. Arieti, pp. 665–73. New York: Basic Books.

Guggenbühl-Craig, A. 1977. *Marriage—dead or alive*. Zurich: Spring Publications.

Harding, M. E. 1945. *The way of all women*. New York: Longmans, Green.

Heilbrun, C. G. 1973. *Toward a recognition of androgyny*. New York: Harper & Row.

Hill, G. S. 1978. Patterns of immaturity and the archetypal patterns of masculine and feminine: a preliminary exploration. Doctor of Clinical Social Work dissertation, Institute for Clinical Social Work.

Hillman, J. 1973. Anima. *Spring* 1973:97–132.

_____. 1974. Anima II. *Spring* 1974:113–46.

Johnson, R. A. 1977. *He: understanding masculine psychology*. New York: Harper & Row.

Jung, C. G. 1928*a*. The relation between the ego and the unconscious. In *Collected works*, vol. 7, pp. 121–239. Princeton: Princeton University Press, 1953.

_____. 1928*b*. The therapeutic value of abreaction. In *Collected works*, vol. 16, pp. 129–38. Princeton: Princeton University Press, 1954.

_____. 1954. Concerning the archetypes, with special reference to the anima concept. In *Collected works*, vol. 9, part 1, pp. 54–72. Princeton: Princeton University Press, 1959.

Jung, E. 1957. *Animus and anima*. New York: Spring Publications.

Kohut, H. 1971. *The analysis of the self: a systematic approach to the psychoanalytic treatment of narcissistic personality disorders*. New York: International Universities Press.

Korner, A. 1973. Sex differences in newborns with special reference to differences in the organization of oral behavior. *Journal of Child Psychology and Psychiatry* 14:19–29.

McGuinness, D., and Pribram, K. 1978. The origins of sensory bias in the development of gender differences in perception and cognition. In *Cognitive growth and development*, ed. M. Bortner, pp. 3–56. New York: Bruner Mazel.

Marcus, K. 1960. *The stranger in women's dreams*. Paper #7. Los Angeles: The Analytical Psychology Club.

May, R. 1980. *Sex and fantasy*. New York: Norton.

Money, J., and Ehrhardt, A. 1972. *Man & woman, boy & girl*. Baltimore: Johns Hopkins University Press.

Neumann, E. 1954*a*. On the moon and matriarchal consciousness. *Spring* 1954:83–100.

———. 1954*b*. *The origins and history of consciousness*. Princeton: Princeton University Press.

———. 1963. *The great mother: analysis of the archetype*. Princeton: Princeton University Press.

Ornstein, R. E. 1972. *The psychology of consciousness*. San Francisco: Freeman.

Perry, J. W. 1953. *The self in psychotic process*. Berkeley: University of California Press.

———. 1966. *Lord of the four quarters: myths of the royal father*. New York: George Braziller.

Pleck, J. H., and Sawyer, J., eds. 1974. *Men and masculinity*. Englewood Cliffs, N.J.: Prentice-Hall.

Rapoport, R., and Rapoport, R. 1977. *Dual-career families re-examined*. New York: Harper & Row.

Rupprecht, C. 1974. The martial maid and the challenge of androgyny. *Spring* 1974:269–93.

Schaefer, S. 1974. A study of sex and age differentials in typologies as derived from the test score of 200 adults on the Jungian Type Survey and the Myers-Briggs Type Indicator. Unpublished paper, University of Minnesota.

Schmidt, L. 1980. The brother-sister relationship in marriage. *Journal of Analytical Psychology* 25:17–35.

Singer, J. 1976. *Androgyny: toward a new theory of sexuality*. Garden City, N.Y.: Anchor Press/Doubleday.

Steinmann, A., and Fox, D. 1974. *The male dilemma*. New York: Jason Aronson.

Stoller, R. J. 1979. *Sexual excitement: dynamics of erotic life*. New York: Pantheon.

Ulanov, A. B. 1971. *The feminine in Jungian psychology and in Christian theology*. Evanston: Northwestern University Press.

Whitmont, E. C. 1969. *The symbolic quest*. San Francisco: Harper.

———. 1980. Reassessing femininity and masculinity: a critique of the Eros/Logos concept. *Quadrant* 13/2:109–22.

Zabriskie, P. T. 1974. Goddesses in our midst. *Quadrant* 17/2:34–45.

[16]

PSYCHOPATHOLOGY AND ANALYSIS
Donald F. Sandner and John Beebe

COMPLEXES

JUNG observed that the first dream brought to him by a prospective patient often contained surprisingly specific intimations for the future course of that person's analytic work. In a parallel way, Jung's first published paper, his doctoral thesis, "On the Psychology and Pathology of So-called Occult Phenomena" (1902), contained many prefigurations of important concepts that were to appear in his published work only many years later. The thesis presents a series of séances conducted by a fifteen-year-old girl, Jung's cousin Helene Preiswerk. During the séances, many psychic entities were personified by Helene for the assembled company. If one set aside, as Jung did, the idea that these entities actually were occult "spirits," then the séances became a strong demonstration of the dissociability of the psyche and the autonomy of its personified parts (or splinter psyches), which Jung called feeling-toned complexes. The complexes were, for him, clusters of associated, unconscious ideas that had assumed

Donald Sandner, M.D., is a member of the Society of Jungian Analysts of Northern California and maintains a private practice in the San Francisco Bay Area. He has taught at the C. G. Jung Institute of San Francisco and has been a member and chairman of the certifying board. A graduate of the University of Illinois College of Medicine, he served his psychiatric residency at Stanford University Medical Center, where he was chief resident in 1960. Dr. Sandner is the author of *Navaho Symbols of Healing* (1979); his papers on healing methods have appeared in *Spring* (1972), *Human Nature* (1978), and as a chapter in *Ways of Health*, edited by David Sobel (1979).

John Beebe, M.D., maintains a private practice in San Francisco. He is a member of the Society of Jungian Analysts of Northern California and Editor of the *San Francisco Jung Institute Library Journal*. A graduate of Harvard College and the University of Chicago Medical School, he served his psychiatric residency at Stanford University Medical Center, where he was chief resident in 1971. He is the author of "The Trickster in the Arts" (1981) and, with C. Peter Rosenbaum, the author and editor of *Psychiatric Treatment: Crisis, Clinic, and Consultation* (1975).

in Helene the character of little inner personalities, each with an emotional nature of its own. The feeling-toned complex became for him the foundation for the further development of his theory of psychopathology and psychotherapy.

Watching the mimetic enactments of his cousin during the séances, Jung observed the following images and scenes: inner masculine figures (which Jung would later see as animus personifications); an inner female psychic figure who was more mature and whole than the medium herself (a representation of the Self for Helene); the personifications of many past lives, each with dramatic scenarios (historical archetypes); the development of a psychic cosmology; and finally the spontaneous appearance of a full mandala, an image of potential wholeness. All of these images and scenes were vivid demonstrations of the operation of the feeling-toned complexes, and of what Jung would later recognize as their archetypal cores. At that time, the data were too informal and unscientific to supply firm grounding.

The first hard evidence that he presented to his professional colleagues came from the word-association experiments he conducted during his tenure as resident physician at the Burghölzli Mental Hospital in Zurich under Europe's leading psychiatrist, Eugen Bleuler. Here he developed a series of 100 neutral and emotion-laden words, mixed together, which were presented to patients and to control persons. Jung carefully noted the responses, the response times, and any other unusual features of the interaction. He saw that a prolonged reaction time, unexpected responses, perseveration, failure of response recall, and other indicators gave evidence of the presence, under surface consciousness, of just such complexes as had been projected dramatically by his medium-cousin. Here was evidence, shown by measured reaction times and recorded responses, replicable by any competent person, that would establish scientifically the concept of the feeling-toned complex (1905a, 1905b, 1906b).

Sometimes the association test would elicit responses from the subject that were so emotionally charged as to jeopardize the whole procedure. Jung wrote:

> . . . it was discovered on these occasions that what the method was aiming at, namely to establish the average speed of the reactions and their qualities, was a relatively subsidiary result compared with the way in which the method was disturbed by the autonomous behavior of the psyche, that is, by assimilation. It was then that I discovered the feeling-toned complexes, which had always been registered before as *failures to react*. (1934, p. 93)

This discovery brought Jung worldwide recognition.

Jung's early papers attracted the attention of Freud, who at first saw them as independent corroborations of his psychoanalytic theories (McGuire, p. 3). Freud later discarded the term *complex* in favor of his own word *conflict,* but the evidence was there to show that psychic entities did interfere with conscious functioning; the presence and action of the feeling-toned complexes were firmly established by the word-association experiments.

In a 1906 paper, "Association, Dream and Hysterical Symptoms," Jung showed that responses to the association test could be correlated with dream material. The stuff of dreams gave substance and character to the bare skeleton of the complex that was revealed in the association tests. In dreams, it was possible to trace the complexes as they moved and interacted: the workings of the inner psyche were made visible. That the psyche was actually structured in the form of complexes and that this structure was accessible to observation in dreams became fundamental to Jung's maturing ideas on the basic nature of neuroses.

SPLITTING OFF OF COMPLEXES: NEUROTIC CONDITIONS

Jung contended that neuroses sprang from the tendency of the psyche to dissociate or split in the face of intolerable suffering. He saw this clearly manifested in old Babette, the chronically psychotic woman whom he analyzed for more than seven years while he was working at Burghölzli. She provided the central case material in his first important book, *The Psychology of Dementia Praecox* (1907). He showed that her seemingly meaningless and random productions could be decoded into two coherent complexes, which on further study appeared to form a pair of opposites: delusions of exalted grandeur and feelings of profound inferiority. Later Jung saw such oppositions as the basis of all forms of psychic splitting.

Though Babette was suffering from incurable psychosis, Jung believed that similar splits occurred in neurotic patients as well. In Babette's case, these splits were not only traceable to traumatic childhood experiences with her emotionally disturbed parents, but also demonstrable in the present, as responses to immediate moral conflicts within her psyche. Jung thought that whatever its roots in previous experience, neurosis consists of a refusal—or inability—in the here-and-now to bear legitimate suffering. Instead, this painful feeling or some representation of it is split off from awareness and the initial wholeness—the primordial Self—is broken. Such splitting "ultimately derives from the apparent impossibility of affirming the whole of one's nature" (Jung 1934, p. 98), and gives rise to the whole range of dissociations and conflicts characteristic of feeling-toned complexes. This splitting is a normal part of life. Initial wholeness is meant to be broken, and it becomes pathological, or diagnosable as illness, only when the splitting off of complexes becomes too wide and deep and the conflict too intense. Then the painful symptoms may lead to the conflicts of neurosis or to the shattered ego of psychosis. The way back, the restoration—perhaps always partial—is the work of individuation.

Splitting takes place unconsciously, and it takes many different forms in different individuals, much as a sharp blow with a hammer on one diamond will cause quite a different fracture line than it would on another. Differences in internal structure, planes of structural weakness, and basic temperamental disposition make the difference. Jung described the splitting that occurs in hysteria as follows: "If the patient can maintain his emotional rapport by dissociating himself into two personalities, one religious and apparently transcendental, the other perhaps all too human, he will become hysterical" (1919, p. 224). Thus, hysteria develops from a conflict between two powerful complexes, and it concerns mainly the feeling function. Jung further states:

> There is, however, another form of dissociation, and that is the splitting off of the conscious ego, together with a selected function, from the other components of the personality. This form of dissociation can be defined as an identification of the ego with a particular function or group of functions. It is very common in people who are too deeply immersed in one of their psychic functions and have differentiated it into their sole conscious means of adaptation. (1921, p. 207)

This formulation describes obsessive-compulsive neurosis, in which the thinking function is identified with the ego and is in constant use, while the feeling function is out of contact with consciousness and inferior to the point of producing symptoms.

But the idea of complexes and their interactions had a deeper philosophical meaning for Jung. He wrote: "The existence of the complex throws serious doubt on the naïve assumption of the unity of consciousness . . . and on the supremacy of the will" (1934, pp. 95–96). He defined the complex as the "image of a certain psychic situation which is strongly accentuated emotionally and is, moreover, incompatible with the habitual attitude of consciousness. This image has a powerful, inner coherence, it has its own wholeness and, in addition, a relatively high degree of autonomy" (ibid., p. 96). (A somewhat boyish, immature man, for example, might possess a powerful unconscious father image sternly demanding higher levels of achievement and responsibility from him. This father image would form the nucleus of his father complex.)

Jung finally conceived of the feeling-toned complexes as "living units of the unconscious psyche" (ibid., p. 101), each carrying a splinter of consciousness of its own, a degree of intentionality, and the capability of pursuing a goal. They are like real personalities in that they contain images, feelings, and qualities, and, if they engulf the ego they determine behavior as well. They are caused by conflict, and they are injuries to psychic wholeness. Yet, once formed, they tend to press for recognition and integration by the ego.

The nucleus, the dynamic origin of every complex, is connected to the inner directive center of the collective unconscious, the Self. This connection to the Self introduces a paradox: the production of complexes not only leads to a divisive injuring but also provides a new way of achieving integration. Complexes participate in the Self's effort to replace an initially unconscious state of unity with a conscious state of wholeness. Their dual nature explains how splitting, even to the point of psychic injury and neurosis, is necessary for the evolution of consciousness and ultimate personality integration.

This conception is significantly different from the Freudian idea of repression. According to Freud, all the contents of the repressed complex were once conscious. But according to Jung, this is not so: some of the contents of the complexes may have been conscious and repressed, but many of them have never been conscious. These enter the psyche from the collective unconscious as fresh archetypal images moving towards consciousness.

Furthermore, the concept of the complex in Jungian psychology does not lend itself entirely to the usual medical model, in which illness is regarded as an unfortunate interruption in the patient's state of wellness. In the Jungian model, the patient must endure the illness in order to become well: the illness contains some of the "germs" of wholeness.

Perry has extended Jung's description of the complex by showing that a complex response is bipolar. That is, an emotional object relation comprises two complexes in interaction, one of which invests the ego while the other is projected out upon an object to which the patient is emotionally related. The complex closer to the ego is "ego-aligned," the other is "ego-projected." (This terminology does not mean that the ego creates the alignment or projection itself.) Both ego and object, then, are invested by complexes, and the "essential emotional interaction is then not between subject and object but between two complexes within the psyche" (Perry 1970, p. 4). Perry further argues that such bipolar arrangements of complexes form the structure of the psyche; all of its complexes, he feels, are arranged in complementary pairs.

We would like to extend Perry's observations by exploring the actual interactions of pairs of complexes within neurotic and more severe conditions. In dreams, this interplay of complexes can be strikingly obvious, as when two dream figures make love or quarrel. The same interactions produce symptomatic inner conflicts and, through projective identification, the emotional tangles and misalliances experienced in the transference/countertransference.

We begin with the ego-aligned complex. By this term we mean a complex that is close to the ego and can at certain times take over ego direction. It is often projected, but even then it projects contents that are potentially part of the ego's conscious identity. When projected, it deprives the ego of part of its identity and the energy associated with it. For instance, in the dream described immediately below, the young dreamer's repressed rage is portrayed in his dreams as a wild boar that chases and threatens him. This same rage could just as well be projected in waking experience upon another person, who would then seem to be pursuing and threatening him even when this was not actually so. In both cases the content and the energy that could be part of his ego-identity are not really available to him. If that split-off complex were integrated, he would feel the rage as his own and not meet it in his dreams as a wild animal or in his life as a threatening enemy; he would have regained an important part of his identity. Moreover, the interpretation that this energy is his own would be relatively easy for him to accept. Thus the concept of ego-aligned complexes is similar to, but not identical with, the classic Jungian concept of the shadow, which refers to the part of the unconscious psyche that is nearest to consciousness, even though not fully acceptable to it. Ego-aligned complexes are a broader, more inclusive, category because they include not only unacceptable elements, but also, for example, unrealized ideals, as will be shown further in the examples below.

The portion of the psyche that can become ego-aligned is by no means experienced as a unitary reality. It, too, is split into pieces, some that are identifiably one's own and some that seem quite foreign to one's identity. In forming an identity, as in every other phase of the ego's development out of the unconscious, the ego must confront a pair of opposites. The ego forges its identity by integrating opposite possibilities. Along the way, a wide range of unconscious tensions may be represented in dreams and in life as pairs of opposites, but the pair most often encountered in clinical work consists of instinctual drives on the one hand and spiritual strivings on the other. (The analogy to Freud's id/superego split comes to mind, but Jung, as against Freud, considered spiritual as well as instinctual drives to be prime movers in the unconscious. The ''superego'' in Jung's model would have an inherently spiritual, not just a law-giving, character.) We can learn much about the tension between instinctual and spiritual strivings by looking at its representation in dreams.

The instinctual-energetic complexes are often represented in dreams as wild or dangerous animals, as in this dream of a man in his early twenties who is suffering from a great deal of repressed rage:

> Dream: *I am in a wooded area running down an open road. I am trying to put some distance between myself and a herd of elephants. I am loping along thinking I am ahead, but a small elephant is overtaking me with incredible speed. I turn around and, instead of running, sidestep the charge, and he goes past me. I jump up a hillside into the trees thinking he can't chase me there, but he turns into a wild boar with long tusks. Somebody warns me that boars know the terrain well. As the dream ends I am running and dodging.*

In this dream, the complex is represented first as a wild elephant, then as a dangerous boar, both charging animals possessing aggressive, prominently phallic, features. Thus the split-off complex has an instinctual quality and contains a great deal of energy. The dream-ego tries to escape, but the complex pursues, even changing form to do so. In the treatment, it had become clear that this young man's ego was in an inflated state, and was also inwardly mother-bound and cut off from its natural animal instincts. At the time of this dream, the cut-off instinctual energy is pushing toward integration. In the dream, we see it actively intruding and in the end the inflated ego will have to come to terms with it. Integrated, this masculine drive would be conscious and at the disposal of the ego.

In another example, taken from a professional man in his early thirties, the instinctual energy takes the form of a poisonous snake.

> Dream: *There on the ground lay a rattler all coiled up, hissing and ready to strike. I, or really something in me, made up my mind that I would have to pick it up in spite of its vicious appearance. I very slowly reached my hand towards it, and just as I was about to touch it, it turned into a playful puppy that I picked up and cuddled. The dream had very little feeling in it, no great fear, but just seemed to be a series of images.*

Here the complex takes on a particularly menacing form: the cold, poisonous fury of a hissing snake. But it is approached by the dreamer, with more courage than he himself thinks he has. In its snake form, the complex represents a deeply buried form of vicious, unrelated hatred previously unconscious to the dreamer. In the clinical working through of the dream, the patient was able to accept those negative feelings, thus truly reducing the originally destructive complex to the innocuous level of a harmless puppy, because the viciousness had left the unconscious and become conscious. Such dramatic changes can and do occur. But, if the patient had been unable to understand the necessity for accepting the energy first in its negative form, or had he been unable to do so because of insufficient ego strength, the puppy image might still have appeared, but it would have represented a wishful reaction-formation against the still-unconscious viciousness. The original snake complex might have continued as a deeply repressed complex of high energy charge, capable of suddenly taking possession of the ego and creating a paranoidlike clinical situation. Effective integration of a complex that makes such seductive transformations from malignant to benign forms requires an unstinting honesty from both patient and therapist.

Frequently such instinctual-energetic complexes take the form of tough street gangs, menacing attackers, or, in dreams of white persons, aggressive black men. Here is an example from a man in his mid-twenties:

> Dream: *I was taking a long walk in the city. I found myself in a rough section of the town. A couple of black toughs were following me. . . . I saw they had a knife and finally they blocked my path. I realized I could not escape; I decided to fight. One of the men took his shirt off. I was frightened but I circled him. I attacked him and fell on top of him; I hurt him. Then he was angry and I threw him down. I thought I might have broken his back. I lifted him by his clothes and took him to my apartment. Later I saw a little black boy who had ditched school and needed money for his fine. I gave him the money and he went in and paid the teacher and came out. I looked at him and then kissed him. I had a very strong feeling.*

In this dream, the instinctual-energetic complex takes the form of knife-wielding black toughs. The ego is strong enough to take aggressive action, to counter the attack of the complex, to subdue it, and finally to make peace with it by taking it into consciousness (his apartment), paying the fine to the authorities (the teacher), and giving the little black boy a kiss of love. The resolution here is a very optimistic image of integration.

In women, the symbolism of the instinctual-energetic complex is often masculine, as in the following dream of a middle-aged housewife:

> Dream: *A college-age young man was driving down the street in an old car. He was driving fast and telling me that last night he and*

> *another boy had been driving around and saw some teen-age boys.*
> *He began teasing them and needling them. Finally the boys became*
> *angry and ran after the car. Because the car was old, they just*
> *barely escaped them. The teen-age boys chased them down the*
> *street.*

When asked to make associations between components of her dream and elements of her waking life, the patient said she identified with the college-age boy because she also loves old cars and would like to drive fast in them. She said that in the dream, "she" made the teen-age boys angry, because she loved to tease men when it was safe, but here it almost wasn't. In this dream, the college-age boy, even though of the opposite sex from the dreamer, represents an ego-aligned complex because its energy is very close to the dreamer's ego-identity, and could with a little work become part of her own conscious repertoire of assertiveness. The teen-agers, however, represent a deeper, angry, and destructive kind of energy that she usually experiences in projection as the problem with the men she relates to. In reality, this is a part of herself, a part that Jung called the animus and that here appears in negative aspect. Negative animus energy is often portrayed in women's dreams as gangs of toughs, rowdy young boys, and threatening animals. Yet if this patient were told this, only intellectual agreement might result. Ego-projected complexes are very difficult to recognize as one's own and integrate into one's self-concept, so difficult that Jung called it the masterpiece of one's lifework to do it.

In the dreams of a similar analysand, the energetic-instinctual complex is portrayed as an unruly, spoiled brat:

> Dream: *A little girl took a knife and cut a slit in the sofa. I asked*
> *her why she did it and she said it was because she wanted to use*
> *mending tape to see how it could be mended. I said I would tell her*
> *father on her.*

The little girl is a "shadow" figure who can express rage (an instinctual-energetic complex), but who must at the same time rationalize and deny it. Since this complex was ego-aligned, the patient could begin to integrate it. (The father, a respected aspect of the animus, may offer some possibility for discriminating this part of herself.)

The common characteristic of the complexes portrayed is the presence of strong affect filled with instinctual energy. This energy is often unacceptable to the ego because it is charged with sexual or hateful emotion that goes beyond the current ego-ideal; but this energy is nevertheless essential to life and even health, and cannot be safely ignored.

The complexes of inflated spiritual strivings, on the other hand, elevate the ego at the expense of its connection to bodily instincts. These complexes may be portrayed as persons—often the dream-ego itself—flying or moving about without normal bodily restriction, or standing on mountains, tall buildings, or other high places and looking down on the scene below. They may be portrayed as persons of great wisdom and learning, nobility, royalty, elevated purity or spirituality, and so on. This type of complex may be represented as a hero who is driven to do good works: rescue maidens, free the oppressed, imitate Christ, or take on the sufferings of the world. We use the phrase inflated spiritual striving to designate these complexes because they represent a split-off spiritual potential that has gained the status of religious transcendence and has been severed from the earthy vitality of the instinctual-energetic complexes. Here is an example of such a complex from the dream of a young man:

> Dream: *I was on the crest of a high mountain on a trail. There was a young couple with me. We came to a point on the trail where it seemed to end. I told them to stay behind while I climbed over boulders and rubble. I found the trail on the other side and followed it to a steep embankment. I was very high up. I saw a tree twisted and gnarled . . . I got to the tree and climbed it. Then I was looking far below and saw everything in color. I saw the whole countryside, a river running strong behind its embankments. It was green and swift-flowing . . .*

Here the dreamer's ego is in an inflated state, but he is looking down at the swift flow of life energy (libido) in the countryside below. He is cut off from the flow of life, but it is visible and even attainable if he can find a way down. Here are other dream images of a similar character:

> Dream: *I am able to fly freely through the air. I can twist and turn and do all sorts of stunts to the astonishment of those below . . .*

> Dream: *I can take giant steps and travel like the wind . . .*

> Dream: *I am the master of a vast domain . . .*

> Dream: *I was in the presence of the great king and his royal court. He smiled at me in a friendly way . . .*

Sometimes the dream-ego is inflated with power, watching energy being expended by an opposite complex—perhaps by one filled with destructive energy:

> Dream: *I am on a high place looking out over the city. Below I see bombs dropping on the city. People are running and shouting, and*

many are being killed and wounded. I start to cry because I am frightened . . .

In one of Jung's recorded dreams, we can see an interaction between an instinctual-energetic complex and a complex of inflated spiritual power:

[Dream (18 December 1913):] *I was with an unknown, brown-skinned man, a savage, in a lonely, rocky mountain landscape. It was before dawn; the eastern sky was already bright, and the stars fading. Then I heard Siegfried's horn sounding over the mountains and I knew that we had to kill him. We were armed with rifles and lay in wait for him on a narrow path over the rocks.*

Then Siegfried appeared high up on the crest of the mountain, in the first ray of the rising sun. On a chariot made of the bones of the dead he drove at furious speed down the precipitous slope. When he turned a corner, we shot him, and he plunged down, struck dead.

Filled with disgust and remorse for having destroyed something so great and beautiful, I turned to flee, impelled by the fear that the murder might be discovered. But a tremendous downfall of rain began, and I knew that it would wipe out all traces of the dead. I had escaped the danger of discovery; life could go on, but an unbearable feeling of guilt remained. (1961, p. 180)

The brown savage represents instinctual energy, and the dream-ego is on good terms with it. This complex helps the ego reduce the power of the hero ideal, Siegfried (an inflated, spiritual complex); this had to be ''killed'' before life could flow onward. (Jung said of this dream, ''The dream showed that the attitude embodied by Siegfried, the hero, no longer suited me. Therefore it had to be killed'' [1961, p. 180]. This dream is often understood as Jung's sacrifice of sonship to Freud.)

We now turn to the ego-projected complexes, those that are usually experienced not as parts of the ego's identity, but rather as qualities in other people. Frequently these complexes form the basis for relationships with others. The term *ego-projected* is not meant to imply that the ego does the projecting, but rather that the ego relates to this type of complex in projected form. Although these complexes are theoretically parts of the psyche, located at deeper levels of the unconscious than the shadow complexes, they are commonly experienced by the ego as qualities in other persons. These complexes are of two kinds: (1) those referred to in the classical anima-animus theory of object relations, which places the basis for relations between the sexes upon the projection of one's own contrasexual characteristics upon one's partner, and (2) parental complexes. Parental complexes, the all-important mother and father imagoes, are formed partly from interaction with actual parents and partly from the patterning created by the innate mother and father archetypes. Parental complexes exert a strong influence on the dynamics of the complexes we are discussing, and their analysis is fundamental to any real work in depth. We can only consider them in passing here.

Just as there are splits within the ego-aligned complexes (shadow-level complexes), so there are splits within ego-projected complexes. Again, such splits can usually be characterized in terms of opposite qualities. A common opposition is between the qualities "dominant harshness" and "vulnerable woundedness." For instance, to a young man, the anima may appear in dreams as a dominant, overbearing, commanding, cruel woman, an image of terrifying, ruthless power. In the dreams of one such analysand, this is how the anima looked:

> Dream: *We were all collected in the prison yard and in the center was a cruel woman in black garb. She held a submachine gun and ordered us to crawl around the yard in the dirt.*

Or again:

> Dream: *I was with a pretty girl playing dominoes. When my hand held the dominoes, she said something about my hand shaking. Then the girl changed into a whorehouse madam—her clothes, face, etc. She aged ten years, and changed to a heavy, ugly madam figure. Then it turned out there were whores all around, and it was a heavy sex scene. Then the whore got up and left out of impatience. She had her duties to do. Did I want to buy some of the action? She acted sexy and said it would cost $20. I think I said no and walked out.*

Such a dominating, powerful figure is regularly complemented by an anima image that is vulnerable and wounded—weak, retarded, ill, crippled, deranged, or seriously injured. The wounded pole of the anima complex can be seen in this dream of a young man who was in therapy to free himself from a dominant mother complex.

> Dream: *I am in a strange, rickety Victorian house. I am in bed. Sitting beside me is an old high-school classmate, a girl who was somewhat retarded. I am trying to help her. Sitting across the table is another girl who is deformed, and I am also trying to help her. A fatherly man comes up and kisses me on the temple. Then I am*

in a car and the first girl has her arms around my neck. I am still trying to help her.

Here the wounded anima is seen in two forms, and the dreamer is trying to make a bond with her by attempting to help her. The fatherly man is probably the therapist, whose presence in the dream may indicate the beginning of change. From the dreamer's point of view, he seems to reward the effort to heal the crippled anima.

In the following dream, the wounded anima figure has connections with an aggressive, ego-aligned shadow complex.

Dream: *A young woman I knew was sick in the hospital. I was in the room talking to her. There was a feeling she didn't have any legs, that she ended at the waist. She was going to have her legs sewed back in an operation. I had my arm around her, speaking to her. She said the tragedy was something that happened to her in the East. She had been raped and kidnaped. Afterward, two men walked into the room. They were young ruffians and might want to beat me up but they didn't. I talked to them and saw that they were responsible for her condition, but they weren't going to hurt her any further. They were just there. I walked away as if there were nothing more to do.*

Or the two sides of the anima may interact in the same dream.

Dream: *A young woman was on the operating table, naked, with legs spread wide apart. She was to be operated on by a huge woman. An appendectomy. I was there somewhere, and I and the young woman were very concerned. I told the huge woman she had no right to operate. I thought the knife might cut the vulva. I anticipated the pain. It ended when the huge woman just pushed the cart with the young woman on it through the door into the operating room.*

The animus in the dreams of a woman in psychotherapy often displays an even sharper split, appearing again as two quite different ego-projected complexes. One is the dominating, judgmental, condemning side, personified as a patriarchal father, dictator, judge, executioner, stern priest or rabbi, schoolmaster, robber chieftain, or even menacing animal such as a tiger or panther. These animus personifications seem to attack the woman dreamer, corresponding to involuntary thoughts that may attack her in waking life, saying, ''What good are you? What could you accomplish? All you do is worthless.''

In the same woman, a complementing ego-projected complex may be weak, helpless, or impotent. He may be an oversensitive artist; a deformed, crippled, or crazy boy; a distant, indifferent, or frigid man unable to love; or a weak, helpless animal.

Each person's experience and representation of these complexes is different, but in this discussion we have tried to show the main lines of splitting in the psyche by highlighting significant qualitative differences in dream figures. Both the shadow (ego-aligned) complexes and the anima/ animus (ego-projected) complexes display this characteristic of splitting. To see the split in well-defined form, one must look at the dreams of men and women in the midst of a deep healing process; usually a series of several hundred dreams must be surveyed to see this process in action. The same splits can be felt minute by minute within the dynamics of the transference/countertransference, even if not so clearly seen.

Among the anima/animus complexes, the dominating images are derived from overcontrolling parents, which are in turn complemented by weak and helpless inner love objects. The ego-aligned, identity complexes split between an unconscious instinctual shadow complex and an inflated drive to spiritual power. Both splits are typically present in the struggles of young adults with serious neurotic fixations and impaired object relations. The splits are interrelated and form a complex quaternity, which suggests the wholeness that is being maintained through the neurotic organization, even as it is the key to the psyche's potential for integration.

In figure 1, the arrows connect complexes that form object relations through their interaction. The spiritually inflated boy (ego-aligned complex on the left) forms an object relationship with a dominant and perhaps sadistic woman. But this excludes the primitive shadow complex (ego-aligned complex on the right), which is imbued with aggressive, sexual energy. This complex will enter into an object relationship with a helpless or injured woman anima figure (ego-projected complex on the left).

The implications of this splitting for the analytic transference/countertransference are enormous. The analyst, as the one onto whom the ego-projected complexes are projected, must avoid behaving too much like a critical dominant anima figure, or too passively, like a wounded anima figure, because either extreme of behavior will tend to maintain the reciprocal split in the patient's ego-aligned complexes. In response to criticism, the patient may become a miffed divine child, and in response to excessive passivity, a poisonously aggressive attacker. But, in analytic therapy with a stable father figure (male analyst), or a strong but caring woman (female analyst), the complexes above would tend to integrate (that is, swing together in the diagram). This creates a strong, but still spiritually sensitive,

Figure 1. Schematic Representation of Neurotic Organization in a Man
(puer aeternus)

Outer World

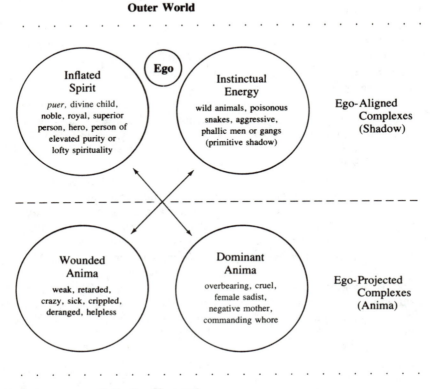

Collective Unconscious

ego-identity (an integration of the left and right ego-aligned complexes),
which can then project a relationship onto a sturdy but caring woman or
onto a man with a stable anima. A stable anima structure is produced by
an integration of the left and right ego-projected anima complexes.

If a young man is well integrated in regard to his instinctual and aggressive shadow qualities, the inflated spiritual complexes may be split off.
Such a person is vulnerable to sudden invasions of these complexes, often
resulting in rapid conversions to intellectual beliefs or religious cult fanat-
icism. (These would also be ego-aligned complexes, and the designation
of them as shadow would have a different meaning than the instinctual-
energetic connotation we usually intend.)

In figure 2, the good little girl, or inflated princess (ego-aligned complex on the left), tends to form an object relationship by projecting the dominant animus complex (ego-projected complex on the right) onto a strong, dominant, and perhaps cruel and sadistic man—often a father figure. But the complex containing aggressive, assertive energy (ego-aligned complex on the right), if it gains influence over the ego, will create the basis for a relationship with a weak, perhaps impotent, young man or boy (ego-projected complex on the left). In therapy, the analyst will have to watch out for being pompously authoritative on the one hand and excessively vulnerable on the other in response to the patient's attempts to place

Figure 2. Schematic Representation of Neurotic Organization in a Woman *(puella aeterna)*

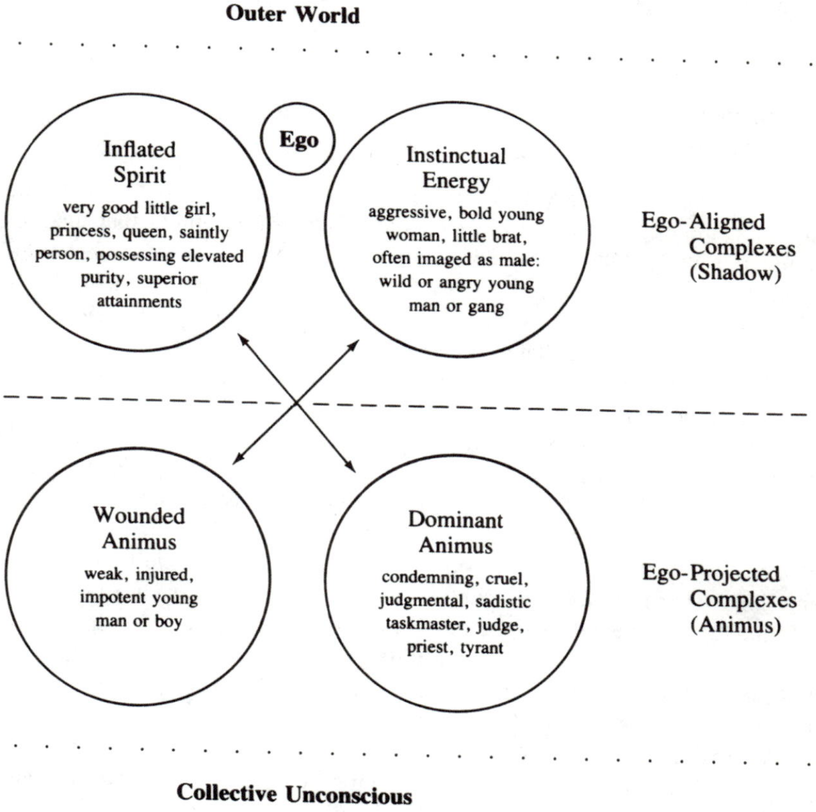

Outer World

Inflated Spirit

very good little girl, princess, queen, saintly person, possessing elevated purity, superior attainments

Ego

Instinctual Energy

aggressive, bold young woman, little brat, often imaged as male: wild or angry young man or gang

Ego-Aligned Complexes (Shadow)

Wounded Animus

weak, injured, impotent young man or boy

Dominant Animus

condemning, cruel, judgmental, sadistic taskmaster, judge, priest, tyrant

Ego-Projected Complexes (Animus)

Collective Unconscious

the analyst in these positions. But, with a strong but approving father figure (male analyst) or with a constant, warm woman (female analyst), the complexes diagrammed above would tend to integrate (swing together in the diagram), thus creating a strong, but still sensitively attuned, ego-identity. She would be capable of experiencing an object relationship with a manly, but still loving, young man or with a woman with a reliable, related animus. A stable animus structure would be produced by integrating both sides of the animus as represented by the complexes in the diagram.

Both of these diagrams show inner psychic structure in schematic, and of course highly simplified, form. In clinical work, relationship patterns are never so simple or clear. Nor does integration, the swinging together of the complexes shown in the diagrams, occur with such ease and elegance in the office as it does in these diagrams. We hope, however, that our schematic representation may provide an overall view of psychic structure, of how the psyche splits, and of how change might be expected to take place within that structure.

POSSESSION BY COMPLEXES: PERSONALITY DISORDERS AND PSYCHOSES

Jung's theory of complexes goes a long way toward elucidating neurotic psychopathology. But Jung himself warned against assuming that just because one understands the theory, one will easily overcome the behavior thus understood. "Everyone knows nowadays that people 'have complexes,' " Jung wrote. "What is not so well known, though far more important theoretically, is that complexes can *have us*" (1934, p. 96).

Here Jung opened the way to a new use for the concept of possession, one of the primitive explanations of mental disease (Ellenberger, pp. 13–33) and long discredited by modern psychiatry as a destructive medieval notion. Jung realized, however, that the concept of possession can be applied to the behavior of complexes in the more serious psychopathological disorders. He observed that there are many conditions in which the ego is "taken over" (that is, "possessed") for long periods of time by complex emotional states. Indeed, without a period of possession, when the contents of the complex are "lived out," integration of the complex into conscious ego functioning could scarcely occur. At the same time, possession is a potentially grave state of affairs while it is occurring, even if it ultimately serves the striving for wholeness.

Possession tends to produce what Jung called "a shadow government of the ego" (1966, p. 87). This is a more thoroughgoing phenomenon than alignment with a complex. Possession of the ego is accompanied by a change in the quality of object relations produced by the anima/animus. Ego-projected complexes become more archetypal, characterized by intense affect and primitive forms of projection, such as extreme idealization and projective identification. The basis for such archetypal forms of projection seems to lie in the archetypal cores of the complexes. During possession, when the complexes have taken over the direction of behavior from the ego, the ego is no longer the center of consciousness. Instead, rationalized archetypal attitudes and viewpoints are dominant. During possession, the archetypes function to structure perceptions of situations, consequent behaviors, and entire styles of being in the world. These patterns not only are compulsively overdetermined, but may also produce reciprocal possessions in significant others. For this reason, everyone in the psychic field of a seriously possessed person, including the analyst, is in risk of some degree of possession.

Possession is the hallmark of serious personality disorders and of psychotic states. Substitution of sectors of the ego by complexes and their archetypal cores results in drastic alteration in normal ego-attributes, such as ethical behavior, reliable reality testing, and a stable level of mood. Possession can happen for various reasons, only one of which is the attempt by the Self as the archetype of healthy wholeness to compensate for a restricted ego-attitude. Just as often, ego weakness is the fault. Biological conditions (like hypoglycemia or hypothyroidism), crushing life circumstances, and the erosion of ego-defenses during uncovering therapy all may weaken the ego's ability to stand up to its complexes and may thereby facilitate a pathological regression into primitive forms of object relation.

An example will illustrate such regression. After a long period of analytic work, a difficult patient, whose conflicts had heretofore presented themselves within the analysis as fleeting ego-alignments with malignant parental complexes that could still be dissolved by careful elucidation, slipped into an excited hypomanic state. This condition began after he recognized the archetypal core of his father complex, the demonic trickster within the sociopathic alcoholic man who had been his father. This father had a history of ruthless and unethical behavior, and so, to a lesser degree, did the patient. This much the patient had always been able to see. But, as the degree to which the patient was unconsciously identified with this father was uncovered, the patient began to lose his ability to maintain his defenses against the identification. These defenses had been largely of a masochistically guilt-inducing, self-punitive kind, based upon the martyred attitude of his mother. The mother had demonstrated in her marriage the uncanny, witchlike ability to finger her husband's weak spot and to use this ability to make him question his very right to be. The patient had a similar ability to punish himself with ruthless self-judgments. He had a suicidal history. In analysis, the patient used what he learned about himself to castigate himself. The analyst tried to stand between the patient and his tendency to criticize himself so harshly. But as the patient began to give up the criticism that had seemed to come from his mother complex, the sociopathy of his father complex apparently began to possess him. He initiated a series of interpersonal maneuvers designed to intimidate and provoke his spouse, his coworkers, and finally his analyst. These actions forced a judgment as severe as any his mother had meted out, even from those who had tried to maintain a caring attitude toward him.

The provocation directed against the analyst was so severe that he could not maintain a forgiving attitude, and he was forced to accept the patient's termination of the analysis even though the patient was far from being psychologically stable. (A former therapist had told the patient, at the time he had sought out this analyst, "I have too much countertransference to see you.") At the time of termination, the now-immobilized analyst dreamed: "I see my patient. His mother and father have returned to live with him for good. They won't ever leave him now."

The analyst's dream proved tragically prophetic. The patient soon started behaving even more maliciously. Such behavior would be followed by guilt-ridden depressions even more severe than the one that had driven him to his last analysis. He went on to several more psychiatrists, but none was able to reverse this cycle of escalating "tricksterism" followed by ever severer self-castigation. The patient lost his employment, his marriage, and, through a final suicide attempt, his own life. The retrospective diagnosis given was borderline personality with depressive features, but the analyst's dream seemed to point to the essential dynamic: possession of the patient by his parent complexes. Presumably, these parent complexes were partly introjects. To explain their formation, we would say that archetypal cores of his parents' own complexes (which had interacted in life like witch against trickster) had activated similar elements within his own psyche. The resultant parent complexes in him were so powerful that they overwhelmed his ego.

This case illustrates the problem of possession as it may surface during analysis. The tendency toward possession may worsen even though analysis is undertaken to ameliorate it, and so the thorny question of analyzability must be raised. Jung has often been criticized by later Jungian analysts for what appear to be rigid views on this subject. Jung often speaks of "latent psychosis," which he thinks contraindicates analysis, even though his writings contain examples of successful treatment of borderline and even schizophrenic conditions by analytic means.

Jung's most famous example of the unanalyzable patient was a doctor, an almost too normal-seeming medical man, who had read of analysis and wanted to enter a training analysis for the purpose of becoming an analyst himself. This man was not accustomed to recalling dreams, but after Jung's suggestion that he try to do so, he dreamed of taking a railroad trip to an unfamiliar city, where he walked to what looked like the town hall at the city's center. In this building, he first encountered rooms that were well furnished with old paintings and fine tapestries. But then, in uncanny darkness, he passed through a series of entirely empty rooms. He realized he had met no one at all in this place. Seeking an exit at what appeared to be the end of the building, he opened a door to find an enormous room in whose center he saw "an idiot child . . . about two years old," sitting on a chamber pot, smearing itself with feces. Jung felt that this image represented a latent psychosis, a content the man could not deal with; predicting to himself that analysis would unleash this man's psychosis, Jung talked him out of taking up analysis (1961, pp. 134–36).

Recent papers by two Jungian analysts, who represent the quite different approaches of Fordham and Hillman, have criticized Jung's handling of this patient (Marriott, p. 131; Hartman, pp. 94–95). They make the point that the presence of regressive infantile content alone is no indication of latent psychosis. Indeed, the analyst's attitude toward such material may be crucial if a patient is to work it through. To many later analysts, it has seemed that Jung's reaction to this patient was prejudiced and opened the door to rejection of many analyzable patients by analysts who become revolted or frightened by their inner contents. This attitude may lead an analyst to discourage a patient even from seeking another opinion.

In a seminar, von Franz clarifies the considerations that led Jung to reject the medical man for analysis (1974, pp. 233–34). She points out that the problem he posed is indicated not only by the image of the baby smearing itself with feces, but by several other factors as well. First, the self-smearing takes place in the innermost chamber of the dreamer's psyche (represented by the room at the interior of this central structure in the town that the dreamer is exploring). The nucleus of the patient's personality, therefore, is occupied by an infantile attitude. In addition, this central complex operates at a great distance from the conscious standpoint of the dreamer, which is seemingly adult. Little or nothing seems to lie between these opposites, the messy infant and the adult professional, to mediate their tension. (The spaces between the initial handsome corridors of the structure and the large back room are ominously empty.) To von Franz, this connotes a tension of opposites that is too great: there is nothing—no intervening humanizing attitude, especially—to prepare the dreamer for the unpleasant reality that lies behind his elegant façade. A gradient of contents that could prepare the patient's ego to accept the reality of his own largely infantile state, or a compassionate or humorous or tolerant attitude toward himself, might have paved his way. But there was nothing, and the shocked dreamer awakened in a panic from the unanticipated discovery. In that reaction, above all, lay the indication that this man would not benefit from an analytic discovery of the Self. Jung rightly saw that the dream warned that an analytic exploration would lead the patient to uncover a big mess from which he might not be able to escape.

Analysis favors spontaneity, but it is a luxury some psyches cannot afford. Thus the analyst, considering in advance what some of the worst possibilities may be, will want to establish a prognosis for the outcome of analysis before he or she allows the patient to embark upon what may be a hazardous procedure. At the same time, an analyst will not want to refuse analysis to any patient who can genuinely benefit from it. Nor is analysis well served by too cautious a stance, which seems to project onto the patient a "weak ego" that is unable to decide what is best for itself (Goodheart, pp. 19–20).

The issue is best considered in terms of the likely behavior of the patient's complexes under pressure. The uncovering process of analysis forces the ego to experience its complexes at progressively deeper levels, and the receptive attitude of the analyst invites buried complexes to surface. This surfacing collapses the tension of opposites that normally exists between the ego and the archetypal cores of the complexes, and it releases the potential energy buried in this dynamism. What ensues can resemble what occurs when the nucleus of an atom is bombarded by another atomic particle. Because of the very high energic charge of some of the archetypal cores—their potential for structuring whole sequences of behavior and for releasing quantities of affect—some temporary states of possession are the norm during the unfolding of an analysis. Jung sometimes speaks of analysis as an artificial psychosis under controlled conditions (1946, p. 267). An ego not sufficiently prepared for such an in-depth experience of the complexes is likely to fall to the invasion, and psychopathology during analysis is the result. Depending upon the strength and quality of the complex responsible for the takeover, the possessed ego may become depressed, manic, paranoid, or schizophrenic—to use, as compass points, four orienting positions of psychotic pathology (Beebe). Such takeovers are obvious in cases of psychotic reactions, but are also present, to a less obvious degree, in cases in which latent personality disorders are manifest.

The Role of Psychological Type in Possession

It is usual in Jungian literature to discuss the psychopathology found in such states of possession in terms of the archetypal cores of the complexes involved. Archetypes tend to structure situations in a typical way, and each psychotic syndrome has an archetypal basis. There is also, however, a personal factor that is quite important in the development of any possessed state, and that is the role of the "psychological type" of the individual suffering the possession.

All complexes contain aspects of the attitudes and functions that have been excluded or inhibited from conscious representation by the dominant attitudes and functions of the ego. Usually, one attitude is dominant, either extraverted or introverted, and this attitude is expressed through one of the functions: thinking, intuition, feeling, or sensation. Often (and it has been left to analysts after Jung to make this clear), an auxiliary function will be of the opposite attitude (Quenk). This pairing of functions of opposed attitude within the ego means, for example, that an introverted thinking type may have at his or her disposal an auxiliary extraverted sensation with which to meet the world. The other two functions are likely to be largely unconscious, and will carry attitudes opposed to those of the superior functions, forming a system of checks and balances.

In the example above, these less conscious functions might be a relatively inferior introverted intuition and a markedly inferior extraverted feeling. The least developed, or inferior function, is particularly apt to exist in archaic form, and it is often represented by the anima or animus. When states of anima or animus possession occur, as in many borderline conditions, this inferior function is activated, producing strikingly inferior attempts at adaptation, often of a compulsive, psychotic character. En route to such full-blown states of possession, or in association with them, the operation of the relatively inferior function can be noted as well.

A case will illustrate such use of inferior functions. A young engineer who had excelled in school and at college, under pressure from a demanding father, was motivated by drug experiences and peers in the counterculture to drop out of his first job after college for the purpose of exploring "varieties of religious experience." He drifted to the West Coast and lived in various communal situations, where he experimented with his sexual as well as his religious feelings. He eventually tried to exchange his dominant heterosexual adaptation for a homosexual one, but he became a most absurd and unsuccessful homosexual, affecting a mincing, false feminine persona and a whorish attitude that were in comic contrast to his normally reserved and masculine presentation of self. He became silly and disorganized under the pressure of these experiments, and he was hospitalized for what appeared to be a psychosis. When he asked to see a "Jungian," he was referred from a day treatment center to an analyst.

After some exploration, the analyst concluded that the patient, in his attempt to undo his father's excessive demands, had turned his psyche inside out. He had fled to his inferior functions in an attempt to discover parts of himself that his father could not organize for him. Normally an introverted thinking type with reliable auxiliary extraverted sensation, he had turned first to his relatively inferior introverted intuition, which he explored through drugs and through participation in a religious cult. Then communal life had stimulated his inferior extraverted feeling, which was normally carried by his anima. He became anima-identified, enacting the part of an inferior extraverted feeling woman. To be sure, he was taking revenge on his father by enacting an unconscious caricature of the "feminine" role he had felt himself to have occupied in his original relation to his father. But the entire compensation, witty though it was, was ruining his life and psychotically distorting his personality. Sadly enough, he was really very like the compulsive engineer his father had wanted him to be.

The analyst took the tack of gently supporting the patient's return to adaptation through his superior functions and quietly discouraged the patient from further exploration of his inferior functions. He firmly refused the more floridly "Jungian" feeling-intuitive approach the patient had at first demanded. With this approach, the patient's near-hebephrenic silliness disappeared. He resumed heterosexual functioning, recovered his dominant introverted personality, and sought work in a less ambitious field related to engineering.

As this case illustrates, a psychotic syndrome can be thought of as an expression of the inferior function. Severe depressions, frequent in high-achieving thinking types, are often the expression of an inferior feeling that is excessively judgmental. Feeling tends to evaluate, but inferior feeling is often felt (and symbolized) as the "judge," the one who decides that the patient has sinned and deserves to be punished. The resulting depression is frequently symbolized in dreams by jails and felt as a confinement from life.

Mania, frequent in compulsive introverted sensation types, often represents the activity of an inferior extraverted intuition, which produces a rapid outpouring of intuitive thoughts and plans that the patient is driven to express or live out.*

Paranoia is a frequent problem for feeling types who have become alienated: the inferior thinking then makes false and dire deductions in an effort to comprehend why others have severed the feeling connection.

Schizophrenia often appears in intuitive types when they are marginally adapted to practical reality, and the sense deceptions as well as the concreteness that appears probably represent the emergence of inferior sensation.

This is not to say that only thinking types develop depressions, feeling types paranoia, and so on. These syndromes appear to reflect disturbances in the different inferior functions, and so they could potentially appear in any person who for some reason was experiencing particular difficulty with that function, regardless of which function was normally dominant. For example, even a sensation type may experience ''inferior sensation'' under the impact of drug intoxication and withdrawal. The typically inferior function is, however, an area of special vulnerability.

Treatment is most effective when it appeals to the patient's dominant function rather than when it reinforces the inferior function's already unsuccessful attempt at overcompensation. Thus, with depressed thinking types, a focus on cognitions, with the aim of rationally contradicting the patient's inaccurate and self-defeating conceptions, can often be highly effective. Practical limit setting and somatic approaches are often helpful to the manic sensation type. Direct expressions of caring and concern, including the sincere effort to explore the patient's wounded feeling, a readiness to take the ''one-down'' position when confrontations occur, and a willingness to disclose one's own inner feelings honestly to the patient, are often dramatically transforming with the paranoid feeling type. And a willingness to listen to the patient's flashes of insight and to explore his or her archetypal imagery as it emerges seems to restore sanity to the schizophrenic intuitive type.

Conversely, exploring feelings with a severely depressed person; amplifying archetypal images with a manic person; contradicting a paranoid person's deductions in logical, thinking terms; and putting sensation pressure on an acutely schizophrenic person by means of severe somatic approaches or by prescribing menial tasks, though frequently invited by the manifest character of the regression at hand, often only exacerbate the difficulty.

---

* W. Detloff: personal communication.

ARCHETYPAL ASPECTS OF POSSESSION

The archetypal aspects of possession have received the most attention by Jungian analysts. Indeed, Jung felt his work on parallels between mytho-logical and psychological processes to belong to "the comparative study of delusional systems" (Jung 1914, p. 188), or, in other words, possessed states. Many dynamic factors determine the course that a possession takes. An archetype provides the implicit structure for an image, an affect, and a pattern of behavior. When these appear, an archetype is said to be con-stellated, and typical preoccupations, feelings, and situations tend to recur. The exploration of specific archetypal figures, and of the patterns of be-havior that they determine, has been an especially fruitful source of a spe-cifically Jungian psychopathology. An understanding of the role played by archetypal figures—such as Saturn (Vitale) and Hephaistos (Stein)—in determining the fate of individuals has not only increased our understand-ing of psychopathology, but extended the range of what may permissibly be considered normal.* The work of Hillman in archetypal psychology and that of Edinger on the deep psychological analogues to alchemical pro-cesses have been especially helpful.

The difficult question is why an archetype is ever constellated. The general Jungian explanation is teleological: archetypes "come up" when they are needed, and they are needed when an adaptational demand cannot be met by the individual's ego. For example, archetypal behavior must emerge in adolescence because the ego that has been shaped by childhood experience simply is not adequate to meet the demands placed upon it when social and biological adulthood approach. The first steps in the adult direction are then, necessarily, structured by archetypes. They will feel appropriate to the individual even when they conflict sharply with aspects of practical reality. *Romeo and Juliet* contains the tragic material that must inevitably surface to some degree in the life of many adolescents.

Analysis, too, places demands upon a patient's ego that it cannot meet unaided. The implicit demand is for acceptance and integration of all the parts of one's personality, and so many different complexes, each repre-senting a different unrealized facet of the total personality, respond. Each complex, like an onion, has various layers from which this response can arise. The more superficial layers of a complex are personal; its deeper layers are archetypal. The shadow and the anima or animus represent pro-gressively deeper archetypal layers. The deepest layer of all is the nucleus, which is rooted in the central archetype, or Self, the directive center com-

---

*J. Hall: personal communication.

mon to all complexes. The response of a complex may arise from any of its layers, and not infrequently deeper archetypal layers respond to the effort at integration well before superficial, personal layers have been uncovered and assimilated.

For instance, at the outset of an analysis, when the patient is first presented with the demand for Self-realization and is still very far from being able to achieve that goal, "deep" dreams involving images of the Self are apt to appear. Compensatory images come from deep layers of the complexes, and these same layers also carry much potential for restructuring the patient's emotions and behavior in accordance with archetypal prerogatives. When deep layers of a complex are stirred, the patient's ego is particularly liable to invasion and possession. When possession of the patient's ego by an archetypal layer of a complex occurs, a typical, recognizable syndrome is the result: stereotyped behavior characteristic of the archetype particular to that layer replaces the more usual, individualized behavior of the patient's ego.

Some patients are especially prone to archetypal possessions during the analytical procedure. The vicissitudes of analysis with borderline and narcissistic individuals, as well as the complexes in the psychological background, have been carefully explored in both their personal and archetypal aspects by Redfearn; Schwartz; Kalsched; and Satinover.

Syndromes of Psychotic Possession in Analysis

In the remainder of this chapter we will present a Jungian perspective on the four major kinds of psychotic syndrome—depression, manic excitement, paranoia, and schizophrenia—in an attempt to provide an understanding of the severer pathologies.

Since each of these syndromes has aspects that resemble the behavior of a different inferior function, we believe, as already mentioned, that each psychological type has its own vulnerability to a particular kind of psychopathology. In addition, the various syndromes appear to arise from distinct archetypal layers. Jung often thought of the shadow, anima/animus, and Self as progressively deeper layers (Jung 1945). When the first layer, the personal shadow, is activated, psychotic depression results. When the archetypal shadow, or trickster, is constellated, manic excitement may emerge. When the projection-making factors, anima and animus, are active, paranoid states may appear. When the deepest layer of all, the Self, the central archetype that pushes for all-inclusive wholeness, is activated, there may be a shattering of a restricted schizoid ego and schizophrenia may result (Perry 1976). We therefore present psychotic syndromes in an order that implies ever more severe activations of the collective unconscious. Yet each poses a different style of problem to the patient and the analyst that is significantly challenging in and of itself. Each syndrome offers a unique potential not only for destruction, but for development as well, within the analytic process.

Psychotic Depression

Patients experiencing psychotic depressions usually have a persistent sense of their own inferiority, often symbolized by delusions that their bodies are rotting, or that they have become poor financially. There is a general lack of energy. These symptoms can be explained partly as the withdrawal of psychic energy from the ego, which is left demoralized, impoverished, and lacking in will. Since persons who are prone to psychotic depressions are often perfectionistic persons whose egos are aligned with complexes demanding high achievement, their depressions usually represent compensatory possessions by the shadow, which has become the reservoir of physical, ethical, and mental inferiority. (In dreams, this shadow may be symbolized by a tramp on a run-down street in the worst part of a city.) During periods of psychotic demoralization, patients may act unethically — stealing, cheating, and lying. Analysts may have to guard against judging them too much in terms of normal moral strength.

Psychotically depressed patients may be seen as experiencing a psychological analogue of the alchemical *nigredo*. They may seem to personify alchemical *prima materia*, felt by their analysts as leaden weights in the consulting room, and by themselves as heaps of excrement. Such patients may seem to be treating themselves to primitive alchemical operations in the attempt to transform their wretched state. They may refuse to bathe *(putrefactio)*, cry uncontrollably *(solutio)*, or burn with interminable resentments *(calcinatio)* (Edinger 1978).

The purposiveness of such depressive states may be apparent to the analyst, and if he or she can communicate to the patient his or her own sense of the meaning of the suffering, the depression can often be integrated because it has been well contained within the analysis. However, there is always the danger that the analytic process will be swallowed by the depression, as by an alchemical dragon. Long periods of insolvency may threaten the financial base of the enterprise, forcing the analyst to change the nature of the containing relationship by altering the financial arrangement. Suicidal behavior may necessitate contacts with family, friends, and other professionals outside the analytical relationship. Hospitalization and somatic treatments may have to be introduced. All these interventions may be necessary and lifesaving for the patient, but they make integration of the possessing shadow more difficult. Very careful interpretation of the hostile and destructive content of the depressive maneuvers can often make it possible for the patient to integrate the emerging material, but this stance takes considerable skill and faith in the analytic process in the face of manifest signals of helpless depression. When the process can be maintained, transformation may occur.

Psychotic Excitement (Mania)

The turn to mania may be understood analytically as an alternative to deepening depression. Mania often represents possession of the ego by an archetypal aspect of the shadow, aptly called the trickster (Radin). Mania involves a progression through stages of *euphoria* (simple inflation), *anger and irritability* (including a hostile belligerence that takes on a distinctly paranoid quality, with the usual paranoid tendency to projection), and *panic* (accompanied by a level of disorganization that looks almost schizophrenic). A psychotic depression may follow. Thus a manic episode can be a great mimic of many psychotic conditions. Although in later stages mania is hard to distinguish from other kinds of psychosis, at first it is hard to recognize as the beginning of a psychosis at all. This ability of manic-depressive illness to disguise itself in the beginning and to mimic other conditions later is only one of its tricksterish aspects.

Characteristic of a manic episode is its disturbing impact on others in the manic patient's life. Manic patients externalize their inner oppositions to an alarming degree. They play those who become involved with them against each other, splitting the significant others into warring camps who think they know best what the patient needs. Thus, the analyst may find him- or herself at odds with the patient's spouse, or the spouse with the rest of the family, and so on. Other forms of "interpersonal havoc" are described by Janowsky and his coworkers in their article, "Playing the Manic Game":

> Possibly, no other psychiatric syndrome is characterized by as many disquieting and irritating qualities as that of the manic phase of manic-depressive psychosis. These characteristics seem specific to the acute attack. . . .
>
> The acutely manic patient is often able to alienate himself from family, friends, and therapist alike. This knack is based on the facile use of maneuvers which place individuals relating to the manic in positions of embarrassment, decreased self-esteem, and anxious self-doubt. (P. 253)

According to these authors, the manic patient uses five types of activity to induce discomfort in those around him:

1. Manipulation of the self-esteem of others: praising or deflating others as a way of exerting interpersonal leverage.
2. Perceptive exploitation of areas of vulnerability and conflict.
3. Projection of responsibility.
4. Progressive limit testing.
5. Alienating family members.

Eventually, everyone is undermined by such tactics. Family members may begin telephoning the analyst, and the annoyed analyst may be provoked into an unwise collusion with the patient against these "intruders" upon the analytic field. All too easily, an analyst is manipulated into believing that others are failing to understand the positive changes resulting from analysis, including a well-rationalized living out of shadow impulses. Or, an analyst sweating out a psychotic interval may feel required to carry the knowledge of the patient's pathology in confidential isolation, imagining that others in the environment are unaware that the patient is out of control and that others are not just as worried as the analyst. Collaborative contacts with significant others in the patient's life may be required to overcome such destructive splitting fantasies, which the patient may be fostering and supporting. All such splits require special handling, and they must be recognized as demonic effects of the trickster archetype at work, externalizing inner splits by throwing individuals into double binds and dividing groups into warring camps. The trickster is a crazy-maker, and patients in the grip of a manic episode regularly try to drive others, including the analyst, crazy.

Again, analysis may founder under the weight of the required interventions, which may include, besides collaborative contacts, much limit setting and pharmacotherapy (often lithium). So much of the analyst's energy is required that there is danger of exhaustion and failure of analysis. Sometimes, sharing such cases with a general psychiatrist permits analysts to maintain their concentration on the analytic work. The strain on the analyst precisely reflects the weight of the archetypal shadow upon the patient's ego, which must shift some of the load onto others to survive.

Interestingly, patients who are prone to develop mania are often persons who were given premature responsibilities in youth. To accomplish adult tasks so prematurely, they had to align themselves with idealized, pseudoadult, moralistic spiritual complexes. These alignments persist into adult life, but at the cost of excluding portions of the shadow, particularly the trickster, that have normally been dealt with before adult life. At the outset of treatment, such patients may look deceptively easy to analyze.

Neither analyst nor patient may recognize that there is a potential for emergence of the repressed trickster and for possession of the patient's ego by this unrecognized unconscious content.

An analyst is wise to note early signs that the strain of being "good" is going to prove too great and that the treatment is simply riding on the patient's superego—in other words, demanding that the patient continue to exclude the shadow. This danger may be recognized by a burdened quality to the way the patient maintains regular payment of the bill, or the appointment time, and the implicit demand that the patient stay physically well during the period of analysis. The patient who finds these usual signs of ego strength impossible to maintain may be signalling to the analyst that it is not psychologically possible any longer to be a good patient; the previously unrecognized trickster core of the shadow problem may be about to surface.

Despite the patient's initial record of cooperativeness, the analyst may now have to confront a most recalcitrant shadow. If the patient cannot accept the analyst's insistence that the meaning of the undermining behaviors be examined, the analyst may have to allow the patient to move away from analysis rather than capitulate to the emerging trickster. But with many patients who exhibit manic defenses as depressive issues are explored, it is possible to interpret the hostility and anxiety that surround emerging contents. Often these reactions can be understood as attempts at assertion by long-buried portions of the Self. The analyst can then point out that the demonic attributes are in part a healthy response to longstanding repression; the analyst can affirm the right of these portions of the patient to enter awareness. Usually such affirmation is enough to enable the patient to maintain an analytic attitude toward the shadow and to allow the work of analysis to continue.

Paranoid States

In contrast to the patient in a manic inflation, who may encourage the analyst to continue what can become a speeded-up caricature of analysis by presenting a grab bag of chaotic material that cannot be integrated, the paranoid patient will slow down the analytic process through obsessive attention to the analyst's every attempt at intervention, in an effort to force the analyst to reconsider every move and so cast doubt on the entire analytic procedure. Although few analysts attempt to work with overt paranoid schizophrenic patients, paranoid personalities and borderline or narcissistic patients with strong paranoid defenses frequently seek analysis. Many other patients with negative mother complexes develop paranoid resistances to the analytical procedure. With such patients, the analyst may feel that nothing can get done. There is no basis of trust, and whenever trust appears to be established, some new crisis of confidence threatens the ground that has been gained. It is as if the analyst's most sincere attempts to help are taken in by the patient as poisons or seductions.

In fact, it is portions of the patient that are poisoning the therapeutic atmosphere or seducing the analyst into believing that his or her own complexes are responsible for the recurrent therapeutic impasses. Jungian psychology assigns this paranoid response to the activity of the anima or animus. The anima employs her "poison of illusion," while the animus tends to plot, setting traps for the unwary analyst. Yet, because the anima and animus are projection-making factors, the patients in their grip will see the analyst as the poisoner, or as the plotter who undermines the therapeutic effort. The kind of projection involved when the patient is in a state of psychotic possession by one of these archetypes is more precisely called projective identification, a particularly insidious kind of projection in which an empathic identification is maintained to the projected content. Often this identification with the patient's own projected content is masked as a therapeutic interest in the analyst's "problem." So a situation may arise in which the patient begins to tell the analyst about what are assumed to be the analyst's unconscious difficulties. Sometimes, this effort includes the use of "double projection," in which the patient makes a projection about what the analyst is supposed to be projecting. So, to a psychologically sophisticated paranoid patient, the reason the analyst makes interpretations that are harming the analysis is that wrong motives are being projected onto the patient out of the analyst's own complexes. All this is forgivable by the patient because the analyst is of course unconscious that such projections are being made, but the patient feels that the analyst ought really to be made aware of what is going on so that it won't keep happening, to the continued harm not only of the particular patient and analysis, but also of other patients. If the analyst protests these intrusive assumptions, the patient may deliver the *coup de grâce:* "But of course I realize you aren't ready to deal with all this."

It takes a strong analyst, with a confident relation to the unconscious, and relatively aware of personal blind spots, to stand up to this kind of paranoid pressure to give up the analytic stance and submit instead to the patient's interpretations. In light of the unconscious involvement any analyst has with any patient, there will always be grains of truth in the patient's double projections. But an analyst must not allow the patient to preempt the animus or anima function with which much of the analyst's work is done. When this is allowed to happen, the state of affairs that Searles has called the "pathological symbiosis" ensues (Goodheart, pp. 5– 8), and the analyst in such a situation may grow frightened, angry, or distrustful of the patient, and very tired. Prolonged experiences in this state are disastrous for the analyst and unhelpful to the patient, and they force a termination without resolution of the problem. But brief periods in this state may enable the analyst to get a taste of what is going on in the patient, who in fact is fearing that his or her own anima or animus will be preempted by the treatment, as it once may have been by intrusive parenting.

These fears surface particularly in patients who are afraid of instinctual-energetic libido, such as the erotic interests toward the analyst that frequently surface in analysis. Such a patient may hide behind spiritual-powerful complexes, which can intimidate the analyst and provide a kind of character armor for the patient. But behind the armor, the patient is afraid of the instinctual-energetic complexes, which he or she has been taught from early childhood are unacceptable. These complexes may represent a variety of issues—oral cravings, exploratory behavior, hetero- and homoerotic interests, and so on—issues that seem to have been viewed in earlier development with suspicion by parental figures who could not tolerate the tension they generated. For this kind of parent, it was the energy these issues required that was suspect. The exhaustion of the analyst in the transference/countertransference seems to repeat the original reaction of the parental figures, but it has been induced by a patient unconsciously identified with these avoidant attitudes.

If the analysis is to continue, the analyst must first of all *survive*. The analyst must communicate to the patient that the energy contained in these repressed complexes is not threatening, and that it is not the analyst, but the patient, who has been made afraid of instinct. The analyst's authority within the transference/countertransference must be maintained, particularly the analyst's authority as the only expert present with regard to the analyst's own unconscious life. In that way, the analyst demonstrates to the patient that it is possible not to fear one's unconscious, whatever scary things others may have tried to persuade one about it. Nor need the analyst be afraid to call a spade a spade where the patient is concerned. In not allowing a patient to disconnect one from one's own experience of oneself and others, one mediates the possibility of wholeness to a patient. In holding on to the analytic prerogative to make interpretations, the analyst retains the right to heal the patient's splits. Paranoid patients are frequently split in their experience of the anima or animus—sometimes strongly identified with the spiritual-powerful pole and able to encounter the instinctual-energetic pole only in projection, and sometimes identified with the instinctual-energetic pole, in which case spiritual-powerful strivings may appear to be the analyst's problem.

For example, a male analysand, brimming with aggressive energy, decided that his female analyst was a castrating negative mother, hideously possessed by what he decided was a pseudoprofessional animus. He came to feel that she lived to destroy her patients' lives. He noted that she sometimes used controlling tactics in the countertransference to ward off strong expressions of instinctual affect, and so he vengefully began to barrage her with just such expressions. Her reactions seemed to him to confirm his conclusions: she became defensive and interpretive. Realistically, much of what she was doing came in an attempt to maintain the analysis in the face of hostile attack. She was not successful in getting him to recognize the impact his hypersensitivity and manipulativeness were having on her, because of a countertransference fear of exposing her vulnerable side to him. The existence of this fear dawned on the patient only after the analysis had foundered and was over, and the insight enabled him to empathize with her real position and apologize for harassing her. Only then could he admit his own fear of his aggressive energies.

There are always large grains of truth in any projection. The analysand is apt to have unparalleled insight into the unconscious life of the analyst, especially in the condition of narcissistic vulnerability that Balint has called "the basic fault." Thus there exists in the analytic situation a vulnerability on the analyst's side that is too seldom recognized in the literature. Few practicing analysts can have failed to notice the evil quality of the unconscious energy that seems to surround the paranoid states that develop in analysis, and most analysts learn to confront and interpret such distortions early, before a female patient's animus possession can take on a dictatorial, Hitler-like aspect, or a male patient's anima possession a witchlike quality. Such confrontations involve a frank admission of the impact the patient is having on the analyst, which is considerable. Patients who progress to full-blown possession by the demonic aspects of the contrasexual archetypes develop an uncanny sense for the weak spot in the analyst, and they regularly stimulate it. Thus analysts in this situation may be put back in the grip of complexes that they thought their own analyses had laid to rest, and it is as if, as one analyst has put it, "my own analysis is continuing."

Presumably, these demonic manifestations of the contrasexual archetypes that are possessing the patient emanate from the dark side of the Self: they are the defenses of the Self (Fordham 1974). The function of these powerful defenses seems to be to maintain, against the analyst's uncovering efforts, repressions that became necessary during development to permit at least partial Self-survival in the face of crushing parental demands and intrusions. The Self, in its positive aspect as an organ of acceptance (Edinger 1972, p. 40), is often conceptualized as standing behind the animus as the wise old woman and behind the anima as the wise old man (Jung 1945, pp. 227–41), but, under threat, the Self may just as well appear as the witch or evil magician. Using offense as the best defense, these dark Self figures convey to the anima or animus, which are archetypes of projected otherness (Hill), their uncanny sense for where to project to do the most damage. As demonic defenses, these negating aspects of the Self lead the anima or animus to make projections that can be ruinously effective. They use the truth as a weapon to exploit and undermine the real vulnerabilities of others, including the analyst. Their purpose seems to be to make sure that the existing splits in the patient's anima or animus are maintained. As a result, the unacceptable parts of the patient's Self can never be mediated to his ego, but only projected onto others.

Projections based on such fundamental splitting are the essence of paranoid development, and the analyst is wise not to let such projections gain too much power. In the early years of his or her analytic practice, an analyst will almost unavoidably underestimate this malignant potential and fail to take up the projective identifications that threaten to undermine the analytic endeavor. Many, if not most, analysts can report several vivid experiences of having felt personally undermined, and so divided from their own well-analyzed sense of Self that they are no longer effective in certain transference situations. Such experiences can have the positive effect of getting analysts to sharpen their technique. For the incautiously sincere analyst who tries to stay humbly related to a paranoid patient who has seized the upper hand, there are considerable dangers. The analyst who makes the common mistake of agreeing to the whole of the projection when only a part is true is not only neglecting the analytic duty to discover the truth but is also denigrating a part of him- or herself. This can only lead the analyst to resent, and even to come to hate, the patient, inasmuch as essential parts of the analyst's own Selfhood are being injured, producing, in consequence, narcissistic rage. What the patient really needs, of course, is not hate (although that may be a helpful clue to what the patient is warding off) but considerable empathy. The patient needs help in facing the unacceptable, often rageful, parts of the personality that were once repressed to accommodate parental demands and avoid annihilating rejection. Such rageful parts will often turn out to be early Self-assertions that were repressed (Wiesenfeld).

When severe paranoid resistances develop in the patient, one signal of the developing malignant regression (Balint) may be that the analyst will start to become paranoid in the attempt to stay related to the patient.*

---

*J. Henderson: personal communication.

Under these circumstances, an analyst may even be forced to curtail the analysis for self-protection, as an induced psychosis is not impossible. But with enough self-respect, with careful confrontation of the first paranoid projections that begin to distort the analyst's intentions, and with a faith that the patient can work through these distortions, a transformation can often be effected before this point of no return is reached. When honest confrontation succeeds in producing a new basis of trust and mutual respect, the analysis can proceed to a satisfactory resolution of the splits in the patient that led to the impasse.

Schizophrenic Conditions

Schizophrenic states appear when the archetype of the Self is constellated within the field of consciousness of an ego unprepared for such an experience. Such individuals are usually schizoid persons who have up to then been under the inner or outer control of a parent figure who has taken the position of knowing what's best for the child. Such a substitution of someone else's judgment for the normal connection to the unconscious severs the ego-Self axis (Perry 1976, pp. 32–35), and any experience of the Self appears thereafter strange and awesome. To such a person, the normal compensating activity of the Self in everyday life is experienced as quite ego-alien, the functioning of an entirely autonomous complex (Beebe). The frankly schizophrenic episode severely disrupts this rigid and restrictive personality organization, but the very disorganization that ensues sometimes permits the individual's personality to reorganize in a more holistic, integrated way. Thus the schizophrenic condition has been interpreted by several Jungian analysts as the severest example of an attempt at healing compensation by the Self. The clearest formulation of this position has been offered by Perry (1976).

In a series of careful observations (1976, pp. 201–21), Perry has defined a small subgroup of schizophrenic individuals who appear to come through six-week psychotic episodes ("forty days in the wilderness") not only emotionally restored, but renewed. Their manifest psychotic episode is one characterized by acute catatonic excitement, although the syndrome may actually be a variant of affective illness. When such individuals are given analytic treatment without drugs, there is an emphasis on affect, leading to recovery of Eros (ibid., pp. 11–22). To Perry, there appears to be a meaningful attempt at reorganization of the patient's Self-image during such psychoses. Returning to Jung's observation that a split (delusions of grandeur versus feelings of inferiority) often existed in schizophrenic patients such as Babette, Perry points out that the split is really between

Self-images, with a deflated Self-image at the ego level and a compensatory Self-image within the unconscious. Often the deflated Self-image is instinctual-energetic, while the inflated Self-image is spiritual-powerful. Perry argues that the schizophrenic process is triggered by some traumatic experience, such as a love failure, which sets off the latent tension existing between contradictory Self-images (ibid., pp. 43–60). Obviously, the uncovering process of analysis can trigger an explosion when this latent dynamism is exposed to consciousness. This can occur when the unconscious worth of the Self is suddenly revealed to a chronically self-devaluing individual, caught in avoidant, passive-aggressive, obsessive, or otherwise restricted behavior patterns. The person may conclude that he or she is royal or divine.

During the psychosis itself, which he understands as an attempt at healing this deepest of personality splits, Perry has noted a cycle of images with obvious, striking parallels to the rituals of kingship in the ancient Near East, which provided a year-end festival with images of renewal of the world center and the death and rebirth of the king. Perry traces a similar pattern in the imagery of the delusions in this subgroup of schizophrenic persons, and often he finds that the inflated image of spiritual power gives way to a new, related sense of instinctual energy at the end of the psychotic period (ibid., pp. 61–164).

Another, probably larger, group of schizoid individuals find their way into Jungian analysis when a massive experience of the Self begins to push upon them through their dreams. Such patients dream classically "big" dreams with great frequency and turn spontaneously to the works of Jung to comprehend and contain this imagery. Often such patients come to analysis bringing as many as twenty or thirty dreams to a single weekly session, as to a haven where this material may be valued and comprehended. Clinically, many of these individuals might seem to belong to the psychotically depressed or ambulatory schizophrenic category. Their outer lives are striking for the paucity of object relationships and vocational functioning, almost to the degree that their inner lives are rich. Some, however, benefit enormously from the integration of the unconscious material over time and eventually find a way to express the richness within themselves. Usually they relate well to Jungian analysts, who enjoy working with them on, so to speak, home ground.

For some patients, the experience of the Self constitutes a disaster, quite deserving the sense of dread and the imagery of world catastrophe that may precede a schizophrenic episode. Such was the fate of Gerard de Nerval, as related by von Franz (1977, pp. 103–4). De Nerval was a French poet who "became schizophrenic and hung himself at a relatively young age after an unfortunate love affair.'' Just prior to his first psychotic episode, he dreamed that an angel had fallen into the narrow confines of a Parisian hotel's back courtyard, its garbage-collection area. The angel "had wonderful wings with feathers of thousands of shining colors, but it was jammed, all hunched up in this backyard," and de Nerval recognized that if it made the "smallest movement to free itself the entire hotel would be wrecked."

De Nerval, a rationalistic Parisian, had met a working-class woman with whom he fell deeply in love. He began to write inspired poems about her as a goddess. But his cynical Parisian side led him to devalue the experience with the remark, "she is an ordinary woman of our time," and he kicked the woman aside. Shortly after rejecting her, he fell into his first psychotic episode. "He tried to have a reconciliation," but "he could not get on with her because of the terrific tension of seeing clearly that she was an ordinary human being and experiencing her as a goddess and not being able to hold these paradoxical things together."

For von Franz, the hotel backyard in the dream typified de Nerval's cynical Parisian attitude toward love, which was simply too narrow to comprehend the mysterious richness of the experience of the Self that had befallen him. (The angel was a symbol of the Self for de Nerval.) She feels that his ego tragically could not grasp that the conflict that confronted him contained the paradoxical essence of love, "which is a divine mystery and at the same time a very ordinary, if not anthropoid, affair." She feels that the Self, caught in the narrow confines of an outlook that could not bring itself to associate instinctual energy with spiritual power, simply exploded de Nerval's ego. The poet hanged himself "in the most horrible way."

This early casualty of the Romantic movement illustrates a typical danger of an ill-timed effort to stimulate individuation. However beautiful the Self may be potentially, the patient's ego must be prepared to contain the experience, or contact with the Self may precipitate disaster. Once constellated, the Self with its tremendous tension of opposites will always attempt to realize itself, even if it must shatter the ego of the unfortunately unprepared individual to do so (von Franz 1977, p. 104). Thus, schizophrenic psychosis is a possibility whenever there is an attempt to integrate the deeper layers of the psyche by an ego that is unprepared for the complexities and power of the experience.

For this reason, analysts attempt to create a containing environment in which Self material can be safely integrated. Often the felt sense of the analyst is the most reliable guide to what the patient can tolerate. It is also inevitable that for long periods during analysis, an analyst must carry the projection of the Self because the patient is not ready for it. The analyst must not force the patient's effort at Self-realization, but rather allow the patient to take back the projection that has been made onto the analyst (or onto analysis) increment by increment (Wiesenfeld). In this way, the patient's own Selfhood can be gradually realized without a psychotic explosion.

SUMMARY

Jung recognized, at the beginning of his professional career, that understanding the dissociability of the psyche is the key to its psychopathology. Splitting off of psychic functions occurs throughout the life of the psyche, in the persona, the shadow, the anima/animus, and even the Self. Just as an individual ego accepts only one part of the persona for the "image" it shows the world, so also does the ego become accustomed to recognizing and aligning itself with only one part of its shadow, to the projection of only one part of the anima or animus in object relations, and to the connection to only one image of the Self in its deep estimate of its individual worth. Rarer, and less comfortable, are alignments that occur with other parts of the shadow, projections of other parts of the anima or animus, and the acceptance of alternate Self-images. These variants tend to occur in analysis only because of the heightened receptivity of the ego during the analytic process, fostered by the empathic encouragement of the analyst. The split-off parts of the shadow, anima/animus, and Self, therefore, have been truly unconscious until they gradually emerge in dreams, symptoms, or affects within the transference, seeking a relation with the patient's ego. Sometimes, in analysis, which has an inductive effect, such unsuspected contents appear suddenly, filled with energy charge and the demonic quality of the returning repressed, to capture and possess the unsuspecting ego. In this high-energy form, they threaten not only the analytic field, but the patient's general behavior as well, which is inevitably altered.

In association with his complex theory, Jung offered two fundamental concepts to formulate the psychopathology that we see in analysis: splitting and possession. Complexes tend to split into complementary poles, such as spirit versus instinct, and one-sided alignments occur between the ego and one of the poles, producing personality imbalance and a latent dynamic tension between the opposed elements. Working through any split requires not only disidentification by the ego from the more familiar pole of the complex, but also affective recognition of the contrary pole. Such recognition requires immersion in the side that has been unconscious. There is an unconscious tendency toward wholeness and relief of tension that fosters the emergence, under accepting conditions such as analysis, of the repressed pole. The consequence is that at least temporary possession by unfamiliar contents is a regular part of life and of the analytic process, an inevitable prelude to the integration of unconscious portions of the Self.

It follows that in addition to the watchful and containing presence of the analyst, a strong and resilient center of consciousness—an ego—is required in the patient to accomplish and survive the cycle of possession, disidentification, and final integration that is the process of analysis. Although some Jungians have denigrated the ego and its defenses as mere identification with the hero archetype, the integrity of the ego's standpoint and its capacity for realistic judgment can make the difference between the success and failure of the analytic enterprise. A task of the analyst is therefore to estimate the capacities of the patient's ego before the difficult work of exploring complexes is undertaken, and carefully to support that ego's efforts at discrimination once the analytic work is under way.

REFERENCES

Balint, M. 1979. *The basic fault: therapeutic aspects of regression.* New York: Bruner Mazel.

Beebe, J. 1975. Evaluation and treatment of the psychotic patient. In *Psychiatric treatment: crisis, clinic, and consultation,* ed. C. P. Rosenbaum and J. E. Beebe, pp. 82–114. New York: McGraw-Hill.

Edinger, E. F. 1972. *Ego and archetype.* New York: Putnam.

———. 1978. Psychotherapy and alchemy: I. introduction; II. calcinatio; III. solutio. *Quadrant* 11/1:5–37; 11/2:63–85.

Ellenberger, H. 1970. *The discovery of the unconscious.* New York: Basic Books.

Fordham, M. 1974. Defenses of the self. *Journal of Analytical Psychology* 19/1:192–99.

———. 1978. *Jungian psychotherapy.* New York: Wiley.

Franz, M.-L. von. 1971. The inferior function. In *Lectures on Jung's typology,* pp. 1–54. New York: Spring Publications.

———. 1974. *Shadow and evil in fairy tales.* Zurich: Spring Publications.

———. 1977. *Individuation in fairy tales.* Irving, Tex.: Spring Publications.

Goodheart, W. 1980. Theory of analytic interaction. *San Francisco Jung Institute Library Journal* 1/4:2–39.

Guggenbühl-Craig, A. 1980. *Eros on crutches: reflections on psychopathy and amorality.* Irving, Tex.: Spring Publications.

Hartman, G. V. 1980. Psychotherapy: an attempt at definition. *Spring* 1980:94–100.

Hill, G. 1975. Men, anima and feminine. Lecture given at C. G. Jung Institute of Los Angeles, 1975.

Hillman, J. 1970. The language of psychology and the speech of the soul. In

Eranos jahrbuch 1968, ed. A. Portmann and R. Ritsema, pp. 299–356. Zurich: Rhein-Verlag.

————. 1975. *Revisioning psychology.* New York: Harper.

————, ed. 1980. *Facing the gods.* Irving, Tex.: Spring Publications.

Janowsky, D. S.; Leff, M.; and Epstein, R. S. 1970. Playing the manic game: interpersonal maneuvers of the acutely manic patient. *Archives of General Psychiatry* 22:252–61.

Jung, C. G. 1902. On the psychology and pathology of so-called occult phenomena. In *Collected works,* vol. 1, pp. 3–88. 2d ed. Princeton: Princeton University Press, 1970.

————. 1905*a.* Experimental observations on the faculty of memory. In *Collected works,* vol. 2, pp. 272–87. Princeton: Princeton University Press, 1973.

————. 1905*b.* The reaction-time ratio in the association experiment. In *Collected works,* vol. 2, pp. 221–72. Princeton: Princeton University Press, 1973.

————. 1906*a.* Association, dream, and hysterical symptom. In *Collected works,* vol. 2, pp. 353–407. Princeton: Princeton University Press, 1973.

————. 1906*b.* The psychopathological significance of the association experiment. In *Collected works,* vol. 2, pp. 408–25. Princeton: Princeton University Press, 1973.

————. 1907. The psychology of dementia praecox. In *Collected works,* vol. 3, pp. 1–151. Princeton: Princeton University Press, 1960.

————. 1914. On psychological understanding. In *Collected works,* vol. 3, pp. 179–93. Princeton: Princeton University Press, 1960.

————. 1919. On the problem of psychogenesis in mental disease. In *Collected works,* vol. 3, pp. 211–25. Princeton: Princeton University Press, 1960.

————. 1921. *Psychological types. Collected works,* vol. 6. Princeton: Princeton University Press, 1971.

————. 1934. A review of the complex theory. In *Collected works,* vol. 8, pp. 92–104. 2d ed. Princeton: Princeton University Press, 1969.

————. 1945. The relations between the ego and the unconscious. In *Collected works,* vol. 7, pp. 123–241. 2d ed. Princeton: Princeton University Press, 1966.

————. 1946. Psychology of the transference. In *Collected works,* vol. 16, pp. 163–323. 2d ed., rev. Princeton: Princeton University Press, 1966.

————. 1961. *Memories, dreams, reflections.* New York: Pantheon.

————. 1966. *The practice of psychotherapy. Collected works,* vol. 16. 2d ed., rev. Princeton: Princeton University Press.

Jung, C. G., and Riklin, F. 1906. The associations of normal subjects. In *Collected works,* vol. 2, pp. 3–196. Princeton: Princeton University Press, 1973.

Kalsched, D. 1980. Narcissism and the search for interiority. *Quadrant* 13/2:46–74.

McGuire, W., ed. 1974. *The Freud/Jung letters.* Princeton: Princeton University Press.

Marriott, K. 1980. On becoming a person. *Journal of Analytical Psychology* 25:125–40.

Perry, J. W. 1970. Emotions and object relations. *Journal of Analytical Psychology* 15/1:1–12.

————. 1976. *Roots of renewal in myth and madness.* San Francisco: Jossey-Bass.

Quenk, A. 1978. Psychological types: the auxiliary function and the analytical process. Diploma thesis, Inter-Regional Society of Jungian Analysts.

Radin, P. 1956. *The trickster*. New York: Philosophical Library.

Redfearn, J. 1980. The energy of warring and combining opposites: problems for the psychotic patient and the therapist in achieving the symbolic situation. In *Methods of treatment in analytical psychology,* ed. I. F. Baker, pp. 206–18. Fellbach: Verlag Adolf Bonz.

Satinover, J. 1980. Puer aeternus: the narcissistic relation to the self. *Quadrant* 13/2:75–108.

Schwartz-Salant, N. 1982. *Narcissism and character transformation*. Toronto: Inner City Books.

Stein, M. 1980. Hephaistos: a pattern of introversion (and) Postscript on Hephaistos. In *Facing the gods,* ed. J. Hillman, pp. 67–86. Irving, Tex.: Spring Publications.

Vitale, A. 1973. Saturn: the transformation of the father. In *Fathers and mothers,* ed. P. Berry, pp. 5–39. Zurich: Spring Publications.

Wiesenfeld, H. 1980. Kohut's self psychology. *The San Francisco Jung Institute Library Journal* 1/3:1–23.

[17]

RECENT INFLUENCES
ON THE PRACTICE OF JUNGIAN ANALYSIS

Edward C. Whitmont

THE basic model of psychotherapy inherited from the days of the founding fathers is a talking therapy. Originally, Freud worked extensively with catharsis and abreaction and stressed reliving the affects of repressed traumatic material. But soon he dropped this in favor of his reconstructive-cognitive approach. Only much later did Fritz Perls and Wilhelm Reich, each in his own way, begin to redevelop those earlier, more body- and affect-oriented, approaches. In this effort, however, they met with a good deal of opposition from most traditional psychoanalysts and with relative disregard from many analytical psychologists.

In the classical approach, analysands are helped to understand their behavior and motivations through the therapist's verbal interpretations of actions, dreams, emotions, and associations. Frequently such understanding does bring about a reorientation and hence an improvement of psychopathology, or even a change in the total personality; but frequently, alas, it does not.

A chief reason for the failure, when it occurs, of the interpretative approach is that a purely reflective and verbal method may not sufficiently "touch" the levels of affect and body awareness. The importance of this fact was evidently not yet apparent at the beginning of the century.

Edward Whitmont, M.D., is Chairman of the Board of the C. G. Jung Training Center of New York and maintains a private practice of analytical psychology in New York City and Irvington, New York. A graduate of the University of Vienna, he is a founding member and member of the teaching staff of the C. G. Jung Training Center of New York, as well as a founding member of the International Association for Analytical Psychology. He is the author of *The Symbolic Quest; Psyche and Substance: Essays on Homeopathy in the Light of Jungian Psychology;* and *The Return of the Goddess: Desire, Aggression and the Evolution of Consciousness.*

Whether this was because a revaluation of sexual mores and a new relation to spiritual meaning had to be dealt with first, or because the quality of our psychic awareness has since undergone a change, or, as I believe, because of both developments, our present psychological state increasingly calls for feeling and body awareness in addition to understanding. It would appear that a new phase in the evolution of consciousness has begun, one that necessitates a wider scope of awareness than intellect alone can provide. The bias of a cultural era is now about to pass.

The dominant attitude of this past cultural phase has been Apollonian and patriarchal; it has been a culture of abstraction, thought, and distance. It has tended to cut individuals off from their matrix: from instincts and affects; from nature, earth; from the body and the containing community. Cartesian dualism and utilitarianism, along with myopic intellectual reasoning, held sway; people lost awareness of what is not directly evident to the senses and what cannot be pragmatically controlled. Soul and meaning were perceived as separate from soma; individuality and ego were seen as separate from group. These viewpoints, still prevalent during the founders' days of psychotherapy, helped shape the beginnings of a theory and practice whose limitations we can only now begin to appreciate.

THE EGO

It has been taken for granted that the familiar sense of "I-ness" that we call ego constitutes an individual motivational system in that it functions as a personal sense of separateness, distinct from other egos, from group, and from environment. Ego is defined as (1) the center and subject of personal identity, extending and continuing through time, space, and cause-and-effect sequences, and capable of reflecting upon itself and of establishing a sense of identity by reasoning and reflection (Descartes's *"Cogito, ergo sum"*); (2) a center and originator of personal choices, decisions, and value judgments, hence, of personally willed actions (Whitmont, p. 232).

Freud held that while id and superego represent influences of the past—the id that of heredity, the superego that of other people and authority figures—"the ego is principally determined by the individual's own experience, that is by accidental and current events" (p. 17). However, two facts are easily overlooked. The first is that experience is not an imprint upon a tabula rasa of unstructured and unconditioned mind, but rather is created or "made" by the active perceiver. The second is that events are not altogether accidental but rather, as our experience with synchronicity is constantly demonstrating to us, occur in a correspondence relation to the psyche—that is, not only to a priori, given structures, but also to conditioned awareness.

As I have detailed elsewhere (Whitmont, p. 236ff.), the ego complex, as Jung called it, is the "actualization" (ibid., p. 119ff.) of a transpersonal Self in a personal shell of conditioned ideas and images of what one has been trained by family and culture to assume one is like or should be like, in terms of standards, values, and aspirations. Hence what we have called our ego turns out to be "determined" by an "experience" that is but the expression of the way the Self has been "actualized" by parental and cultural conditioning. The ego's experience is "made" to fit its previous conditioning.

Throughout the patriarchal period, this conditioning extolled individual separateness and self-responsibility and increasingly minimized the unconsciously continuing group and clan identity. At the same time, it actually defined, indeed prescribed, the shells of individual ego-systems, namely, values, self-images, and aspirations, in thoroughly collective, nonindividual terms. Thus the ego that came into being during the patriarchal epoch was conditioned by the collective superego and persona of that time. Our identity, our personal choices, decisions, and value judgments, are determined—certainly initially and, to a large extent, throughout our lives—by the ways we endeavor to be seen. We express the ideals of our family group and cultural environment, even when we hate or rebel against them or consciously disregard them. Genuinely individual values are more often than not carried by the shadow.

The ego that has so far been developed, then, is more a product of collective values than one is aware of when one chooses and directs one's values and actions, supposedly in a pragmatic fashion. Our ego is not yet as separate and individual as we have assumed it to be. Even the antitraditionalist's value system is still predominantly controlled by group superego or persona, rather than by genuinely individually determined judgments. (What we are impelled to fight against, we still are.) Our ego still rests upon patriarchal rationality, the patriarchal hero ideal and its rigid "shalt" and "shalt-not" concept of ethics inherited from the Decalogue, even where one "shalt" may have been replaced by another, more modern "shalt." Our patriarchal superego standards, with their outer-directedness, have until now determined our ego qualities even when we fought them or the authority figures that represented them. Good and evil are still defined predominantly for most people in terms of the standards of their community, whether they were born into it or rebelliously chose it, rather than by a genuine individual conscience, the *vox Dei* arising from the Self. And this patriarchally conditioned ego, with its learned need to control and to dominate, its rationality, its extraversion, and its sense of isolation from body, emotion, group, and world, we have considered to be *the* ego.

INDIVIDUATION

Analytical psychologists have held that during the first half of life, this reasoning, willful, and discipline-based ego needs to be developed. In the process, ego and Self are to be separated (Whitmont, p. 250ff.). In the second half of life, there is a surrender of the ego, or at least a relativization—that is, a loosening of its dominance—as the ego experiences and comes to relate to the Self.

Since this ego has been predominantly outer-directed—Jung defined it as a "synthesis of the various sense-consciousnesses" (p. 614)—such surrender or relativization has been held also to entail a shift away from extraverted interest. In the classical view of individuation, external object concern and relations are now to take second place to introversion.

We are discovering now, however, that the rational, patriarchal ego is not the only possible one, but a particular form of ego. It is being transcended in what appears to be a new step in the evolution of consciousness. A new ego, genuinely subjective or, rather, directly Self- and inner-determined and motivated, is beginning to make itself felt in our time. In contrast to the patriarchal ego, this emerging ego is oriented not so much by outer-directed action, concept, and thought, as by nonverbal experience. As it emerges at first in a person, it is closer to the magical dimension of the psyche—repressed in the patriarchal value system—and hence, to affect and emotion than to the rational frame of reference; only secondarily does it function conceptually (Whitmont, p. 221; Gebser). In its first emergence, this new ego is still preverbal and functions somewhat like an inarticulate, affect-laden child. With respect to the values of our collective world, this ego is a newcomer and easily feels itself to be an outsider or an outlaw, unaccepted, unloved, rejected. It tends to preserve itself in an inimical environment by staying hidden or by reacting with defensive isolation and dissociation. Its sense of not fitting into our heroic and predominantly outer-directed life (seen from its vantage point as judgmental and rejective, or at least inhospitable) may then be compensated by fantasies of heroic grandiosity.

Prior to a full, authentic experience of itself in terms of its affects, this new ego is easily drowned in traditional superego and persona expectations. Premature therapeutic interpretations or conceptualizations tend to be misunderstood as "thou shalt . . ." Expressions of anger and aggression are especially felt to be difficult, and are prohibited, as they have been by the patriarchal cultural code. The inhibition against expressing anger is experienced, in turn, as a denial of individual power and selfness, and hence is turned against the ego and felt as threats of destruction. Or, alternatively, defensive identification with the superego aggressor leads to passive aggressive or outrightly self-destructive behavior, as well as to isolation behind the persona mask of the old, no longer viable, persona-ego, which at this stage increasingly tends to become a pseudoego. The so-called borderline and narcissistic syndromes can be understood as expressions of this development. Yet, this narcissistic phenomenon is not merely an exaggerated introversion or preoccupation with self, but, teleologically, it is an as yet unadapted response to the needs of a newly emerging Self-motivation. Narcissism is thwarted individuation.

Individuation need no longer be seen then in the light of a need to renounce the ego for the Self, but rather as the development and differentiation of a new ego position, of a Self-oriented, truly individual ego, in which outer and inner directions are balanced. Nor need individuation be considered limited to the second half of life, nor defined exclusively in terms of introversion. Individuation now comes to mean a "becoming consciously what one is or is meant to be" (Whitmont, p. 48), an aware and conscious living commitment to one's experienced reality, an aware and responsible enacting, rather than acting out, of one's motivating impulses, including those of the inferior function, which need differentiation and conscious training.

Choices and responsibilities remain with the ego, which, however, has to maintain a receptive openness to the necessities of the individuating Self, to inner reality, and to outer relationship and adaptation needs. The ego must at no time one-sidedly renounce this responsibility in favor of a "decision of the unconscious." In the first half of life, ego development may already have included the cultivation of Self-motivated values, if one is attuned not only to social reality and to the development of will and discipline, but also to one's own individual uniqueness and needs. To the second half of life belongs the differentiation of the inferior function. The second half of life, then, does not necessarily require a shift in emphasis away from extraversion and outer object relations. On the contrary, when extraversion has been the inferior function during the first half, in the second half external persona and interpersonal and group adaptation may have to be deliberately cultivated for the sake of fulfilling one's reality, of "becoming what one is meant to be." The call of the spirit is also the call for an incarnated and individual way of being in the world of objects and persons, and a call for individual relatedness to a Thou and a We. In one way or another, this task begins at birth. It is not limited to the second half of life.

For our time, individuation means not only a conscious relationship to the archetypal world, but also a conscious relationship to interpersonal reality and social collectivity. It includes developing the ability for introspection no less than for experiencing, playing with, feeling for, and fulfilling one's calling in outer reality.

Relatedness is not a feminine principle, nor is it an Eros function; it is the extraverted aspect of individuation for both sexes. Relatedness is the fruit of the ego's becoming aware of its Self-motivation and of its having succeeded in the difficult task of differentiating its capacity and need for interplay with one and many others. This awareness of the importance of interpersonal relatedness as an aspect of the individuation urge constitutes, I believe, a step in cultural development, and hence in the differentiation and evolution of consciousness, that, during the earlier days of Jung's work, certainly at the beginning of the century, was not apparent.

Relatedness, rather than *"Gemeinschaftsgefühl"* (social interest), is also the answer to the inferiority-complex/power-urge dichotomy discovered by Adler, who was unable, however, to show a satisfactory way toward its integration. Social interest, more often than not, merely masks the power urge. Relatedness, on the other hand, assigns this urge a place in the overall pattern, where it may operate responsibly. Relatedness thus constitutes the "big third," in addition to sexuality and religious or spiritual meaning, in the call for integrative fulfillment in our time.

During the first half of this century, the acceptance of sexuality and the rediscovery of religious, transpersonal significance, accomplishments of Freud and Jung, were vital steps toward individuation, and provided adequate answers to the healing of psychological suffering. In our time, seemingly, a new psychological need has arisen, namely, the need for the integration of affect, especially of anger, aggression, and infantile neediness for personal validation, regardless of whether these affects are "good" or "bad." *These* needs are expressions of the archetypal feminine, which values subjective experience, affect, and feeling. Throughout the patriarchal period, this dimension was repressed. Then, the Self manifested itself primarily in outer-directed, rational, and heroic standards that looked upon affect and neediness as weaknesses to be overruled and disregarded by the ego. Affirmation of these needs, on the other hand, leads to an affirmation of "being as it is" rather than "being as it should be," and hence to an acceptance of Self in the here-and-now regardless of expectations of perfection in collective persona categories. Yet, this Self-acceptance occurs with an attitude of respect for and empathy with the needs and sensitivities of partners and partnership. This transition from superego or persona-ego to Self-motivated ego thus heralds new forms of relationship between individuals and in groups.

EXPERIENTIALNESS

Interpretation and reflection do not necessarily suffice for differentiating and incarnating the newly emerging Self-motivated ego. In fact, at times, they may even be counterproductive to efforts at bringing about awareness of the preverbal level of emotion, affect, and motivation. Interpretation is essentially based on thought and concept. It offers ways of understanding and a frame of reference that are different from, and presumed to be better than, the direct experience of the affect. Hence, it offers a temptation to bypass the direct and authentic experience of the affect in favor of this "better understanding." Furthermore, since this "better understanding" can be provided only by a trained therapist, a reliance upon another person is often created. This reliance can function as a shield against authentic Self-experience and against reliance upon one's own motivations and impulses. Moreover, conceptualization often tends to cause one to miss the direct impact of the moment. While vitally important, to be sure, it often fails to link up adequately with the level of the still preverbal, groping "being in feeling," which, like a small child, grasps for orientation and expression in the here-and-now. Before being able to deal with meaning, this child-ego needs space for the experience of its immediate reality, and it gets it through supportive acceptance of its experimenting and "playing" with self and others.

Affect and emotion need to be experienced directly in order to be tested against reality and differentiated. A quasi-experimental exploration and "feeling through" of affects in relation to concrete persons is necessary. If it is to promote symbolic living, psychotherapy not only must facilitate understanding, but must also be experiential. Unless the implications of symbolic perception can also be lived and reality-tested in concrete life and relationships, reflection upon the symbolic dimension is ineffectual, even potentially isolating, and can contribute to inflation and ego inadequacy.

When other persons arouse my resentment, I may realize that a shadow projection has occurred. I may know that I projected my own pride or arrogance upon them. But merely knowing this and deciding to "take the projection back" will not help matters. The affect cannot be assimilated and transformed unless and until it has been "born into the world" by having been given deliberate and conscious expression vis-à-vis the other person, both as a feeling toward the other and as my own subjective state. The affect needs to be repeatedly and concretely experienced in terms of the tensions and emotional turmoil it creates in oneself and between oneself and the other. In addition, the frustrated needs and aggressions for which the pride has served as a defensive screen have to be discovered, experienced, and expressed in relationship to (and received by) another person. All these hitherto repressed and split-off emotions need to find viable channels of expression in the external world. If I am to discover what and how much is possible in an interpersonal relationship, I need to be able to experiment with my expressions. It does not suffice only to "work at it internally." And, I will have to find out what it is in the reality of the other person that drew me into this encounter in the first place, so as to make me bump up against my projections. Lastly, I will be able to measure the degree of assimilation of my projections by the degree of clarity in the kind of I-Thou relationship that eventually becomes possible, in the freedom to be close or to let go. (I prefer the term assimilation to "taking back," which seems to imply a deliberateness that does not exist here.)

Likewise, in the opposite situation of a fascination or of falling in love, a "working out" of animus or anima problems in isolation from the other person, merely accepting and registering the qualities in question as parts of the inner self, rarely relieves the problem. Nor does it lead to fruitful integration. Desire, need, love, anger, disappointment must be reflected upon, but they also must be expressed and lived through in a real relationship if they are to be relieved of their obsessive character. Self-motivation occurs primarily through affect and emotion; only secondarily is it conceptualized. Compulsive affects, therefore, need to be consciously expressed and reality-tested, "suffered through" in the world of objects and relationships, if they are to become conscious feelings. The ego is an incarnation of the Self, the new affect- and feeling-ego no less than the patriarchal, heroic, rule- and reason-oriented ego. While the old ego had to gain its reality through discipline and obedience to outer rules, the new ego has to gain its reality by discovering the logic, rules, and reason of feeling and relatedness.

If analysis is to reach out into this deepening of experience, it cannot continue to limit itself to verbal and interpretative methods. They are important for clarification, but can feel overpowering and, at times, too narrowly focused to permit a truly holistic experience.

A greater emphasis may also be called for than has hitherto been placed, at least by some Jungian therapists, on the working through of the personal unconscious, not only prior to but also as part of making the archetypal dimension more real. In practical terms, this means laying greater stress on the allegorical than on the symbolic dimension of dreams, and regarding interpretations as insufficient unless they sum up or are preliminary to a working through of the affects, impulses, or emotional memories that the dream touches upon. For the purpose of this working through, moreover, therapists may also resort to the use of enactment—verbal or nonverbal—body awareness, guided imagination, and analysis in a group setting. And finally, since therapists' attitudes and feelings critically determine what patients can permit themselves to experience, the importance of the countertransference deserves more attention than it has hitherto received (cf. chapter by Machtiger, above).

DREAMS

In Jung's definition, a symbol points to a content that is essentially beyond knowing, beyond even rational understanding. An allegory, on the other hand, is a figurative description or expression of something that could be, and indeed, as far as we are concerned, is in need of being, known and understood directly and concretely. Personal behavior, personal psychological qualities, thoughts, affects, and feelings are represented in dreams and fantasies as images that call for allegorical understanding. While they are presented to us in images, which is the aboriginal language of the psyche, these contents of the personal unconscious can and should also be known and understood concretely, in daily experience, by consciousness. Before dealing with symbolic significance, the personal, allegorical dimensions of the dream need to be felt through.

For instance, a dream of a brutal Nazi soldier who kills children can be understood and worked through in terms of the dreamer's identification with the ruthless self-assertion and will to control that threatens the dreamer's child side—that is, his or her neediness, helplessness, playfulness, dependency, or sensitivity and growth potential, whatever the dreamer happens to associate with childlikeness or childishness. These factors are knowable and ought to be known and expressed directly. Both the Nazi and the child will have to be experienced as currently acting feeling and behavior patterns, here and now. They also can and need to be worked through by means of recalling and consciously reliving, perhaps with the help of guided imagination, childhood memories of traumatic experiences and of harsh or rigid disciplining or deprivations that may have led to the Nazi attitude. It will have to be discovered how both the Nazi and the child express themselves in interpersonal relations and in the dreamer's relationship to the analyst in the transference. The same issues will appear as well in the countertransference reactions they evoke in the therapist. Only when this groundwork has been completed will it be of help to explore the archetypal symbolism, the dimension of possible meaning in the overall life destiny pattern, as alluded to perhaps in the motif of the "murder of the innocents" or whatever arises through association and amplification.

It is not sufficient to interpret dream figures simply as animus, anima, shadow instinct, and so on, without working through the specific characterological attitudes that are represented. Take, for instance, the "dark-haired woman": what particular dark-haired woman does she remind the dreamer of? If none, can the dreamer visualize the dream figure or any dark-haired woman that may come to his or her mind right now? What is she like as a person, as the dreamer looks at her and sizes her up? The dreamer should feel him- or herself into her, express her attitude, feelings, moods. When does the *dreamer* feel like that? Similarly, the sinister man, and even animals, are to be experienced in terms of the attitudes or "personality traits" that they allude to and "impersonate"—for example, a lion as rulership, pride, perhaps reckless daring; a shepherd dog as the capacity to keep the flock together, watchfulness; a poodle as irritable nervousness, and so on. These figures may be helpful or threatening depending upon the nature, ecology, or particular dramatic emphasis of the dream action or the myth or fairytale.

For psychological awareness, the working and feeling through of these specific characterological tendencies may be more important than their classification as shadow, animus, anima, Self, or whatever. The same viewpoint should obtain when dealing with any other archetypal or mythological motifs. Rather than adhering to a set of amplificatory understandings (water = purification, dissolving, feeling soul; black = shadow, earth, death; pig or bear = mother, and so on), analysts should always elicit dreamers' associations, personal feelings, reactions to and ways of experiencing the images, by having them meditate, reminisce, enact, or even talk to the figures or objects of the dream.

A lack of relation to the archetypal dimension results in spiritual impoverishment and a sense of meaninglessness in life. But insufficient anchoring and incarnating of the archetypal in the personal realm—that is, speculating about archetypal meaning rather than trying to discover this meaning through living concretely the prosaic and "trivial" problems and difficulties of everyday feelings and relationships, results in mere "head trips" and is the hallmark of narcissistic pathology. Then the symbol fails to heal and may, indeed, insulate analysands from the unconscious, rather than connect them to it.

The achievement of a solid grounding in the personal dimension is also aided by work on the seemingly trivial, "little," nonarchetypal dreams. These dreams furnish the bulk of the personal context. But even in working with seemingly or even obviously archetypal dream material, the personal associations and context and the allegorical significance need to be carefully considered first in order to avoid missing important points. Consider the following example:

An analysand dreamed of a landscape dominated by a centrally located, brilliant, square-shaped quartz crystal. A voice was heard saying: "It is the four in red." Then she dreamed that she considered whether or not to eat breakfast.

The classical approach would be to treat this as an individuation dream, and to elaborate upon the motif of the center, of the *lapis;* upon the significance of quartz as permeable to ultraviolet light and as regulator of electricity or the matrix for gold; upon the significance of four as pointing to wholeness; upon the alchemical *rubedo,* perhaps pointing to the need for allowing in more feeling or passion. This imagery of wholeness, centering, and emotion might be explained and interpreted as compensating for an insufficiently focused and introverted conscious attitude. The breakfast dream might be taken as indicative of a hesitation to get ready for the day's work, or perhaps of a resistance to committing oneself to life or to the process of therapy.

In fact, the patient had already "worked" on that material and herself "understood" it that way and proudly recited it thus to the therapist. I had the somewhat uncomfortable feeling of a "head trip," and felt that there must be more to the dream than had been brought out. So I asked the patient first to "act" the crystal without saying anything, then to tell me in the first person what she felt as the crystal, and then to talk to the crystal.

In being the crystal, she stood rigidly and tensely in the middle of the room and just stared. Then, speaking as the crystal, she said: "I feel hard, immobile, straight, and tense. I cannot move, and I resent being pushed around by other people." When she asked the crystal what it wanted, it answered: "I want to be released and taken out of the box I have been put in. I feel confined there and scared."

Now I asked the analysand to "stay" with all those reactions. This unleashed a flood of associations and memories quite different from the previous "interpretations." The crystal now reminded the dreamer of her father's mineral collection. Her father made a good deal of fuss over this relatively small and insignificant collection. It was repeatedly and painstakingly arranged, rearranged, labeled, classified, reclassified, pigeonholed, and cleaned. From here the associations led to her father's general perfectionism, his small-minded, pedantic, and rigid orderliness and overcritical attitudes, by which she had felt suffocated and inhibited from giving expression to her own sensitivities and artistic interests.

The four reminded her of the grading system in the European school where she had received her early education. Grades of one to four were used to indicate excellent, good, satisfactory, or unsatisfactory, with four the dreaded failing grade. Her papers were graded in red ink by a professor as exacting and perfectionistic as her father. And now, as she reminisced, she remembered how often she dreaded school so much that she did not want to eat breakfast.

Thus her dream portrays her "inner landscape"; it is dominated by a rigid and pedantic animus that tends to put things, and herself, into boxes; that makes her fear and have a sense of failure; that deprives her of intrinsic value and renders her unable to live as a full person and to experience her potential. Feeling through the breakfast dream, she now got in touch with her fear of ever risking herself in authentic living. Mythological reflections had helped her to turn her attention from her fear of risking herself toward a sort of vicarious or substitute spirituality. Focusing on individuation symbolism without a prior working through of the personal inferiority and confinement complexes, along with the petty perfectionism, would engender here an unrealistic inflation on top of a sense of failure. Only after these elements have been realized, made real on the level of actual here-and-now experiencing, not of merely knowing about them, could the individuation implications of the "indestructible core" or of the "stone which the builders have rejected" (see Ps. 118:22; Matt. 21:42; Mark 12:10) be of real help in bringing about a *"metanoia,"* a change of attitude.

ENACTMENT

Enactment is an adaptation of Gestalt and psychodrama methods to the Jungian process. But it also includes nonverbal pantomiming, which often comes closer to the expression of preverbal affect than standard Gestalt and psychodrama technique do. In contradistinction to Perls and Moreno, who intended to address themselves primarily, if not exclusively, to the experiencing of the immediate here-and-now and hence rejected interpretation, I do not hesitate to use interpretation after, but not before, the experiential working through. Interpretation, as well as active or guided imagination, may frequently be helpful and even essential in amplifying the affect experience and integrating it into the overall pattern of the transformation process and of meaning.

Enactment can be considered an auxiliary technique for deepening, intensifying, and working through whatever unconscious material, personal or archetypal or both, happens to be constellated in the course of our accustomed analytic process. As a method in itself, it is not adequate to replace the analytic process, as Perls, who was unfamiliar with Jung's work, thought.

Enactment is not to be confused with "acting out." Acting out is compulsive behavior and, more often than not, destructive to varying degrees; hence it is frowned upon in psychotherapy. It is an attempt to relieve tension. Enactment, on the other hand, is conscious and deliberate psychodrama. Initially, at least, it does not relieve but rather increases tension and anxiety, through the deliberate contact with the anxiety-charged complexes. It is constructive in its effect by virtue of enlarging consciousness and experiential awareness.

In enactment, analysands are asked to imagine themselves as a particular image, object, complex, or archetypal figure; or as a dream figure, friend, or spouse with whom they may happen to have a problem. They are to feel themselves into the figure, move as they feel it moves, then verbalize what they feel while being the figure, using the "I" form. Then they may engage the figure or object in a conversation and listen to "its" responses. An experiential *"Auseinandersetzung"* (encounter) with partial personalities or subpersonalities occurs that, unlike verbal interpretation alone, rarely if ever increases a sense of splitness, but always reconnects and increases a feeling of wholeness.

For example, take a shadow problem. A man who sees himself as a warm-hearted, tolerant chap dreams of a repressive dictator, a harsh military martinet. In the interpretation, this would be explained as his unconscious shadow aspect. It is hoped that he will understand. Yet all too often he *merely* understands; he does not necessarily *realize*. He does not really see how or when he is himself this dictator. In a group setting, he may be caught *in flagrante,* acting out the dictator in some sense that the group picks up, but he may still protest that he is being misunderstood. What he needs is a chance to experience himself consciously as a dictator.

Now he may be asked to try deliberately to be a dictator, to feel himself into and enact the dictator of the dream. At first he performs without words, by pantomime, expressing the attitude of the dream figure. Then he speaks in the first person and tells how he feels about himself in this role and about the world and other people. His attention is drawn by the therapist or by the group to the way he moves, to his posture, to tensions in his body. He is asked about what he feels, and about where he feels his emotions to be embedded in his body, whether in the back, the shoulders, the gut, or wherever. He is then instructed to "stay" with the awareness of these newly discovered tensions and see what associations, memories, or emotions arise "out of them." He is also told to pay attention to when and under what circumstances similar tensions and feelings arise in every-day situations. He may also be asked to talk to the dictator or to enact the dictator's responses by alternatingly playing both parts.

Now the dictator is being experienced and given space for expression and self-explanation by the analysand's attending to body signals usually ignored and to emotional and imaginal material previously not recognized. But the dictator is also given a chance to express his own needs, perhaps for more attention or assurance, which, unheeded, can only express them-selves "dictatorially." In latching on to any of these, the analysand may be led to realize when he is acting the dictator at other times. In verbaliz-ing his role, he may say something like: "I do not care what other people feel; I am always right; I know better," or "I need to control everything so as to assure attention." There is no need to interpret this. The therapist need merely comment, "Did you hear what you said? You described your-self. Now look for the times when you can catch this feeling in yourself. Look for the times when you yourself give too little attention to your needs."

This method leads directly to the core that usual verbal associations often tend to meander around; furthermore, the emotional and hence trans-formational impact, through acute awareness, is indescribably greater than in merely reflective interpretation.

The enactment technique can also be of help in elucidating dreams when associations cover such wide or indefinite areas that the implications remain obscure, or when a dearth of personal associations leaves only a general archetypal understanding that cannot be adequately related to a concrete personal situation.

Take, for example, the dream of a young woman who was subject to seemingly groundless outbursts of rage that tended to punctuate a generally conventional and anxiously inhibited personality pattern. She dreamed of a swineherd who killed a mourning dove because its twittering bothered him. Interpreted in terms of conventional association and amplification, the dream led to a consideration of how her identification with the sensation function—the hardnosed, prosaic concern with concrete work reality (swineherd)—tended to kill the spiritual or poetic side in her. While this was theoretically correct and accurately described her overall situation, the interpretation did not add anything that had not been said and understood before. She had known as much from previous material, but the affect experienced in the dream, the terror of the brutal act, could not be understood by associating to anything in her present situation.

She was now asked to enact the various figures of the dream. The swineherd elicited nothing new. But in "being" the dove, she started with a few dancing steps and then suddenly stopped, saying that she felt terribly inhibited about going on, and she did not know why. Now this was peculiar. One does not expect dancing from a dove, and the sudden inhibition suggested that something important was at hand. I now proposed that a bit of music might bring back the dancing mood. As I proceeded to put on a record, I noticed that she was standing in the middle of the room as though panic-stricken. Tears were pouring from her eyes. She was unable to offer any explanation. I suggested that she simply hold on, intensify if possible what she was feeling and express any impression, memory, or image that arose regardless of rational thought or order. She stretched out her hands and began to cry, "No! No! No! Keep away, keep away!" She then described a gypsy girl or perhaps a young witch dancing in the moonlight in a forest glade, being attacked and killed by brutish peasants.

Later, the scene was reenacted in the therapy group setting. The group members took the roles of the threatening, brutish peasants. This reproduced one of her typical, hitherto unexplainable, rages, which now clearly showed the features of angry despair and panic, of someone helplessly cornered. Her inhibitions, formerly seen merely in personal terms of conventional standards, were experienced in a much more profound way as the terror of the young witch.

Now she not only knew but felt and experienced how the fear of being ostracized or attacked as a maverick "witch" led her to brutalize her intuitive and sensitive feeling sides; it did not allow her to dance. For the first time, she was connected to the reality of emotional experiencing, heretofore untapped, but she was connected by an affect and energy potential that mere discussion of her dreams had failed to reach.

Seemingly obvious and simple dreams may also reveal new facets when dealt with in this way, as shown in the following case. The dreamer, a most unassertive and self-effacing person, was attempting to walk through a hilly countryside. Each time she approached a hill, it would rear up before her and turn into an impassable mountain. The message is clear enough: for her, every molehill becomes a mountain. The dreamer understood this. But in terms of her subjective experience, unfortunately, every molehill *was* a mountain. I now suggested that she act the dream—act not herself, but the mountain. Here the irrational element appeared. In being the mountain, instead of rearing up as the dream-mountain did, she flattened out on the floor! Now that was a revelation to us both. It brought home to her as nothing else could have how she perceived obstacles, expecting them to be flat and insignificant. It also showed her how she really behaved when she thought she was "rearing up" or standing up to difficulties: she actually flattened herself out and then invited others to step on her. The dream and her enactment now converged to bring home to her that it was her failure to stand up for herself that turned even small obstacles into mountains. What was really an inner personality trait confronted her as "outer" destiny. No amount of theoretical explanation could have provided better illustration of destiny and synchronicity as expressions of one's own psychological reality.

The extent to which unconscious motivation can be clarified through nonverbal physical expression is illustrated in an example from a group session. A man and woman got involved in one of those seemingly endless and pointless anima-animus squabbles in which the real issues become more and more obscured with every word uttered. I suggested that they try a nonverbal way of discovering what was really at stake. They were instructed to place themselves at opposite ends of the room and, while walking toward each other, express nonverbally whatever arose in themselves about the other person.

We were in for a surprise! The man slowly and ploddingly moved toward the woman. She remained rooted to the spot. As he came nearer, she began to sway in a sinuous dance, a highly suggestive movement. When he came close and reached out to her, she abruptly turned her back on him. When he rather clumsily tried to force her to turn to him, she vigorously resisted and eventually flew at his throat. In a moment they were in vicious combat, wrestling and rolling on the floor. I now stopped them. It had become obvious to onlookers as well as participants that the woman's motivation was to arouse the man's aggression at any cost. She would risk violence, perhaps even desire it, in order to be noticed erotically as a woman. Yet when she succeeded, she was unable or unwilling to face up to the implications of her urges, out of the very sense of inferiority that she projected onto those who would not take sufficient notice of her.

The man, in turn, rather naïvely identified with the role of conquering hero, the breaker of hearts unable to resist a woman's allurement; he was bent only on "proving" his manhood by a show of plodding strength that disguised his inferiority feelings. The mutual projection of their similar complexes by virtue of animus and anima expectations were now matters of experience, and they became quite obvious once the main dynamic of their behavior was explained to them.

Now the roles were reversed. The woman acted the man's part, and he played her side. He thereby got a sense of how her attitude was also a reflection of his own unconscious seductiveness and desperate wish to attract attention. The woman, in turn, got in touch with her "macho" superego and the brutality of her rejecting animus, which decreed the inferiority of feminine values and of her as a person. They both now came to realize the extent to which they had been caught in mutual projections.

In another instance, in order to bring home to an analysand her tendency to ask constantly for help, but to reject it when it was offered, I asked her to give me "something." I would not specify what. Whatever she gave me—pen, pencil, water—I refused, but I continued to say, "Give me something. No, not that." "What then?" she asked. "I don't know; give me something." After a while the message registered. She really experienced how she came across to others.

Now we reversed roles. She played the one who always rejected what was offered and I acted her part. This brought her back to her childhood and made her aware of how she identified with and replayed the roles of her perfectionist parents. She never could offer the "right" or good enough responses to them, and hence was made to feel inadequate and unacceptable. In playing her part, I, in turn, got in touch with the hopeless feeling of "nothing is good enough" that pervaded her. This experience helped me gain a greater awareness of the patient's hopelessness and diffidence that came across only as stubborn negativism and resistance to the process of therapy. The ensuing change in my attitude, and the change in the countertransference, made an important difference in the therapeutic process from there on. It is the quality of the countertransference that creates or denies the "enabling space" that is so important for the outcome of the therapy process.

Enactment lends itself to the conscious realization of complexes, as well as of their archetypal cores, and to the realization of transference and countertransference dynamics. A mother-dominated man could be asked to enact, and thereby get in touch with, the oppressed child he felt himself to have been. But he might also be asked to "be" the mother who oppressed and "devoured" him. The latter, especially, connects him with the archetypal power that tends to undermine his independent selfhood (through unassimilated anima emotionality). He may gain a sense not only of what he tends to project, but also of how the actual carrier of his projections is likely to feel. A way may thereby be opened to reach beyond mere defensiveness toward sympathy and understanding of the other. Likewise, as the preceding example shows, the therapist can also get a better insight into transference and countertransference dynamics by "playing" first his or her own and then the patient's part.

The dynamics of the archetypal dimension can become a more vivid experience when the grand figures, as they arise in dreams as well as in raw emotions, are consciously embodied and felt. Pain, terror, anguish, joy, love, the hero, the martyr, the witch can be felt and expressed through body movement—in posture, gesture, or tension—and come closer to reality. It is a traditional precept of the East that, in order to connect with a god, one must "become" that god.

Vague and undefined tensions and anxieties, or "free-floating" emotions, may be brought to more distinct awareness, first by focusing attention on where and how they are felt as body tensions, and then by moving in some way, or doing something, that discharges or relieves those tensions. Relief and awareness may come from a grimace, an exclamation, or a symbolic gesture, such as clenching the fist or perhaps hitting a pillow or the floor.

The postures or words are then to be repeated like a mudra or mantra until, spontaneously, images, memories, or associations, verbal or nonverbal, arise that cast light on the situation. These may be scenes of anguish, such as the example of the gypsy girl, or repressed impulses or affects. They are now experienced in their present affective implications rather than as abstract memories of past events.

It may be objected that the above techniques constitute invitations to identification and inflation. This possibility, I believe, exists no more, and probably considerably less, than in the use of active imagination (cf. chapter by Dallett, above). In fact, the body techniques may well be considered an expansion or amplification of active or guided imagination (to be discussed later), extended to embrace not merely the eidetic but the total-body, proprioceptive image level. Except for instances of overt schizophrenia or near-schizophrenic states (where this method would be contraindicated), the possibility of the ego's being assimilated by a complex or archetype is mitigated by the conscious effort it takes to embody a role or object that is deliberately chosen. The very effort required clearly marks the boundary line between ego and the complex or image. It may even be made part of the exercise to move back and forth between the assumed part and the normal ego-state in order to establish their different feelings, when and if this should be deemed necessary. What actually takes place is disidentification from obsessive states as well as from inertia, rather than identification with them: one is set free. For, essentially, the method aids in the formation of conscious ritual, a form of activity that makes archetypal energy consciously available, grounds the archetype, and thus connects one with the *numinosum* in a safe fashion. Psychologically, enactment and ritual help overcome inertia and obsessional states by offering an experimental, reality-testing stage for archetypal energy to "become flesh," rather than remaining on a level of inaccessible threat or unacceptable fantasy.

Ritualization and enactment help make available to consciousness the energy of seemingly unproductive daydreaming or frightening and repulsive fantasies, frequently sexual or aggressive in nature. The first step is to rework the fantasy as a playwright might do for a stage performance (perhaps a private performance for consenting adults), while still preserving the emotional or affective content of the original. The material is thereby condensed into its essential symbolic core; it has become nondestructive and acceptable, yet remains dynamically and affectively authentic. The libidinal content is thereby made available for integration. The metamorphosis of "eating the god" into the ritual of the Mass is a collective example of this process. The possibilities inherent in the conscious use of this modality, both for psychotherapy and for culture, are, in my opinion, as yet unforeseeable.

Contrary to the usual expectation, the inclusion of nonverbal enactment does not complicate transference problems, but tends to help in working them out. It does so by clarifying, through direct experience, the qualities of transference and countertransference. Mutual resistances and their unconscious motives are brought into focus. In the case of an authority, dependency, or inertia problem, the therapist may suggest that the analysand react to being pushed around the room. Or the therapist may suggest handwrestling. A dance movement often points up rigidities and resistances. It is most surprising to analysands that their resistance or lack of it comes out quite contrary to their own ideas of how they will react. In a group this discrepancy can be more dramatically emphasized. For instance, the group members may form a tight circle around a person who then responds or fails to respond to being hemmed in—forcefully trying to break out, pleading, or even giving up in resignation. Or, they may form an independent circle of exclusiveness, to which the outcast is challenged to react. The physical enactment of one's attitude to such situations comes as quite a revelation.

Other preverbal, experiential approaches include dialogue drawing (Finley) and various forms of play therapy, primarily sandplay, but other forms as well. There are many ways of improvising a play situation consistent with the early preverbal forms of adult-to-child or child-to-child communication: building with blocks together, singing, Indian wrestling, rocking, holding, touching—whatever may appeal to, connect with, and help nourish the infant ego. Any form of libido expression—need, desire, affection, and, last but not least, anger—as it happens to arise spontaneously is to be given value and a channel for expression and experimentation, consistent, of course, with the possibilities and limitations of the interacting personalities. When the libido is fundamentally accepted in its primitive form, it can itself accept the need for more mature or adequate channels of expression. Only then can interpretation and understanding of meaning begin to be helpful.

TOUCHING

There has been a good deal of controversy over whether physical body contact, beyond the polite handshake between analyst and analysand, should be permitted. Here, too, the traditional outlook has been heavily influenced by the culture's bias against body and bodily experience. In the last few years, there has been an increasing awareness of the helpful, indeed healing, effect of touch, judiciously used.

Touch helps to overcome a sense of isolation and lack of communication with both self and others. Repressed or split-off emotions are embedded in muscular constrictions and areas of body tension. Touching and being touched by the therapist, or by one's fellow members in a therapy group, facilitates "getting in touch" with one's tensions; hence it helps in grounding the awareness of the affect level. For many people, relating and "being in touch" do not become real until, and unless, real bodily touch and contact occur. Many women analysands, in particular, have repeatedly expressed that they can comprehend what comes through the body much more readily than what comes through words and explanations alone. We know that for the infant, bodily contact is a vital biological necessity as a channel of relatedness. For many contact-starved adults, the intensity of this need remains a hunger as strong as the infant's, and thus a psychological necessity if they are to learn to trust relationships.

Much of what appears on the face of it to be a sexual transference may really be a masked, unrecognized urge to have physical body contact, to have one's reality affirmed in bodily concreteness by the therapist. If the therapist is too ready to dismiss this as a projection to be handed back to the analysand for internalization, it may result in increased resistance at best, and depression and sexualization, the very thing the therapist would like to avoid, at worst. The infant's need for contact is then redirected, prematurely, into the adult channel of genital sexuality, when the primary and original form of the need has remained unfulfilled. No amount of overt sexual expression is found to be satisfying, since it fails to meet the pregenital needs.

The short-circuited energy may now play havoc with transference and countertransference. Either the therapist continues to resist what to him or her appears as sexual demands or tempting seductiveness, thereby creating and enlarging what the analysand's infant ego experiences as a wall of isolation and rejection; or, if the therapist responds in kind with sexuality, he or she may overtax the infant ego's ability to deal with sexuality and to stand up for its own relationship needs. In either case, the preverbal ego is being rejected and deprived of space and nurturance. Either eventuality is experienced as a betrayal in the depths of the psyche.

THE COUNTERTRANSFERENCE

The importance of the countertransference has become clearer during the last few years. Previously, difficulties arising in the therapy process tended to be discussed primarily in terms of the analyst's techniques, or of the analysand's failure to cooperate, or of transference problems. Yet many, if not most, impasses in the therapy process have their roots in an inability or unreadiness of the therapist to respond in an emotionally accepting way to the patient's personality and affective demands, to be able to see potential values in the patient's foibles and complexes, and hence to value libido even in that seemingly objectionable form in which the therapist may first perceive it. Yet this offensiveness is likely to be accounted for by the responses of the therapist's own complexes, now projected upon the patient. The less therapists happen to take this fact into account, the less they are in touch with the complexes in themselves that were constellated by the encounter, and the more the complexes will act as barriers in the process.

The major thrust of the transformational encounter occurs on the magical level of subject-object identity (Whitmont, p. 27ff.; Gebser), *particularly* in the "narcissistic" and "borderline" pathology of the new ego dynamic. On this level of mutual identity-merging, the healing influence is determined not by what therapists say or do, nor by the school or system they believe in, nor by their skill in interpretation, but by what they feel and "are"; by their own readiness to tune in, to be open to the unfamiliar; by their capacity and willingness to accept relatedness, intimacy, and personal closeness, to live with shadow, to touch and be touched, both metaphorically and concretely. It is vital that therapists be willing and able to look at themselves, at their own resistances and their own terrors of "nakedness" and exposure, at every difficult point of the journey. It does not help the process if they hide behind a professional persona, behind ready interpretations of the patient's reactions as projections to be "taken back." Eventually, to be sure, projections need to be dealt with. But a nascent ego needs the affirmation of its feelings first and the example of his or her partner's capacity to accept negative feelings. Not until the infant ego has felt itself accepted in an open human-to-human encounter, meeting and "touching," and therefore not until the therapist has dealt with and even, on occasion, owned up to his or her own feelings and complexes (when it seems clear that it will help rather than burden the patient), can the projection aspect of the transference be dealt with.

Moreover, the awareness of countertransference reactions can also serve as a sensitive indicator of what is happening within analysands' psyches, provided their therapists are familiar with the range of their own reactions and cautious enough first to check them out as possibly their own. The revulsion, boredom, erotic response, and so on, that therapists happen to feel may indeed be their own; but when recognized as out of character in intensity or quality, these reactions may also be expressive of what is happening on the other side. They may be the analysand's unrecognized reactions registered by the therapist. In either case, they are indicative of what needs to be explored and mutually clarified in the relationship at that particular juncture.

A relatively simple example will illustrate. My patients are asked to take off their shoes in my office since we sit, lie, and even roll on the floor, particularly in group meetings. When, at her fourth or fifth session, an analysand deposited her shoes right in the middle of the room on the rug, I remarked rather curtly, "Not on the rug—please put them over there." This patient, attuned to a critical and perfectionistic father, responded rather sharply and emotionally to what she perceived as a reprimand for being "too stupid" to remember where to put her shoes. She felt rejected and worthless. Before dealing with her obvious overreaction in terms of the underlying projection, I noted my own fleeting sense of impatience and the momentary grouchiness that had prompted the tone of my remark. I said to the patient that I appreciated her feeling, and that indeed I myself have an overcritical, perfectionist, and impatient side. While I am aware of it, it nevertheless, and contrary to my intentions, tends to run away with me at times and then can be quite hurtful to others; it is just one of the shadow problems I have to live with. To this she responded with a sigh of relief and said, "My father would never have admitted that." And then we were able to look at her side and to investigate her overcriticalness and self-rejection that stood behind her projection.

The above example also serves to illustrate how any seemingly trivial incident between analysand and analyst can, and indeed should, be used to concretize psychological dynamics. Ordinarily, interpretation deals with yesterday's and tomorrow's happenings, and understanding thereby remains separated from living. But if the personal relation between analyst and analysand is to be used as a model for the living experience, it must be an open two-way street of two equal human beings. To be sure, therapists are expected to be superior in terms of experience and know-how. But they must permit themselves to be the equals of their partners in terms of vulnerability, openness, and receptivity, to give and take, and to share their reactions and blind spots when appropriate.

GUIDED IMAGINATION

Guided imagination is an office procedure in analytical psychology for exploring specific areas of unconsciousness. It is a form of working through, amplifying, or completing fragmentary dreams or visions, a way of tuning into old memories or forgotten experiences. It is also a way to reexplore attitudes or situations that are suspected of being, or have been shown to be, faulty or dangerous. Therapists actively participate in the descent into the image world by imaging with their clients. By way of first-hand coexperience, they remain in close touch with what is constellated. They function as companion-guides, add the reassurance of their presence, and help analysands to focus on what their experience has shown them to be essential. Therapists thereby allay fear and can provide help in difficult situations. They can also prevent avoidance of important but painful issues that the patient might try to by-pass by wandering off into peripheral issues, and they can suggest possible alternatives when an impasse seems to have occurred. An example may illustrate this.

An experience of active imagination was started by picking up on a dream about a needed descent. The imagination led into a dimly lit cavern with many doorways leading in different directions, all locked but one. This one, the analysand found, opened quite easily and he wandered along a corridor whose walls were covered with "interesting" symbolic signs and images. Presently he found himself outside again, exactly where he had started from. The process had short-circuited itself through all-too-easy wandering along a path of symbolic speculation. Something important had been missed in by-passing the difficulties of the locked doors (cf. chapter by Dallett, above).

Now I entered the process: I suggested that he go in again, and this time try to open any of the other doors. At first, no luck; they were tightly closed. Now I asked him to look around in the space for any sign or indication of what to do. Nothing was to be seen; there was not enough light to make out any details. Evidently more "light" was needed, so I suggested he look around for matches, candle, or flashlight. Since nothing could be found on the outside, owing to the darkness, the only place to look would be in his own pockets. And behold, a fairly adequate flashlight was indeed discovered in his right pants pocket. As he now directed its beam around the cave, he discerned in a dark recess the figure of a man chained to a rock. I asked him to talk to the man and ask him what he needed. The man in response begged him to set him free. Yet he could not loosen the chains. They were padlocked.

Again the patient was ready to give up and wander off in a different direction. Instead I suggested that he again search his own pockets for a helpful tool or key. This time he came up with a screwdriver. With this he managed to unscrew some bolts and free the man, who offered to show him the way into the interior through a slippery passageway. This by-passed the locked doors, which could be opened from within if so desired.

I now asked the patient to have a close look at his newly found guide and to describe him. To his surprise, he discovered a close resemblance to an uncle of his who had been held in contempt by his conventionally minded parents as a "slippery" maverick, but whom he himself admired and loved. In this figure, he had met his guide to the interior. His pathway was to be found through setting free his own "maverick" independence of thought and feeling, which had been shackled by his parent-identified de-valuation of his individuality. This self-denigration had robbed him of ini-tiative and self-confidence to the extent that he would not look for light and tools in his own pockets.

We terminated the imaging by first thanking the guide and promising to seek him out again if it was all right with him, to which the guide graciously assented. The patient then retraced his steps out of the cavern in the reverse order of that in which he had entered. These steps are helpful for keeping in touch with the figures of the unconscious and assuring a full return to the concrete here-and-now.

Subsequently, for the sake of grounding the experience, I asked the patient to feel himself into the man he found in the cave, to be him and enact him, to experience the stance and attitude of this figure. In doing so, he touched upon an inner sense of what independent male daring might feel like. He made an emotional contact with his own repressed originality, without which he had wandered around in the dark corridors of inertia, of symbolically decorated daydreaming.

Another patient dreamed that she was pursued by a raving monster. Starting imagination, she first tried to run away. When that did not work, she turned about and tried to strangle the monster. That seemed to work well enough. The monster hung limp, but the patient now felt a choking sensation in her own throat, which uncomfortably reminded her of a recurring psychosomatic symptom. Thereupon I intervened and suggested that, since in choking the monster she was evidently choking something important in herself, she had better try a different approach, perhaps befriending the monster, offering to feed it or trying to talk to it. Even though very scared, yet assured by the therapist's presence, she dared to touch the monster gently and hesitantly and asked it who or what it was. The monster now responded quite positively and changed into a little girl, in whom she recognized the "little monster" she had come to consider herself in response to the constant nagging criticism of her lively temperament by her mother and the private school principal of her early adolescent years.

Both enactment and guided imagination can be helpful, also, in unraveling affect that has been frozen in bodily tensions or somatic symptoms. One can "be," or talk to, a pain, a constricted area, or an internal organ or limb. In fantasy, one can descend into the interior of one's body and seek out a disturbed function or organ. I recall a rather dramatic example of this method with a patient with advanced cancer. She was undergoing chemotherapy and during her hour with me was plagued by intense nausea. I suggested that she talk to the nausea and listen to its answer. This is what the nausea "said": "I hate you. I want to destroy you. You always make a mess of things. You never accomplish anything worthwhile. Whatever you do is wrong." Not only was she shocked to discover the degree of her destructive self-hatred, but, amazingly enough, the nausea disappeared.

I suggested to another patient during a light asthma attack that she visualize what was happening to her chest. She imaged a huge black spider squeezing her. Staying with and intensifying the spider image brought up memories of her angry helplessness when she felt herself manipulated by her domineering mother. Giving vent to her feelings, even by screaming and crying out her anger at the imaged mother, relieved the spasm and the asthma and paved the way for working on her self-assurance.

One might compare the relation between the traditional active imagination and the newer guided imagination to the relation between free association, which is a form of monologue, and the more centered association method that Jung introduced that takes place as a dialogue between analyst and analysand. As in the latter technique, the participation of the therapist in guided imagination makes it a dyadic rather than a solitary process. This participation can be a help or an interference (as has sometimes been suggested in criticism of guided imagination), as can the interaction with the therapist in any other analytic dyadic process. It is vital that therapists respect the freedom and autonomy of the unconscious process and offer their reactions as no more than that, namely, as suggestions of possibilities. Whether or not they are relevant and helpful will have to be determined by the reaction of the unconscious, by the response of the images and the patient's "Aha" feeling, by that dim sense of affirmation that tells us, regardless of rational doubts, that an interpretation has "hit home."

The guidance and constellating power of the therapist's participation help to bring about a depth and intensity of experience, as well as a sense of relative security, that makes it possible to touch in full consciousness levels of experience that hitherto have been accessible only with the help of LSD or hypnosis. These include memories of early childhood, of birth, of prenatal sensations and possibly even of past lives, analogous to the cases that have been described by Grof and by Netherton and Schiffrin. Such material is often helpful in deepening the process of reductive working through.

Whether experiences such as the dancing gypsy girl lynched by the peasant mob represent fantasy or actual past-life memories may be theoretically interesting, but clinically such speculation is of secondary importance. It reminds one of the quandary Freud found himself in regarding the incest fantasies he encountered in his early work. Whether actual memory or "just" fantasy, their importance lies primarily in their allegoric and symbolic significance for the here-and-now. It lies in the psychological dynamic they bring home in "as if" terms. It is a remarkable fact, however, which may give us food for thought, that such "historic" fantasies carry an emotional impact incomparably greater than that of the bona fide memories of actual and verifiable childhood events and traumata.

GROUP THERAPY

Jungian analysis in a group setting is a particular therapeutic modality. It is not a shortcut in therapy. In fact, it does not shorten therapy at all. On the contrary, it amplifies it, and, by offering an additional dimension of exploration, may even lengthen analysis. It is not mass analysis nor merely a means of adapting to collectivity. It is individual analysis in a particular pluralistic setting that offers a quasi-laboratory situation in which certain direct experiences become possible to a degree not found in individual analysis. These include reality-testing of one's self-validations and insights, relationship encounters, the experience of the group archetype, and the realization and resolution of the group transference.

The group also provides a place in which to work through experientially one's sibling and family problems and rivalries, the competition and power complexes, the sense of not being accepted, supported, protected, or sheltered, and problems with trust and openness. All this can occur in a setting that is questioning, confrontative, and yet also supportive. The group thus offers a chance not only of seeing oneself as one is seen by others, from various perspectives and different value systems, but also of experimenting with new ways of relating in a fashion not usually encouraged or allowed in our present culture. In this function, the group experience is of vastly greater help, by and large, to the introverted personality than to the extravert, who tends to take such relationship problems more easily in stride.

Group and individual analysis are complementary; they constellate complementary archetypes and transferences. And, like every archetype, the group archetype is bipolar. When consciously confronted, experienced, and related to, it can be potentially constructive and an individuation factor. It can also be a source of obsessional complexes, mob psychology, "churchy" dogmatism, and group bias. Owing to their complementing each other, group and individual analysis will give the best results when they can support each other and be carried out simultaneously. In my own experience, starting with individual analysis prepares the analysands by giving them an understanding of the dynamics of the unconscious. The relative ego-strengthening effect of this understanding enables them to utilize more adequately the irrational impact of the group encounter and to hold their own in the face of the potentially inundating and ego-threatening impact of the group archetype. Sometimes, however, the opposite procedure may be called for. Starting with group therapy or with both modalities simultaneously may be indicated, especially in people with strong intellectual defenses or impersonal attitudes, or when the individual analysis would bog down from the very beginning in the face of a resistance that purports to "understand" everything and enjoys symbol hunting as a defense against feeling.

One of the most important characteristics of the analytic experience in a group, as compared to individual sessions, is precisely its greater concreteness and ability to add reality impact. In individual therapy, it all too often happens that after a problem or dream has been worked on and "understood," the analysands have difficulty translating their insights realistically into their own life situations. Typical life situations do not necessarily occur in the consulting room. Too often the analysands carefully avoid confronting raw reality even with the one person they supposedly trust. They would rather talk about reality as yesterday's happenings, as they perceive it, coloring it with their own biases. Hence the importance of emotionally working through whatever comes up in the hour. Frequently, however, the therapist, too, prefers a certain professional distance and shies away from an emotional involvement of too personal a nature. The relationship problems and complexes of analysands are talked *about,* but they are actually outside of the analytic encounter. Moreover, the "talking" can only be dealt with in terms of the analysands' viewpoints, as they report situations. Their reports are distorted, however, by the very complexes that made analysis necessary. Dreams, it is true, point up the nature of the distortion, but this in itself does not solve the problem of where and how to connect the understanding of their message with the actuality of emotions and behavior.

In the group, on the other hand, complexes are not merely discussed as yesterday's events; they are apt to occur right there and are discussed during the course of mutual interaction. One's peers can and do provoke complexes, and also manage to catch a greater variety of affect reactions, than the single person of the analyst. Group members have no compunctions about professional distance, and they have a greater need for direct interaction than the therapist has. In a group, one is more likely to be caught *in flagrante,* creating one's own difficulty. It is much harder to get away with rationalizations and evasions in a group. But there is also greater sympathy in the group for the shadow side, inasmuch as everyone present has his or her own unacceptable aspect. It is an astounding and profoundly moving experience when one's nonprofessional peers not only fail to react with disgust and condemnation at terrible, shameful secrets, but confess similar difficulties. Even the therapist is discovered to have a shadow, to be "human," and that can bring great relief and rejoicing! For in groups, it is not only possible, but inevitable and desirable, for therapists to allow their shadows to participate. This may be one of the reasons, incidentally, why some therapists fear working with groups.

The possible shock effects of a therapist's shadow expressions, which might prove shattering to oversensitive analysands, can be diluted if the therapist directs these reactions at a stronger group member and lets this interaction be witnessed by the other analysands. Some of the most stubborn transference and countertransference illusions can thereby be alleviated. Timing is crucial, of course; so is individual follow-up in analysis. The reality dimension thus gained helps both transference assimilation and self-acceptance.

Yet the most unexpected potential of analysis in a group, which to my knowledge has not been mentioned heretofore, is its peculiarly individualizing capacity. This capacity is quite at variance with the bias so frequently expressed among Jungians with little or no practical experience of the group. The law of opposites is at work under the influence of the group archetype, no less than in other archetypal situations; the group's helpful potential becomes manifest when its dangerous ''mob'' aspect is consciously confronted.

There is frequently a common theme or motif in the problems, dreams, or other unconscious material brought into a session by several group members. By some the theme is centered upon, by others it is circumambulated. But all of the coinciding is quite unintentional, as though constellated a priori by the unconscious. The themes and reactions tend to elucidate and complement each other. At the same time, there is a marked difference in the way the process occurs for each individual. It is as though a common theme or themes were constellated by a superordinated center that at the same time assigns individual aspects or qualities of that shared theme to the various members of the group. They thereby experience a shared human commonness and the necessity of individual differences. Whereas in its first phase, the group experience offers a protective, sheltering dimension, which in extreme form may degenerate into a regressive herd attitude, later it also constellates the opposite dimension, a vector toward individual structuring. The result can be a greater immunity against identifying with, or yielding to, collective or authority pressures, while still being able and ready to take one's place as an individual, cooperating member of that collective. This relationship to the extraverted, collective dimension of human functioning is one of the weaker areas in Jungian therapy and has often been dismissed as unimportant. The position usually taken is that the outer functioning in society will follow when the inner picture is clear. This is no doubt true, but only up to a point. In the group we have a working model in action, a place where abstractions can become concretized and understood affectively. The inner picture may also need a social structure in order to reach clarification.

The intent of this presentation is to reemphasize the importance of the very concern for wholeness and holistic living that was Jung's most central concern throughout his lifetime. In dealing concretely with soul-body, preverbal-verbal, imaginal-conceptual, dyadic-group, transference-countertransference, daily life-archetypal realm polarities, we enrich and complement, rather than replace, the time-tested verbal methods of analysis. We remember Jung's dictum that, regardless of theoretical assumptions, no one single method can cover all contingencies, and that in the multiplicity of individual encounters and problems, the ''right'' approach is that one that proves most helpful.

REFERENCES

Finley, P. 1975. Dialogue drawing: an image evoking communication between analyst and analysand. *Art Psychotherapy* 2:87–99.

Freud, S. 1949. *An outline of psychoanalysis*. New York: Norton.

Gebser, J. 1949. *Ursprung und Gegenwart*. Stuttgart: Deutsche Verlags Anstalt.

Grof, S. 1975. *Realms of the human unconscious*. New York: Viking.

Jung, C. G. 1960. *The structure and dynamics of the psyche. Collected works*, vol. 8. Princeton: Princeton University Press.

Mindell, A. 1982. *Dreambody*. Los Angeles: Sigo Press.

Netherton, M., and Schiffrin, N. 1978. *Past lives therapy*. New York: William Morrow.

Whitmont, E. 1978. *The symbolic quest*. Princeton: Princeton University Press.

THE
EDUCATION
AND
TRAINING
OF
JUNGIAN
ANALYSTS

PART FIVE

[18]

THE EDUCATION OF THE ANALYST
June Singer

THE education of the analyst extends beyond anything that can be verbally expressed. It is, more than anything, an experience of transformation in which one comes to know one's own soul and to befriend it. In the process, it is hoped that one may become what one really is. People enter analytic training programs with a variety of conscious motives, some from a genuine desire to help, some from an insatiable curiosity about matters of depth in the human psyche. What they learn is not necessarily what they came seeking. The education of an analyst is extremely personal. The psyche is divested of its protective coverings and laid bare in the personal analysis, which is also the training analysis. In this process one feels terribly alone, even though the analyst is standing by. The analyst-to-be, like anyone else, enters the dark nights with their dreams and the terrors of the day, alone and unprotected. But the difference in those who submit themselves to be trained as analysts is that they know they must go through the process no matter what, and neither turn back nor be led astray. They must confront all the difficulties and demons that beset the path, if they are to become the' ones who will support others in their soul-journeys.

The education of the analyst provides the context for the analytic journey. The education, as distinguished from the personal-training analysis, is meant to give the neophyte a map of the territory that must be traversed.

June Singer, Ph.D., is Director of the Transpersonal Center and member of the core faculty of the California Institute of Transpersonal Psychology in Menlo Park. She is a founding member of the Inter-Regional Society of Jungian Analysts and of the Chicago Society of Jungian Analysts. She graduated from the C. G. Jung Institute of Zurich and received her Ph.D. from Northwestern University. Dr. Singer is the author of *Boundaries of the Soul: The Practice of Jung's Psychology* (1972), *Androgyny: Toward a New Theory of Sexuality* (1976), and *The Unholy Bible: A Psychological Interpretation of William Blake* (1970); with Mary Loomis, she is the coauthor of the Singer-Loomis Inventory of Personality.

Yet this is hardly possible, for the territory is unknown, unconscious. So any map must be based on the stories told by people who have been there, on myths and legends, on the "scientific" statements made by those whose way is quantifying and measuring, and on the faith expressed by those who follow the way of religion. The stories are many and each points out some of the possible routes, along with the milestones along the way, the dangerous curves, and the vista points. More than providing the maps, the education of the analyst is a teaching of how to read the maps and a help toward recognizing the limitations of the maps.

These maps are not given to everyone. To read them requires a particular gift for psychological exploration—just as not everyone can scale high mountains or descend into the depths of the sea. Also needed are the gifts of tenacity and perseverance, and last, but certainly not least, the capacity for self-reflection and self-examination. The education of a Jungian analyst, therefore, is more than preparation for a profession, and more than a drawing out of innate potentials. It includes a lengthy training process during which it is hoped that analysts-in-training will become more psychologically sensitive to their own complexes, reactions, fantasies, and motives, and to those of others, and that they will learn, too, to use themselves as analytic instruments in the service of their analysands' individuation processes. The didactic elements in the training program serve the goal of increasing this basic capacity of using oneself as an instrument.* The education of the analyst also creates a basic "Jungian attitude" or set of attitudes in the analyst.

The process of becoming a "Jungian" may present problems. Those who apply for Jungian training are often nonconformists, persons seeking individual fulfillment as well as membership in a psychological community. Issues of authority versus individuation surface in the educational process. We are reminded that Jung himself was ambivalent about the Jung Institute precisely because of the paradox inherent in trying to "train" and "individuate" at the same time. An important task of the training program is encouraging the trainee to try to hold these opposites in creative tension and not to let them split into irreconcilable antagonists.* If there is anything that characterizes the analytic process, it is the continuing differentiation and reconciliation of psychic elements within the human soul. This process cannot be accomplished by the application of mere techniques, yet there are certain competencies that can be developed in training that will enhance the ability of the individual to deal with the infinite variety of

---

*M. Stein 1981: personal communication.

material that emerges in the course of analysis. What the analyst does is not as important as who the analyst is, for ultimately the quality of the work depends on the character of those who take part in it. Jung raised the questions "Who is applying the technical skill? In *whose* hands does this power lie?" (1958, p. 534).

WHO IS THE ANALYST?

Personal qualities are of prime importance in the candidate for training. Unless they are present, no amount of general or professional education or clinical training will prepare the person for the life commitment that analytic work demands. Analysis is nothing if it is not a way of life. Those who look upon this education as a way to secure yet another credential to attest to therapeutic competence will discover that the cost is far too high in terms of the reward. One heeds the analytic calling because one must. All other reasons for applying for training are secondary. Yet as with any vocation, not all who are called can finally be chosen. An admissions committee looks for certain essentials in selecting training candidates. From my experience of sitting on numerous such committees, I believe I have a general sense of what is being sought in those who apply. The criteria indicated below will surely omit some important considerations and include others upon which not all analysts will agree, but they will give some impression of what is being looked for.

There is, inevitably, the sense of vocation. Something in the person of the applicant is profoundly attracted to the mystery of the human soul, is fascinated by its complexity, and finds nothing more entrancing than to explore its labyrinthine paths. Some people feel this as a quiet sureness; for others it has the strength of a demonic possession; and still others waver between the two extremes. With some it takes the form of confidence in the purposive nature of the psyche, as though the psyche had its own pattern for development. This confidence allows some people to enter into training not altogether certain that it is the right course, but sure enough that the pattern for their lives will be revealed in the course of time and in the analytic process. Meanwhile it may be necessary to tolerate a sense of disconnected drifting, of being lost, and of waiting for the mist to clear.

A sense of the symbolic dimension of life is sought in considering the applicant for training. When a person possesses the capacity to recognize that phenomena and events occur at many levels of meaning, symbolic thinking connects these levels and adds infinite richness to experience.

Words and images are seen not only in their surface dimensions, but also as keys unlocking buried emotions, lost memories, potentials for the future, unsuspected dangers, reasons for hope, and causes for fear. Since it is well known that in analysis the presenting problem is not necessarily the real problem that brings a person to seek help, analysts must see through the symbolic presentation into what lies behind it. They must also possess the ability to communicate through the use of symbols, as in utilizing the mythic image to reflect an archetypal configuration in which a person may be caught.

The person who undertakes the education required of an analyst needs to be committed to a process of personal growth through reading and study, through continuing self-observation, and through ongoing analytic work with the unconscious materials that emerge. Dreams, fantasies, and creative productions are to be viewed analytically. But growth is not always apparent and, like a seed in wintertime, the would-be analyst often has to endure long periods of inaction, of aimless waiting, of confusion and "de-integration," of being "in the dark." It is necessary at times to just "let it be," and analysts who cannot tolerate this in themselves cannot be expected to supply the patient husbandry that the analysand will require when the time comes. Part of analysis, as in any growth process, requires that one just wait, and the waiting sometimes may end with death rather than with a new birth. In this case, death must be accepted as a part of the life cycle and hence a part of the analytic life.

Personal integrity is a prerequisite for the wholeness toward which an analytic candidate will be guided. This wholeness is, of course, a goal that is rarely achieved; nevertheless, the commitment to seek it is crucial. This means that one is to take personal responsibility for what one says and does, not to seek excuses or scapegoats. Conventionality is not important, for the person of integrity is not necessarily bound by collective standards. When these standards conflict with the person's own sense of the meaning and purpose of life, the person must have the courage to take the unpopular stand. Integrity means a willingness to be critical of oneself, not only of others, to admit error, to be honest in communications, and to be open to change. It is important not to need to be liked, for the analyst must perform tasks when confronting the darker elements in the soul of the other that will incur the anger and fear of the analysand. Preparation for this work requires confronting one's own shadow—not only in the analytic process but also in interaction with one's peers in the group learning situation.

Flexible self-presentation makes it possible for the analyst-in-training to bring out different aspects of personality to meet the changing conditions that constantly occur. Often applicants come into a training program with a set view of how to meet "the collective." Through the process of education, the candidates can be led away from the too-rigid personae, and given the nurturant setting in which the real human being is encouraged to show through. The candidates learn not to dispense altogether with personae, which would leave them exposed and vulnerable. The appropriate persona is flexible and can be set aside when it is not needed—and this develops in the course of training when things go well (cf. Jung 1928, pp. 154–60; Singer 1972, pp. 187–202).

A genuine liking for people as individuals will help the candidate learn to foster the development of the analysand within the context of that person's innate capacities. Analysts-in-training will learn to accept others just as they are, knowing that unless a person feels accepted in the present moment there can be little movement or change. The candidate comes to transformation through self-acceptance. Caring for the other rests on caring for oneself. Analysts who neglect their own welfare inevitably end up resenting their analysands for imposing upon them, or else exploiting their analysands as the analysts feel they themselves have been exploited. By cultivating their own paths, analysts show their analysands that all people must survive the ordeals of birth and death individually, and take care of themselves. Only then can persons be sufficiently independent to enter into relationships of mutual interdependence, where Eros furthers but does not inhibit or compromise individual development.

To be able to love without possessiveness, and to be able to hate without the need for retribution, are abilities that must be developed if one is to be able to deal with issues of transference and countertransference. Deep feelings, whether positive or negative, need to be fully experienced when they are present, but also to be looked at from a reflective perspective. This capacity for reflecting upon experience is bone and sinew of the analytic process. Without it, the work comes to naught.

There is a quality of psychic energy that the candidate for analytic training must possess. It is difficult to describe, but easily recognized. It empowers the individual to proceed through the training program and to accept the many tasks that are presented in the process. One senses: here is a person who can take strain and stress, suffer disappointment and loss, endure embarrassment and shame, yet not crumble. Analysands will feel that this is a person they can trust, one to whom they can be fully open, who will not take advantage of them, and who will not break down under the burdens that they may bring. Analysands want to feel that the analyst can stand the dirt and stench of another's life and not turn away. An analyst is needed who is not only wise and compassionate, but also singed, scorched, and seasoned: someone who understands how tough life really is.

The person who undertakes education for the analytic profession must already have undergone education for life. This means the acquisition of wisdom and maturity, which can only come from experience. And how should this have been obtained? William Blake perhaps expressed it better than any training committee ever could:

What is the price of Experience?
  do men buy it for a song?
Or wisdom for a dance in the street?
  No, it is bought with the price
Of all that a man hath, his wife, his children.
Wisdom is sold in the desolate market
  where none come to buy,
And in the wither'd field where the farmer
  plows for bread in vain.

What Do Analysts Do?

The education of analysts must prepare them for the work that is to be done. Thus it is important to summarize the various aspects of the process that will constitute their lifework. Many Jungian analysts have reflected on this question and each sees it through the eyes of personal experience. There are, however, some common themes.

Analysts act as companions to the soul on its path, which is called "the way of individuation" (Jung 1968, pp. 275–384; Jaffé, pp. 76–94; Jacobi 1942, 1967; Neumann 1954; Harding; Singer 1972; Whitmont). Analysts are called upon to join a person at a particular place on the path, usually a place where the way has gotten rocky or where the person is stuck in despair, or when something mysterious has happened that the person cannot understand. Analysands bring their entire history to this moment, and analysts bring an understanding of the territory of the unconscious psyche—being in possession of maps and having done previous exploration. The two kinds of knowledge are joined and the two participants proceed in the mutual endeavor of analysis.

Analysts recognize a responsibility to the entire organism, of which the psyche is only one expression. Analysts need to be aware of the limits of their own competence, and to know when and to whom to refer analysands for needed help that lies outside the scope of the analyst's own knowledge, training, or experience.

Analysts recognize developmental patterns and are able to distinguish growth patterns from pathology, as well as, sometimes, to see the growth potential in "pathology."

Analysts recognize typological differences among individuals (Jung 1921), and are sufficiently flexible themselves to adapt their ways of working to their analysands' particular cognitive styles or ways of knowing (Loomis and Singer). They are cooperative with their analysands' more effective attitude and functions at the same time that they help to make the less well-developed ones more conscious (cf. chapter by Quenk and Quenk, above).

Analysts help to bring into sharp focus the unique individuality of the person with whom they work. To do this it is necessary that analysts be able to distinguish individual patterns from collective patterns, and genuine expressions of the psyche from conditioned responses to the environment.

Analysts ally themselves with the creative potential of the analysands, by helping analysands to recognize and remove, circumvent, or transcend obstacles to creative functioning.

Analysts seek to provide a solid reference point in ordinary reality, an ego standpoint to support the analysand's own ego when that support is needed for the confrontation with the unconscious. This reference point is especially needed when the psyche is out of balance, as, for example, in neurosis or psychosis, or under the influence of ordinary or extraordinary life stresses or intensely numinous experiences.

Analysts look for the purposive dynamism of the psyche in each analysand, which manifests in unconscious myths, conscious desires, and motivations. Analysts help their analysands in working toward the transformations that enable individuals to become what they are meant to be. This is done by observing the individuation process as it reveals itself, by setting goals in keeping with the psyche's own statements about itself, and by continuing the dialectic between the ego and the unconscious—with all the latter's various components (Jung 1928).

Analysts note carefully the transference-countertransference aspects of the analytical encounter, making these as conscious as possible both to themselves and to their analysands at the appropriate times (Jung 1946). Analysts recognize the need for consulting another analyst when more detached objectivity is needed, and they willingly do so. They also refer the analysand to another analyst or appropriate resource when it appears that they are not able to work productively with the person.

TRAINING INSTITUTES

The first institutes for the training of Jungian analysts in the United States were established in New York, San Francisco, and Los Angeles. In recognition of the need for the training of analysts between the coasts, the

Inter-Regional Society of Jungian Analysts began a training program in 1973. More recently, new training centers have been formed by groups of Jungian analysts who are members of the International Association for Analytical Psychology. The International Association determines when a group of analysts is sufficiently well established and experienced to begin training, and then authorizes the group to do so. Diplomates of these training institutes become eligible for membership in the International Association for Analytical Psychology, as well as in their own local societies.

The training institutes differ in their entrance requirements. None prepares its candidates to meet professional certification requirements that may be mandated by various states; this work remains the responsibility of the individual candidate. The institutes are, in this sense, postprofessional, deepening and widening the earlier professional training of the candidate. Every Jung Institute requires of its candidates some personal analysis before they apply. The amount of time spent in personal analysis varies upward from a minimum of 100 hours. All of the institutes require some clinical experience before completion of their training program, but only one (Northern California) requires completion of and certification in a clinical specialty before an applicant may enter the program. Even here, exceptions may be made in certain cases.

Some institutes provide clinical experience in their own clinics for analysts-in-training during all or part of their training period. Others maintain facilities where trainees may do supervised analytic work as part of their analytic training. Still others expect their trainees to do their clinical work under supervision outside the analytic institution, either before entering or during their analytic training.

Not all persons who enter Jungian training programs come with backgrounds in psychiatry or psychology. Most institutes seek persons with a variety of backgrounds, including, but not limited to, the so-called helping professions (medicine, psychiatry, psychology, pastoral counseling, psychiatric nursing, psychiatric social work). Persons from fields such as education, literature and the arts, communications, religion, anthropology— any field in which there is concern with human development and/or healing—are also considered. These persons may be asked to augment their backgrounds with courses in general psychotherapy and related areas, outside of the Jungian training program.

CONTENT OF THE TRAINING PROGRAM

The content of the training program centers around three major areas: the personal and training analysis, didactic material in the area of analytical psychology, and the practice of analysis.

The first of these is discussed in detail elsewhere in this book (see chapter by Kirsch, below). Essentially, the training analysis *is* a personal analysis, and the analyst-in-training enters into the analytic process for its own sake and for the self-understanding that may come of it, regardless of any implications it may have for the progression through the training program. In most institutes, the personal analyst has little or nothing to say about the trainee's movement in the program. Thus the analysis is allowed to be the heart of the training experience—for it is here that the analyst-to-be goes through the difficulties and trials necessitated by the transformative process. The personal training analysis follows its own path. There is no requirement that the trainee try to observe it from the outside or to conform it to any theory. Theoretical considerations may enter into the analytic process along the way, or the experience itself may provide its own teaching.

The didactic material that forms the corpus of Jung's work is presented to the analyst-in-training in various ways, depending on the style of the particular institute. Certain basic areas are covered by all of them, however. These include a study of how Jung conceptualizes the structure and dynamics of the psyche, his work on psychic energy and its transformations, his experimental research, and the work on psychological types. In addition, a rich overlay of archetypal materials, with their endless images and symbols, provides a collective background against which to view the personal unconscious and conscious position that emerges from the psyche of the individual in analysis.

Analysts-in-training learn to observe and to trust their own observations as they discover how Jung's empirical studies at the Burghölzli Klinik and in his private practice led him to develop a cohesive theory of how the psyche is formed and how it functions (1928, pp. 154–60; 1960a). Of particular interest in this context is the work described in *Experimental Researches* (1973), during the course of which Jung discovered, independently of Freud, the psychological mechanism of repression. The trainee will be learning much about the history of analytical psychology by studying these early researches of Jung, as well as recognizing their influences in contemporary forensic psychology and other areas in which the intricate relationships of psychological and physiological factors are experienced and treated.

From these early beginnings, Jung recorded his observations and explored their implications, then expounded upon his ideas in lectures and articles. His range of interests is astounding, and the richness and variety of his allusions testify to his diligent pursuit of any information that could possibly relate to the theme he might be pursuing. His *Collected Works* include his major theoretical works as well as his findings as he pursued the imagery arising from archetypal bases. These works are studied by the analytic candidate in such a way as to develop a sense of the Jungian approach to the care of souls. A competent grasp of the basic material prepares the trainee for working with the vagaries of the psyche as they appear in analytic work.

The study of the history of analytical psychology leads to an appreciation of the sources of Jung's ideas and to a sense of the social and intellectual milieu out of which his thinking developed. We can see Jung's work in part as an expression of a particular *Zeitgeist*. On the other hand, this history provides an excellent viewpoint from which to study some of the newer psychotherapies. Students of Jung are often surprised to recognize in the "new" therapies adaptations of ideas enunciated by Jung. These appear in the Gestalt psychology of Fritz Perls, in the existential therapy of Rollo May, and in the psychosynthesis of Roberto Assagioli, to name only a few. Furthermore, the current enriching of contemporary American psychology by the assimilation of psychological and religious influences from the Orient was anticipated by Jung in many of his works. He introduced, and wrote the foreword for, the English version of Wilhelm's translation of the *I Ching or Book of Changes* (Jung 1958, pp. 589–608); he also wrote commentaries on the *Tibetan Book of the Great Liberation* (1958, pp. 475–508), the *Tibetan Book of the Dead* (1958, pp. 509–26), the Taoist *Secret of the Golden Flower* (Wilhelm and Jung), and other works on yoga, Zen, and Eastern meditation (Jung 1958).

What Jung had to say about the appropriation of foreign philosophies and foreign psychologies may well prove a helpful way of approaching these ideas when they emerge in the newer therapies. Jung's recognition that much of what passes for "oriental wisdom" in the West is superficial and misleading is an important lesson for the analytic candidate to learn.

Jung never meant his writings to be regarded as sacred dogma. He often expressed his awareness that theories are workable for a while, then pass away or are superseded. I believe he intended that his writings would inspire those who came after him to revise and reinterpret his ideas in ways consonant with other times, other situations. People who are training to become analysts are encouraged to see how Jung's ideas apply to their own times, their own analytic cases, and, of course, themselves. While Jungian analysts tend to be individual in their approach, it is necessary that Jung's original perspectives and thoughts be mastered in the process of finding one's own way.

An understanding of psychological typology (Jung 1921) is an important part of the education of the analyst. Jung's theory of psychological types, along with the considerable work that has been done with typology by Jungians more recently (Gray, Wheelwright, and Wheelwright; Loomis and Singer), has been viewed as useful for recognizing individual differences in cognitive styles, and for the analysis of these differences and their effects on human interactions. Typology is far from being a mere categorization of types. It is a guide to the movements of psychic energy along certain paths, depending on the particularities of individual personalities. Trainees not only need to understand typology as a system, but must also have a grasp of their own personal typology and the ways in which it may interact with that of an analysand. Jung showed that typological differences between people often accounted for their seeing the world through different eyes.

Evidence for the genetic or innate character of typology has recently been collected in studies of identical twins reared apart (Farber). Research indicates that these persons with identical genetic make-up develop in surprisingly similar ways, not only in physical appearance, size, weight, body movements, and posture, but also in personal mannerisms, choice of vocation and mates, and hobbies—all clearly "psychological" choices—regardless of the differences in their environments. This is not to say that environment has no influence on the development of personality or typology, but it strongly suggests that Jung was correct in his view of the psyche as patterned from the beginning (1934; 1936; 1960a, pp. 237–97). If we knew the cognitive style of individuals, we could provide them with the kind of experience that would further, rather than obstruct, their natural tendencies. Hence an important part of the education of analysts includes learning to distinguish and measure typology, and to work with the issues that typology presents (Jung 1921; von Franz and Hillman; Gray, Wheelwright, and Wheelwright; Myers-Briggs; Loomis and Singer).

Dreams often reveal psychological processes not otherwise accessible to consciousness. Understanding the content of dreams, therefore, is essential for gaining a more complete view of the whole person—the conscious and unconscious aspects and their dynamic interaction. Jung formulated a theory of dream interpretation (1934; 1936; 1960a, pp. 237–97) that involves reflection on the affective content of the dream, personal associations to dream contents, and amplification from collective material, including archetypal material. Candidates will have been working on their own dreams since the beginning of their analyses. This work continues and intensifies throughout the period of training, as they learn about the nature of the dreaming process and become competent at applying this knowledge, along with a good amount of intuition, to their own dreams and to those of others (Hall; Mattoon).

The individuation process is a lifelong journey and the analyst is at first a pilgrim, then a guide; but analysts never stop being pilgrims either. For it is well known that people cannot lead others further than they have traveled themselves. As Jung described the process, it has two aspects and neither can be separated from the other. One is the development of the individual as a person unique upon this earth; the other is the knowledge that we of this human race are all members of a cosmic family, sharing many common patterns of growth and development, and that we exist in a state of continuing interaction with "the collective," which is our human, social, political, and physical environment. So we participate in the individuation process, sometimes as the archetypal heroes striving after distant goals, and sometimes waiting quietly as grains of sand upon the seashore. We are both actors and the ones being acted upon; one iota and the stuff of the universe. To find a creative balance between the personal and the collective aspects of the psyche and the world is the essence of individuation. To become an analyst means to take on the struggle against the lack of that balance, when it is observed, and to hold firm to the conviction that one can work toward its restoration.

Jung provided maps to indicate where and how the tendencies toward fragmentation of the psyche may be met. One of these is his theory of complexes. The feeling-toned complex, Jung wrote, "is the *image* of a certain psychic situation which is strongly accented emotionally and is, moreover, incompatible with the habitual attitude of consciousness. This image has a powerful inner coherence, it has its own wholeness . . ." (1960a, p. 96). Complexes are often discovered in the dissonances of the individuation process, when emotional reactions have become more and more intensely charged. Jung wrote, "Everyone knows nowadays that people 'have complexes.' What is not so well known, though far more important theoretically, is that complexes can *have* us" (ibid.). How to recognize complexes and how to follow their course through the personal history and associations is something the trainee learns through observation of self and others. The interpretation of complex behavior can be as fruitful as the interpretation of dreams. Both are overt manifestations of unconscious processes. Often, they lead us to the archetypal nucleus.

Archetypal images are the raw material of the psyche. Forged in the unknowable depths of the archetypal world, they come to light in the form of myths and fables, folklore and fairy tales, as well as in many religions, ancient and modern. Archetypal material is of fundamental importance in the education of the Jungian analyst, for it stages the psyche's own drama in the psyche's own symbolic language. Although it often speaks in very personal ways, as in dreams and fantasies, its origins go back to the common experiences of family, clan, tribe, nation, and race.

Mythology and folklore belong to particular regional and national groups. They express the characteristic flavor of their own areas; they dramatize the particularity of a people. Folklore deals primarily with the little people—human beings and familiar spirits of human and smaller-than-human dimension, fairies and elves, dwarfs and gnomes, who inhabit a certain region. Often folklore tells of how things came to pass in the "old days." Filled with humor and mystery, these tales are all very human; even the animals have human qualities, as, for example, those in Aesop's fables and the tales of Br'er Rabbit.

Mythologies resemble folk tales, except that their figures have been expanded to superhuman proportions; yet myths do not lose their human qualities, either. Gods and goddesses of every land receive the projections of the people they are believed to rule over. Larger than life, they reflect the beliefs, ideals, and fears of those people through whom they speak. Myths are the productions of the collective unconscious. Connected as they are to unrecognized but powerful motivating forces in the human psyche, they provide rich resources for the analyst's understanding of the substructure of dreams and fantasies. Naturally no analyst can make a comprehensive study of all mythologies, but each is expected to study at least one or two mythological systems or motifs in considerable depth. In addition, an overview of mythological patterns is necessary, and here the works of such specialists as Campbell, Hamilton, Eliade, and Singer (1976) are helpful.

The interpretation of fairy tales in the light of Jung's psychology has been presented with great clarity by von Franz in her several works on the subject (1970, 1970a, 1972). The fairy tale is important because it is impersonal. Its characters exhibit very little individuality; on the contrary, they represent psychic principles common to all. The old king who struggles to maintain his position while the young king strives to overthrow him, the simple son with purity of heart who manages to outdo his wiser and craftier brothers, the young virgin who is awakened from her innocence by a daring and tricky lover, the wicked witch who is outwitted by children and cooked to a crisp in her own oven—all of these speak of fantasies common to all of humankind, regardless of where they live or whether they are rich or poor. When analysands recount a preferred fairy tale, they tell the analyst much about themselves—and, conversely, the use of fairy tales by the analyst can help to show analysands how universal and archetypal the condition is that they regard as terribly and uniquely their own.

The study of religion is part of the education of the Jungian analyst. Foremost in Jung's psychology is the acknowledgment of the archetype of the Self as the principle of wholeness, the universal principle. The Self functions as an ordering principle, but since it is all-inclusive, it also embodies the opposite of order—that is, chaos. The Self, as overarching archetypal power, is eternally engaged in making order out of chaos, only to watch the order dissolve again into chaos, and to reorder it, again and again. Religions, whatever else they may be, are expressions of the human need to relate to the ultimate source of being, the guiding power of the universe. Jung was interested in the psychology of religion rather than in the justification of any particular religious system. He regarded religious experience as the experience of the *numinosum*, "that is, a dynamic agency or effect not caused by an arbitrary effect of will" (1958, p. 7). Jung dealt with the psychological aspects of religions—that is, the ideas and images that human beings ascribe to the *numinosum*. These may be among the most ennobling contents of the psyche, or the most fearsome. To understand something about the workings of these images and ideas in the psyche, it is important that the education of analysts include some study of at least one religion other than the one into which they were born. Through comparing different religions, psychological parallels and differences may be understood as different ways of interpreting phenomena that are archetypal and coherent in nature no matter where they appear. In this way, the analyst is able to see not only how the psyche is shaped by a belief system, but how the psyche itself may give shape and form to a belief system.

All archetypal contents of the unconscious are expressed in symbolic form. The analyst therefore needs to be familiar with the use and interpretation of symbols. Indeed, Whitmont has called the analytic work "the symbolic quest." His book by that name deals with symbolic structures in analytic work. Because the unconscious is preverbal in nature, it manifests mostly in images. These emerge into consciousness and can sometimes be traced back to their archetypal sources. To make these connections it is necessary to think analogically. Such thinking is not always easy today, especially for scientifically trained people. It is the language of the right hemisphere of the brain; it tends to be holistic and diffuse and often primitive or childlike. The various methods of analytical psychology, such as attention to dreams and fantasies or active imagination, help to develop the capacities needed in working with archetypal material.

The third major area of concentration in the education of the Jungian analyst is the practice of analysis. While this is a focus of the entire training program, it is generally concentrated in the latter half of training, after the basic principles have been reasonably well assimilated by the candidate and a facility for working with archetypal material has been developed. Now the analyst-in-training is actually doing analytic work with analysands, and it is different from any clinical experience in a non-Jungian setting that may have preceded it.

The study of psychopathology in the Jungian training programs includes the use of the general categories of mental disorders as employed across therapeutic styles and theoretical orientations (American Psychological Association), but it is by no means limited by these categories. Psychopathology is redefined in terms of the symbolic content of its manifestations. It is understood as part of the psyche's own language, formulated to point to areas of disturbance, frustration, difficulty, misunderstanding, and, sometimes, unrecognized physical illness. Jung never forgot the interrelationship of psyche and body. "Since psyche and matter are contained in one and the same world," he wrote, "and moreover are in continuous contact with one another and ultimately rest on irrepresentable transcendental factors, it is not only possible but fairly probable, even, that psyche and matter are two different aspects of the same thing" (1960a, p. 215). Thus Jung's view of psychopathology is in agreement with contemporary research on the biological basis of psychological functioning. Jung adds to this a consideration of the meaning of symptoms as communication from unconscious sources that apparently cannot make themselves heard in other ways. This particular way of viewing psychopathology is part of the education of the Jungian analyst (Perry 1953, 1971; Jung 1960b, 1968; Jacobi 1967).

Developmental psychology and psychopathology need to be understood in terms of each other. We never know what is "normal" unless we know what is "abnormal," or, taken the other way around, we never know what is abnormal unless we know what is normal. Jung was particularly interested in what constituted normal development throughout life, and his work on the second half of life (1960a) has influenced some contemporary research, as acknowledged by Levinson in his *Seasons of a Man's Life*. Analysts wishing to concentrate on psychotherapy or analysis with children will turn to Jung (1954b) and to some of his followers who emphasized work with children. Among these should be mentioned Fordham and the London analysts, Neumann (1973) and the Jerusalem child analysts, and Sullwold, working in the United States (cf. chapter by Sullwold, above). In addition, Kalff has introduced her sandplay therapy as a technique for working with children and adults. The Hilde Kirsch Children's Clinic in Los Angeles is a setting for the training of Jungian analysts especially interested in working with children.

Analysts-in-training who are doing analytical work under supervision are working with dreams of their analysands, as well as continuing to work on their own dreams (Hall). The dream work may be carried forward with the technique of active imagination (Jung 1960a, pp. 67–91). Analysts, in their education, are also prepared to use other means of eliciting unconscious material from their analysands, especially nonverbal means. Opportunities may be provided to learn to utilize various expressive techniques, including painting, sculpture, music, dance, and, more recently, film and videotape.

Picture interpretation is one way of learning to use material elicited in active imagination. It is particularly revealing of psychic material, since so many components go into the making of a picture, from the choice of a medium to the uses of color and shape, to the general dynamism of the production. All of these elements express the psychic state of the creator of the picture. Interpretation of other unconscious material may yield rich ore as well. One may well ask, how do we know when such material is truly from the unconscious? The analyst-in-training is challenged to learn how to differentiate what is natural and spontaneous from what is artificial and contrived.

Problems of transference and countertransference are dealt with as part of the analyst's education in two ways: in the individual supervision of cases (called ''control work''), and in case colloquia where the candidates bring their cases for discussion with colleagues and with a training analyst. Until recently, the supervising analyst has in most cases relied on the candidate to report on the salient features of the case. Voice recordings have not been encouraged because of concern for the privacy of the analysand. More recently, however, questions have been raised about the relative value of privacy versus greater accuracy in portraying and assessing the work that is being done. Inasmuch as the case is being discussed anyway (with the analysand's informed consent, of course), the privilege of privacy is already waived—or perhaps it would be better to say that it is extended to the confines of the professional supervisory group. Some argue, therefore, that it is more effective and useful to present the situation in analysis as it actually occurred, rather than to deal with the analyst's imperfect recollection of the events. Some training programs are using videotaped recordings of analytic sessions for the purpose of improving the quality of the supervisory work. Those analysands who are willing to participate in this kind of process, and there are many, are able to get direct feedback on their process in a way that would not otherwise be possible. One can only wonder what Jung would have said, had he been faced with the possibility of reflecting upon the analytic process in this new way. (Perhaps he might have liked the presentation of the analysts' uncovered shadows.)

In summary, vast amounts of material can contribute to the education of analysts. But ultimately the most important tool that analysts have is their own way of being-in-the-world. Everything else can be added if the essential tool is in good condition, finely honed, and ready for the analytic work. Candidates must be educated in the intrapsychic area, through the personal and training analysis. They must be educated in the interpersonal area, through experiencing relationships with analysands in clinical and analytic practice. And they must also be educated in the transpersonal area, by gaining familiarity with archetypal material, shared in common by all people in all places, and with its widely varied manifestations in image and symbol.

REFERENCES

American Psychiatric Association. 1980. *Diagnostic and statistical manual of mental disorders*. 3rd ed. Washington, D.C.: APA.

Blake, W. 1957. Vala or the four zoas. In *Complete writings of William Blake with all the variant readings,* ed. G. Keynes, p. 290. New York: Random House.

Campbell, J. 1949. *The hero with a thousand faces*. New York: Pantheon.

———. 1959. *The masks of God: primitive mythology*. New York: Viking.

———. 1962. *The masks of God: Oriental mythology*. New York: Viking.

———. 1964. *The masks of God: Occidental mythology*. New York: Viking.

———. 1972. *Myths to live by*. New York: Viking.

———. 1974. *The mythic image*. Princeton: Princeton University Press.

Eliade, M. 1958. *Rites and symbols of initiation*. New York: Harper & Row.

———. 1960. *Myths, dreams and mysteries*. New York: Harper & Row.

———. 1961. *Images and symbols*. London: Harvill Press.

Farber, S. 1980. *Identical twins reared apart: a reanalysis*. New York: Basic Books.

Fordham, M. 1969. *Children as individuals*. New York: Putnam.

Franz, M.-L. von. 1970. *An introduction to the interpretation of fairy tales*. Zurich: Spring Publications.

———. 1970a. *The problem of the puer aeternis*. Zurich: Spring Publications.

———. 1972. *Problems of the feminine in fairy tales*. Zurich: Spring Publications.

———. 1973. *Interpretation of fairy tales*. Zurich: Spring Publications.

Franz, M.-L. von, and Hillman, J. 1971. *Lectures on Jung's typology*. Zurich: Spring Publications.

Gray, H.; Wheelwright, J. B.; and Wheelwright, J. 1964. *Jungian type survey*. (The Gray-Wheelwrights' test.) San Francisco: Society of Jungian Analysts.

Hall, J. 1977. *Clinical uses of dreams: Jungian interpretations and enactments*. New York: Grune and Stratton.

Hamilton, E. 1940. *Mythology*. Boston: Little, Brown.

Harding, M. E. 1965. *The 'I' and the 'not-I', a study in the development of consciousness*. New York: Random House.

Jacobi, J. 1942. *The psychology of C. G. Jung*. New Haven: Yale University Press.

———. 1967. *The way of individuation*. New York: Harcourt, Brace & World.

Jaffé, A. 1971. *The myth of meaning*. New York: Putnam.

Jung, C. G. 1911–12/1952. *Symbols of transformation. Collected works,* vol. 5. Princeton: Princeton University Press, 1956.

_____. 1921. *Psychological types. Collected works,* vol. 6. Princeton: Princeton University Press, 1971.

_____. 1928. The relations between the ego and the unconscious. In *Collected works,* vol. 7, pp. 119–239. 2d ed. Princeton: Princeton University Press, 1966.

_____. 1934. The practical use of dream analysis. In *Collected works,* vol. 16, pp. 139–61. New York: Pantheon, 1954.

_____. 1934/1950. A study in the process of individuation. In *Collected works,* vol. 9, part 1, pp. 290–354. 2d ed. Princeton: Princeton University Press, 1968.

_____. 1936. Individual dream symbolism in relation to alchemy. In *Collected works,* vol. 12, pp. 41–223. Princeton: Princeton University Press, 1953.

_____. 1939. Conscious, unconscious, and individuation. In *Collected works,* vol. 9, part 1, pp. 275–89. 2d ed. Princeton: Princeton University Press, 1968.

_____. 1946. Psychology of the transference. In *Collected works,* vol. 16, pp. 163–321. New York: Pantheon, 1954.

_____. 1950. Concerning mandala symbolism. In *Collected works,* vol. 9, part 1, pp. 355–84. 2d ed. Princeton: Princeton University Press, 1968.

_____. 1954a. *The practice of psychotherapy. Collected works,* vol. 16. New York: Pantheon.

_____. 1954b. *The development of personality. Collected works,* vol. 17. Princeton: Princeton University Press.

_____. 1958. *Psychology and religion: west and east. Collected works,* vol. 11. Princeton: Princeton University Press.

_____. 1960a. *The structure and dynamics of the psyche. Collected works,* vol. 8. New York: Pantheon.

_____. 1960b. *The psychogenesis of mental disease. Collected works,* vol. 3. Princeton: Princeton University Press.

_____. 1968. *The archetypes and the collective unconscious. Collected works,* vol. 9, part 1. 2d ed. Princeton: Princeton University Press.

_____. 1973. *Experimental researches. Collected works,* vol. 2. Princeton: Princeton University Press.

Kalff, D. 1971. *Sandplay: mirror of a child's psyche.* San Francisco: Browser Press.

Levinson, D. J. 1978. *The seasons of a man's life.* New York: Random House.

Loomis, M., and Singer, J. 1980. Testing the bipolar assumption in Jung's typology. *Journal of Analytical Psychology* 25/3:351–56.

Mattoon, M. A. 1978. *Applied dream analysis: a Jungian approach.* Washington, D.C.: Winston.

Myers, I. B. 1962. *The Myers-Briggs type indicator.* Palo Alto: Consulting Psychologists Press.

Neumann, E. 1954. *The origins and history of consciousness.* New York: Pantheon.

_____. 1973. *The child.* New York: Putnam.

Perry, J. W. 1953. *The self in psychotic process.* Berkeley: University of California Press.

_____. 1971. *Reconstitutive process in the psychopathology of the self.* San Francisco: C. G. Jung Institute of San Francisco. Reprinted from *Annals of the New York Academy of Science* 96/3:853–76.

————. 1974. *The far side of madness*. Englewood Cliffs, N.J.: Prentice-Hall.

Singer, J. 1972. *Boundaries of the soul*. New York: Doubleday.

————. 1976. *Androgyny: toward a new theory of sexuality*. New York: Anchor Press/Doubleday.

Whitmont, E. C. 1969. *The symbolic quest*. New York: Putnam.

Wilhelm, R., and Jung, C. G. 1931. *The secret of the golden flower: a Chinese book of life*. New York: Harcourt, Brace & World, 1962.

Wilhelm, R. 1950. *The I Ching or book of changes*. Princeton: Princeton University Press, 1976.

ANALYSIS IN TRAINING

Thomas B. Kirsch

JUNG was the first to recognize the necessity of the training analysis, and did so while still a Freudian psychoanalyst. Freud acknowledged the importance of this contribution when he stated: "I count it one of the valuable services of the Zurich school of analysis that they have emphasized this necessity and laid it down as a requisition that anyone who wishes to practice analysis of others should first submit to be analyzed himself by a competent person" (p. 116). One year later Jung wrote the following: "Just as we demand from a surgeon besides his technical knowledge, a skilled hand, courage, presence of mind, so we must expect from an analyst a very serious and thorough psychoanalytic training of his own personality before we are willing to entrust a patient to him" (1913, p. 200).

Thus, the importance of the personal analysis for analytic training was central for both Freud and Jung from the beginning, before the First World War. In Jung's later writings, he continued to place the personal analysis of the analyst at the core of training, all the while recognizing its limitations: ". . . anybody who intends to practice psychotherapy should first submit to a 'training analysis,' yet even the best preparation will not suffice

---

Thomas Kirsch, M.D., is currently Second Vice-President of the International Association of Analytical Psychology and Clinical Assistant Professor of Psychiatry, Stanford University Medical Center. He teaches at the C. G. Jung Institute of San Francisco and maintains a private practice in Palo Alto. A graduate of Reed College, of Yale Medical School, of a psychiatric residency at Stanford University Medical Center, and of the C. G. Jung Institute of San Francisco, he is past president of the Society of Jungian Analysts of Northern California. He is the coeditor of the Jungian section in the *International Encyclopedia of Psychiatry, Psychoanalysis, Psychology, and Neurology* (1977). His published papers include "The Relationship of REM to Analytical Psychology" (1968), "A Clinical Case of Puer Identification" (1975), "The Practice of Multiple Analyses" (1976), and "Dreams and Psychological Type" (1981).

to teach him everything about the unconscious. . . . A complete 'empty-ing' of the unconscious is out of the question if only because its creative powers are continually producing new formations'' (1946, p. 177).

In the field of analytical psychology, before the formation of training institutes, the way to become a Jungian analyst was through personal analysis with Jung and/or one of his assistants. An analysand usually attended seminars, but a letter from Jung saying that the individual was ready to practice analysis was virtually the only way to become a Jungian analyst prior to World War II. The first generation of analysts came to analysis primarily out of personal need, with little conscious thought of becoming analysts themselves. The early analysts were quite literally transformed into practitioners of their profession through their analyses. I would refer to this transformative aspect of the analysis itself as the individual calling to become an analyst.

Today's potential candidates have some notion of what it means to be an analyst before starting training. Usually they have been exposed to the analytic community through seminars, public lectures, workshops, and so on. They also have some idea, however filled with projections, of what the professional analytic community is like, and they want to become part of it. It is my hope that the individual sense of vocation will not get lost through all the group exposure to Jungian psychology. This chapter focuses on the personal analysis of the candidates as a feature of their training. A discussion of the academic requirements, goals, and selection of candidates may be found elsewhere in this book (cf. chapter by Singer, above).

Prior to entering training, the potential candidate's analysis is not very different from other therapeutic analyses. When the analysand applies for candidacy, some changes may take place. What role does the analyst play in either encouraging or discouraging the analysand to apply for training? The task is somewhat easier when the analyst in good conscience can encourage the applicant. The analyst is an ally of the candidate, which has implications for the transference-countertransference. Sometimes an apprentice model is constellated, in which the candidate becomes a ''disciple'' of the particular analyst.

However, what happens if the analyst does not believe the analysand would make a good candidate? Should the analyst be the one to tell such analysands that they are not suitable to become analysts? When I definitely feel that the person would not be suitable, I have discouraged the analysand from making application for training. Often, the analysand then realizes that being an analyst is not what he or she really wanted. In one case, the analysand knew that he preferred dealing with psychotic patients using medication and short-term treatment. He realized on his own that he did not need or desire analytic training after having initially thought it would be good for him. When I do not have a sense of whether particular analysands should be candidates or not, I encourage them to apply and let an admissions committee evaluate them. Naturally, in all cases, the decision is up to an admissions committee, but here we are examining the role of the personal analysts vis-à-vis their analysands in the application process.

Jung's statements, quoted above, emphasize the importance of the personal analysis of anyone wishing to become an analyst, but they do not elucidate what a training analysis is, nor is a distinction made between it and other types of therapeutic analysis. In the English-language Jungian literature, only one article specifically addresses itself to the subject of training analysis (Fordham 1971). I define the training analysis as the analysis of a person who is in analysis for the express purpose of becoming an analyst. The person generally has entered analysis because of some form of suffering, but at some point has decided to become an analyst.

In addition to training analysis, the institutionalization of training has produced "training analysts," which implies that some analysts are better suited to train candidates than others. This adds another goal to the increasingly hierarchical structure of training, which I strongly resist. Ideally, analysands or candidates should be free to choose their own analysts based upon the personal characteristics of the analysts, rather than being limited to certain preselected analysts, no matter how qualified they may be. The argument usually given against this freedom is that trainees will pick analysts who have the same defenses they have and thus will not work out their neurotic conflicts. However, I have noticed that in reality candidates usually work with more than one analyst during their training and that this problem takes care of itself. It is also true that, in analytic societies, candidates tend to gravitate toward a select few analysts who see most of the candidates in a given institute, but the choice seems to be based upon the psychological authority of these analysts rather than on their political power.

Unfortunately, I have seen among my psychoanalytic confreres the situation in which a potential candidate had to change analysts because the first was not a training analyst. In one case this change was extremely disruptive. For these reasons, San Francisco, Boston, Chicago, San Diego, and the Inter-Regional Society do not have the category "training analyst." In New York and Los Angeles, one applies to a local certifying board to become a training analyst, although the importance of the training analyst category has diminished. One may point out that this step presents another hurdle for young analysts to pass in the pursuit of their own psychological authority.

Regardless of whether the analyst is called a training analyst or not, the process of being in analysis is considered central in all Jungian training programs throughout the world. What this central process of analysis involves varies tremendously from place to place. An enormous range of differences exists in such matters as the frequency of sessions, the couch versus the chair, the relative importance of transference, and the reductive versus the prospective aspects of analysis.

The length of time of an analysis varies, of course, from individual to individual. Most training institutes demand a certain minimum time in analysis before application for training. The usual minimum number of analytic hours required to complete training is approximately 300, and the maximum is unlimited. Some institutes require candidates to be in analysis throughout their training. From my point of view, this requirement is an intrusion of institutional demands into the individual analytic relationship. Analysis cannot be legislated. If the person no longer requires analysis, he or she should be free to terminate it. For instance, some potential candidates have had long and deep analysis prior to their training, and it makes no sense to require further analysis. On the other hand, in order to circumvent a resistance to analysis, the termination of an analysis during training should be with the approval of the personal analyst. As the analytical process is a lifelong pursuit, analysts themselves will go back for further analytical work from time to time, often many years after they have finished formal training.

Once training has begun, what role does the analyst play in promoting the ongoing candidacy? This seems to be one of the issues in which there is a real divergence of opinion. Hillman stated the central position of the Zurich Institute, which was the pioneer Jungian training center:

> At the Institute in Zurich this clear separation of training and analysis does not exist. Training analysts, seminar leaders, supervisors, examiners and curatorium have been and still are, more or less, the same people. This reflects the attitude that training *is* analysis and so cannot be separated from it. . . . But the analyst gives in writing to his colleagues his opinion as to the suitability of the candidate. This opinion remains crucial. If the analyst is opposed to the candidate's further candidacy, the curatorium will not override his judgment . . . the primary training takes place in the dialectic between candidate and analyst. (1962*a*, p. 8)

Today, however, the personal analyst no longer has such a central role in the evaluation of the candidate in Zurich.*

The earlier Zurich approach to training analysis would seem to overburden the already difficult work of analysis. If the training analyst has the

---

*A. Guggenbühl-Craig 1980: personal communication.

power to pass judgment upon the candidate, it seems that candidates might withhold information, fearing that it could be used against them. I am told that this has been a problem in psychoanalytic training. Many newly qualified psychoanalysts will choose to have a posttraining analysis, just so they can have an unpressured therapeutic experience no longer under the scrutiny of an analyst who is also an authority figure.

For this reason, the San Francisco Jung Institute has taken a position opposite to the Zurich one. In San Francisco there has been a complete separation of the training analysis from the rest of the training process. The training analyst is not allowed to give any specific information to the certifying committee. The philosophy behind this is that no matter what happens, the candidate is entitled to an honest analysis. The task of evaluating the candidate then falls to a certifying body that collects information from seminar leaders and supervisors, and then has personal interviews with the candidate. Not having the input from the personal analyst of course makes the task of the certifying body more difficult. Since the training analyst does not have an evaluative function in training, there is a freer exchange and a more genuine analytic experience. Other American Jungian training centers are divided in their approach to this issue. In the beginning, New York and Los Angeles followed Zurich's example, but these societies moved to a position closer to San Francisco's as they began to find the training analysis overburdened, for the reasons mentioned.

Even if the analyst does not have an official voice in the evaluation of a candidate, the analysis of a candidate is different in many ways from an ordinary therapeutic analysis. Persons who enter analysis with the idea of becoming analysts have a definite aim or goal beyond their own therapy. They wish the analysis to serve the end of their becoming Jungian analysts, an ego aim. Such an aim is clearly different from that of a person who comes with no specific goal other than to get treatment for suffering. In the nontraining analysis, there is an end point at which the analyst and analysand separate, whereas in the training analysis there is continued connection in their shared professional world.

As a result, in the latter situation, unconscious material is constantly being influenced by the pressure of ego demands, such as seeking inclusion in the professional community and the training program. These ego demands may be quite similar to those of the analyst him- or herself. Some candidates' dreams may deal only with personal unconscious material, for example, and they may be concerned that their dreams do not include enough archetypal material, so that they doubt their "Jungian identity." Or, candidates may strongly resist having their material interpreted in a Jungian way. This resistance may manifest itself in several ways. In order not to conform to collective expectations, they may not want to discuss dreams or other unconscious material. If they do present dreams, they may be resistant to their symbolic meaning, again, so as not to conform to the Jungian expectation.

What we are dealing with in the analysis is the archetype of initiation (Henderson; Micklem). The analysand as initiate may have a resistance to emerging unconscious material. The analyst as one of the elders may be seen as the wise old man or priestess in the initiation process. Furthermore, the analyst is a member of the group into which the candidate as initiate wishes to enter. There is a necessary ordeal and trial of strength that the analysand as initiate must undergo in order for the *rite de passage* to take place. It is an archetypal situation in which both the personal analyst and training institute carry the projection of the group of elders or *communitas*.

Von Franz has discussed the vocation of analyst in the context of shamanic initiation. In primitive tribes, the shamanic initiate is the one who experiences a breakthrough of the collective unconscious and is able to master the experience, a feat many sick persons cannot achieve. Von Franz emphasizes that such an experience must occur in the analysis of a candidate as part of the training of an effective analyst. It is the perspective of initiation that differentiates the Jungian point of view from that of some Freudians. The latter often see resistance as the product of the parental introjects, now projected onto the analyst and institute. For the Jungian, resistance includes not only those aspects, but also the dimension of shamanic initiation, which evokes the collective unconscious.

The persona of the analyst, as well as the sum of collective, conscious attitudes that have developed toward the profession of analyst and toward the local training institute, may become critical concerns to a candidate. In every training analysis, questions about a particular seminar leader, or about how a certain person ever became a Jungian analyst, will surface. The candidate may question why the institute has a particular rule or a certain seminar topic and not another. These issues tend to surface within the training analysis, but in my experience they are often used as a form of resistance to some more personal issue for the candidate. Although one must deal with their content, it is important for the training analyst to recognize the resistance aspect and deal with it. My own tendency, out of my concerns about the training program, has often been to focus on the content issue and miss the resistance aspect.

An even deeper issue involves the tension between individuality and collective responsibility. Training analysts must, on the one hand, honor the individual expression of the analysand; on the other, they have a collective responsibility to the Jungian community to affirm certain values basic to the practice of Jungian analysis. Candidates are in a profound search for their own identity and will often question the value of becoming analysts. Eventually, the candidate may cause the training analyst to question the value of analysis itself, with thoughts like these: after all, analysis can help so few people; some are not helped at all; analysis itself may be just a luxury. Training analysts must be secure enough in what they are doing to stand the "test."

More agonizing still for the candidate is that he or she, like all analysands, must eventually realize that there is no point of security outside the analysis itself to provide a sense of direction, and whether a personal transformation will take place cannot be known beforehand. All training institutes say that they honor the individuality of the candidate, but at the same time they emphasize certain collective values and attitudes about the meaning and importance of Jungian analysis. Beyond that, the different institutes embody certain styles and emphasize certain aspects of the analytic process, and individual candidates have to come to terms with these nuances of emphasis with which they may not agree.

A further complexity in most training analyses is the fact that the majority of candidates are in the first half of life when they enter training, even though Jungian psychology often emphasizes changes that take place in the second half of life. The usual training analysis therefore deals with problems of the first half of life. This creates a tension between the candidate's own experience in analysis and certain aspects of Jungian theory and practice. Moreover, the institute wonders how the candidates will develop as they mature. What one hopes for in the training analysis is that enough genuine dialogue with the unconscious will be experienced to foster a commitment to continue the process. This does not always turn out to be the case.

A large issue in any analytic relationship is the transference-countertransference (cf. chapters by Ulanov and Machtiger, above). In a training analysis, this phenomenon has many complications not found in a normal therapeutic analysis. Training analysts are potential models for the candidates. In their analyses, the candidates experience how their particular analysts work. If there is a transference, the trainees will introject the analyst and will begin their own practices by using a similar style. After all, who else's work has the candidate experienced at such close hand and so intimately?

The problem is, though, that the training analyst's style may not work for a particular candidate. Differences in psychological type (cf. chapter by Quenk and Quenk, above) and personality may mean that the analyst's style cannot be imitated by the trainee. If, for instance, an introverted thinking type is attracted to an analyst whose typology is extraverted feeling, the experience may be good for the trainee but will serve poorly as a model for the trainee's own analytic practice. The training analysts, on the other hand, may have considerable difficulty in letting the candidates go in directions that are not consonant with their own dominant attitudes and orientations. It is hard for an analyst to judge whether differing attitudes derive from differing psychological typologies or from unresolved transference-countertransference issues.

Fordham has offered insight regarding the irreducible pathological core in any transference-countertransference situation. All analytical psychologists value the individuating factor, but the shadow of human nature surfaces when candidates' individuation contradicts their mentors' most sacred tenets. How the training analyst and candidate handle this complex impasse is extremely important, not only for them but for their institute. If genuine differences are not accepted, they can lead to splits within the training institute after the candidate becomes a qualified analyst. The training analyst therefore is both a role model and a person against whom the trainee can react.

Extraanalytic contacts, rivalry with "sibling" patients, and decisions about self-disclosure by the analyst are factors that frequently generate psychological issues in training analysis. Although the relationship to the analyst is initially restricted to the consulting room, this situation often changes when analysands become candidates. It is then probable that they will have contact with their training analysts outside of analytic hours. Candidates' experiences of seeing their analysts as seminar leaders are often initially fraught with difficulty. One typical reaction of the candidates is to feel exposed. They feel as if their analyses are continuing right there in the middle of the seminar, and that everyone else is noticing how vulnerable they are at that moment. They may feel as if their analysts are talking directly to them, while in reality they are addressing the whole group. It may also be hard for training analysts to talk to their patients in a seminar.

Sibling rivalry is often constellated in candidates who "share" their analysts with other students in a seminar. In the analytic hour, the trainees have their analysts all to themselves and do not have to share them with anyone else. They may have the fantasy of being the analyst's only patient, or perhaps at least the most special one. In the seminar situation, on the contrary, trainees see others who are in analysis with their analysts, and fantasies of rejection or of being less preferred than others may surface under these conditions. Furthermore, how others in the seminar react to their analyst becomes an issue. The candidates want their analyst to look good in the eyes of their peers. Thus transference issues are carried out of the consulting room into other areas.

These transference factors, inherent in training situations, allow more contact between analyst and analysand than in the therapeutic analysis. As a result, the candidates tend to have more real knowledge about their analysts than ordinary analysands, and consequently there are more "hooks" on which to hang projections. Now there occurs a temptation for the training analysts to be more self-disclosing in an effort to validate their patients' perceptions and to welcome them prematurely as colleagues. A certain collegial attitude can enter into the analysis, which affects the transference-countertransference relationship. Perhaps this temptation also reflects the isolation and loneliness of being an analyst and the desire to share one's experiences. Casualness may mask deep unresolved problems.

Personally, I find that my increasing sensitivity to the problems posed by the collegial attitude have led me to become less self-revealing with potential candidates than with other analysands. I have become more conscious of the transference-countertransference level of interpretations with candidates. I want to minimize the differences between the training analysis and the therapeutic one, and especially to lessen the effects of the extraanalytic contacts.

Such emphasis on the transference and countertransference causes the analysis to last longer, as more of the unconscious material is interpreted in the light of the transference. In London, where one group of Jungians practice analysis using the couch, a regressive transference is fostered, and hence more infantile psychopathology is evoked. This can be extremely helpful to trainees, for they can experience certain psychopathological states in themselves within the transference relationship rather than merely learning about them from textbooks and clinical exposure. Fordham specifically encourages providing conditions wherein psychopathological states can be experienced in the training analysis (1971). His thesis depends upon the concept that psychopathology is the result of quantitative, not qualitative, variations in the experience of unconscious conflicts. The hope is that the candidates can experience and transform their own areas of psychopathology so that they can help patients who have similar problems. Equally, the trainees can learn what parts of themselves are healthy and therefore do not require analytic work.

In line with the view that the training analysis should involve the maximum exposure of a candidate's complexes, it has been suggested that training should include more than one analyst/analysis, as they would most likely emphasize different aspects of the analysand's psyche according to the dialectic that is established. On the other side, it has been argued that this dilutes the intensity of analysis. Proponents of both points of view expressed themselves in a "Symposium on Training" published in the *Journal of Analytical Psychology* (Fordham 1962, p. 26; Plaut, p. 98; Hillman 1962*b*, p. 20). A review of the debate was published by this author (Kirsch).

Multiple analyses—that is, the practice of seeing more than one analyst during training—has long been an accepted pattern among analytical psychologists. It dates back to Jung, who would often refer his analysands to a female analyst at the same time that he was seeing them himself (Wheelwright). Multiple analysis has two main advantages. First, if carried out with a male and a female, it may activate the inner polarity between male and female components of the psyche. A man's anima will be experienced differently with a woman analyst than through the anima of a male analyst. Obviously, sexual fantasies will also be experienced differently depending upon the sex of the analyst.

In addition, seeing a second analyst gives the analysand an opportunity to experience a therapist of a different psychological type. As mentioned earlier, an analysand often starts analysis with someone who is of a similar psychological type. Later on in the analysis, it may be important to have the experience of someone of an opposite type and function. Theoretically, therefore, a wider consciousness of anima and animus and of one's psychological type will be experienced through multiple analyses. Since a future analyst should have the widest possible analytic experience, multiple analyses are to be recommended.

On the negative side, there is the justified concern that this practice leads to transference "leakage." Any analysand may transfer to another analyst when an unconscious block develops with the first analyst. Analyst and analysand may, with the best of intentions, work out a transfer or an addition of another analyst without realizing that they are avoiding a resistance.

An extremely important issue is how a candidate's analysis ends. The ending of analysis is a difficult and complex subject in its own right. There is the realization that an analyst needs to continue self-analysis forever, and that there will be periods of returning to one's original analyst or going to another one. Fordham has described the termination of a training analysis as depending upon

(1) the patient's history, embodying past separations, capacity to feel grief and gratitude, (2) the overt transference situation, (3) clues obtained from one or a series of dreams, (4) the reality situation of the new Society member, (5) an

assessment of the ongoing individuation processes at work in the unconscious, and last but not least, (6) the training analyst's countertransference. (1971, p. 181)

Fordham emphasizes the idea that an unresolvable pathological nexus exists between any patient and his or her analyst, consisting of the irreducible part of certain complexes in both analyst and patient that cannot be analyzed away. Fordham discusses this idea in terms of the actual traumatic situations that have occurred for both analyst and analysand that can be elucidated but cannot necessarily be changed, and also to the theme of the "wounded healer" referred to by Jung. Fordham maintains that the full elucidation of this pathological nexus is frequently overlooked through insufficient concentration on reconstructing infancy and childhood. I would point out that the elucidation of the pathological nexus is critical in a training analysis, since it may be the only way to help potential analysts recognize the damaged parts of themselves that are likely to come up in their future professional work.

Fordham states that a candidate's pathology is all too often displaced into the local society in which the future analyst will practice. The local professional society carries the projection of family, and members react to it as such. Concurrent with this are all the individual transferences and countertransferences among the individual members that can never be fully resolved. These mutual projections flare up from time to time, and it is hoped that they can be contained within the local society. But, when that unresolved pathological nexus is too large, it becomes a nidus out of which hatch tendencies for one or more members to split off from the larger whole. This situation is what makes the basically rewarding job of being a training analyst disillusioning as well.

This chapter has encompassed a delicate subject. Personal analysis of the candidate is the core experience in the making of a Jungian analyst. It needs to be the most individual and subjective of experiences, and yet, at the same time, candidates are evaluated by a certifying body that probes their relationship to their own psyches. How does one protect the individuality and creativity of the analytic process, and yet at the same time produce analysts? The very mention of the word "training" constellates complexes, because analysts all have their own strong ideas of what the analysis of a candidate should be. In this chapter it may seem that I have focused too much on some of the problems of the analysand in training. If that is the case, it has been because of my desire to retain as much of the core analytic experience as possible for the candidate, and not have it diluted by the institutional demands of training.

REFERENCES

Edinger, E. 1961. Comment. *Journal of Analytical Psychology* 6/2:116–17.

Fordham, M. 1962. Reply. *Journal of Analytical Psychology* 7/1:24–26.

———. 1971. Reflections on training analysis. In *The analytic process,* ed. J. B. Wheelwright, pp. 172–84. New York: Putnam.

———. 1976. Comment. *Contemporary Psychoanalysis* 12:168–73.

Franz, M.-L. von. Beruf und Berufung. In *Die Behandlung in der Analytischen Psychologie,* ed. U. Eschenbach, pp. 14–32. Fellbach: Verlag Adolf Bonz.

Freud, S. 1912. Recommendations to physicians on the psychoanalytic method of treatment. In *Standard edition,* vol. 12, pp. 109–20. London: Hogarth, 1958.

Guggenbühl-Craig, A. 1971. *Power in the helping professions.* New York: Spring Publications.

Henderson, J. L. 1967. *Thresholds of initiation.* Middletown, Conn.: Wesleyan University Press.

Hillman, J. 1962*a.* Training and the C. G. Jung Institute, Zurich. *Journal of Analytical Psychology* 7/1:3–18.

———. 1962*b.* A note on multiple analysis and emotional climate at training institutes. *Journal of Analytical Psychology* 7/1:20–22.

Jung, C. G. 1913. The theory of psychoanalysis. In *Collected works,* vol. 4, pp. 85–226. New York: Pantheon, 1961.

———. 1946. Psychology of the transference. In *Collected works,* vol. 16, pp. 163–321. New York: Pantheon, 1954.

Kirsch, T. 1976. The practice of multiple analyses in analytical psychology. *Contemporary Psychoanalysis* 12:159–67.

Marshak, M. O. 1964. The significance of the patient in the training of analysts. *Journal of Analytical Psychology* 9/1:80–83.

Micklem, N. 1980. Paper read at *Symposium on Training,* Eighth International Congress of Analytical Psychology, 5 September 1980, San Francisco.

Newton, K. 1961. Personal reflections on training. *Journal of Analytical Psychology* 6/2:103–6.

Plaut, A. 1961. A dynamic outline of the training situation. *Journal of Analytical Psychology* 6/2:98–102.

Spiegelman, M. J. 1980. The image of the Jungian analyst. *Spring* 1980:101–16.

Stone, H. 1964. Reflections of an ex-trainee on his training. *Journal of Analytical Psychology* 9/1:75–79.

Wheelwright, J. B. 1975. A personal view of Jung. *Psychological Perspectives* 6:64–73.

GLOSSARY

Amplification   C. G. JUNG: " . . . first of all, when you handle a dream you say, 'I do not understand a word of that dream.' I always welcome that feeling of incompetence because then I know I shall put some good work into my attempt to understand the dream. What I do is this. I adopt the method of the philologist, which is far from being free association, and apply a logical principle which is called *amplification*. It is simply that of seeking the parallels. For instance, in the case of a very rare word which you have never come across before, you try to find parallel text passages, parallel applications perhaps, where that word also occurs, and then you try to put the formula you have established from the knowledge of other texts into the new text. If you make a new text a readable whole, you say, 'Now we can read it.' That is how we learned to read hieroglyphics and cuneiform inscriptions and that is how we can read dreams." (*Collected Works*, vol. 18, p. 83)

Anima and Animus   C. G. JUNG: "The collective unconscious as a whole presents itself to a man in feminine form. To a woman it appears in masculine form, and then I call it the *animus*. I chose the term anima because it has always been used for that very same psychological fact. The anima [and animus—ed.] as a personification of the collective unconscious occurs in dreams over and over again. I have made long statistics about the anima figure in dreams. In this way one establishes these figures empirically." (*Collected Works*, vol. 18, p. 89)

"The animus and the anima should function as a bridge, or a door, leading to the images of the collective unconscious, as the persona should be a sort of bridge to the world." (*The Visions Seminars*, Book 1, p. 116)

"The projection-making factor is the anima, or rather the unconscious as represented by the anima [or animus—ed.]. Whenever she appears, in dreams, visions, and fantasies, she takes on personified form, thus demonstrating that the factor she embodies possesses all the outstanding characteristics of a feminine being. She is not an invention of the conscious, but a spontaneous product of the unconscious." (*Collected Works*, vol. 9, part 2, pp. 13–14)

Archetypes and the Collective Unconscious   Jung observed characteristic images that come from the deep layers of the psyche that he called the collective unconscious. He wrote: "These collective patterns [and images—ed.] I have called *archetypes*, using an expression of St. Augustine's. An archetype means a *typos* [imprint], a definite grouping of archaic character containing, in form as well as in meaning, *mythological motifs*. . . ." (*Collected Works*, vol. 18, pp. 37–38)

The products of the unconscious that cross the threshold of consciousness can be divided into two classes: images from the personal unconscious and images from the collective unconscious. The former, as far as we can determine, are made up of personal elements. As human beings, we all share a pattern of the deep unconscious that is peculiar to humanity in general; this is the *collective unconscious.*

C. G. JUNG: "In spite or perhaps because of its affinity with instinct, the archetype represents the authentic element of spirit, but a spirit which is not to be identified with the human intellect, since it is the latter's *spiritus rector.* The essential content of all mythologies and all religions and all isms is archetypal." (*Collected Works,* vol. 8, p. 206)

"The dynamism of instinct is lodged as it were in the infra-red part of the spectrum, whereas the *instinctual image* [archetypal image—ed.] lies in the ultra-violet part. If we remember our colour symbolism, then, as I have said, red is not such a bad match for instinct. . . . Violet is a compound of blue and red, although in the spectrum it is a colour in its own right. Now, it is, as it happens, rather more than just an edifying thought if we feel bound to emphasize that the *archetype* is more accurately characterized by violet, for, as well as being an image in its own right, it is at the same time a *dynamism* [Jung's italics] which makes itself felt in the numinosity and fascinating power of the *archetypal image.* The realization and assimilation of instinct never take place at the red end, i.e., by absorption into the instinctual sphere, but only through integration of the image which signifies and at the same time evokes the instinct. . . ." (Ibid., p. 211; italics added)

"Archetypes were, and still are, living psychic forces that demand to be taken seriously, and they have a strange way of making sure of their effect. Always they were the bringers of protection and salvation, and their violation has as its consequence the 'perils of the soul' known to us from the psychology of primitives. Moreover, they are the unfailing causes of neurotic and even psychotic disorders. . . ." (*Collected Works,* vol. 9, part 1, pp. 156–57)

Complex   C. G. JUNG: "Complexes are autonomous groups of [feeling-toned—ed.] associations that have a tendency to move by themselves, to live their own life apart from our intentions. . . . We like to believe in our will-power, and in our energy and in what we can do; but when it comes to a real show-down we find that we can do it only to a certain extent, because we are hampered by those little devils the complexes." (*Collected Works,* vol. 18, p. 73)

"The complexes, then, are partial or fragmentary personalities. When we speak of the *ego-complex,* we naturally assume that it has a consciousness because the relationship of the various contents to the centre, in other words to the *ego,* is called consciousness. But we also have a grouping of contents about a centre, a sort of nucleus, in other complexes." (Ibid., p. 73; italics added)

The complex "has a sort of body, a certain amount of its own physiology. It can upset the stomach. It upsets the breathing, it disturbs the heart—in short, it behaves like a partial personality. For instance, when you want to say or do something and unfortunately a complex interferes with this intention, then you say or do something different from what you intended. You are simply interrupted, and your best intention gets upset by the complex, exactly as if you had been interfered with by a human being or by circumstances from outside." (Ibid., p. 72)

Jung's research using the word-association test (see *Collected Works,* vol. 2) led him to the discovery of complexes. At one time, Jung's psychology was called "Complex Psychology."

Ego   C. G. JUNG: "We understand the ego as the complex factor to which all conscious contents are related. It forms, as it were, the centre of the field of consciousness; and, in so far as this comprises the empirical personality, the ego is the subject of all personal acts of consciousness. . . .

"The ego, as a specific content of consciousness, is not a simple or elementary factor but a complex one which, as such, cannot be described exhaustively. Experience shows that it rests on two seemingly different bases: the *somatic* and the *psychic* [Jung's italics]. . . .

"Clearly, then, the *personality as a total phenomenon* does not coincide with the ego, that is, with the conscious personality, but forms an entity that has to be distinguished from the ego. . . .

"I have suggested calling the total personality which, though present, cannot be fully known, the *self*. The ego is, by definition, subordinate to the self and is related to it like a part to the whole." (*Collected Works,* vol. 9, part 2, pp. 3–5; italics added. See also *Complex* and *Self*)

Extraversion   C. G. JUNG: "Extraversion is an outward-turning of *libido*. . . . I use this concept to denote a manifest relation of subject to object. Everyone in the extraverted state thinks, feels, and acts in relation to the object, and moreover in a direct and clearly observable fashion, so that no doubt can remain about his positive dependence on the object." (*Collected Works,* vol. 6, p. 427)

Extraverted persons, therefore, find their orientation in the objective, outer environment, through other people and institutions.

Individuation   C. G. JUNG: "In general, it is the process by which individual beings are formed and differentiated, in particular, it is the development of the psychological *individual* . . . as being distinct from the general, collective psychology. Individuation, therefore, is a process of differentiation . . . having for its goal the development of the individual personality." (*Collected Works,* vol. 6, p. 448)

"Under no circumstances can individuation be the sole aim of psychological education. Before it can be taken as a goal, the educational aim of adaptation to the necessary minimum of collective norms must first be attained. If a plant is to unfold its specific nature to the full, it must first be able to grow in the soil in which it is planted." (Ibid., p. 449)

"But again and again I note that the individuation process is confused with the coming of the ego into consciousness and that the ego is in consequence identified with the self, which naturally produces a hopeless conceptual muddle. Individuation is then nothing but ego-centredness and autoeroticism. But the self comprises infinitely more than a mere ego. . . . It is as much one's self, and all other selves, as the ego. Individuation does not shut one out from the world, but gathers the world to oneself." (*Collected Works,* vol. 8, p. 226)

"The centring process, is, in my experience, the never-to-be-surpassed climax of the whole development, and is characterized as such by the fact that it brings with it the greatest possible therapeutic effect.'' (Ibid., p. 203. See also M.-L. von Franz, ''The Process of Individuation,'' in *Man and His Symbols,* by C. G. Jung et al.)

Introversion   C. G. JUNG: ''Everyone whose attitude is introverted thinks, feels, and acts in a way that clearly demonstrates that the subject is the prime motivating factor and that the object is of secondary importance.'' (*Collected Works,* vol. 6, pp. 452–53)

Introverted persons derive their orientation from within.

C. G. JUNG: ''The apparently trifling difference between the extravert, with his emphasis on externals, and the introvert, who puts the emphasis on the way he takes a situation, plays a very great role in the analysis of dreams. From the start you must bear in mind that what the one appreciates may be very negative to the other, and the high ideal of the one can be an object of repulsion to the other.'' (*Collected Works,* vol. 18, p. 218)

Persona   *Persona* was the Latin name for masks worn by actors.
C. G. JUNG: ''The persona is thus a functional complex that comes into existence for reasons of adaptation or personal convenience, but is by no means identical with individuality. The persona is exclusively concerned with the relation to objects. The relation of the individual to the object must be sharply distinguished from the relation to the subject.'' (*Collected Works,* vol. 6, p. 465)

''It is only because the persona represents a more or less arbitrary and fortuitous segment of the collective psyche that we can make the mistake of regarding it *in toto* as something individual. It is, as its name implies, only a mask of the collective psyche, a mask that *feigns individuality,* making others and oneself believe that one is individual, whereas one is simply acting a role through which the collective psyche speaks.
''. . . Fundamentally the persona is nothing real: it is a compromise between individual and society as to what a man should appear to be. He takes a name, earns a title, exercises a function, he is that or that. In a certain sense all this is real, yet in relation to the essential individuality of the person concerned it is only a secondary reality, a compromise formation, in making which others often have a greater share than he. The persona is a semblance, a two-dimensional reality, to give it a nickname.'' (*Collected Works,* vol. 7, pp. 155–56)

Self   C. G. JUNG: ''The self as an archetype represents a numinous wholeness, which can be expressed only by symbols (e.g., mandala, tree, etc.). As a collective image it reaches beyond the individual in time and space and is therefore not subjected to the corruptibility of *one* body: the realization of the self is nearly always connected with the feeling of timelessness, 'eternity,' or immortality.''(*Collected Works,* vol. 18, p. 694)

Particularly in dreams and the various forms of active imagination, it is possible to observe the significance of symbols of the Self in the healing process. (The term *self* was not capitalized in the *Collected Works.* In this book, however, we have chosen to capitalize this term used by Jung.) Manifestations of these symbols of wholeness and balance often appear just before new ego development, as well as in times of disorientation.

C. G. JUNG: "Just as conscious as well as unconscious phenomena are to be met with in practice, the self as psychic totality also has a conscious as well as an unconscious aspect. Empirically, the self appears in dreams, myths, and fairytales in the figure of the 'supraordinate personality' . . . such as a king, hero, prophet, saviour, etc., or in the form of a totality symbol, such as the circle, square, *quadratura circuli*, cross, etc. When it represents a *complexio oppositorum*, a union of opposites, it can also appear as a united duality, in the form, for instance, of *tao* as the interplay of *yang* and *yin*, or of the hostile brothers, or of the hero and his adversary (arch-enemy, dragon), Faust and Mephistopheles, etc. Empirically, therefore, the self appears as a play of light and shadow, although conceived as a totality and unity in which the opposites are united. . . . It thus proves to be an archetypal idea . . . which differs from other ideas of the kind in that it occupies a central position befitting the significance of its content and its numinosity." (*Collected Works*, vol. 6, pp. 460–61)

Shadow   C. G. JUNG: "The shadow personifies everything that the subject refuses to acknowledge about himself and yet is always thrusting itself upon him directly or indirectly—for instance, inferior traits of character and other incompatible tendencies." (*Collected Works*, vol. 9, part 1, pp. 284–85)

The nature of the shadow "can in large measure be inferred from the contents of the personal unconscious. The only exceptions to this rule are those rather rare cases where the positive qualities of the personality are repressed, and the ego in consequence plays an essentially negative or unfavourable role." (*Collected Works*, vol. 9, part 2, p. 8)

In dreams and fantasies, the shadow appears as the same sex as the dreamer.

INDEX

Acting out, 150, 339, 347

Active imagination: and anima/animus, 284–85; versus art, 184–85; body movement as, 192, 194, 195, 198; components of, 177–83; conscious ego and, 175, 179; as creative function, 184; dangers of, 186–88; as dialogue, 174–77; and enactment, 352; ethical attitude in, 181–82; expressing unconscious in, 179–80; versus Gestalt techniques, 184; in group therapy, 229; versus guided fantasy, 184; importance of play in, 178–79; versus meditation, 183–84; participants in, 175, 179; and play in childhood, 206; versus prayer, 183; reducing ego interference in, 178; resistance to, 188–89; ritual for, 178; and sandplay, 204, 212, 213; using conclusions of, 182–83; using dreams for, 178; value of, 189–90

Adler, Gerhard, 52

Affect-ego, 127, 134

Alchemy, 20–21, 49, 52, 141, 142, 143; well-sealed vessel of, 57

Allegory, 343

American Jungian movement, 11–15; revisions of Jung's theories in, 15; women in, 11–13

Amplification, 139–42

Analysis versus psychotherapy, 15–16, 33

Analysts: absolute rules for, 64; and archetypal material, 378–79; backgrounds of, 374; and child patients, 248–49, 253–54; and clergy, 27; as companion-guides, 357; and complexes, 378; and curing souls, 27-28, 376; and dream interpretation, 377; education of, 367–72, 375–83; and experiencing patients, 60–62; extraverted, 21, 22; and friendship with analysands, 116–18; and individuation, 368, 377–78; initiation of, 391; introverted, 21, 22, 220; introverted intuitive, 21, 144; introverted sensation, 21, 144; intuitive, 21–22; Jungian training institutes for, 373–74; learning by, to practice analysis, 380–83; life experience of, 50, 372; motivations for becoming, 94–95, 367, 369, 387; as nonconformists, 368; and older patients, 257, 262; and parents of child patients, 245–46; personae of, 370–71; personal growth of, 370; personal integrity of, 370; personal qualities needed in, 368, 369–72; providing protected space for children, 235, 239, 248, 249; psychic energy of, 371; psychological development of, 49–50, 370; and recognizing unanalyzable patients, 312–14; and relationship with patients, 29–32, 52–53, 116–18, 165–68; and religion, 379–80; resistance of, in training analysis, 391; responsibilities of, 48–49; screening potential, 369–72, 387–88; training analysis of, 375, 386–96; as transitional object, 59; and treatment of complexes, 307–10; treatment by multiple, 111–12, 395; typology of, 21–22, 49, 96, 144–45; and typology of patients, 373, 376–77; vocation of, 369, 387, 391; vulnerability of, 326, 327; work of, 372–73

Analytical psychology, 10, 29

Analytic ritual, 42

Analytic sessions: frequency of, 53, 63, 100; setting for, 113, 114

Analytic structure: allowing for patient's projections in, 56; alterations in, 58; based on patient, 50, 55; for dealing with misunderstandings, 59; flexibility of, 63–65; fundamental features of, 60; major components of, 47; for narcissistic disturbances, 59–60; reserve of analyst in, 61; stages of, 54; for standard neuroses, 55; sublimation of transference in, 52–53

Androgyny, 282

Anima/animus, 73–84; and active imagi-